A **CREATIVE WRITING**
HANDBOOK

DEVELOPING DRAMATIC TECHNIQUE, INDIVIDUAL STYLE AND VOICE

A **CREATIVE WRITING** HANDBOOK

DEVELOPING DRAMATIC TECHNIQUE, INDIVIDUAL STYLE AND VOICE

EDITED BY **DEREK NEALE**

A & C Black Publishers Ltd
in association with The Open University

Published by

A & C Black Publishers Limited
38 Soho Square
London
WID 3HB
www.acblack.com

in association with

The Open University
Walton Hall, Milton Keynes
MK7 6AA
United Kingdom

First published 2009

Edited and designed by The Open University.

Typeset by SR Nova Pvt. Ltd, Bangalore, India.

Printed in Malta by Gutenberg Press Limited.

This book forms part of an Open University course: A363 *Advanced creative writing*. Details of this and other Open University courses can be obtained from the Student Registration and Enquiry Service, The Open University, PO Box 197, Milton Keynes MK7 6BJ, United Kingdom: tel. +44 (0)845 300 60 90, email general-enquiries@open.ac.uk

http://www.open.ac.uk

British Library Cataloguing in Publication Data: applied for

Library of Congress Cataloging in Publication Data: applied for

ISBN 978 1 4081 0941 0

1.1

Contents

Contributors

The authors are current members of the English Department at The Open University.

Derek Neale is Lecturer in Creative Writing and has helped launch the Open University's new generation of writing courses. He is co-author of *Writing Fiction* and *Life Writing* (both 2008, Routledge) and has written about literary approaches and techniques in several genres. He is an award-winning fiction writer and dramatist, and his stories have appeared in various anthologies and periodicals. He taught creative writing at the University of East Anglia for a number of years, lecturing in both dramatic writing and fiction writing. He completed his Creative Writing MA and his PhD in Creative and Critical Writing at UEA. He has also facilitated writing activities in a prison – poetry, plays, fiction and even song writing – and has edited two collections of prison writing.

Bill Greenwell is a poet, parodist and life writer. His collection *Impossible Objects*, published by Cinnamon in 2006, was short-listed for the Forward Prize for Best First Collection; he won the *Mail on Sunday* Poetry Prize in 2004. He was *New Statesman*'s weekly satirical poet from 1994 to 2002. His poetry and parodies have appeared in more than forty anthologies, and in many poetry magazines, as well as on BBC Radio 3 and Radio 4. He also contributes to *The Independent*. Before becoming a Lecturer in Creative Writing at The Open University, he taught poetry and fiction at the University of Exeter and University College, Falmouth. He was Head of Performing Arts, Languages and English at Exeter College, Exeter, from 1986 to 2002.

Linda Anderson is Reader in Creative Writing at The Open University. She is the editor of *Creative Writing: A workbook with readings* (2006, Routledge/OU), which has been acclaimed as a 'major contribution to the pedagogy of creative writing'. She is an award-winning novelist (*To Stay Alive* and *Cuckoo*, both published by Bodley Head) and writer of short stories, poetry, performance pieces and critical reviews. From 1995 to 2002 she was Head of Creative Writing at Lancaster University, where she designed the first computer-mediated postgraduate writing course in Britain. She has also worked as a producer and director for BBC Radio Drama. In 2007 she was awarded a National Teaching Fellowship by the Higher Education Academy in recognition of her outstanding impact on the student learning experience.

Introduction

Derek Neale

'If there is no wind, row' goes the Latin proverb. This is handy advice for a writer. You are on the boat already – you have begun to write – and then the wind starts to drop. The dream you are attempting to put down in words still compels you, yet in order to make something of that early inspiration you need technical knowhow. *A Creative Writing Handbook* is for writers who have already started, for those who want to go on and to develop their style and approach. One of the key suggestions offered in this book is that dramatic writing is connected to other forms of writing. Developing a fuller understanding of this connection can revive the way in which you generate ideas, improve the drafting of your stories and poems, as well as extending the range of forms in which you write.

All writing benefits from the writer's decision to pause at vital moments, to follow the hunch that something could be improved, however slightly. When the writer waits, puts the story or poem away in a drawer, takes another look not in five minutes but in a few days, this is not procrastination or avoidance. The habitual, assiduous rearranging of words, without promise of immediate reward, appears in most accounts of writing practice. Yet such drafting and redrafting is not done in a vacuum. Each consideration is an amalgam of a very personal inquiry – what do I want to say? – and an awareness of technique – how do I want to say it?

The American novelist Joyce Carol Oates (2003) has suggested that without craft, art is too private; and that without art, craft is just hackwork. Oates says that art comes from the personal, from the idiosyncrasy of a compelling idea. Yet it is nothing without the scaffolding of technique. This book will talk about many approaches to the craft of writing, some of them familiar, some of them new to you. It will suggest methods of generating ideas but also explore new ways in which you can review your work. According to Oates, rewriting, revising and re-imagining your work are the lifeblood of the creative process. It is this dedicated attentiveness to the original conception that can transform an idea, and it is this approach that can improve and develop your writing style.

This Handbook forms one of the core components of an Open University writing course (A363 *Advanced creative writing*). It is appropriate for use on other writing courses. It can be used by writers' groups and by individuals working alone. It is suitable for a range of writers: from those who have not yet settled on a preferred form to those more experienced writers who want to expand their range, to seek new directions and genres or to hone the subtlety of their style. It may be worked through sequentially or used as a resource book for writers and writing tutors.

This book contains a series of writing activities which will prompt you to write both brief and more extensive pieces of work. These activities are designed to be worked through progressively, but can also be used out of sequence. They can complement writing workshops by helping to generate new work and by prompting complex discussion about approaches and techniques. Each chapter will provide you with immediately relevant practice in an aspect of writing. Many of the writing tasks will be challenging. You may get hooked on activities, even on ones that you initially find difficult. Such tussles can sometimes be productive. On occasions you may find that an exercise grows into something unexpected – a character resists being confined to a page; a scene suggests a whole story; a personal memory evolves into a poem. Some tasks might generate substantial new work. These writing activities are also places to return when you are seeking ideas. Many of them are designed to be repeated or to be tried in a variety of ways.

A writer can, and often will, discover different ways of writing in what he or she reads. Each of the following chapters uses examples by established writers. You will see poems, extracts of fiction, life writing, films and plays which suggest a range of possible approaches to the question of marrying form and content, craft and idea. Reading can help your writing in a number of ways. As the playwright Mark Ravenhill says:

> Feeling how a dramatist's words feel on your lips and your teeth, how it feels in your stomach, what it does to your chest is really, really important ... I think if people want to write, they should pick two or three dramatists whose work they really like and learn some of it and actually walk around the house, or if you feel very bold, at the bus stop, and speak that stuff aloud and see how it feels.
>
> (Ravenhill, 2007)

A Creative Writing Handbook has been written by three published writers who are also experienced tutors. We have taught writing in workshops in a wide range of institutions, including the universities of East Anglia and Lancaster, both of which pioneered the teaching of Creative Writing in Britain. Our approach covers three main genres – fiction, poetry and drama – but also with some appropriate consideration of the often connected genre of life writing. Many chapters feature more than one genre and a key approach of the book is that we advocate an integrated approach to your writing. For instance, we often discuss writing novels alongside writing films, and writing poetry alongside writing short stories and memoirs. You will encounter many different ways of writing and be asked to consider how your own writing might benefit from these various methods.

The book is arranged in four parts. Part 1, 'Ways of Writing', explores some of the close links between reading and writing. In considering the importance of revision, research, conflict and contrast, we examine the influential role of genre, and, in particular, encourage you to investigate the importance of drama in your writing.

Part 2, 'Writing Drama', develops this awareness. We introduce some principles of dramatic writing in the context of stage drama, offering script layout guidance for the playwright and suggesting ways of adapting stories for the stage. We also explore approaches to writing dialogue and creating subtext, and consider staging, status, exposition and action. We then look at radio drama, again offering layout guidance specific to the medium, exploring the possibilities of radio adaptations, and considering how to create aural contrasts. We go on to explore writing films, offering layout guidance and advice on writing film adaptations. You will examine how to write more visually, how to construct scenes and how to use the juxtaposition of images.

In Part 3, 'Developing Style', we work on improving your techniques in prose and poetry. By taking different approaches we aim to generate new and exciting momentum, encouraging writers to be bold in their experiments, and to be diligent and brave in their redrafting. We explore how some of the methods used in writing scripts for dramatic performance can be used to revise and improve your writing in other genres. For instance, you will examine the similarities between a novel's narrative voice and a dramatic monologue; you will be encouraged to approach fiction with a film-maker's eye, creating visually rich stories with graceful transitions between scenes and even between sentences. We go on to examine the use of rhetorical techniques such as repetition, variation and understatement to improve your writing style. You will see how variation in the use of analogy can improve your fiction, life writing and poetry. You will investigate the paradox of poetic form – how the constraint of a traditional way of writing can be liberating. We conclude this part by looking at how the vital elements of time and theme can create cohesion and unity in your writing.

Part 4, 'Readings', contains examples from established writers in all the genres, and for all the media, explored throughout the book. These readings demonstrate how certain techniques can be achieved. We have chosen a rich blend of writers and styles to illustrate the range of possible ways of writing. As you progress through the book we will refer you to these readings, posing questions and linking discussion with each example. This will enable you to reflect upon what the particular extract might mean to you and your own writing strategies.

Reading will always help you to carry on writing; you will want and need to read, and not just the extracts contained here. These were chosen because they display possible methods; they represent solutions to problems of form and the personal responses of various writers to those problems. The writer will always be faced with such dilemmas. As Oates says:

> *I have to tell* is the writer's first thought; the second thought is *How do I tell it?* From our reading, we discover how various the solutions to these questions are; how stamped with an individual's personality. For it's at the juncture of private vision and the wish to create a communal, public vision that art and craft merge.
>
> (Oates, 2003, p.126)

This book's aim is to refresh and sustain you as a writer, by showing, explaining and inviting you to try, various ways of writing. By illuminating the potentially fruitful connection between different genres, and especially the influential connection of drama to other forms of writing, we hope to help you to create work which is both crafted and artful.

References

Oates, Joyce Carol (2003) *The Faith of a Writer*, New York: Ecco.

Ravenhill, Mark (2007) Interview, *Ian McMillan's Writing Lab*, BBC Radio 3, podcast [online], http://www.open2.net/writing/markravenhill.html (accessed 30 December 2007).

1   Playing with genre

Derek Neale

When writing a short story called 'Violin Lessons' (reproduced as Reading 1 on p.279) I worked in the evenings in an upstairs room across from my seven-year-old daughter's room. At the time she was obsessed with a children's story called *The Man* (Briggs, 1992). No matter what else she read or we read to her at bedtime, she had to listen to an audio version of *The Man* as she fell asleep. This story often played in the background, permeating the evening hours, as I wrote.

Though not conscious of its effect at the time, I can see now that the story I had written during those evenings inverts or plays with many of the things that happen in Raymond Briggs's story. Instead of a miniature, pocket-sized man turning up in a boy's private space, his bedroom (as happens in *The Man*), I have a schoolboy, not oversized but rather precocious, turning up in my man's private space, his workshop. Briggs's man introduces homely items such as Oxford marmalade and Gold Top Channel Islands' Jersey milk to the boy's bedroom; the schoolboy in my story brings condoms and the rumour of sex to the man's workshop.

In adopting and adapting such details I was playing with genre, though I did not quite realise it at the time; shifting the tale from a children's story to a story for grown-ups, while retaining some discrete elements of the original style. This chapter will explore what genre means and look at ways in which you might use the elements of style from different genres when writing fiction.

The audio version of any story amounts to a dramatic adaptation. I think this was another factor which affected the way I wrote my story. A lesson was subliminally learned while *The Man* played in the background: narrative fiction, whether for children or adults, is a form of dramatic performance. Usually the solitary reader performs the narrative voice and all the dialogue voices of a story, hearing and enacting them inside his or her head. Interestingly, the original book version of *The Man* is written totally in dialogue.

This chapter will examine the strong links between fiction and drama, looking at what key terms such as 'dramatic' and 'scene' might mean in the context of fiction writing. You will start to explore how varying the pace and using different voices might improve your fiction.

What is genre?

Genre is derived from the Latin word *genus*, meaning 'kind' – and simply refers to what 'kind of writing' is being read or written. Is it fiction? Is it poetry? Is it drama? These are the three over-arching genres that have evolved from Plato's and Aristotle's initial discussions of genre some two and a half thousand years ago. There is a whole constellation of other kinds of writing – sometimes called sub-genres – branching from these three main genres. Children's fiction is a sub-genre of fiction, for instance, as are historical fiction, romance fiction and science fiction. Here, I will be using the term 'genre' in the widest possible sense, to mean both main genres and sub-genres.

A reader brings expectations about genre to a piece of writing; these are shaped by previous reading of similar works. On a simple level – if the reader sees a lot of space around the text on a page, he or she may assume it is a poem. This is a basic recognition of genre, but readers are capable of more subtle and sophisticated recognitions.

ACTIVITY 1.1 Reading	Look at the following passage:

> The church clock strikes eight, so those villagers who are awake know without checking that it is six. A cock crows. A body lies across the doorstep of the church, a line of crumb-carrying ants marches across the fedora covering its face. There is a serene, momentary quiet after the chimes cease. A figure glides past the church wall, before the silence is cracked by a baby crying.

Now read the passage several times, each time applying a different title from the following list. After each reading, consider what 'kind of writing' you think it is. Write down what elements of any particular genre suggest themselves in the style, voice and content of the story.

Murder in the Morning;

Woman in the Wind;

The Life History of Guillermo Brown;

The Betrayal;

My Problem with Peyote.

DISCUSSION	You, as a reader, may have started constructing events beyond the details you were given, guessing at what sort of story this might be. The role of the title is to ignite initial speculation. Some kinds of story may be more familiar than others, but unfamiliarity does not prevent a reader from trying to establish which type of narrative they are involved with.

'Murder in the Morning' suggests a thriller or detective fiction – because of the body, the prominence and confusion of time, and the possibility that the gliding figure might be the murderer. 'Woman in the Wind' might suggest romance, partly because of the alliteration. It also suggests a mystery or ghost story; it refocuses the reader towards the gliding figure, and the possibility that this is a spirit. 'The Life History of Guillermo Brown' suggests a fictional or real biography, in which the reader must try to decide whether the body with the fedora or the baby is the subject of the narrative. 'The Betrayal' redirects the reader to the symbolism of the cock crowing, and raises the question: is the gliding figure an adulterer returning to the marital bed? The final title, 'My Problem with Peyote', suggests an autobiographical, confessional narrative – but one that might concentrate comically on hallucinations, and which recasts the body as alive but intoxicated.

We are given no historical clues other than the fedora: the scenario has to be after 1882, when fedoras were first worn. Just imagine how your perception of the story would change if that one item were different – a stetson, a mantilla, a beret, a headscarf, a bowler or a coif. That simple prop in the narrative can betray a whole cultural, and sometimes historical, setting.

Using genre

Jonathan Culler says:

> To write a poem or a novel is immediately to engage with a literary tradition ... The activity is made possible by the existence of the genre, which the author can write against, certainly, whose conventions he may attempt to subvert, but which is nonetheless the context within which his activity takes place, as surely as the failure to keep a promise is made possible by the institution of promising.
>
> (Culler, 1975, p.116)

By including certain elements that suggest a genre the writer is making a form of promise to his or her reader. Yet promises are kept in degrees of fidelity. You might suggest a genre ambiguously, include elements that could be interpreted in a number of ways, and which may lead different readers to think they are engaged in different sorts of promises. You can see such possibilities from the brief passage just discussed.

ACTIVITY 1.2 Writing	Choose one of the titles from the list in Activity 1.1, or one you invent yourself, and write the next two or three paragraphs of the story (up to 500 additional words) – altering the first given paragraph in any way you see fit.

DISCUSSION	From your attempts to develop the passage you no doubt saw the potential for playing with your reader's expectations and developing the sort of promises Culler suggests. It is a vibrant way of approaching a project. Yet you have to be aware of what you are doing. You can end up confused by being overly ambitious, and if this happens then your reader will be confused too. It is important that you are in control of the stylistic elements associated with each genre. It is better to use fewer genres initially – one or two at most. In your development of this scenario did you find that you were focusing on a particular character? Whatever decisions about genre you make it is still important to think most about the character and characterisation, because genre on its own will not lend enough life to your story. And you have to attend to the other fundamentals of the writing – the setting, the action and the vital, revealing details – in order to bring the fiction alive.

Genre is everywhere

One of the most effective ways in which a writer can use genre is to evoke and intensify the reader's generic expectations only to confound them. By doing this the writer might 'induce in [the] reader a series of intellectual reflections and emotional experiences very like those being enacted in and by the work itself' (Dubrow, 1982, p.37). In this way form and content work in harmony to simultaneously trick and alert the reader to a larger meaning in the writing.

As I suggested earlier, my story, 'Violin Lessons', has a connection to the genre of children's fiction. Yet it is playing against this generic influence and is a story that uses other genres more prominently.

ACTIVITY 1.3 Reading	Read the short story 'Violin Lessons' (Reading 1 on p.279). • What generic elements are at work in the narrative? • What makes the story dramatic?

DISCUSSION	Did you recognise how the naive narrative voice might be related to children's fiction? The man's voice appears more childlike and unknowing than that of the boy, revealing a strange sexual naivety. The narrative voice becomes, in effect, a dramatic monologue. This is perhaps another aspect

which connects the story to the dramatised audio version of *The Man*. All information has to be sifted through this peculiar sensibility, which the reader might not trust entirely. The story is also dramatic because it is arranged in scenes of conflict between the boy and the man. When a particular episode is concluded, the narrative moves on to the next scene.

Controlling genre

The man in 'Violin Lessons' is a craftsman who makes chair legs, but who is in search of a new project. He wants to make something else, but does not yet know what this might be. He is visited by a boy. This encounter provides the story with an ongoing sense of danger, a feature I was certainly aware of generating. When the story was read before publication (in a writing workshop), several readers commented on the similarity of my main character to that of Norman Bates in Alfred Hitchcock's film *Psycho* (1960). This alarmed me – it was not a murder story – yet it pleased me at the same time. Some part of my aim had been realised, even if these readers had taken the element of danger further than I had intended. The association was suggested in part because the character, at that point in the story's drafting, had a dominant, if offstage, mother, just like Norman Bates. The story was using the same sort of tactics as a Hollywood thriller (an isolated situation and a lonely encounter), but I did not regard my main character as psychotic or similar in any way to the character from *Psycho*. I wanted my character to be more rounded. I wished to maintain the threat from the thriller genre, but to exert more control over it, to make it less stereotypical, and to turn away at the last moment from the thriller's conventional moment of climax – murder. I decided that my man's mother was an unnecessary character. Changing this part of his background, I hoped, would put more emphasis on the inner life and integrity of my character, while maintaining the dramatic tension of the encounter.

When writing this story I was also aware that my character's dilemma was similar to that of its writer – wanting to create something new, but having barely a glimmer of what that something might be. Not all readers will see this connection between making things in wood and making things in words – two different 'genres of creativity'. Not all writers will identify with the sort of narrow obsession depicted in the story. In this reading the story is a thriller, but also a 'story about craft', and part of my intention was to show the thrilling, dangerous and illicit side of making things. You might well have noticed other generic elements, especially when the boy reveals what happened to his sister. Here the narrative turns away from being a thriller and into a very different kind of writing.

Going against the grain

You can write with or against the grain of a genre. You could say that we do the latter a lot of the time without realising it – by dramatising the mundane; by writing comedic elements into a funeral scene; by using a first person 'I was there' testimony in our fiction. This latter tactic suggests a confessional or witness narrative, as if the fiction is really autobiographical. It is a commonplace in fiction, and has quite a lineage – for an early example look at Daniel Defoe using it in *Robinson Crusoe*, first published in 1719:

> I was born in the Year 1632, in the City of *York*, of a good Family, tho' not of that Country, my Father being a Foreigner of *Bremen*, who settled first at *Hull*:
>
> (Defoe, 1983, p.3)

This opening works like a conventional autobiography, starting with the birth date and place names; the narrative then goes on to give family names, details of the narrator's early career and 'rambling thoughts' about going to sea.

Some first-person voices address the reader directly and admit they are fictions more readily:

> Good morning! Let me introduce myself. My name is Dora Chance. Welcome to the wrong side of the tracks.
>
> (Carter, 1992, p.1)

This is the narrative voice of one of the Chance twins in Angela Carter's *Wise Children*; the playfulness is immediately apparent, not only in what she says but also in her name.

Some first-person narratives are more discursive than Defoe's early model. This can be seen in John Lanchester's *The Debt to Pleasure* (1997), where we are five pages into the narrative before the reader learns, in a sub-clause, that the main character is situated on a cross-channel ferry. However, the reader is aware far earlier that various genres are at work. The novel is written as if it were a series of seasonal menus. The narrator, Tarquin Winot (another playful name), journeys from Portsmouth to Provence; it is also a travel narrative. And, of course, it is a comedy, one in which the narrator's immodesty is often exposed:

> I myself have always disliked being called a 'genius'. It is fascinating to notice how quick people have been to intuit this aversion and avoid using the term.
>
> (Lanchester, 1997, p.18)

We are always being led to read between and behind what Tarquin says, to infer how he might really be perceived. The deluded character is set up as a snob and a bigot:

> There is ... a deliriously vulgar 'caviare bar' at Heathrow Terminal Four, just to the right of the miniature Harrods.
>
> (p.18)

The narrative plays a mesmerising game with genre, telling us where to buy some ingredients, listing the methods for various dishes:

> Blinis. Sift 4 oz. buckwheat flour, mix with ½ oz. yeast (dissolved in warm water) and ¼ pint warm milk, leave for fifteen minutes. Mix 4 oz. flour with ½ pint milk, add 2 egg yolks, 1 tsp sugar, 1 tbs melted butter, and a pinch of salt, whisk the two blends together. Leave for an hour. Add 2 whisked egg whites. Right. Now heat a heavy cast-iron frying pan of the type known in both classical languages as a *placenta* – which is, as everybody knows, not at all the same thing as the caul or wrapping in which the foetus lives when it is inside the womb. To be born in the caul, as I was, is a traditional indication of good luck.
>
> (p.14)

You can see from this passage that the concrete information of the recipe leads into an odd, self-obsessed divulgence, typical of the narrator's digressions. Interestingly, the autobiographical part of the passage is seen as discursive; the food writing is the genre fronting the narrative. Yet even while Lanchester's novel may not conform to the usual sequencing of events and dramatic scenes, and while the possible genres accrue – travel, food, autobiography, family history, comedy – character is still its most central and essential feature, just as with the more straightforward *Robinson Crusoe*.

ACTIVITY 1.4
Reading

Read the following passages. Identify the elements of style or content related to genre that are at work in each.

Passage 1

Through rotting kelp, sea cocoa-nuts & bamboo, the tracks led me to their maker, a white man, his trowzers & Pea-jacket rolled up, sporting a kempt beard & an outsized Beaver, shovelling & sifting the cindery sand with a tea-spoon so intently that he noticed me only after I had hailed him from ten yards away.

Passage 2

Let's begin. Usually, I start by asking interviewees to recall their very earliest memories. You look uncertain.

I have no earliest memories, Archivist. Every day of my life in Papa Song's was as uniform as the fries we vended.

Passage 3

Old Georgie's path an' mine crossed more times'n I'm comfy mem'ryin, an' after I'm died, no sayin' what that fangy devil won't try an' do to me ... so gimme some mutton an' I'll tell you 'bout our first meetin'.

DISCUSSION

Remarkably these passages are taken from different sections of the same novel, David Mitchell's *Cloud Atlas* (2004, pp.3, 187, 249), a novel in which there are six such juxtaposed sections in different genres. The anachronistic clothing, word choice, spelling and the use of ampersands suggest that the first passage is a historical narrative. The words 'kelp' and 'Pea-jacket' suggest that it may be a narrative about the sea. In the second passage the first genre that strikes the reader is 'interview'. As you read the response to the question you realise there is something strange about the voice, culminating in the use of the word 'vended'. Why not 'sold'? The idiom seems odd, and offers a clue to the peculiar nature of the situation being presented. It becomes clear later in the narrative that this is a futuristic world. The third passage seems to be in dialect, with many apostrophes used to stylise the phonetics of the character's speech. This narrative voice, like the others, holds a connection to time. It seems to be brutalised and uncivilised. The reader later learns that this is because the narrator is situated in a post-apocalyptic world.

Trying out voices

The other three generic sections in Mitchell's novel include an epistolary strand set in the 1930s, a farce set in the 1980s, and a thriller set in the 1970s, this latter the only strand to use a third-person narrative. With these, as with the sections you have just glimpsed, the idiom – the words the narrative uses and the way those words are arranged – is crucial in establishing the narrative voice and style. In first-person narrations there is a vitally important link between character and narrative voice.

ACTIVITY 1.5 Writing	Invent your own characters and situation and write the first page of a story (up to 500 words) containing elements of style from one of the Mitchell narratives you have seen – historical seafaring; futuristic interview; post-apocalyptic story – or one of the genres you have not looked at – epistolary; farce; thriller. Consider the ways in which you might be writing with or against the grain of a particular genre.

DISCUSSION	Some critics of Mitchell comment that the different genres in *Cloud Atlas* only link tangentially, that the stylistic ventures seem gratuitous – the point of it all is too enigmatic. How did you find the activity? Did you find you were restricted or liberated by trying to write in this way? Such an exercise can sometimes revitalise your writing, freeing you from too personal an approach. You may also have found that the constraints of a particular kind of writing provoked you into writing against the grain of that genre. You may have found that you altered or elaborated upon the style of the genre. Often you will find that one genre combines with another: for instance, the interview genre is playing with the futuristic genre in the second passage from Mitchell's novel.

There is no denying that such energetic manipulation of 'kinds of writing' can be vibrant and highly inventive, and a potent hook for the reader. Yet it has its dangers too. It is essential to have a strong enough unifying element (such as character) to underpin the narrative.

Dramatised narratives

Along with poetry and fiction, drama is one of the major genres, and one that influences narrative fiction in important ways. Mitchell's *Cloud Atlas* uses the dramatic device of impersonation in each of its strands, and in many of your narratives you too can use this form of mimicry. Mitchell makes the narrative voice into more of a spoken voice. This is a way of bringing the storytelling alive and giving it dramatic energy.

There are various ways in which a story might be made more dramatic. Raymond Carver rewrote his story 'The Bath' (1985a) after it was first published. The story tells of a mother ordering a cake for her son's eighth birthday. The boy gets knocked down by a car on the same day and falls into a coma. The parents are hassled by phone calls from the baker who wants the cake collecting and paying for. The story is bleak in that no communication seems possible between the distraught parents and the baker, and there is no resolution to the conflict or to the fate of the boy at the end of the narrative.

Carver's second version of the story, 'A Small, Good Thing' (1985b), was written two years later. The characters are the same but are now given names (in 'The Bath' they were simply 'the mother' and 'the father'); the story is twice the length, and scenes are developed; there are more aggravating phone calls from the aggrieved but ignorant baker, which has the effect of ratcheting up the dramatic tension. The story now seems gripping, whereas the previous version held a different kind of interest, more concerned with the impassable spaces separating people. In the second version the boy dies. Yet the clinching difference is that the mother and father have a confrontation and final resolution with the baker which, despite their son's death, offers the ritual sacraments of food and drink, recovery and hope. Carver thought there was a truth in each version of the story, and continued to publish both. The rewritten version offers an example of the way in which the same story can be retold and rejuvenated by adding more points of dramatic tension, by reinforcing the rising action and by offering a resolution scene. In Robert Altman's film *Short Cuts* (1993) – an adaptation of a poem and nine of Carver's stories – the latter version of the story is used because it has more of the ebb and flow of conflict, and there is a rising tension more suited to dramatic adaptation.

When writing and rewriting your stories, make sure you attend to the pace of the storytelling. Ensure that your reader is always kept interested. Editing for pace often involves tightening your scenes. Below are some useful points to remember in creating dramatic scenes in your fiction:

- Beware of preambles, where characters enter scenes one by one.
- Beware of lengthy resolutions, waiting for the teacups to be drained and all the characters to depart.
- Think of the momentum you want to gain from a scene's ending.
- Remember you can sometimes use the theatrical black-out, ending a scene suddenly, in order to cut to the next sequence of action.
- Bear in mind that it is important to orchestrate decisively when your reader enters and leaves particular scenes in your narrative.

ACTIVITY 1.6
Editing

Look back over one of the stories you have started in the activities in this chapter, or a story you have previously written. Try to improve the dramatic shape and structure of your scenes and how they fit together by using some of the suggested approaches above and from the Carver example.

DISCUSSION

It is important to identify the right climactic points in your narratives, seeing where the tension in the stories rises and falls. It is also important to look for strong ways of ending scenes. Economy in the way you write and link your scenes is certainly something to be gained from drama. How to start and cut a scene at the appropriate moments is an essential storytelling skill.

Migration between genres

Although there are some novelisations of dramas – *Star Wars* and *The X Files*, for example – the most common, modern-day migration of stories is from the novel form to the dramatic adaptation. Adapting from existing sources has an established pedigree in radio, film, television and theatre. Shakespeare drew heavily on the 1587 edition of Raphael Holinshed's *Chronicles* for many of his plays. Films are often adaptations of novels, and quite a number are then remade in different eras.

ACTIVITY 1.7
Reading

Read the story 'A Real Durwan' by Jhumpa Lahiri (Reading 2 on p.287). Note down any stylistic elements related to genre, and the aspects of the way the story is told, that interest you most.

Imagine you were given the task of writing a dramatic adaptation and answer the following questions:

- What dramatic medium would best suit the story – stage, screen or radio?
- Why have you chosen this medium?
- Note some key elements that would feature in such an adaptation – any images, dramatic exchanges, dialogue, descriptions.
- What would you discard?
- What would you like to keep but would be unable to retain in such a dramatisation?
- Would you keep the same running order as Lahiri's version of events, or would you alter it?

DISCUSSION

The tenants of the flat-building do not know in which genre Boori Ma is telling her personal stories about the past. When she talks of her former life, is she lying, or is it a tragic tale? Is it a 'riches to rags' story, or a corrupt form of snobbery? This is an Indian story, a post-colonial story, but it also has a universal aspect. It has some powerful images and similes: the hair knot the size of a walnut, for instance. It is a story about the dispossessed, about someone who talks all the time, but who has no voice. Boori Ma loses her bed to mites, then to rain. This foreshadows what happens later in the story when her vulnerability in the building is fully exposed, just as it was when she lived in East Bengal.

The story establishes a very strong habitual world with the inclusion of clauses beginning – 'every rainy season', 'lately', 'twice a day'.

How would you transfer this into a dramatic script? Perhaps you chose film as your dramatic medium, so you could capture the image of the walnut-sized bun. You might have chosen radio because this could potentially retain something of the original's tone of narration. Would you give Boori Ma more of a voice than is in the story, or less? The story does give her more dialogue than any other character, but it also implies she talks much more voraciously than is illustrated. You might, in your dramatisation, put Boori Ma at the front of the stage, the building behind her, delivering a monologue to the audience.

The effect of genre and drama

You will be looking at 'A Real Durwan' again in Part 2, where you can explore more thoroughly the techniques involved in dramatic adaptation. As you have seen in this chapter, readers' imaginations are informed by various genres. Genre in its many guises is an exciting tool to use, to rebel against, to play with – but most of all to be aware of. There are subtle and intriguing ways in which you might alter the genre of your stories as you revisit them to redraft and edit. Drama is an influential genre and its various media offer rich possibilities in terms of telling and retelling stories. You have looked briefly at some dramatic methods and how to use these when writing and revising your fiction. In later chapters you will learn more about how dramatic methods can influence your style, starting in the next chapter with the importance of contrast and conflict.

References

Briggs, Raymond (1992) *The Man*, London: Julia MacRae.

Carter, Angela (1992) *Wise Children*, London: Vintage.

Carver, Raymond (1985a) 'The Bath' in *Stories*, London: Picador, pp.214–20.

Carver, Raymond (1985b) 'A Small, Good Thing' in *Stories*, London: Picador, pp.331–52.

Culler, Jonathan (1975) *Structuralist Poetics: Structuralism, linguistics and the study of literature*, New York: Cornell University Press.

Defoe, Daniel (1983 [1719]) *Robinson Crusoe*, Oxford: Oxford University Press.

Dubrow, Heather (1982) *Genre*, London: Methuen.

Lanchester, John (1997) *The Debt to Pleasure*, London: Picador.

Mitchell, David (2004) *Cloud Atlas*, London: Sceptre.

Psycho (1960) film, Alfred Hitchcock and Saul Bass (directors), Joseph Stefano (writer).

Short Cuts (1993) film, Robert Altman (director), Robert Altman and Frank Barhydt (writers).

Further reading

Kaplan, David Michael (1998) *Rewriting: A creative approach to writing fiction*, London: A & C Black.

Kaplan offers useful testimony about how a writer makes his stories more dramatic, and is especially enlightening when talking about his story 'Trips'.

2   Conflict and contrast

Bill Greenwell

If your writing is to engage a reader's attention and hold their interest,
your original source material needs to be carefully honed and refined.
You probably know people who tell a story so entertainingly that listeners
ask to hear it again and again. Sometimes you hear the compliment,
'She should be on the stage'. A good storyteller, whether an amateur
raconteur or professional stand-up comedian, makes use of a variety of
anecdotes, sometimes short or, sometimes, very long. He or she holds an
audience by constantly gauging its reaction to a story, and by editing the
content and refining the timing to increase the appeal of the material.

As you read in the previous chapter, one way of making your writing more
interesting is to make it more dramatic. In Chapter 1 you learned how to do
this by playing with the reader's understanding of different genres. In this
chapter you will look at another technique: using conflict and contrast to
build dramatic tension.

ACTIVITY 2.1 **Writing and** **editing**	Consider a story that you have told to others several times – for instance, a story about a family event or an incident with friends. Note down the answers to these questions:

- What are the story's key points?
- What kinds of response would you aim to elicit? Astonishment?
  Laughter? Tears? And at what points in the story?
- Have you edited the events of the story when you have told it to others?
- Does the story contain tension? If so, what causes this tension?

DISCUSSION	You may have realised that you almost automatically omit any detail that slows the storytelling. The key moments might be in the middle or at the end, and be preceded by moments of tension. Would you rearrange these if you were trying to elicit a different response?

Think of other stories you have told which you have borrowed – for
instance, from a friend or relative. Many of them have probably 'grown' in
the telling. This doesn't mean you are like the proverbial fishermen who
exaggerate their catches. It means you have adjusted and edited your story
for maximum impact. You have left material out, placed more emphasis on
some elements than on others, refined the language, and phrased your story
in a way that ensures you hold an audience.

One way to practise holding a reader's attention is to take relatively unshaped material and to search through it for potential conflict or contrast, tension or contradiction. In the next section you will see how I used this method with a personal letter.

Potential sources

Many forms of writing are intended for a limited audience – for instance, diaries, notebooks and private letters. Here is an extract from a letter written by a distant relative of mine. It was written in the 1940s by an uncle to a nephew he had not seen since the nephew was three. The younger man was by this time nearly thirty. The uncle, trapped in New Zealand by the war and by lack of funds, was the nephew's mother's brother. Like most letters, it is casual about 'correctness'.

> I received photos of wedding group some days ago from your Mum very good but sorry she looks so sad she is disappointed with your photo tho the one leaving the church is more like you not so serious eh! however marriage is a serious matter & I think must be an ordeal at least for the man. Pity you had such bad weather for the great day & hindered a lot of the guests from attending. The postal dept ask for all letters to be sent unsealed to facilitate the operation of censorship & to be sent early, so I will post this away tomorrow when I go to Auckland on my weekly outing. Now I have one or two more chits to send so you must excuse short note, it is really more for the stamp that I thought you might be interested in, that I write you.

At first glance, this might seem unpromising – but all material is promising if you look closely. Here are my initial thoughts. There is a tension between the 'not so serious' look on the young man's face and the sudden, odd thought of the older man that 'marriage is a serious matter & I think must be an ordeal *at least for the man*' (my italics). There is a tension between the way the photos are 'good' and yet the mother at the wedding 'looks so sad'. There is a tension between the 'great day' and the 'bad weather'. There is a conflict between the compliment on the quality of the picture ('very good') and the alternative reason for sending the letter ('it is really more for the stamp that I thought you might be interested in'). And there is also a contrast between the sender (unmarried, far away, older) and the recipient (newly married, close to family, younger).

Tensions, contrasts and conflicts are the stuff from which dramatic writing emerges. You could use this material in many ways. You could write a short story, developing the reasons for the mother's apparent sadness.

You could write a passage of dialogue in which the older man, absorbed in his thoughts, fails to notice that the young man is absorbed in his own glee. You could open a longer fiction, recasting the wedding on a wet day as a funeral on a bright day – in which case, why are so few people there? You could base a poem on the contrasts between the two men.

In other words, an apparently mundane letter is brimming with possibility. The trick is to see, and to develop, that potential.

ACTIVITY 2.2
Writing

Choose a letter, diary or other document, and look for examples of contrast, conflict and tension within it. List the number of potential pieces of writing that it might spark.

Write a poem (12–20 lines) or a brief passage of fiction (up to 500 words) which exploits the use of contrast, conflict and tension.

DISCUSSION

Here is the draft of a poem in which I have tried to contrast the two men involved with my letter – the writer and recipient.

> ### Uncle, New Zealand, 1941
>
> The curtains part; the drop descends, a scrim
> behind which, shimmering, you move your hands.
> A wave divides us. Still, these moistened eyes
> study the snaps, the monochromes of home:
>
> which is here, or there, I hardly know the words.
> As deaf as this ink, in which our silence breaks,
> I fathom out faces – yours, wearing the smile
> of a bridegroom; mine, with a faraway look,
>
> but lost beneath sea. The sonar fails, unless
> I press the phones to my ear, and hear your faint
> theatricals of marriage. Someone (I don't know)
> is gazing at me through this glaucous glass.
>
> I make you out. Your mother has sent me these,
> which please me obscurely, almost like the girl
> I never met, nor wrote to, did not touch.
> You do not know how much it troubles me
>
> to glimpse you, dimly. I think it an ordeal
> that you must marry, far from me, unreal
> as limelight, stage light. So I write, beguiled,
> and send you this, just for the stamp, dear child.

My aim was to bring out the tension in the letter writer, who feels as close as if watching a play, but separated, like an audience (hence the image of the 'scrim' at the opening, the 'theatricals' of marriage, the 'limelight, stage light' at the end). I also wanted to create some kind of distance, and to do this, I introduced a recurring image of being divided by water, of the communication being as if underwater. This is the reason for the images of sea and sonar. The letter writer is confused by what 'home' means – it 'is here, or there'. He does not 'know' the nephew – hence the play on words, as in 'Someone (I don't know)'. The form of the poem is dictated by this uncertainty. Although the lines are written in a shifting iambic pentameter, they do not rhyme until the conclusion, which tries to close the poem with the same unsatisfactory reference to the stamp as in the letter. At the same time, a sequence of echoes is threaded through the poem, as in 'unless/ press', 'touch/much', and others. And there are repeated ideas of division ('part', 'break', 'faraway', 'glass'), to counteract the attempt to connect. The tension in the poem is intended to come from the paradox of writing intimately to someone no longer intimate enough to write to.

Conflicting points of view

Some of the best source material – drawn from personal experience, or from reading – is that which contains debate, and which therefore causes debate. Think how often you have had conversations about events you have witnessed. The most interesting are likely to be those in which there has been a disagreement, a falling-out, a difference of opinion, an argument, or where there have been contrary points of view. In life, we may side with one person against another. If you want your audience or readers to be absorbed by conflict, however, it makes good sense to force them to have problems choosing 'sides'.

One way to complicate the issue, and to make it richer, is to create characters who see from a point of view with which you are in disagreement.

ACTIVITY 2.3
Reading

Read the poem below, 'We Remember Your Childhood Well' by Carol Ann Duffy (1990, p.24). You will see that the points of view diverge. What is the difference between what 'we' in the poem think, and what 'you' think?

We Remember Your Childhood Well

Nobody hurt you. Nobody turned off the light and argued
with somebody else all night. The bad man on the moors
was only a movie you saw. Nobody locked the door.

Your questions were answered fully. No. That didn't occur.
You couldn't sing anyway, cared less. The moment's a blur, a *Film Fun*
laughing itself to death in the coal fire. Anyone's guess.

Nobody forced you. You wanted to go that day. Begged. You chose
the dress. Here are the pictures, look at you. Look at us all,
smiling and waving, younger. The whole thing is inside your head.

What you recall are impressions; we have the facts. We called the
                                                              tune.
The secret police of your childhood were older and wiser than you,
                                                            bigger
than you. Call back the sound of their voices. Boom. Boom. Boom.

Nobody sent you away. That was an extra holiday, with people
you seemed to like. They were firm, there was nothing to fear.
There was none but yourself to blame if it ended in tears.

What does it matter now? No, no, nobody left the skidmarks of sin
on your soul and laid you wide open for Hell. You were loved.
Always. We did what was best. We remember your childhood well.

DISCUSSION

The speaker(s) in Duffy's poem (they do seem rather forbiddingly to be in
the plural) suggest in an unpleasant way that 'they' have the 'facts', while
the addressee has 'the impressions'. Their voices are made dominant by
the way Duffy uses strong internal and final rhymes ('moors', 'saw', 'door'
in the first stanza, 'occur', 'blur' in the second stanza, and so on).
The poem is also structured so that the first, third and fifth stanzas open
with an emphatic, short phrase beginning 'Nobody ...'. We can tell that the
speaker(s) are intended to be overbearing because Duffy makes them
carelessly refer to themselves as 'the secret police of your childhood'.
What Duffy has done is to contrast one view with another. Neither is
necessarily reliable, although we are plainly meant to side with the
addressee.

The power of Duffy's poem comes from the decision to speak from the
bullying adults' point of view. When you are writing in the first person, it
is invariably more arresting if you create a character or characters either
with whom the reader is on poor terms, or about whom the reader is
uncertain. This tension between the speaker and the reader may not be
obvious at first – or may become more obvious as the piece proceeds. You
may want your reader to be surprised into coming to terms with your
character; or you may want your reader to become surprised when your
character, having gained the reader's trust, goes on to break that trust.

ACTIVITY 2.4
Writing

Draw on any experience you have of a conflict between a figure or figures in authority and someone on whom they are trying to impose their point of view. Choose the point of view with which you disagree. Imagine that the proponent of this point of view is speaking disapprovingly to the other person or persons. Write a passage of prose (200–300 words) or a poem (16–24 lines) in which the viewpoint of the listener is implied by what the speaker says, and the way it is said. For instance, a librarian might tell a group of people to stop talking, because they are interfering with the concentration of other readers. In this case, you might write from the viewpoint of one of the talkers, answering back.

DISCUSSION

What kind of language was used by the speaker(s) you selected? You might have found it helpful to think of a list of statements, using the second person ('you have', 'you will', 'you must', 'you should not', 'you did not'). You might have thought about ways in which you could make the position of the speaker or speakers firm and emphatic. You could have used repetition, or have quoted the other person's words back to them, or have used a determined, assertive rhythm. All of these would make it clear that the speaker's point of view was too overbearing to be trusted.

Contrasting characters

When you look at material you intend to retell and reshape, make sure that you are not letting your own point of view dominate. A good example of a writer muting her own view occurs in Caryl Churchill's play *Top Girls* (1982). Churchill's aim was to make her audience debate what was meant by 'a successful woman'. Did the phrase refer to a woman who had succeeded, as Margaret Thatcher had recently done, in reaching high office in politics? Were the American feminists correct when they praised the promotion of women to senior posts in large corporations? As Churchill explained in a BBC interview (1988), this was not her definition of success. However, she wanted to ensure that her play was not a simple political tract, but an invitation to the audience to debate the issue.

Marlene is the dominant character in the play. In many ways she is attractive: she is articulate, and she challenges a male view of the world. Churchill pits Marlene against her sister, Joyce, who is often unattractively bitter and argumentative. There is a heated debate between them in the final act. The audience is encouraged to side with Joyce's point of view, even though Marlene is represented as having more charisma. Put simply, Churchill has encouraged her audience to leave the theatre more sympathetic towards Joyce's point of view, but less sympathetic to Joyce. This kind of contradiction is what makes the play strong drama.

Rivalry is always fertile ground for a writer. This is particularly true of sibling rivalry, because the siblings you create will have as much in common (their childhood experience) as they have differences. However, your contrasting characters do not have to belong to the same family. They might be lovers or partners. They might even be allies, or they might work together. The essence of Laurel and Hardy films is that the two are yoked together, but do not, most of the time, get on. Indeed, you can make rivalry more dramatic because it takes place between two characters who have much in common.

ACTIVITY 2.5 Reading	Read the story 'The Fly in the Ointment' by V.S. Pritchett (Reading 3 on p.296). What tactics does Pritchett use to create dramatic tension between father and son?

DISCUSSION	Pritchett's story shows you a very good way in which to build up tension and conflict. There are only two characters, father and son, and it is the father who has fallen on hard times. At the start of the story we are encouraged to feel sympathy for the son. We collude with him, because he is presented to us as decent and trustworthy. And because we see from the son's point of view, we are misled into feeling the son's sympathy for the father, who is even compared to the genial figure of a 'snowman'. It comes as a surprise, therefore, when we see that there are two sides to the father.

Dramatic tension often springs from an alliance that gradually sours. Characters in conflict also do not need to share the same perception of their differences. You can make a piece of writing more absorbing by having one character fail to realise the extent of the conflict. One character may be quite naive about the conflict, the other highly aware. You can create great drama by persuading the reader that one view is correct and then amending that view, perhaps even turning it on its head.

ACTIVITY 2.6 Writing	Make preliminary notes about two characters who are brought together, but who have differing views. Here are some suggestions: a magician and a magician's assistant; neighbours in adjacent flats; a prisoner and a warder. Try to make their views a mixture of similarity and difference. Think about how you can bring out the tension between them without resorting to stereotypes.

Write a passage (up to 400 words) which brings out this tension, in your descriptions of the characters, in their behaviour, and in what they say.

DISCUSSION

You might have created the tension between them by using contrast. Contrast between characters springs from personality rather than position. In the Dick Clement and Ian La Frenais television series *Porridge*, set in a prison, the conflict between the warder, McKay, and the inmate, Fletcher, does not come from their being on 'opposite sides'. It comes from the difference in their personalities. McKay is prickly, twitchy, a stickler, humourless. Fletcher is bumptious, relaxed, breezy, witty.

Contrast could equally consist of having one character being active and another passive. In Caryl Churchill's play *Owners* (first staged in 1972), for instance, two of the main characters, Marion and Alec, are defined by the difference in their attitudes to life: one of them is belligerent, the other accepting what takes place and allowing events to take their own course. In her introduction to a published collection of her plays, Churchill explains that she used the revivalist marching hymn, 'Onward Christian Soldiers', as her inspiration for Marion, and a Zen poem, 'Sitting quietly, doing nothing. / Spring comes and the grass grows by itself', as her inspiration for Alec (Churchill, 1985, p.4). The contrast is deliberate: she is undermining the stereotype of women being less active than men. Bringing the characters face to face means that each attitude is brought into sharp relief.

Conflicting evidence

You can learn a great deal from seeing one event from two points of view. Witnesses' memories are unreliable and, as a writer, you can make dramatic use of the tension that comes from that unreliability. The next two activities focus on the differences between two accounts of the same event.

In 1982, two writers were engaged upon separate journeys. Paul Theroux was travelling by train in a clockwise journey around Britain, a journey he describes in *The Kingdom by the Sea* (1983). At the same time, Jonathan Raban was sailing his boat, *Gosfield Maid*, in an anticlockwise direction around the British coast, an experience he describes in *Coasting* (1986). Theroux and Raban crossed paths at Brighton, and both described their meeting.

ACTIVITY 2.7
Reading

Read the passages by Theroux and Raban, which describe this meeting (Reading 4 on p.303 and Reading 5 on p.304).

- What techniques do the passages have in common?
- In what ways are they different?

DISCUSSION

Both pieces borrow from fiction. Both writers characterise each other and themselves. Both use dialogue to create the characters. Both make the scene come dramatically alive by setting up a sort of comic antagonism between the two of them.

However, the focus of each piece is different. Raban is far more verbal. Theroux does not really use metaphor at all, although he allows the interior of the boat to hint at what he thinks of Raban – very 'comfy and literary'. Raban, by contrast, wastes no time in depicting Theroux as a kind of comically sinister figure. He wears 'Papa Doc' sun-glasses ('Papa Doc' Duvalier was a murderous Haitian dictator). He concentrates to a far greater extent on sensory experience and analogy. He picks out 'the lavender-smelling gleam of the woodwork', the 'crinkly, tongue-shaped spill of red wine' on the log-book. He compares himself and Theroux to Britain and Argentina (the Falklands conflict was taking place at the same time both journeys were undertaken). He describes Theroux's instruction to the photographer as 'clipped and military'. In fact, he devotes much more time to the incident with the photographer, which Theroux dismisses in a single sentence.

The Theroux and Raban pieces were marketed as travel writing. Yet both Raban and Theroux were plainly writing a species of autobiography. Between the publication of their two books, Raban and Theroux had contributed to an edition of travel writing published by *Granta*. Its editor, Bill Buford, drew attention in his introduction to the writers' 'sheer glee of storytelling, a narrative eloquence that situates them, with wonderful ambiguity, somewhere between fiction and fact' (1984, p.7).

These passages are stylistically different from each other. The authors have reinvented what took place. The two accounts show how there can be differences of opinion about real events, and how the emphasis in an account can be shifted. They also reveal that autobiography is a creative literary form, in which the factual representation of events is not the only consideration.

ACTIVITY 2.8
Writing

Go for a walk, or on a journey, with another person. Agree to write down your observations, and to discuss what you saw a few days later.

Use these observations to write two first-person narratives (up to 200 words each) which draw on the two separate experiences. See if you can exaggerate the differences between them – inventing details, if you like.

DISCUSSION

Your perception – your focus, your sensory experience – is likely to have been quite different from the other person's. You will no doubt have found that you have left out all kinds of details which the other person has put in, and vice versa. What was most important to you in the journey will probably not be what was most important to the other person. As in the Theroux and Raban extracts, your pieces of writing could be very different, not only in substance, but in tone.

Language and sentence structure
Sound and rhythm

You can also create contrast by using different rhythms and sound-patterns. One voice might seem cool and unflustered, the other agitated and hectic. You can build these effects into the language by using very different patterns of syllables, vowels and consonant clusters. This kind of contrast can take place in a single character, as the poem in the next activity suggests.

ACTIVITY 2.9
Reading

Read the following poem, 'Bat', by D.H. Lawrence. What devices does Lawrence use to bring out the conflict between what his speaker sees and feels at the opening of the poem, and what his speaker sees and feels at its conclusion?

Bat

At evening, sitting on this terrace,
When the sun from the west, beyond Pisa, beyond the mountains of
Carrara

Departs, and the world is taken by surprise ...

When the tired flower of Florence is in gloom beneath the glowing
Brown hills surrounding ...

When under the arches of the Ponte Vecchio
A green light enters against stream, flush from the west,
Against the current of obscure Arno ...

Look up, and you see things flying
Between the day and the night;
Swallows with spools of dark thread sewing the shadows together.

A circle swoop, and a quick parabola under the bridge arches
Where light pushes through;
A sudden turning upon itself of a thing in the air.
A dip to the water.

And you think:
'The swallows are flying so late!'

Swallows?

Dark air-life looping
Yet missing the pure loop ...
A twitch, a twitter, an elastic shudder in flight
And serrated wings against the sky,
Like a glove, a black glove thrown up at the light,
And falling back.

Never swallows!
Bats!
The swallows are gone.

At a wavering instant the swallows give way to bats
By the Ponte Vecchio ...
Changing guard.

Bats, and an uneasy creeping in one's scalp
As the bats swoop overhead!
Flying madly.

Pipistrello!
Black piper on an infinitesimal pipe.
Little lumps that fly in air and have voices indefinite, wildly
vindictive;

Wings like bits of umbrella.

Bats!

Creatures that hang themselves up like an old rag, to sleep;
And disgustingly upside down.
Hanging upside down like rows of disgusting old rags
And grinning in their sleep.
Bats!

In China the bat is symbol of happiness.

Not for me!

(Lawrence, 1999 [1923], p.87)

DISCUSSION

At the opening of this poem Lawrence's speaker is depicted as 'sitting quietly', taking comfort in the sight of the sunset and the flight of some swallows he is watching. As he gradually realises that the swallows are, in fact, bats, he reacts in panic, and begins to denounce what he sees in vigorous terms, at first in particular, and then in general.

The creatures in flight at first seem soothing to the speaker, but in the course of the poem they come to seem erratic and threatening. The way in which Lawrence suggests this change in the speaker's mood is by altering his speech pattern. The poem begins with extremely long lines, containing many pauses and ending in ellipses, and full of long vowel sounds and soft consonants. By the time the speaker, increasingly hysterical, has identified the creatures as bats, Lawrence has changed the pattern of his speech so that it is quick, irregular, staccato, and full of short vowel sounds and clipped and noisy consonants.

The second line of the poem has five beats, but twenty syllables. It qualifies what is being seen at leisure by repeating the pattern of the phrases ('when ... beyond ...'). Later in the poem, you can hear a frantic quality instead. The lines become erratic, emphatic, abrupt. The line that begins 'Little lumps ...' has twenty syllables again, but this time it has eight beats. Words like 'Pipistrello', 'infinitesimal', 'indefinite' and 'vindictive' have a series of quick, short 'i' sounds, and the words have to be pronounced in a finicky way. The images are contrasting, too – the romantic image of a 'tired flower' is replaced by an image of a 'little lump' or of 'bits of umbrella'.

'Bat' is an extreme example of how contrast can work in a poem, but it illustrates how you can make words, sounds and rhythms dramatise a mood.

Changing the pace

You can experiment with passages of fiction to see how this works. I have rewritten a passage from Jonathan Coe's novel *The House of Sleep* in which a character wakes feeling disturbed. This character has been taking part in an experiment to do with sleep patterns. Here is my version of the passage:

> He unglued himself, untangled the electrodes. He left the bedroom, saw Lorna, waved good morning. She was crouched over her computer screen, and her habitual cup of tea. He went to the terrace, watched the sun rise. It came over the headland. It was five o'clock.

That sounds quite fractious, because of the relative shortness of the sentences and the way they move abruptly on. Contrast this with the much more complex pattern of clauses in Coe's original:

> Carefully ungluing and disentangling himself from the electrodes, he left his bedroom, waved good morning to Lorna (crouched bleary-eyed over her computer screen and habitual cup of tea) and went on to the terrace to watch the sun rising over the headland. It was five o'clock.

> (Coe, 1997, p.206)

The original uses two sentences, whereas my version uses six. Coe begins with participles, whereas I have used active main verbs; his original uses parentheses, and a steady sequence of connecting words to create a seamless and gentle transition from bed to terrace. He is using sentence structure to create the effect of feeling, as his character does, 'profoundly refreshed'.

ACTIVITY 2.10 Writing	Write a passage of prose (300–400 words) or a section of poetry (up to 20 lines) in which the character or voice is either calm, reflective and at ease, or agitated, irritated and distressed. When you have finished, try rewriting the material so that you come as near as possible to the opposite effect.
DISCUSSION	Practising rhythmical and tonal shifts like this is a good way to become aware of the potential for contrast within a piece of writing. It will also increase your ability to judge the appropriate tempo of your writing at any given point.

Conclusion

In this chapter, you have explored ways of creating tension by seeking out potential sources of conflict and contrast in your original material. You have looked at ways of creating tension by bringing contrasting characters together, by devising voices that are in conflict with others, and by using material that reveals the world from different viewpoints. You have also looked at ways of using language to increase or decrease that tension and conflict. In the next chapter, you will research an original piece of writing, and revise it in different ways.

References

Buford, Bill (ed.) (1984) *Granta 10: Travel Writing*, Cambridge: Granta.

Churchill, Caryl (1982) *Top Girls*, London: Methuen.

Churchill, Caryl (1985) *Plays: One*, London: Methuen.

Churchill, Caryl (1988) Interview, *Omnibus*, BBC1, November.

Coe, Jonathan (1997) *The House of Sleep*, London: Viking.

Duffy, Carol Ann (1990) *The Other Country*, London: Anvil.

Lawrence, D.H. (1999 [1923]) *Birds, Beasts and Flowers*, Harmondsworth: Penguin.

Further reading

Raban, Jonathan (1968) *The Technique of Modern Fiction*, London: Edward Arnold.

Long before his first published fiction and life writing, Raban discussed the close relationship of the two genres. This is a good general introduction.

Buford, Bill (ed.) (1991) *The Best of Granta Travel*, London: Granta.

This gives some excellent examples of travel writing in which the writers sustain interest by exploring conflict within themselves, and between themselves and their environments. It includes a piece by Raban, 'Sea-Room', which is an earlier, cancelled chapter of *Coasting*.

3   Vision and revision

Bill Greenwell

In Chapter 2, you looked at how you could identify potential sources of conflict and contrast in your source material, and use these to build dramatic tension. In this chapter, you will look at ways in which to use research and rewriting to intensify the drama of a piece of writing.

Research

Many think that finding material involves only mining direct experience. Yet Stef Penney, whose novel, *The Tenderness of Wolves* (2006), is set in Canada, had never been there. Nor had Sid Smith been to China, where his first novel, *Something Like a House* (2001), is set – unless you count his one hour at Hong Kong airport. 'The only ticket you need,' he said, 'is a library ticket' (Smith, 2002). As Aldous Huxley explained, 'I had no trouble finding my way around the English part of *Brave New World*, but I had to do an enormous amount of reading up on New Mexico, because I'd never been there. I read all sorts of Smithsonian reports on the place and then did the best I could to imagine it' (quoted in Dick, 1967, p.158).

Research can be primary or secondary, or a mixture of the two. A 'primary' source means that your information has been obtained from original documents, or is based on your own first-hand experience; a 'secondary' source is a book or website someone else has already prepared.

| **ACTIVITY 3.1** Research | Find a story in a current newspaper or a magazine, in which a real-life event is being described. See if you can work out what kinds of research have gone into the story. Ask yourself the following questions: |

- Is the story first hand?
- Does the story rely on more than one source?
- How has the story been shaped – what does it seem to have left out?

Now imagine the story set at least fifty years in the past. What kind of work would you have to do to make the story 'believable' if it was set in a different time in this way? Spend some time undertaking that research – using online and library sources.

| **DISCUSSION** | Some types of writing plainly demand more research than others. If, for instance, you are writing a piece set in a past decade or century, it is important to make your detail believable, and even informative. After all, we often read fiction for the pleasure of the information as well as for the |

pleasure of the narrative, character and setting. And you can be sure, especially in the case of historical novels, that astute readers will spot the smallest factual error.

Looking for potential

It is also useful to think of researched material as that which has the potential to be adapted into something more dramatic. Suppose you were writing a story in which a character worked in the preparation of flax (a plant from which linen is made). You might find the following extract useful.

> Flax byssinosis occurs mainly but not exclusively in those preparing flax for spinning. After a number of years of exposure the worker begins to experience chest symptoms on a Monday. These are tightness in the chest, breathlessness and a cough. The symptoms get worse as the day goes on. As time passes the trouble comes on a Tuesday too, and then successively on other days of the working week. At the weekend there is relief, and on the Monday following another exacerbation. Monday is always the worst day. Eventually the condition may become very severe and the patient be disabled. On the other hand it may remain moderate. The physical signs are non-specific, and merely those of a wheezy emphysematous chest. There is no abnormal shadowing in the X-ray of the lungs.
>
> Diagnosis depends on the existence of the chest disease, the history of exposure to flax dust, the Monday exacerbation, and in some cases improvement when the patient leaves the industry. Improvement is likely to take place, but the degree varies. Some workers are affected and some are not. This may depend on variations in the dose of flax dust received, or on differences in individual susceptibility.
>
> (Logan, 1961, pp.178–9)

Since it is taken from a clinical account, you would have to use the detail in this extract very carefully. Looking at it, you will see that the language is far too technical for fiction, drama, poetry – or even, if you happened to be writing about flax working, for life writing. Words such as 'byssinosis' and 'emphysematous' would be too complex and, in the context of a story, so too would 'exacerbation', 'individual susceptibility', 'exposure', and even 'shadowing'. That is because they are being used here in a clinical context.

However, if you set your mind ticking, you might see that there is some potential here. The medical condition described has some unusual features – it affects some people more than others; some are not affected at all. A sufferer has respite at the weekend, but suffers badly on a Monday. The symptoms do not appear for several years. They disappear, sometimes, when people leave the flax industry. There seems, in other words, to be a great deal of chance involved, and a great deal of contrast and a process of change. Chance and contrast and change are fundamental aspects of fiction. Perhaps there is a story to be written here about someone who suffers and their relationship with someone who doesn't; perhaps a story that focuses on the contrast between Sunday and Monday – and perhaps that story doesn't need to be written about flax at all. In researching your idea for a story, you might hit on something quite different. The difference between Sunday and Monday might make you think of other situations in which someone is afflicted in a dramatic or random way.

Apart from putting you off ever working in the flax industry, this extract should make you think about how you can use researched material, how you can adapt it to give it more potential, and how you can even discard it but still gain from it. You do not need to look for learned journals. I once asked a group of students to write a piece based on the idea of a stain. One of them, Frea Lockley, came up with a monologue spoken by a woman whose job was to mind the children of, and to clear up after, a couple, each of whom was having a clandestine affair:

> Dishes done. Time to tackle the laundry. Although it will often take all day, I read the silent language of the clothes with acid pleasure. Kids' clothes are easy – mud's no problem; brush and then 40°, which blasts out the felt-tip too. His will take a little longer. Lipstick is unforgiving on £80 shirts, but I take pride in my skills. All fine so long as he never wears silk, no way of shifting lipstick from that. Hers is tricky today; 'someone' gave her lilies. The secret with lily pollen is, never rub or wet the mark; go gently, gently with Sellotape or a Hoover nozzle to lift it off, and no-one will ever know how you rolled on them in the taxi last night.
>
> (Lockley, 2006)

As the piece moved on, it became clear that the speaker was completely obsessed with cleaning, to the extent that she had a comic lack of interest in the adulterous secrets she was sharing with the reader. The source of Lockley's research was an article in the January 2004 edition of *Good Housekeeping*, '101 stain-removing problems solved'. Obsessive behaviour is always dramatically interesting, and the article on stain removal gave Lockley everything she needed to start writing.

In the next activity, you will read work by a writer who has made use of a wide range of source material. Sarah Waters's novel *The Night Watch* (2006) is set in the Second World War – well before Waters was born, but in the living memory of many people. In particular, she focuses on the experience of conscientious objectors, and on the experience of women, including gay women, in London, during the Blitz.

ACTIVITY 3.2 Reading	Read the extract from Waters's *The Night Watch* (Reading 6 on p.305). The setting is an ambulance station, in 1944. • What details in the passage suggest the period in which it is set? • Why do you think Waters has included so many period details?
DISCUSSION	The period detail here is quite considerable: the playing cards picturing glamour girls, the oil-stove, the astrakhan coat, the dark tortoiseshell frames, the woollen knickerbockers worn by the dance tutor. There are slang phrases in the conversation ('Penny a pop?', 'We're in for it tonight, kids!', 'my Aunt Fanny') and slang and terminology to do with the Blitz (ack-ack, wallops, R and D, nuisance raiders, photograph flares). Waters has plainly taken great trouble to give her novel an authentic and accurate flavour. This is not to say that Waters has simply given us a 'picture' of life in an ambulance station when bombs are falling. It is more that, by researching the background, she has helped to propel her novel along. *The Night Watch* is interesting for its characters and their conflicts; it is not a documentary. But the novel is set in a particular time and place, and her research adds colour, depth and drama to the narrative.

How much research?

Not all writers acknowledge their sources in the way that Waters does in *The Night Watch*. Her acknowledgements give a very full idea of the process through which a writer might go. She acknowledges forty published non-fiction sources alone (Waters, 2006, pp.471–3) as well as numerous conversations.

The next activity asks you to think about what research a writer may have done. Liz Jensen's novel *War Crimes for the Home* (2002) contains a passage in which the main character, Gloria, is remembering an incident during the Second World War, when she falls for a GI stationed in her home town. Gloria is a munitions worker who has that day witnessed a horrific accident in the factory where she works.

ACTIVITY 3.3 Reading	Read the extract from Jensen's *War Crimes for the Home* (Reading 7 on p.307).

- What kind of research and sources do you think Jensen would have had to undertake to write this extract?
- What information in the passage suggests the period Gloria is remembering? List the phrases and information that you think refer to the period.

DISCUSSION	In *War Crimes for the Home*, Jensen was less prolific in her use of sources than Waters. She used an anthology, *The New Yorker Book of War Pieces*, from which she says that she 'occasionally ... quoted directly ... but mostly [she] modified and re-invented their accounts to fit [her] story' (Jensen, 2002, p.227). She also used a contemporary diary, and an account of GI brides, whose author, Pamela Winfield, read Jensen's manuscript, and helped Jensen to spot any accidental incongruities. Jensen also received a travel grant to visit a GI bride who had moved to California after the war. This mixture of reading and conversation is powerful. If your work is set in the not-too-distant past, it is as vital to talk to those who are in the know as it is to consult archive material.

You'll have seen in the passage, I think, that Jensen has added a little period slang, some wartime jokes ('one Yank ...') and the occasional contemporary reference (Clark Gable, doing the 'boomp', the song she quotes). Jensen needs to do less work than Waters because her narrator is actually an elderly woman, looking back, fifty years later.

The following activity gives you the opportunity to try some further research, and to use this research to produce a piece of writing.

ACTIVITY 3.4 Research and writing	First, choose one subject from this list:

- the lindy-hop;
- the work of a rat catcher;
- cloud formations;
- sleep apnoea;
- doll collecting.

Now, work through the following steps:

1 Make a list of sources you might use to research your chosen subject. You could start by looking at the British Library catalogue, which can be found online (British Library, 2007). You could also

use your local library catalogue, or look through any index to newspapers held there – most libraries carry *The Times*, either on CD-ROM or microfiche.

2 Make a copy of what you find – articles, extracts, passages, definitions – and list the possibilities they offer for a story.

3 Write up to 400 words on your initial idea.

4 When you have finished, go back to your research sheet and use a highlighter to pick out what you have lifted. What did you choose? What did you reject?

DISCUSSION

It is always important to allow yourself to use this kind of research as a springboard. If you find yourself being attracted by another idea in the process, follow your instinct and discard the original suggestion. You might well find that you rejected all, or almost all, the research, and headed off in a new direction entirely.

Using what you know

Some writers who might seem to have done a great deal of research have done much less than people think. Mark Haddon's *The Curious Incident of the Dog in the Night-time* (2003) uses a narrator, Christopher, who has Asperger Syndrome, a form of autism – colloquially known as Asperger's. Haddon testified that he:

> did no specific research at all. Many years ago I worked with people with a variety of disabilities (all of them more seriously disabled than Christopher), so I feel comfortable writing about the subject and have what you might call an interested layperson's knowledge of autism and Asperger's. Beyond that I reasoned (rightly, I think, in retrospect) that the novel would work best if I simply tried to make Christopher seem like a believable human being, rather than trying to make him medically 'correct'. In short, if I treated him like any other character and didn't make him a special case ... These days, if you have a reasonably large group of friends and you are as nosy as I am about people's personal lives, you will almost certainly know people with a child who has been diagnosed with autism or Asperger's ... [I used] a little personal knowledge, [did] no research and [used] a lot of imagination ... Christopher's character was, to a large extent, patched together by taking habits, opinions, patterns of thoughts and bits of behaviour from a range of people I know very well,

none of whom would ever be labelled as having a disability (the maths, for example, is me; the refusal to eat different foods which are touching is my niece ... and so on).

(Haddon, 2004)

Haddon's research was primary, personal. Without at least some research, your writing is likely to be less absorbing. In some cases, your primary sources will be your own experience, your own notebooks, your own diaries, and your own memory – and these will be very rich sources indeed, provided that you put them to work.

When you research, you are undertaking the first stage of preparing for writing. As you research, be prepared to go off at a tangent, to allow your mind to explore new possibilities. You may find that the research itself triggers new directions for your work. A minor character may become a major character, for example, or a new thread may enliven your work in an unexpected way.

The same is true when you begin to work. As you write, you will revise, and as you do so, you will sharpen and focus your original idea. Drafting and editing are both creative processes, and, effectively, they are forms of active research. In drafting and editing, you are researching the pattern of your own ideas. You are adapting the material to make it more dramatic.

Rewriting
Cutting

You will almost certainly find that research gives you far too much material, and the hardest thing will be deciding what not to use. It is always tempting to include slabs of detail which is in itself inherently interesting. This is as true of life writing as it is of fiction – indeed, there is a strong temptation to include every known fact about an individual in a piece of life writing, but you need to suppress any instinct you have to become an archivist.

For her television play *Housewife, 49*, Victoria Wood drew on the same material as *Nella Last's War*, a first-hand account of one woman's experiences in the Second World War. It was compiled from the archives of the Mass-Observation project, which invited volunteers to send in accounts of their daily life to a central unit. These accounts were never intended for broader publication, although it was always understood that extracts might be used in bulletins.

Richard Broad and Suzie Fleming, the editors of *Nella Last's War*, reduced the original material from about two million words to about 100,000 – they cut 95 per cent of the material in order to make character, voice, place and time come alive.

ACTIVITY 3.5 Reading	First, read the extract from *Nella Last's War* (Reading 8 on p.310). Next, read the extract from Wood's television play *Housewife, 49* (Reading 9 on p.311). • In what way has Wood transformed the material to make it more dramatic? • What has Wood selected, and what has she left out?
DISCUSSION	This scene in *Housewife, 49* is the only one that has an almost exact parallel in *Nella Last's War*. Wood (who drafted the script nine times) successively reinvented and developed the characters, and added several others. Yet even in this scene, you can see that Wood has condensed the material into an argument which takes about one minute and fifteen seconds, and which is set in the evening, at bedtime. The scene concludes with Nella opting to sleep in the Morrison shelter (earlier in *Nella Last's War*, there has been reference to Nella and her husband sleeping separately, but not as the result of an argument). The storm is not allowed to 'blow over', and the scene is not resolved by Cliff's return. Indeed, one of the features of *Housewife, 49* is that it develops the husband's character considerably (he is rarely mentioned in Nella Last's account), both as a pompous and semi-comic character.
ACTIVITY 3.6 Writing	Find a section of memoir or autobiography (you might like to choose some further Mass-Observation material, some of which can be viewed online; see Mass-Observation, 2007). Write a draft of a short scene which draws on the material you have chosen (you should see this very much as a preliminary sketch). Annotate the original so that you can see what you have crossed out and what you have inserted. When you read it aloud, it should last no longer than two minutes. • What decisions have you made about what to change? • What have you cut? What have you added?
DISCUSSION	You will find that you need to remove a great deal of extraneous material from any source you use. As you cut, you will sharpen the focus. Condensing material is essential to the process of adaptation.

You will be looking more closely at the process of dramatic adaptation in Part 2.

Changing styles

You can learn a great deal about the process of drafting by adjusting the style of a piece of writing. This is not unlike the process of translating from one language to another (and sometimes back again). For instance, if you take a passage of densely written prose and simplify it, you will gain an insight into the process through which the original writing has gone. The following lines are from Dylan Thomas's *Under Milk Wood*:

> It is night in the chill, squat chapel, hymning, in bonnet and brooch and bombazine black, butterfly choker and bootlace bow, coughing like nannygoats, sucking mintoes, fortywinking hallelujah ...

> (Thomas, 1977 [1954], p.2)

I might clarify them like this:

> The chapel is small and cold and dark, but it somehow sounds as if the congregation of women are in there, despite it being night-time.

What I have written is clear. However, it is very *un*-dramatic. What Thomas has done, in a highly ornate and poetic fashion, is to develop a concentrated sequence of expressive images. He has also manipulated the rhythm of the lines so that it is rich and strange, almost other-worldly.

ACTIVITY 3.7
Writing

Take a passage from a novel, short story, poem or some life writing, preferably a passage with which you are unfamiliar. If it is prose, choose about ten sentences; if it is a poem, choose about ten lines. Choose a passage that is rich and complex. Now work through these four stages:

1 Rewrite the passage so that it is much plainer, and concentrates on the information provided.
2 Leave what you have written for a day or two.
3 Now rewrite your piece in a more expansive style, without consulting the original. Try to introduce a distinctive rhythm, and some fresh and unusual words or analogies (in this context, this means using similes or metaphors).
4 Compare your rewritten piece with the original. What do you now notice about the way the original has been constructed?

DISCUSSION In going through this process of alteration and adaptation, you will see that the drafting process can be one both of reduction and of expansion. At every step, there will have been choices to make. You will have changed the shape, the rhythm, the tone and the density of the language. Perhaps you will have found that, when you expanded the piece, you were too lavish with your language. A much-quoted passage from *On the Art of Writing* by Sir Arthur Quiller-Couch recommends that you obey any impulse to 'perpetrate a piece of exceptionally fine writing' – and then 'delete it before sending your manuscript to press. Murder your darlings' (Quiller-Couch, 1946 [1916], p.157). It can be very fulfilling to overwrite, to get the words out of your system, and then to cut.

Rewriting someone else's words can be hard, but it can also be rewarding. It is an exercise which will always teach you a great deal about patterning, about variation and about style. You will return to this in Chapter 13.

In the next reading, you will see how Sylvia Plath drew on her own, highly detailed notes, to create a poem – by expanding, reducing, changing and reshaping her material.

ACTIVITY 3.8
Reading

Read the extract from Sylvia Plath's journals about a journey taken with her husband, the poet Ted Hughes (Reading 10 on p.312), to visit a local bee-keeper in Devon.

Then read Plath's poem 'The Bee Meeting' (Reading 11 on p.315). Look at the language of the poem; how does she borrow from her own journals to create her poem?

DISCUSSION

You can see that Plath is a working writer who is consciously looking for material she can use, storing it up for its potential – both for poetry and prose. She wrote this journal entry in June 1962, but only used the bee image in early October.

You can learn from Plath the importance of looking for dramatic images even while you take notes. In the journal, Plath constantly uses adjectives and comparisons to fix how she felt. One woman looks 'as cadaverous as a librarian'. The coat she is given looks like that of a pharmacist's assistant; the bees look as if they are 'zinging ... dancing ... as at the end of long elastics'. This image of elastic will survive into the poem.

Through the process of writing in a journal or notebook, you can find sudden moments of focus. The crucial part of Plath's journal entry comes when she comments: 'The ugliness & anonymity very compelling, as if we were all party to a rite.'

It is the ritual aspect of the process that sticks in her imagination. In the journal, she notes that she feels alienated, an outsider, 'bare'. The poem turns this into a much more surreal affair, in which the central image is of being the victim of a ritual.

In moving from a notebook or journal to a poem or story, you will find that much mundane material is stripped away. Plath's poem isolates the speaker immediately, whereas in her journal, she knows several people by name and is with her husband. She accentuates the feeling of being 'bare' by introducing uncertainty as to why she is being 'met', and turns the people into hostile figures by having her speaker feel in need of 'protection'. In the original, Plath has just forgotten to bring a sweater. In the poem her speaker is being kept in the dark deliberately. The people are smiling, but this is seen as sinister, as if they have a secret.

The rector, the midwife and the secretary of the society are all retained in the poem, but Mr Pollard ('dark, nice brown eyes') has gone. There are no names, and the secretary becomes 'the secretary of bees', a more formal and peculiar title, as if part of a threatening and remote order.

Plath shows how writers, having made notes as themselves, can transform the material into something new, different, unusual. Plath makes her speaker much more vulnerable, not only to the people, but to the bees. Her cuffs are buttoned, as if she is a mentally disturbed patient being restrained. She is like a prisoner, being led through the beanfield. In the journal, Plath is like everybody else, 'slowly fil[ing] after Charlie Pollard'.

Her observations of the environment in the journal are fairly neutral. In the poem, the speaker sees the environment as dangerous and hostile. The hawthorn is threatening ('etherising'); the gorse has 'spiky armoury'. What Plath has done is to cut out the understanding she has of the process. Her speaker is not involved in any conversation (as Plath is), and is being inducted into a semi-religious ceremony.

The bee expert from Exeter undergoes a great transformation. In the journal, he is even named; the speaker in the poem sees a surgeon, an apparition who hides his identity. Surgeons are associated with knives; so are magicians. By the end of the poem, the speaker seems to have been ritually sacrificed and placed in a long white box. The original irritation at being cold has been turned into a sort of death.

The journal does not describe a nightmare. The poem *creates* a nightmare, by the use of so many questions, and by the apparent indifference of the bystanders. The domestic detail has gone. Instead, the emphasis is on the voice, on the hypnotic repetition of states of fear. What Plath has done is to create a new world out of an actual one, and in the process she has turned the experience into a sequence of emotions, rather than a sequence of events.

Using a journal or notebook in this way will energise your writing. By keeping a journal, you will find that you become more and more alert to the potential of your ideas. Part of the process is about safe-keeping, but another part is about generating your own material. It is a good idea to wait a week or more after making your notes before looking at them again, to see what details seem potentially dynamic and dramatic, and pick out what is most useful.

Conclusion

This chapter has illustrated how source material is important and how its use can be potentially complex, demanding and interesting. Research will also provide you with the necessary detail you need to give fiction an air of authenticity. As you can see, the use to which research can be put can lead to very different outcomes, even when you are writing autobiographical and biographical material. Research and revision are the way you transform the words you set down – and the process of transformation is at the heart of drama, the genre you will explore in Part 2.

References

British Library (2007) *British Library Integrated Catalogue* [online], London: British Library, catalogue.bl.uk (accessed 24 October 2007).

Dick, Kay (ed.) (1967) *Writers at Work: The Paris Review interviews*, Harmondsworth: Penguin.

Haddon, Mark (2003) *The Curious Incident of the Dog in the Night-time*, London: Random House.

Haddon, Mark (2004) Interview, *Guardian Unlimited* [online], 2 February, http://books.guardian.co.uk/departments/generalfiction/story/0,,1137378,00.html (accessed 23 November 2007).

Jensen, Liz (2002) *War Crimes for the Home*, London: Bloomsbury.

Lockley, Frea (2006) 'The Stain' (unpublished).

Logan, J.S. (1961) 'Flax byssinosis: a clinical account', *Occupational Medicine* (London), vol.11, pp.178–9.

Mass-Observation (2007) *The Mass-Observation Archive* [online], Brighton: Mass-Observation, http://www.massobs.org.uk/index.htm (accessed 24 October 2007).

Penney, Stef (2006) *The Tenderness of Wolves*, London: Quercus.

Quiller-Couch, Arthur (1946 [1916]) *On the Art of Writing*, Cambridge: Guild.

Smith, Sid (2001) *Something Like a House*, London: Picador.

Smith, Sid (2002) 'Case study 7 – Enriching the imagination: Sid Smith's travels in the interior', *Twenty-ninth Annual Report and Accounts, British Library* [online], London: British Library, http://www.bl.uk/about/annual/arcasestudies.html#7 (accessed 24 October 2007).

Thomas, Dylan (1977 [1954]) *Under Milk Wood*, London: Dent.

Waters, Sarah (2006) *The Night Watch*, London: Virago.

Further reading

Garfield, Simon (ed.) (2004) *Our Hidden Lives: The everyday diaries of a forgotten Britain, 1945–1948*, London: Ebury.

Sheridan, Dorothy (ed.) (1990) *Wartime Women: An anthology of women's wartime writing for Mass-Observation 1937–45*, London: Heinemann.

Both these anthologies of Mass-Observation writing are not only full of powerful source material for your own adaptations, but are also excellent examples of editing from substantial archive material.

4   Writing stage plays

Derek Neale

This chapter will start to explore ways of writing drama. You will examine some dramatic principles that apply across all media, focusing in particular on writing stage plays. Besides creating original scenes, you will also start to examine methods for adapting stories for the stage. The short story 'Violin Lessons', discussed in Chapter 1, will be used as an adaptation text, enabling you to see what a stage version might look like (in Chapters 7 and 8 the same story will be used to create radio and film adaptations). In this chapter you will also start to explore ways of writing dialogue, surveying some typical features of speech that your characters might use, and working on these in order to develop more individual voices and characters.

Contrast creating conflict

Writing drama, for whatever medium, involves the challenge of creating contrasts – between characters, between voices, between what is seen and what is heard. Contrast and differentiation create both clarity and conflict in the storytelling. Such contrast is not arbitrary or created for the sake of variety. It is generated by the events of the story and the action of the narrative. This chapter will elaborate on what this might mean when you come to write scripts for the stage. We will concentrate on dialogue and establish some scripting principles.

When two characters walk on a stage, the audience immediately tries to distinguish between them – one is tall perhaps, and he uses odd words; another wears a yellow dress and has a bandage round her hand. Once the audience has distinguished between the characters it must try to guess at the conflict between and within them. Why is the character with the yellow dress looking away from the character who uses the odd words? Does the character with the bandaged hand feel sad or angry about her wound? The attention of the audience is immediately engaged by the need to gather clues about the conflict, and to anticipate its depth and subtlety.

Samuel Beckett's *Waiting for Godot* begins with a simple conflict: Estragon is struggling in vain to remove his boot. Eventually he exclaims: 'Nothing to be done.' Vladimir enters and says:

> Vladimir: I'm beginning to come round to that opinion. All my life I've tried to put it from me, saying, Vladimir, be reasonable, you haven't yet tried everything. And I resumed the struggle.
>
> (Beckett, 1985 [1956], p.9)

Straightaway the audience is given a contrast in the characters. Both have conflicts of their own – one is involved in a simple, physical struggle and is rather terse, the other is more loquacious and philosophical. Difference is comically established, even in this simple setting, with two characters – a double act – who have no recognisably 'real' agenda. They don't go to work, or go home – they are just waiting.

When Hamlet comes on stage with Horatio and Marcellus in Shakespeare's *Hamlet* (Shakespeare, 2001a, Act 1, Scene 4, pp.298–9) and they are faced with the ghost of Hamlet's father, the audience soon sees the difference between the characters – a difference in their status – but also, crucially, a different conflict within each character. Horatio's conflict springs from his concern for his friend, Hamlet. Should he protect him from this ghost? How can he? Marcellus is fighting his fear of the spectre. Hamlet's conflict comes from his suspicion of his mother's infidelity with his uncle, whom he also suspects of killing his father. Does the ghost confirm these suspicions? Should he, Hamlet, seek revenge? These differences motivate the actors in how they perform the scene.

ACTIVITY 4.1 Research	Watch or listen to two or three minutes of drama – on television, film or radio. Spot the contrast between each of the characters. Identify the conflict between and within the individual characters.

DISCUSSION	Conflict is a universal element of drama across all media. Sometimes a drama's conflict will be quite complex, as with Hamlet; at other times it can be apparently trivial, as with Estragon and his boot. It will rarely be expressed in abstract terms in the script, but will be shown rather than told. For instance, a character would not instantly declare that she is torn between her lover and her children: it would be shown in the action of the drama. A character would not say that he despises himself as a failure: it would be shown in the things that he does. Without conflict the audience's interest would evaporate. It is created and harnessed by palpable contrasts – it is shown by differences in appearance and action, not by explanation.

Writing stage scripts

Dramatic scripts are performed, and only later and in some cases read as literature. In writing scripts you are writing, in the first instance at least, for a specific readership – directors and actors. Your lines will be enunciated, your stage directions will be enacted, and your set descriptions will be realised. In this sense play writing is a collaborative venture, involving director, actors and stage designers. You are writing a set of instructions for others to follow so that in turn they can present the story you are trying to tell. Paradoxically, while the instructions have to be clear and exact, they also have to give the performers scope to use their own imaginations. It is important to remember this in the scripts that you write. Ask yourself the following questions:

- How well does what you have written work as a set of instructions?
- Is the story clear – are the necessary narrative elements in place?
- Can your story be told well enough, given the lines and stage directions you have provided?
- Have you given the cast and theatrical crew enough to engage with, but not so much that they are unable to use their imaginations?
- How do you think your script would read to a potential actor, to a potential director and to a potential member of the audience?

Drama is a form of childlike play, embracing a naive and vibrant energy, both in its conception and performance, yet it is far from ill-disciplined and can create a most sophisticated form of narrative. Stage scripts are a condensed form of storytelling, tightly honed, and with no excess. On the page they can look a little like poems, with generous spaces and stanza-like word clusters. On first appearance plays might even appear bare and stark, lacking colour and detail. Only on closer scrutiny is it apparent that the elements contained in the script are the essential, storytelling kernels. We will now look at how a script is set out on the page, and how this layout conveys information concisely and clearly.

Script layout for the stage

Look at Figure 1, a sample page from a stage script containing details of particular features. What do you notice about the way in which the script is laid out?

This is an appropriate layout for a stage script, and you should refer back to it when writing your scripts. In Chapters 7 and 8 you will learn about the layouts for radio plays and film scripts.

You can see at once that there is clear differentiation between the spoken and the unspoken elements, indicated by generous spacing between sections of the script. This is because the actors need to be able to see their lines immediately, and to be able to identify any relevant stage directions at a glance. This example is what is called a 'submission script' – one that you might submit to an agent or theatre. You will notice that it differs radically in its formatting from published scripts, including those extracts of plays appearing in this book. For instance, the lines of dialogue don't wrap under the name of the speaker in this layout; there is a clean,

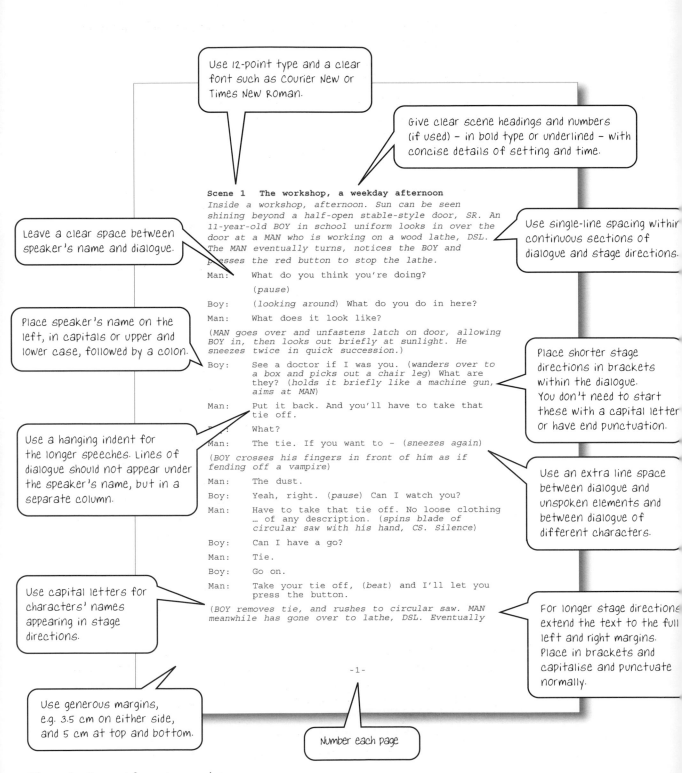

Use 12-point type and a clear font such as Courier New or Times New Roman.

Give clear scene headings and numbers (if used) – in bold type or underlined – with concise details of setting and time.

Leave a clear space between speaker's name and dialogue.

Place speaker's name on the left, in capitals or upper and lower case, followed by a colon.

Use a hanging indent for the longer speeches. Lines of dialogue should not appear under the speaker's name, but in a separate column.

Use capital letters for characters' names appearing in stage directions.

Use generous margins, e.g. 3.5 cm on either side, and 5 cm at top and bottom.

Use single-line spacing within continuous sections of dialogue and stage directions.

Place shorter stage directions in brackets within the dialogue. You don't need to start these with a capital letter or have end punctuation.

Use an extra line space between dialogue and unspoken elements and between dialogue of different characters.

For longer stage directions extend the text to the full left and right margins. Place in brackets and capitalise and punctuate normally.

Number each page

Scene 1   The workshop, a weekday afternoon
Inside a workshop, afternoon. Sun can be seen shining beyond a half-open stable-style door, SR. An 11-year-old BOY in school uniform looks in over the door at a MAN who is working on a wood lathe, DSL. The MAN eventually turns, notices the BOY and presses the red button to stop the lathe.

Man: What do you think you're doing?

          (pause)

Boy: *(looking around)* What do you do in here?

Man: What does it look like?

(MAN goes over and unfastens latch on door, allowing BOY in, then looks out briefly at sunlight. He sneezes twice in quick succession.)

Boy: See a doctor if I was you. *(wanders over to a box and picks out a chair leg)* What are they? *(holds it briefly like a machine gun, aims at MAN)*

Man: Put it back. And you'll have to take that tie off.

Boy: What?

Man: The tie. If you want to – *(sneezes again)*

(BOY crosses his fingers in front of him as if fending off a vampire)

Man: The dust.

Boy: Yeah, right. *(pause)* Can I watch you?

Man: Have to take that tie off. No loose clothing … of any description. *(spins blade of circular saw with his hand, CS. Silence)*

Boy: Can I have a go?

Man: Tie.

Boy: Go on.

Man: Take your tie off, *(beat)* and I'll let you press the button.

(BOY removes tie, and rushes to circular saw. MAN meanwhile has gone over to lathe, DSL. Eventually

-1-

Figure 1   Layout for a stage script

44

continuing margin between the names of the speakers and their dialogue. Below are some further tips on layout.

Stage scripts – some tips

- Put a cast list at the start of each play. Include in this the essential information for each character – usually only one or two words. Don't write mini-biographies.
- Always make it crystal clear who is on stage at any one time – this is often included in the opening stage directions.
- Avoid over-directing. Sometimes – only when the story demands it – you may have to position characters in particular places on the stage. Never overdo this. Use the following abbreviations:

    CS – centre-stage
    SL – stage left (i.e. the actor's left when facing the audience)
    SR – stage right
    DS or D – downstage (i.e. the front of the stage)
    DSL – downstage left
    US or U – upstage (i.e. the rear of the stage)
    USR – upstage right

- Clearly mark the characters' exits and entrances, designating the direction if appropriate ('BOY exits SL', for instance).
- Stage position is more difficult to establish when you are writing for a theatre-in-the-round stage, in which case it is conventional, if such instruction is necessary, to nominate one aspect as the front of the stage.
- Write the stage directions in a pared down style – use the present tense and cut out unnecessary verbs, pronouns, articles and descriptions.
- Within the dialogue, beware of indicating emphasised words and phrases in bold or italic type or with underlining – if there is an emphasis within a line, make sure it is written using syntax and diction, and without relying on typographic features.
- If a line needs to be shouted, put the instruction in the stage directions (if it isn't obvious) and don't type the line in capitals.
- Remember, the actors need to find the meaning and emphasis in lines themselves.

It is important to use an appropriate layout when submitting your work for consideration. Dramatic scripts are always written for a particular medium, and which medium this is should be instantly apparent from the script's layout. In this respect drama is a conservative form of writing, and the physical appearance of the script is the first impression that agents, directors and producers will have of the work. If a script is not laid out appropriately for its given medium it is liable to remain unread.

Using the correct script layout will also enable you to assess the play's running time. Timing a script is notoriously difficult. The best way is to read it through in real time, so that all the actions and pauses are assessed accurately. As a very rough guide, using the layout advice given here would give an average performance time of just over a minute for each A4 page of script. Be aware, though, that this is an average and not an accurate gauge for individual pages, or for all scripts.

Adaptation for the stage

You probably recognised that the characters in Figure 1 were those from the short story 'Violin Lessons' (Reading 1 on p.279). In adapting any story you will have to decide which parts of the original to keep and which to discard. We will now go on to consider in more detail some of the decisions to be made when adapting a story for the stage.

ACTIVITY 4.2
Reading

Read the script below – a stage adaptation of the start of 'Violin Lessons'. It begins at the point when the boy first enters the man's workshop (Reading 1, p.279). Try to look at the script from each of the recommended perspectives – those of the actors, the director and the audience.

Scene 1   The workshop, a weekday afternoon

Inside a workshop, afternoon. Sun can be seen shining beyond a half-open stable-style door, SR. An eleven-year-old BOY in school uniform looks in over the door at a MAN who is working on a wood lathe, DSL. The MAN eventually turns, notices the BOY and presses the red button to stop the lathe.

Man: What do you think you're doing?

    (pause)

Boy: *(looking around)* What do you do in here?

Man: What does it look like?

(MAN goes over and unfastens latch on door, allowing BOY in, then looks out briefly at sunlight. He sneezes twice in quick succession.)

Boy: See a doctor if I was you. *(wanders over to a box and picks out a chair leg)* What are they? *(holds it briefly like a machine gun, aims at MAN)*

Man: Put it back. And you'll have to take that tie off.

Boy: What?

Man: The tie. If you want to – (*sneezes again*)

(*BOY crosses his fingers in front of him as if fending off a vampire.*)

Man: The dust.

Boy: Yeah, right. (*pause*) Can I watch you?

Man: Have to take that tie off. No loose clothing ... of any description. (*spins blade of circular saw with his hand, CS. Silence*)

Boy: Can I have a go?

Man: Tie.

Boy: Go on.

Man: Take your tie off, (*beat*) and I'll let you press the button.

(*BOY removes tie, and rushes to circular saw. MAN meanwhile has gone over to lathe, DSL. Eventually turns to see BOY whizzing the blade of the circular saw with his hand.*)

Man: Get off that.

Boy: You said I could have a go.

Man: Not that. Here, that's too ... and I only said you could press the button. Where did you put your tie?

Boy: (*going over to lathe*) Where'd you think?

(*MAN points at green button on wall, BOY presses, lathe starts, wood spins.*)

Man: Behind me, okay? Keep away from it.

(*Pause, before MAN feels assured the BOY is still, then he picks chisel from bench, starts working the wood. BOY watches MAN, who is intent on his work.*)

DISCUSSION

As well as going to see plays, it is important to read as many play scripts as you can. Besides the examples given in this book, take out your favourite plays from the library and start reading these in different ways – from the various perspectives of the actors, director and audience. Do you think there is enough scope in the script above for the director and actors to be able to interpret events, and to be able to engage imaginatively with the action? Note how the conflict is heightened in this adaptation, and how the dialogue is never cumbersome; it conveys only the necessary story information. The dialogue is a part of the action, creating a sense of movement in the storytelling.

Overwriting

Agents, directors and producers are seriously discouraged by scripts which are clearly overwritten. Look at this alternative version of the script:

Man: What do you think you're doing?

Boy: What's your name?

(The boy looks around in a way that makes the man wonder. When the boy speaks it seems as though his voice echoes. The man doesn't get many visitors.)

Man: William, what's yours?

Boy: Jonathan, but my friends call me Jonny. What do you do in here? There's a lot of dust, isn't there? You must have a problem with your breathing.

Man: My sense of smell is the aspect which is most severely affected, Jonny.

Boy: What do you mean, William?

Man: Come in if you like, Jonny, have a look around. Have to take that tie off though. If there's a rule worth having it's that one: **no loose clothing of any description**. Before you know it the circular saw will have it. Or else it'll get wrapped around the lathe. And you'll go with it.

Boy: Can I have a go, William?

Man: No, Jonny, but you can press the button if you want to see me in action.

Boy: Okay, I'll press the button.

(Boy presses the button and the lathe starts and whirs, the oak begins to spin.)

This adaptation translates the short story too literally, taking not only all the lines of dialogue from the original but also including passages of description. There is too much information. Actors would find the lines difficult to say: some of them are too grammatically correct, presented as written sentences not as spoken phrases, and many of them overuse names. Characters on stage only use the addressee's name in certain circumstances, perhaps to emphasise a point or to distinguish the addressee from a third character, or sometimes to heighten status – but they rarely do it regularly like this, between supposed strangers and without rhetorical purpose. Writers new to drama often overuse character names inadvertently, so watch for this. It is always good to give your characters names, but it is not always necessary to use these in the dialogue.

It is best not to use bold or any other typographic effect for emphasis, as happens here – the emphasis should be achieved in the line, in the way you arrange the words. Beware of over-instructing the actors. Some of the dialogue in this version tends to narrate what is already apparent in the visual action on stage – as with the pressing of the button at the end. This sort of duplication is wearisome for the audience and can appear unintentionally comic. The narrative is implausible in part because it gives too much information. When adapting stories, do not feel obliged to put in all the dialogue from the original story, and feel free to invent lines. Make sure lines follow the thoughts of the characters. In this version there is no dramatic logic to the way the characters act and speak, and without such logic it is unlikely that the audience will be interested in, or come to care about, the characters.

Characters and idiom

You can see from these two possible adaptations that, in terms of dialogue, less often means more – greater clarity in the storytelling but also greater scope for the actors and director to use their imaginations in performance. This also illustrates the vital function of dialogue: it is action. It is not arbitrary or included for decoration. It always serves a purpose. It propels the story forward, while at the same time revealing and developing characters.

In one sense, dialogue functions to reveal information about the characters – who they are, where they have come from, where they are going to, what their desires and fears are. Yet often dialogue will do all of this discreetly; it will hint at and imply character information. Characters often hold back about themselves, and sometimes they tell lies. The audience must try to surmise the truth in what is being said, and in what is not being said. In many ways that is how the audience comes to care about the characters, by imagining the parts of the story that are missing. For the playwright, finding the appropriate voice and way of talking is a crucial part of character creation and development.

Some playwrights create characters who speak in a certain idiom or dialect – a variety of language usage which is peculiar to a limited district, ethnic group, class of people or section of society. The dialect of such characters is stylised in the script by focusing on certain aspects of the language such characters might use. Tanika Gupta often writes with an alert ear for the ways in which different groups in society use language.

ACTIVITY 4.3
Reading

Read the extract from *Sanctuary* by Tanika Gupta (Reading 12 on p.316). Try to identify the elements in the dialogue that typify the way that the various characters speak.

DISCUSSION

Here we have:

- Afro-Caribbean English – Sebastian, typified by the use of words like 'man' and 'brother', and his use of expletives for emphasis;
- middle-class English – Jenny, a vicar, typified by the haste with which she pronounces complete thoughts;
- Asian-English – Kabir, who often uses a continuous present tense: 'Don't be talking about the past'; 'we are needing';
- African-English – Michael, who is formally correct in his manner and therefore usually in his sentences too, rarely using contractions (i.e. he says 'you are' rather than 'you're').

Sometimes it is necessary to instruct the actor that a character should talk with a certain accent – a London or an American accent, for example. Gupta does that here with Michael – instructing the actor to say his lines with an African accent. She has to give instruction with Michael because his lines might otherwise be pronounced in a different way. Sebastian's and Kabir's lines do not need such specific instruction because the word choices and idiosyncratic grammar in their lines make the idiom self-explanatory, especially when coupled with their descriptions in the cast list: 'middle-aged Afro-Caribbean man' and 'Asian man' respectively. Such voices are useful to the dramatist because they help create instantly recognisable characters. Yet the obvious danger here is that you can inadvertently perpetuate negative stereotypes based on class or ethnic background. Gupta often uses such typical voices in her comic writing – types are good in comedy. In this instance, in more serious mode, she uses such voices to create contrasts, and in the rest of the play deals with how such ethnic stereotyping sits against the reality of individual sensibilities and life histories.

Beware apostrophes

In her play *Caravan*, Helen Blakeman establishes that all her characters talk with Liverpool accents by giving the following instructions in the initial cast list: 'The women of the play are from the south Liverpool suburbs, the men are from north Liverpool' (1998, p.v). She also uses phonetic spellings in the lines. Mick, one of the first characters on stage, says 'orright' and 'dunno' repeatedly. Kim, the play's main character, speaks more volubly and many of the beginnings and endings of her words are cut off, or have other kinds of phonetic spellings. Here Kim reveals what she thinks about a suggestion that her family might own the caravan, the location for the play:

> Kim: Ya jokin' aren't ya? I'd go off me 'ead comin' 'ere all the
>   time with me mum an' me sister.
>
> (Blakeman, 1998, Act 1, Scene 1, p.2)

Such a line exhibits both the strengths and weaknesses of phonetic spelling and the use of apostrophes. The line certainly realises the dialect, but without the initial instruction – that the characters speak with Liverpool accents – the phonetic spelling in this line might be interpreted, and then enunciated, in a number of different ways. It is far better when first writing dialogue only to use phonetics and apostrophes when you really have to. In the hands of those new to writing dialogue, overuse of apostrophes often leads to a more confusing script – for the actors and the audience.

You will see even from the short quote above that finding the right choice of word is very important in establishing how your character speaks. In this instance, Blakeman's character says 'me' instead of 'my'. Rather than using phonetics, try to choose idiosyncratic words and word order to typify a way of speaking. Steven Berkoff's play *Greek*, set in the East End of London, uses no apostrophes but instead has key phonetic spellings of words – 'abaht' instead of 'about'; 'nah' instead of 'no'; 'lorst' instead of 'lost'; 'orf' instead of 'off' (1994 [1982]). These key words typify the London accent – almost to the point of lampooning it. You can use such phonetic spellings, but beware of the danger. Do you want to lampoon that particular way of speaking? If not, then you need to find a subtler way of writing the accent.

ACTIVITY 4.4
Writing

Pick one of the following situations and write a one-page script (one to two minutes long, up to 350 words) using at least two distinct voices, one of which should reveal a particular idiom or dialect:

- at the passport desk at a foreign airport;

- at the half-time hot-dog stall at a football match;
- at the cloakroom desk at a charity ball.

The key to writing particular idioms is to be selective in the detail you use to stylise the language. You need to give enough to the actor but not too much. Generally be wary of using too many apostrophes. Sometimes the instruction in the cast list or before the character's first line – to speak with a Scottish or Irish voice, for example – will be enough. But you should also be wary of being too general. A 'Scottish voice' might be enough in some instances, but there are many varieties of Scottish voices – compare the accents of Glasgow to those of the west coast, for instance. Blakeman offers a fine differentiation between north and south Liverpool in *Caravan*. In *Sanctuary* Michael is described as having an African voice, which gives the actor a pretty wide scope for interpretation – that of a whole continent. It is up to you to decide how precise you want to be, and you can usually decide that on the basis of the needs of your story.

It is important in your writing that, when you use idiom to create a character, you consider the wider consequences of your representations. Using typical ways of speaking is useful up to a point, since it taps into universal knowledge about the way certain people talk and behave. But you need to develop such voices in individuals, to avoid the negative connotations of such stereotypes – and, of course, to interest your audience by developing rounded characters. Flat, stereotypical characters are instantly recognisable but have only a limited appeal.

Individual voice

Of more importance than idiom is a character's idiosyncratic speech patterns, the form of expression and use of language peculiar to an individual. This is often referred to as a character's idiolect.

A character's dialogue should always be consistent rather than correct, reflecting his or her individuality. This means that the dialogue should be regular according to the character's own way of speaking. It should engage in his or her diction, by using favourite words, and excluding others. It should engage with the character's personal sense and use of grammar, including odd verb usage and the use of strange syntax – the character's idiosyncratic way of ordering words. So, for example, be careful about having a character saying 'ain't' throughout and then suddenly 'is not' – unless, of course, there is a good reason for that shift (i.e. perhaps the character is trying to effect emphasis or be polite).

Whether or not a character's dialogue typifies a place, class or their ethnic origins, it is important, especially with your main characters, that their voice reveals an individual sensibility. For instance, you might create a character with a Norfolk voice; her dialect is such that she will often slip the word 'now' incongruously into what she is saying – 'I now go down the road'. There is also a slippage in tense here. The meaning of the sentence is 'I have just been down the road', but the line uses the present tense. This use of 'now' and the tense slippage typify how someone from Norfolk might speak. The line uses diction, grammar and syntax – and is not littered with apostrophes and contractions.

So far, so good; the line has achieved a certain familiarity, and an audience may recognise where it comes from. You have also managed to avoid using phonetic spellings. Yet you have still not achieved an individual voice. Knowing the language tricks that can typify a way of speaking is not enough in itself. In order to make a voice more individual you need to imagine the character more fully; imagine her life history, what she might look like, her social relations, her work, her age, her desires, her fears, her traumas, her major life events and so forth. Her voice will be shaped in subtle ways by all these elements. And it will also be shaped by being placed in the context of a story. Compare the line above with this development of the line:

> I now go down the road to see him, but he's drove off. And ... and I ... well you know, don't you, you know how I, what we were like together. You saw us. I now go down there and he's ... well, he's gone.

Now we have an individual's thoughts, as well as the local dialect and the buds of a story. Given a context the lines start to come alive with the tempo of natural, individual speech repetitions and variations (notice the use of 'you'). The more scripts you read, and performances you see and hear, the more you will witness this. The way a character speaks is often what makes him or her distinct and can often give that subtle inflexion of an individual sensibility to your portrayal of the character. In your stage writing, remember to check the following:

- Can the lines be spoken, or are they too 'written'?
- Are the lines too grammatically correct, or do they follow the grammar of the character as they should?
- Is there a clear enough difference between the voices in the dialogue?
- Is the idiom or dialect clearly established in the lines and in bracketed instructions?
- Are the voices of your main characters those of individuals?

Overheard phrases

Many of the characters you create will not have voices with a regional or ethnic timbre. Recently I heard a professor giving a speech. The professor had a middle-class – what might be termed 'BBC English' – voice, clear and precise but perhaps a little bland. Because he was giving an important talk his speech was littered with cautious qualifiers – 'it seems to me'; 'that is to say'; 'as it were' – and sometimes one of these phrases was repeated two or even three times in a single line. Such clauses will sound familiar to most teachers and people who have to speak publicly. They are oratorical devices that can slow or increase the pace of what you are saying, or add emphasis. He did not, one hopes, go home and use such phrases when addressing his cat or children, and it is intriguing to imagine what phrases he might use in those circumstances. The contrast between what people say in private and in public is always fascinating. But the point is that in any particular context, an individual's speech patterns can be distinct because they use the simplest of repeated words or phrases. In Alan Ayckbourn's *Just Between Ourselves*, the character Vera is lacking in confidence:

> Vera: It's quicker to walk really. And then there's the parking and
> all that. It's very bad these days trying to park. Dreadful.
> (*slight pause*) And then, well really I found I didn't really
> enjoy driving really. I used to get so tense, you know. All
> the other traffic and, er, I couldn't seem ... well, I'm not a
> very good driver.
>
> (Ayckbourn, 1979 [1977], Act 1, Scene 2, pp.37–8)

Vera's hesitations (marked in the script by pauses, incomplete clauses and ellipses), and repeated use of 'really', signal her disposition. This seems to reach a peak with the double use of 'really' in one line. A character's idiolect can be signalled with these most basic and familiar bits of language.

The voice of Iago in Shakespeare's *Othello* is sometimes distinguished just by its overuse of the first person. For instance, when planting the seeds of jealousy in Othello's mind, his speech is littered with 'I':

> Iago: I am glad of this: for now I shall have reason
> To show the love and duty that I bear you
> With franker spirit. Therefore, as I am bound,
> Receive it from me. I speak not yet of proof:
>
> (Shakespeare, 2001b, Act 3, Scene 3, p.959)

This avowal, of course, is riddled with betrayal, and the repeated 'I' signals the devious way in which Iago adopts multiple identities within the play.

ACTIVITY 4.5
Research and
writing

Listen to conversations on the street, in cafes, in your workplace – even people talking on the radio. Note the diction, some phrases, repeated words, word order, and types of words. Were the words long or short? What parts of the speech were used? What patterns arose? Were there any that typified each person?

Listen to the differing speeds of delivery, the crescendos and lulls. Try to identify favoured words or word formations – use of 'really', use of 'quite', terms of endearment or affiliation (love, dear, mate, pal), and use of expletives. Note down as much as you can, and identify two voices, or turns of phrase even, that you think you could develop. From this start, work up two characters. Even if you didn't hear these voices at the same time, put them together in a setting and get them talking together – sketch some lines in your notebook (up to 300 words).

DISCUSSION

What you probably found when listening to conversations was that people often fail to complete sentences and that words conceal meaning as much as reveal it. You might also have noticed that some people hesitate and stumble over words. Some race through whatever they want to say, whereas others take their time.

Random conversational voices are also without plot and are not shaped. They would be of little interest to an audience. As soon as you start working on such voices you start shaping them, developing implicit backgrounds and character traits. There will be more work on individual ways of speaking when you get to the chapter on radio writing. For now let's consider in a little more detail the importance of pace and rhythm in dialogue.

Pace and rhythm

David Mamet suggests that:

> in English, we speak colloquially in iambic pentameter: 'I'm going down to the store to buy the cheese,' 'I told him, but he didn't hear a word,' 'I swear I'll love you till the day I die,' 'not now, not later, never. Is that clear?'
>
> If we listen we can hear people in a dialogue complete the iambic line for each other.
>
> 'I saw him on the street.'
> 'And what'd he say?'
> 'He said leave him alone.'

'And what'd you say?'
'What do you think I said?'
'Well, I don't know.'

(Mamet, 1998, p.66)

Many playwrights embrace this natural rhythm in the way we speak; Shakespeare, for instance, used iambic pentameter in his plays. Mamet's example of an exchange, quoted above, echoes the Latin mass or catechism: a statement and response, or question and answer. The regular and insistent pace of such an exchange is familiar to us.

Yet lines of dialogue do not always get a response of equal measure; questions do not always get answered. Some questions, even in Mamet's brief example, are answered with another question. Sometimes the pace in stage dialogue varies – and needs to vary. One character might speak more than another or the exchange might be more littered with one-word, staccato exchanges, or filled with hesitations and pauses. The story and the characters force the pace and rhythm of particular exchanges, rather than any arbitrary need to create contrasts. But it is important to be aware of the effect. Longer lines full of assonance generally slow the pace, and shorter lines with monosyllabic words quicken it.

Punctuation and pauses always affect the speed of exchanges, so it is important that you are precise in how you 'give breaths' to your actors. The script extracts you have read in this chapter contain illustrations of a hierarchy of breaks in the dialogue. The briefest break is signalled by a comma (,) and a slightly longer break by a full stop (.). A longer break is signalled by an ellipsis (...), longer still by (*beat*), then (*pause*), then (*silence*). These are your basic tools of rhythm in a line. Note that an ellipsis at the end of a line indicates that the speech trails off. A dash at the end of a line signals that the speech is interrupted or otherwise curtailed. It is up to you to set the pace using these instructions, as well as carefully gauging the length, sound and content of each line.

Conclusion

In this chapter you have seen how a stage script might be laid out. You have started to engage with stage voices, creating idiomatic voices and considering the idiolect of individual characters. You have seen how individual and typical speech patterns are often realised by using very simple parts of the language. You have been shown the correct layout for submission scripts for stage plays. You have been introduced to some techniques of stage adaptation, learning how to go about picking the parts of a story that need filleting or including, while also considering the dangers of overwriting. The next chapter will look at more methods that are used in stage plays, some of which can also be used when writing for other dramatic media.

References

Ayckbourn, Alan (1979 [1977]) *Just Between Ourselves* in *Joking Apart and Other Plays*, London: Chatto and Windus.

Beckett, Samuel (1985 [1956]) *Waiting for Godot*, London: Faber and Faber.

Berkoff, Steven (1994 [1982]) *Greek* in *Plays 1*, London: Faber and Faber.

Blakeman, Helen (1998) *Caravan*, London: Samuel French.

Mamet, David (1998) *Three Uses of the Knife*, New York: Columbia University Press.

Shakespeare, William (2001a) *Hamlet* in *The Arden Shakespeare Complete Works*, London: Arden.

Shakespeare, William (2001b) *Othello* in *The Arden Shakespeare Complete Works*, London: Arden.

Further reading

Ayckbourn, Alan (2002) *The Crafty Art of Playmaking*, London: Faber and Faber.

This is a concise testimony from the perspective of a seasoned practitioner, a playwright and director. It gives insight into the practical concerns of stagecraft while at the same time giving wide-ranging tips about play construction, with especially helpful advice on writing and punctuating dialogue and the function of characters.

Mamet, David (1994 [1978]) *Duck Variations* in *Plays: 1*, London: Methuen.

This play offers an entertaining double act in which two old men muse about the mating ducks in a park, knowing nothing about them but claiming to know a great deal. The short scenes are especially interesting in the context of what Mamet says about dialogue, and in terms of their potential for creating varieties of pace – very fast, short-line exchanges are mixed with slower, wordier exchanges.

Taylor, Val (2002) *Stage Writing: A practical guide*, Ramsbury: Crowood.

This offers specific advice on stagecraft and storytelling in different theatrical venues. It also gives clear advice on the appropriate layout for stage scripts.

5   Revealing secrets

Derek Neale

A play consists of a stream of information communicated from stage to audience. The art and craft of the playwright make that information interesting, presenting it in a form that makes the audience want to know more. The writer must turn his or her story into a secret, while at the same time advertising its allure and appearing gradually and incidentally to divulge its details. This chapter will examine different ways of presenting information to your audience, through the use of dialogue and monologue, and by revealing important elements of a story by using subtext – the hidden meaning that lies beneath the spoken words. You will be exploring how dramatic irony works and learning how to heighten the contrasts and conflicts in your scripts, in particular by looking at the nature of status relationships between your characters. You will examine how this might be a useful tool to use in helping to move the story along. Many of the methods discussed in this chapter will be applicable to other dramatic media, but here you will be writing for the stage. You will have the opportunity to adapt parts of stories you read in Part 1 – 'A Real Durwan' and 'Violin Lessons' – and to adapt and develop your own stories.

Exposition

The delivery of information to the audience is called exposition. All exposition should be planted as invisibly as possible, so the audience is unaware of being informed. Characters are key to this. As the playwright Mark Ravenhill says:

> The characters will reveal [the exposition]. If you pitch them into the middle of the situation, if you give them really strong needs ... they want stuff from each other, they're trying to do stuff to each other through the language, then exposition will happen naturally, and suddenly you'll say oh she's just told him what I wanted the audience to know.
>
> (Ravenhill, 2007)

Exposition should be motivated by the characters' intentions and aims, and in this way the delivery of exposition becomes less obtrusive.

One way to do this is to have a character who needs and wants to know information: a character whose major trait is to be inquisitive, or one who is on a quest. Or you could introduce an outsider, a newcomer, someone who needs to ask questions, to familiarise themselves with this new world, just as the audience does. A detective is a traditional device for exposition, as is a courtroom setting. Some of the unlikeliest plays are set up as courtroom investigations. Sophocles' *Oedipus Rex* is a play in which the protagonist, Oedipus, sets out to investigate the problems besetting the city of Thebes. In so doing he discovers that he has unknowingly murdered his father and married his mother and is the cause of the city's problems. Oedipus is both the chief prosecutor and, it transpires, the perpetrator of the crimes (Sophocles, 1982).

The best approach to exposition is always to ask the question: how can I dramatise this information? There is a technical challenge concerning exposition in any play. This is especially true in a naturalistic play, which promises some degree of psychological realism and where the dialogue attempts to create the illusion of normal, everyday exchanges. It is essential to avoid two characters coming on stage and telling each other things they should already know – 'Hello Father, back from work at five as usual?'; 'Yes, daughter, you must have been back from school for an hour.'

A play that does not offer the illusion of psychological realism has different tricks at its disposal. Such a non-naturalistic play can relay information via a narrator. Wang the water seller, for instance, in Bertolt Brecht's *The Good Person of Szechwan*, written in 1941, talks directly to the audience and reveals the premise of the story: three gods are coming to earth to discover if goodness is possible, given the pressures of life (Brecht, 1993). Brecht's plays are noted for their expository devices. Some of them use projections of pictures and slogans on the walls of the set, some use a chorus to narrate, and some use music and song. Such methods are possible when the style of a play acknowledges the presence of an audience and talks directly to it.

Yet in a more naturalistic play, where there is a different pact between performers and audience, there is a more subtle art to revealing information. Here the illusion that the events on stage are real is maintained. Any blatant exposition, such as a direct address to the audience, risks disturbing that illusion. In a naturalistic play, you will want to convey detail about location – the set will reveal a certain amount to the audience, but may not convey enough information. You will often want to tell the audience of some events that preceded the start of the play. You may also want to convey the relationships between the characters.

You will recall that Caryl Churchill's play *Top Girls*, which you briefly considered in Chapter 2, deals with the theme of women in society. In the first act of this play, the main character, Marlene, celebrates becoming managing director of 'Top Girls Employment Agency' in surreal fashion, by hosting a dinner to which she invites famous women from the past. These women all have considerable backstories to reveal.

ACTIVITY 5.1 Reading	Read the scene, and the notes on characters and layout, from *Top Girls* by Caryl Churchill (Reading 13 on p.321). • What is the effect of Churchill's innovative use of marks in the dialogue to designate interjection? • What methods are used to dramatise the exposition?
DISCUSSION	The attention that Churchill gives to interjections and the flow of conversation, using obliques (/) and asterisks (*), lends the restaurant scene a highly realistic pace, filled with crescendos and lulls. It feels peculiarly modern despite the array of historical characters. There is a sense in which the characters in combination become a chorus of womanhood, communicating more than their individual stories. In performance, the clarity of some of the dialogue is lost in the overlap between the lines, but the meaning of the overall exchange is always retained. In this sense the dialogue is highly musical. Many writers acknowledge that such overlaps occur in performance but not all orchestrate them in the script, preferring to leave that level of pacing to the director and actors in rehearsal. This is a decision you will have to make about your scripts. In Churchill's play, the pace of the dialogue assists the exposition, with realistic surges and troughs in the conversation. Certain lines are given prominence. There is suspense in the telling of the story and the diners echo the audience in wanting to know more. Even though the scene is non-naturalistic, it uses realistic techniques to reveal the various stories around the restaurant table. Look at the pivotal way in which the serving of food is used to structure the scene and how it unites the characters in the universal pursuit of eating.

Telling stories

The psychology of the participants is portrayed in the *Top Girls* scene as if these were contemporary characters of the same era. There is a rising tension in the scene, partly prompted by Marlene's impatience but also by the different reactions of the other characters to Griselda's story. It is this variety of well-motivated responses that dramatises Griselda's exposition, and several nuggets of exposition concerning the other characters are smuggled in almost invisibly. For instance, look at Marlene's introductions when Griselda enters, and note what we learn of Lady Nijo by the end of this extract.

Marlene is antagonistic towards the story; she is familiar with it and does not like it. She is full of disdain and impatience, and in many ways is the opposite of Griselda. She even mockingly delivers some of the exposition. Pope Joan is incredulous of the story, but especially of Griselda's accepting manner. Isabella Bird reacts similarly but seasons her incredulity with attempts at empathy and by making frequent comparisons with her own life, her familial relations, and her own resentment of domestic demands. Dull Gret is silent but intrigued. She is a powerful physical presence on the stage, as silent figures often are. Total reticence in a character can be a strong source of tension. Lady Nijo, like Isabella Bird, compares and contrasts her own life with that of Griselda. She sees herself much more as a fellow sufferer, as having lived through comparable experiences, yet tragically without the same outcome as Griselda: she was never reunited with any of her children.

Remember that substantial expositions such as Griselda's, though sometimes necessary, can often be avoided. The ideal way to handle exposition is by dripping it invisibly into the action, bit by bit, and only when it is needed – as is the case with Lady Nijo's exposition here. It is important to gauge when to inform the audience of certain things. If you reveal too much information too early then there may be no reason for the audience to watch the rest of the play.

ACTIVITY 5.2 **Writing**	Set three or four characters round a dinner table, in a restaurant or at home. Give them distinct voices. Focus on each character's individual use of diction, (bad) grammar and syntax to create particular speech patterns.

You can use characters you have created in your notebook, or you can develop characters from 'A Real Durwan' or 'Violin Lessons'. Write an exchange (up to 300 words) that starts to deliver an exposition about one of the characters, revealing the information in subtle and motivated ways. Think of pace and rhythm, and use interruption. Use Churchill's method of marking the script if you wish, or use the more conventional dash at the end of a line to mark when speeches are interrupted or curtailed prematurely.

DISCUSSION	Creating the dynamic between a group of characters can be exciting, and delivering a substantial story about one character can present a technical challenge. Such stories have to serve the action of the whole play. They should not be included as a matter of duty. It is important to make all the characters play a part in the storytelling. Try to visualise the actors on stage and what each might be doing and how they are reacting as the story is being told. Always ask yourself if you have correctly gauged the level of interruption and the function of each character in relation to the story. For instance, do all the characters need to be on stage?

Repeated exposition

In some circumstances, important exposition should be repeated. Some exposition can be vital to the plot, and to the understanding of the whole play. Imagine a play about a woman having an affair. If a member of the audience coughs just at the moment at which the woman explains a complex reason why she can never leave her husband, the rest of the play might be meaningless. So this sort of information needs reinforcement; it needs to be confirmed. You will notice that in *Top Girls* Churchill repeats certain key elements in the plot. She uses the device of having a character, Marlene, who knows Griselda's story well, and who intermittently repeats key parts of the exposition. This need to emphasise certain details applies to only a minute percentage of a play's exposition; most information is conveyed once only.

A note on stage monologues

One of the main ways in which stage characters can reveal personal details about themselves, and get close to the sort of intimate, interior narrative you can achieve in a novel, is through monologues. Hamlet's soliloquies chart the progress of his tortured thoughts on whether he should pursue the quest for revenge. Many modern dramatists use monologues to reveal aspects of their characters' interior lives. In Jane Thornton's and John Godber's *Shakers Re-stirred*, four waitresses in a cafe-bar engage in fast one-line exchanges mostly with each other, revealing their individual stories as well as their contempt for many of their customers. Yet at regular intervals the tempo changes, the lights dim and a spotlight falls on one of the waitresses. This is part of Carol's monologue in Act 1:

> Carol: I can't help it, I hate it when people just assume that because you do a job like this, you're thick. You know there's some nights I just can't stand it, I can't. I want to stand up on top of the bar and shout, I've got 'O' levels, I've got 'A' levels and a Bachelor of Arts Degree. So don't condescend to me, don't pretend you feel sorry for me and don't treat me like I can't read or talk or join in any of your conversations because I can. I see these teenage-like men and women with their well-cut suits and metal briefcases, discussing the City and the arts and time-shares in Tuscany, and I'm jealous, because I can't work out how they've achieved that success. It's so difficult. You see I want to be a photographer, take portraits. I won a competition in a magazine. It was this photo of a punk sat in a field on an old discarded toilet. It was brilliant.

Anyway, after college I had this wonderful idea that I'd go to London with my portfolio. I was confident that I'd get loads of work. But it wasn't like that. The pictures were great they said, but sorry, no vacancies. My mum said I was being too idealistic wanting it all straight away. My dad said I should settle for a job with the local newspaper, snapping Miss Gazette opening a shoe shop. No thanks. Now he thinks I'm wasting my degree. I was the first in the family to get one so it's not gone down very well. My head's in the clouds, he said, life's not that easy. But it is for some people, like I said, I see them in here. So why should I be different, have they tried harder or something?

(Thornton and Godber, 2001 [1993], p.217)

You can see that there is internal conflict woven through this speech, motivating the lines. The monologue exposes two tussling sides of Carol, one filled with despair, the other clinging to a dream. Though one single voice, it contains dialogue with other characters. Some information is revealed explicitly, but other things are implied. For instance, when Carol declares how 'brilliant' her photograph was she reveals the spark of hope and resilient faith she still has in herself. Also note how the rhythm and pace varies. There are some long, breathless sentences with few commas, such as when she talks about what she would say to her customers. But there are also some sentences of very few words – 'No thanks'; 'It's very difficult'.

ACTIVITY 5.3 **Writing**	Write a monologue (up to 300 words) in the voice of a character, choosing one of the following options:

- one of your dinner guests created for Activity 5.2, in front of a mirror in the bathroom, talking about one or more of the other diners;
- the character of Boori Ma from 'A Real Durwan', talking about the problem with her bedding.

DISCUSSION	You may have found that writing a monologue acquainted you better with your character; it may have helped you to get to know him or her. Monologues can be a great assistance in character creation and development, and also in finding the voice of a character. This can be true even if the monologue produced is not used in the final version of the play.

Monologues should be used as part of the storytelling only if the logic of events demands it. A prolonged speech from one character can slow the action, and you always have to consider what the other characters are doing while this is happening. While Carol speaks in *Shakers Re-stirred*, the other characters freeze on stage. Remember that you still need to generate suspense and tension, even during long speeches. This is done by not giving everything away. Leave something for your audience to invent. Your first obligation is to keep with your character and not to be ruled by the amount of information you want to deliver to the audience. Try to make your long speeches dialogic by including other voices, as in Carol's monologue. When editing, look long and hard at any monologues and ask: does the play really need this?

Subtext

David Mamet (2004) attests that for him much of the process of writing plays consists of cutting out excessive exposition, always getting the characters to say less because invariably in the original scripting they say too much. By ruthless editing he hopes to engage the imagination of the audience in actively constructing the dynamic of the scenes. Much successful naturalistic dialogue gives little obvious information; rather it masks the real, underlying meaning of the exchange. One of the thrills of good dialogue for the audience is being able to perceive characters thinking on stage, and being able, almost palpably, to feel the atmosphere between characters, even though the dialogue does not reveal this explicitly.

At the start of the first act of Ibsen's *Ghosts* Regina prevents her father, Engstrand, from entering the Alving household, even though it is raining heavily outside.

> Regina: *(lowering her voice)* What do you want? Stay where you are, you're dripping wet!
>
> Engstrand: It's God's good rain, my girl.
>
> Regina: It's the devil's rain, that's what it is!
>
> (Ibsen, 1984 [1881], p.21)

As this opening exchange continues, Regina forbids Engstrand from making any noise in case he wakes the sleeping 'young master', Osvald. Many things are revealed instantly here, including Engstrand's insidious persistence and the class division between Engstrand and the Alvings: Osvald Alving can take an afternoon nap while Engstrand has to be out and about. The subtext woven beneath Regina's lines is 'Go away, I'm ashamed of you, I've bettered myself and don't want anything to do with you.' Also, when Engstrand calls his daughter 'my girl', he is saying 'Yes, I know what you think of me but there might be something of interest here for me. I'm going to hang around to see what I can get.' Ostensibly this is just a conversation about weather. The beauty of the exchange is that the conflict and the subtext are so much richer and more complex than the words that are spoken.

Words can often act as a mask for real meaning. In the next activity you will read a scene in which Harold Pinter uses his famous pauses to create a rhythm of thought in the characters, and see an even more subtle example of subtext. In this scene, Teddy and his wife Ruth have returned from America after an absence of six years; they arrive in the night when everyone is in bed and they let themselves into the house. Ruth has never met Teddy's family.

ACTIVITY 5.4 Reading	Read the scene from *The Homecoming* by Harold Pinter (Reading 14 on p.329). What do you think the subtext might be about in this scene?
DISCUSSION	The rhythm of the exchange – the surges, lulls and silences – reveals the characters' differing responses to their arrival. It is the sort of dialogue that leaves out much, allowing the audience to invent the intentions of the characters. Teddy is effusive and enthusiastic, Ruth is tired and not tuned in to Teddy's excitement – more than half of her responses include the word 'no' and this negativity seeps into the mood of the scene. The audience tunes into her rejection of Teddy, something that is borne out by the end of the play. The audience is also made aware that Teddy doesn't quite comprehend his wife. He fails to offer her anything she might accept, or to suggest anything to which she will respond favourably. Finally she leaves the house at the end of the scene. There is a fundamental fracture in the way they relate to one another. Many of Pinter's plays involve characters trying to leave or not leave rooms; it has come to be seen as a basic premise of his dramas.

Dramatic irony

Creating subtext is the most exciting of writing tasks, but one of the most difficult. It requires you to imagine fully the psychologies of your characters. It depends on you establishing agendas and desires for each of them. When done badly it can produce banal writing in which the hidden exchange is too deeply buried. All the audience is left with is mundane surface banter, while the substrata of feeling and 'real action' remains obscure. Pinter's subtext is subtle, but Ruth's negative lines give strong clues as to what is going on. Make sure you offer such clues. Creating a subtext on stage often depends on the contrast between what is said and what is seen. In *Ghosts*, for instance, the dialogue is contrasted with the heavy rain and the sight of a daughter refusing entry to her crippled father. Such contrasts can lead to discrepancies in perceptions – the audience might see things that one or more of the characters do not. This is the basis of dramatic irony.

ACTIVITY 5.5
Writing

Develop your restaurant scene from Activity 5.2, in which you have at least three characters, by having two of them wanting a third to leave the room. Write a further page of the scene (one to two minutes long, up to 350 words) in which they try to make this happen without explicitly requesting or telling the character to go – so their wish must exist between the lines, in the subtext.

DISCUSSION

By developing this restaurant scene you have used another form of dramatic differentiation or contrast (as introduced at the start of Chapter 4). This type of contrast could be called 'discrepancies in knowledge'. Two of your characters know something that at least one other character does not. This is a powerful dramatic tool. Tension and suspense are immediately created when some characters know things and others remain ignorant, and when the audience becomes privy to such knowledge. An audience will be far more engaged with events if it is given access to secret information. Tension is created if the audience is made more aware of events and their wider meaning than some of the characters on stage. Think, for instance, of Shakespeare's *Macbeth*, and of Duncan's arrival at Macbeth's castle. Duncan gives a warm tribute to his hosts, while the audience is already aware of how his murder has been plotted by Macbeth and his wife (Shakespeare, 2001, Act 1, Scene 6, p.779).

Status

Actors, when approaching performance, tend to view the subtext of a play and the dynamic between characters as very much connected with power shifts and the opposing wishes or desires of the characters. As Mamet says: 'If the two people [in a scene] don't want something different the audience is going to go to sleep' (2004, p.75). The actors will always seek to make use of those differing desires.

Status is another way of talking about how different desires and power plays work in drama. On one level, status is a subliminal system of social behaviour that works on a hierarchical basis. The master/servant relationship is an example of this, as are the teacher/student, doctor/patient and shopkeeper/customer relationships. A servant is low status, and his or her master or mistress is high status, a student low status and a teacher high, and so forth. This is sometimes termed social status.

Yet status also operates on a more immediate level. This is sometimes called interactive status. It is less predicated on affluence and position and is the dynamic that exists in each specific exchange. For instance, with interactive status, it would be possible for the patient to act with a higher status than the doctor.

ACTIVITY 5.6 Reading	Read the extract from 'Status' by Keith Johnstone (Reading 15 on p.334). Make notes on how status might be important for the playwright.
DISCUSSION	You will see that Johnstone calls interactive status 'the played status'. Although his ideas are directed at actors who are learning techniques for improvisation, he has also run workshops for playwrights, and the principles he uncovers offer valuable insights about characters' motivations and desires. According to Johnstone no situation is free of status. He perceives status as the see-saw principle on which power shifts in relationships; it is the shadow that accompanies conflict. Subtle status shifts occur all the time in real-life exchanges between people – with our neighbours, with members of our family, with people we meet at work. This happens even when we are not aware of being competitive or status-minded.

Playing with status

Assigning status to your characters is a useful way of differentiating between them. The play between social and interactive status can be interesting – think of the boy and the man in 'Violin Lessons', for instance. The man has a social status which is high (he is older), but in his interactions with the boy his status is constantly being eroded, first by the boy's precocious behaviour, then by his own reaction to the disappearance of the boy's sister. The dynamic status relationship between the boy and man has the potential for making something shift and for moving the drama forward.

In the scene from *The Homecoming* that you read in Activity 5.4 there is subtle status play between the two characters, which eventually amounts to a dramatic reversal. At the start Teddy seems to be of high status and Ruth low, but by the end the status relationship between them has been reversed. It is this sort of reversal that often provokes significant movement in drama.

In the following extract from Act 2 of George Bernard Shaw's *You Never Can Tell*, there is a family reunion around a lunch table which involves more characters than actually speak, as you can see from the stage directions. You might spot something interesting about the status relationships in the scene.

Dolly: Is your son a waiter, too, William?

Waiter: (*serving Gloria with fowl*) Oh no, miss: he's too impetuous. He's at the Bar.

M'Comas: (*patronizingly*) A potman, eh?

Waiter: (*with a touch of melancholy, as if recalling a disappointment softened by time*) No, sir: the other bar – your profession, sir. A QC, sir.

M'Comas: (*embarrassed*) I'm sure I beg your pardon.

Waiter: Not at all, sir. Very natural mistake, I'm sure, sir. I've often wished he was a potman, sir. Would have been off my hands ever so much sooner, sir. (*Aside to VALENTINE, who is again in difficulties*) Salt at your elbow, sir. (*Resuming*) Yes, sir: had to support him until he was thirty-seven, sir. But doing well now, sir: very satisfactory indeed, sir. Nothing less than fifty guineas, sir.

(Shaw, 1911 [1898], p.255)

Dolly Clandon is a character who never says a lot, but always asks the pertinent question. She could be seen as an expository device, and here she serves that purpose well, initiating the revealing dialogue. What is intriguing about this brief exchange is how the status reversal is achieved; by the end the waiter seems to be the boss of the scene. He is in physical command, facilitating everyone's eating. They are all made to seem incompetent, like children. He has eyes and hands everywhere. The exchange also involves social status in the servant/master relationship – and when the waiter's son is revealed to be a QC, the embarrassment of M'Comas, the family solicitor, at misinterpreting 'bar' is even eased by William, as if he is merely showing him where the salt is on the table. The revelation is made even stronger, raising William's interactive status higher, by the fact that it is made in the form of a contradiction rather than a boast. To cap it all the waiter is indifferent to such high social status. He has his reasons, but this in effect raises his 'played' status to the roof, a feat that is compounded by the repeated 'sir', punctuating practically every clause. This adds a deeply ironic resonance for the audience.

Status shifts

Shaw's stage directions are very elaborate. We will look at those again in the next chapter – and consider the dangers of his method – but for the moment it is important to notice how the drama in his scene unfolds in both the physical action and the dialogue. If you visualise William, the waiter, standing over the table throughout, he is the most physically active but also the tallest of all the characters.

An interview offers an intriguing dramatic situation in which to explore status further. Often interviewees go to such occasions with relatively low status. They are humbly seeking reward for their efforts, but at the same time they might have to boast about themselves. Paradoxically, when they do so, characters' status can be lowered.

Look at the following scene:

B: Mr ... er?

A: Jones, Mr Jones.

B: Jones.

A: With a J.

B: Fine.

A: Took me a while to find you.

B: And you've come about one of the marketing posts, Mr Jones?

A: Yes. Good job I allowed enough time.

B: First test of initiative, shall we say. Now, about the vacancies – before we go to the interview room, could you just tell me a little about yourself? Add a little to what you have already put down on the form. Do you have any experience?

A: Experience? Oh, yes. I should say so.

This is a relatively bland scene – the start of an interview. It gives no real clues as to the interactive status between the characters, and there is no change of status in the exchange, though there might be an expectation about the characters' social status. There are no stage directions, and the characters have no names. The lines could be interpreted in a number of ways. If you tried to perform this script as it stands, the audience might, in Mamet's words, 'fall asleep'. In the next activity, you will attempt to make it more interesting.

Using the script above, try to give the actors some instruction about interactive status – the status the characters should play. Edit and rewrite four different versions of the script. Cut and change elements. Add stage directions, names, hesitations, odd words and phrases, as you see fit, to make it viable as a dramatic script containing a status dynamic between the characters. Write the following versions:

1 with character B as high status, character A as low;
2 with character A as high status, character B as low;
3 with both characters as either high or low status;
4 try to create a shift in status during the course of the scene. So, for instance, it might start as in version 1 but end as in version 2.

DISCUSSION

With version 3 you may well have produced comedy. As Johnstone says, characters are always see-sawing back and forth. Quick vying for status can induce laughter. For versions 1 and 2 you might have created low-status characters with hesitant lines – using ellipses and incomplete sentences. You might also have had the low-status character seated low down, or even lying on the floor. The high-status character might have shouted or constantly interrupted the other, and been physically dominant. Version 4 was possibly the most difficult to achieve because you had so little time to first establish the status relationship, and then find a way to shift it. Yet you may have found that, as you extended the first two versions, your redraft naturally achieved what was asked of you in version 4. This natural shift in the status played by one or more characters has the potential to generate poignant and captivating dramatic movement in your scripts.

If you managed a shift in version 4, you no doubt went some way beyond thinking mechanically about status and started imagining your characters more fully, giving them motivations, fears and desires. Status will not replace the extensive invention and individual care needed to create characters. However, it is a useful template to place over your characters. It can establish difference and be a dynamic tool by which to generate conflict in a scene, move the action forwards and reveal a character's motives.

Conclusion

In this chapter you have looked at ways of revealing information to your audience, by dramatising exposition, telling stories about characters and by having characters deliver monologues. You have also looked at subtler ways of revealing information, through subtext and via the dynamics of status. You have seen how status can move the story on. In the next chapter you will be concentrating on visual narrative and looking more at the vital ingredient of plays – dramatic action.

References

Brecht, Bertolt (1993 [1941]) *The Good Person of Szechwan* (trans. John Willett), London: Methuen.

Ibsen, Henrik (1984 [1881]) *Ghosts* in *Ghosts and Other Plays* (trans. Peter Watts), Harmondsworth: Penguin.

Mamet, David (2004) Interview with David Savran in *David Mamet in Conversation* (ed. Leslie Kane), Michigan: Michigan University Press.

Ravenhill, Mark (2007) Interview, *Ian McMillan's Writing Lab*, BBC Radio 3, podcast [online], http://www.open2.net/writing/markravenhill.html (accessed 30 December 2007).

Shaw, George Bernard (1911 [1898]) *You Never Can Tell* in *Plays Pleasant and Unpleasant II*, London: Constable.

Thornton, Jane and Godber, John (2001 [1993]) *Shakers Re-stirred* in John Godber, *Plays 1*, London: Methuen.

Shakespeare, William (2001) *Macbeth* in *The Arden Shakespeare Complete Works*, London: Arden.

Sophocles (1982) *Oedipus Rex* in *The Three Theban Plays* (trans. Robert Fagles), London: Allen Lane.

Further reading

Friel, Brian (1996) *Faith Healer* in *Plays: 1*, London: Faber and Faber.

This is a play about a travelling faith healer, his wife and his agent. It is interesting because it consists of four monologues, and also because of the mix of Irish and Cockney voices.

Pinter, Harold (1961) *The Applicant* in *A Slight Ache and Other Plays*, London: Methuen.

This revue sketch offers an extreme version of the sort of status play possible in an interview scenario, and is funny, alarming and very theatrical. The revue collection in which it is contained also contains more typical, subtle Pinter scenes, such as *Last to Go*.

Shakespeare, William (2001) *The Tempest* in *The Arden Shakespeare Complete Works*, London: Arden.

In the second scene of the play there is an example of the technical difficulty of a long, convoluted exposition. The backstory is essential in order for the play to make sense; Shakespeare enacts the possible reaction of the audience by having Miranda fall asleep as her father, Prospero, tells his long tale.

6   Staging stories

Derek Neale

A play usually contains spoken words, but always contains action. There are two aspects to this action – the physical action of characters walking across a stage, for example, and the dramatic action. The latter is less tangible than physical presence, yet it is the essential momentum that drives a play's story from start to finish. This chapter will explore the two types of action: developing your ability to create a visual narrative on stage, and exploring how this might contribute to the storytelling.

You will: explore the techniques involved in writing set descriptions and charting scenes; examine what dramatic action might be and why it is often seen as the single most influential principle in drama – across all media; and look at how it might inform individual scenes as well as the larger structure of a play. Again, in trying some play writing techniques, you will be using 'A Real Durwan' as an adaptation text, as well as creating your own settings and characters.

Physical action

Stages

When writing plays it can be helpful – and is sometimes essential – to be aware of the type of stage for which you are writing. It may influence the way you arrange the story. For instance, you might have very different approaches when writing for:

- a theatre-in-the-round stage, where the audience surrounds the stage on all sides;
- a thrust stage, where most of the audience faces the stage except for an apron of stage area which juts out into the auditorium, and on which the actors will be surrounded on three sides;
- a proscenium arch stage, which has a clear divide between performers and auditorium, with the audience facing the stage.

Many concerns about staging are production matters, which will involve the director, set designer and stage manager rather than the writer. Yet being aware of staging possibilities will, at the very least, help you to imagine an eventual performance. In order to write for the stage it is imperative that you picture the live enactment.

Consider your own experience of drama. You may have participated in or witnessed school plays, or seen performances staged in venues such as church and village halls. Some performers (such as 7:84 and Creation

Figure 2   A theatre-in-the-round at the Stephen Joseph Theatre, Scarborough. (Photo: Tony Bartholomew Photography Ltd)

Figure 3   A proscenium arch stage, auditorium of the Empire Music Hall, Newcastle, 1891. (Photo: © University of Bristol Theatre Collection)

Figure 4   A modern thrust stage at the Crucible, Sheffield, 1995. (Photo: © Gerry Murray Photographer)

Figure 5   Bandstand. (Photo: © Jack Eastick)

theatre companies) have staged plays in more unusual spaces, for example at conferences and in factories. You may have witnessed street theatre, in which the space between performers and audience is very different from the type of intimate performances staged in small studio theatres. Some plays will be more suited to certain types of stage, but the most unlikely venues can prove to be surprisingly versatile.

ACTIVITY 6.1 Writing	Choose one of the stages pictured in Figures 2–5, or another of your own choice, and imagine a character on stage with a mobile phone – just hanging up or reading a message. He or she is laughing or crying or bemused or alarmed. The character can be one of your own creations or one you have encountered in your reading.

Write down the visual narrative of what happens in the next few seconds, keeping as much as possible to stage directions only, with little or no dialogue (up to 100 words).

DISCUSSION	What sort of stage did you choose? How did this affect your story and the way it was told? Stages such as the bandstand in Figure 5 are often used in 'theatre in the park' productions or for street theatre performances. Some stages (the proscenium) lend themselves to a greater degree of realism and the establishment of detailed naturalistic sets; others (particularly theatres-in-the-round) seem to suggest the barest use of set and props. The challenge for the writer with an in-the-round stage is to keep the audience engrossed and focused on the action on stage, even though some members of the audience may be able to see straight across the stage and into the eyes of the audience on the other side. However, the intimacy of such a confined acting space can unexpectedly add to the mood and domestic feel of quite naturalistic dramas.

Be careful not to write the directions as a prose fiction story. You are writing for the stage, and for actors. These are performance instructions. They should be concise and in the present tense. Look back at the stage directions in the adaptation of 'Violin Lessons' in Activity 4.2. You will see that the style of many instructions appears abrupt: for instance, 'looking around' and 'going over to lathe'. There are few definite or indefinite articles. It is 'MAN spins blade', not 'The MAN spins the blade'. You have to gauge this carefully, so that the concision does not obscure the instruction.

ACTIVITY 6.2
Writing

Now develop the scene a little, remembering which stage you are using, and including as little dialogue as possible.

Try to identify what might be your main character's aim. What is stopping the character achieving this aim? Make these elements implicit in the action.

Imagine a rising action, building towards something, and then a moment of resolution.

Introduce another character if you wish, but no more than one.

DISCUSSION

It is easy to think that a character's aim has to be something grand, and it can be a relief to realise this need not be so. The aim could be as simple as exiting or entering a room, or wanting to get rid of the phone. For example, the character with the phone could be the boy from the story 'Violin Lessons'; the phone could belong to his sister. He is on stage with just the phone and her violin case. He has read a message on the phone and is shocked, but also realises he has the phone in his hand, has opened the message and can hear his sister approaching. The venue could be a theatre-in-the-round, which would emphasise the sense that there is no place to turn. The stage directions for the boy's actions might have him attempt to hide the phone, turn it off and stuff it into his shirt pocket. His sister, offstage, might be heard approaching, getting louder, shouting: 'Has anyone seen my phone?' The phone could be seen flashing in his shirt pocket, visible to the audience. The resolution might come when she shouts that she is looking for her violin as well. He hides the phone in the violin case.

Sets

A set is what the designer creates in performance and uses to realise the location of the story. You, as writer, have to designate the location, and you can suggest elements of the set too. You can locate plays anywhere: on tube trains, in gardens, on aeroplanes, in football stadiums, in bedrooms, in the desert, on tops of mountains.

In deciding the location of your plays you will be ruled by the story. An adaptation that sticks closely to the original version of 'Violin Lessons', for instance, would need to be set in the man's workshop. There are then a range of choices about how you represent the workshop – how you create the set. You could divide the possible sets into three broad categories: a bare stage; a split set; a full set.

The seventeenth-century French playwright Molière famously said that all you need to create a play is a plank and a passion. When using a bare stage, with only one or two props to suggest place, the audience's imagination is actively involved in creating the location. In Edward Bond's *Saved*, a character walks onto the empty stage with a fishing rod and sits down looking out at the audience, and the scene at the water's edge is instantly established (1969 [1966], Scene 6, p.47). On a bare stage an umbrella can suggest immediately that the action is outside; a kettle can signify indoors. The man's workshop in 'Violin Lessons' might be created by one or two props, the red and green buttons perhaps, and by the man holding a chisel. A bare stage is the most malleable of sets and can change instantly without any need for scene shifters. With the introduction of a violin, for instance, the space could be transformed into Mr Bouillon's study and the scene of the violin lessons. Alternatively, just a shift in the lighting and the use of a fiddle could signify the man's dream of the violinist in the woods.

A split stage offers great potential for creating different locations and sometimes eras without having cumbersome scene changes. Traditionally actors freeze or exit when the action does not involve their scene. The problem is that the frozen characters sometimes attract the audience's attention. So, with 'Violin Lessons', if there was a split set between the workshop and the study for the violin lessons, the challenge would be to prevent the audience from looking at Mr Bouillon and Veronica when they are supposed to be looking at the scene involving the man and the boy. Remember, splitting the stage can be – and often is – achieved with lighting as much as with set furniture and props.

A full set offers greater material detail in the realisation of a location, and suggests a form of naturalism and what is often referred to as a 'fourth wall illusion', as if the audience is looking in on a slice of reality. Such a set is far less flexible in terms of changing locations. Once you have filled the stage with bookcases, for instance, it is difficult then to clear the space for the next scene. With 'Violin Lessons', a full set might involve filling the stage with wood, wood shavings and other objects, such as a working lathe and circular saw, illustrating the man's workplace. You might even see beyond the split door, outside towards the trees. But even in a full set, the writer needs only to detail in the script the objects that are essential for the telling of the story. The director and set designer will make key decisions on how a particular production of a play looks.

ACTIVITY 6.3
Reading

Read the following set descriptions. What is significant about each one? Are there any full, split or bare sets among them?

The Wild Duck by Henrik Ibsen

Hjalmar Ekdal's studio. The room, which is fairly large, appears to be an attic. On the right is a sloping roof with large panes of glass, half covered by a blue curtain. Up in the right-hand corner is the entrance door; downstage on the same side, a door to the living-room. In the left wall there are again two doors and between these an iron stove. In the rear wall is a broad double-door, so constructed as to slide back to either side. The studio is cheaply but comfortably furnished and decorated. Between the doors on the right a sofa with a table and some chairs are standing a little out from the wall; on the table is a lighted lamp with a shade; by the fireside an old easy-chair. Various pieces of photographic apparatus and instruments are standing here and there about the room. Against the back wall, to the left of the double-door, is a book-case with some books, small boxes, flasks of chemicals, different kinds of instruments, tools and other things. Photographs and some small articles, such as brushes, paper and the like, are lying on the table.

(Ibsen, 1952 [1884], Act 2, p.163)

Greek by Steven Berkoff

Place: England

Time: present

Stage setting: kitchen table and four simple chairs. These will function in a number of ways. They can be everything one wants them to be from the platform for the SPHINX to the café. They also function as the train; the environment which suggests EDDY's humble origins becoming his expensive and elaborate home in Act Two. The table and chairs merely define spaces and act as an anchor or base for the actors to spring from. All other artifacts are mimed or suggested. The walls are three square upright white panels, very clinical and at the same time indicating Greek classicism. The faces are painted white and are clearly defined. Movement should be sharp and dynamic, exaggerated and sometimes bearing the quality of seaside cartoons. The family act as a chorus for all other characters and environments.

(Berkoff, 1994 [1982], Act 1, p.100)

Comedians by Trevor Griffiths

A classroom in a secondary school in Manchester, about three miles east of the centre, on the way to Ashton-under-Lyne and the hills of east Lancashire. Built 1947 in the now disappearing but still familiar two-storey style, the school doubles as evening centre for the area and will half-fill, as the evening progresses, with the followers of yoga, karate, cordon bleu cookery, 'O' level English, secretarial prelims, do-it-yourself, small investments and antique furniture. Adults will return to school and the school will do its sullen best to accommodate them.

This room, on the ground floor, is smallish, about a dozen chipped and fraying desks, two dozen chairs set out in rows facing the small dais on which stands the teacher's desk, with green blackboard unwiped from the day's last stand beyond. Two starkish lights, on the window side of the room, are on, flintily, lighting about a third of it. A clock (real: keeping real time for the evening) over the board says 7.27. Cupboards of haphazard heights and styles line the walls, above which the dogged maps, charts, tables, illustrations and notices warp, fray, tear, curl and droop their way to limbo. Windows on the left wall show the night dark and wet.

The SCHOOL CARETAKER, old, gnarled, tiny, is trying to sponge recent graffiti from the blackboard, in the lit segment of the room. He has done away with the 'F' fairly successfully and now begins on the 'U'. C, K, O, F, F, N, O, B, H, O, L, E stretch out before him.

(Griffiths, 1985, Act 1, p.7)

Philadelphia, Here I Come! by Brian Friel

When the curtain rises the only part of the stage that is lit is the kitchen, i.e. the portion on the left from the point of view of the audience. It is sparsely and comfortlessly furnished – a bachelor's kitchen. There are two doors; one left which leads to the shop, and one upstage leading to the scullery (off). Beside the shop door is a large deal table, now set for tea without cloth and with rough cups and saucers. Beside the scullery door is an old-fashioned dresser. On the scullery wall is a large school-type clock.

Stage right, now in darkness, is Gar's bedroom. Both bedroom and kitchen should be moved upstage, leaving a generous apron. Gar's bedroom is furnished with a single bed, a wash-hand basin (crockery jug and bowl), a table with a record player and records, and a small chest of drawers.

These two areas – kitchen and Gar's bedroom – occupy more than two-thirds of the stage. The remaining portion is fluid: in Episode I for example, it represents a room in Senator Doogan's home.

The two Gars, PUBLIC GAR and PRIVATE GAR, are two views of the one man. PUBLIC GAR is the Gar that people see, talk to, talk about. PRIVATE GAR is the unseen man, the man within, the conscience, the *alter ego*, the secret thoughts, the id. PRIVATE GAR, the spirit, is invisible to everybody, always. Nobody except PUBLIC GAR hears him talk. But even PUBLIC GAR, although he talks to PRIVATE GAR occasionally, never sees him and *never looks at him*. One cannot look at one's *alter ego*.

Time: the present in the small village of Ballybeg in County Donegal, Ireland. The action takes place on the night before, and on the morning of Gar's departure for Philadelphia.

(Friel, 1996, pp.26–7)

DISCUSSION

Items used on stage are often referred to as props (short for properties). The less you put on stage, the greater its significance. Objects and what happens to those objects will have symbolic resonance. Many of the props used in these sets hold multiple meanings.

Note how the set in Ibsen's *The Wild Duck* establishes that Ekdal's studio is like a photograph itself. It is full of meticulous, realistic detail – but it is a shared, and therefore quite poor, workspace. (The workshop in 'Violin Lessons' would be a very different location if it were shared with others.) All the doors in the set of *The Wild Duck* signify access to other spaces. The double doors lead to the room housing the wild duck, a literal and symbolic space which represents the unconscious life of the family, with its history of deceit and betrayal. Doors on a stage will always hold a heightened significance, since they are gateways to more private or public worlds, contrasting with the world of the stage. In Sophocles' *Oedipus Rex*, Oedipus sits or stands in front of the doors of his palace, but only at the end of the play retreats into that private space (Sophocles, 1982, p.232). Doors are also, of course, functional exit and entrance points for the actors.

Berkoff's play *Greek* is a rewriting of the Oedipus story: a man discovers he has killed his father and married and had children with his mother. The story is reset in the East End of London. The stage is relatively bare and what is there serves many functions. In this type of drama the actors often play multiple parts, and less effort is made to create the material illusion of reality. At another extreme, the gritty realism of Griffiths's *Comedians* can be seen in the set. The location is a comedians' night class. The would-be comics have been preparing for this final showcase night when they will perform in front of an agent who is 'up' from London.

Friel's *Philadelphia, Here I Come!* is a play that centres on a young man, Gareth (Gar) O'Donnell, and his intended move to Philadelphia. As you can see, the stage is divided into two fixed sets and one flexible space on the stage's apron. The action of the play not only switches between the three spaces but splits between a public Gar and a private Gar, played by different actors, both of whom operate across all areas of the stage.

Sets need characters

The character of Private Gar in *Philadelphia, Here I Come!* offers an example of the way in which a character can sometimes function in the same way as a prop or as part of the set. Polly Teale's play *After Mrs Rochester* (2003) has a character who functions in a similar way. It is a biographical play about the novelist Jean Rhys. One character – Bertha Mason – is on stage from the start, silently accompanying the main protagonist, Rhys. Bertha is a fictional character from Charlotte Brontë's novel *Jane Eyre*. She gains voice only in the second half of the play, after Rhys's grip on reality is seen to be slipping. In the first half of the action Bertha acts almost as a piece of stage furniture or a prop. She symbolises a raft of things, largely to do with Rhys's unconscious: Rhys's obsession with Brontë's creation; her similar background to Bertha, coming as she did from the Caribbean; her fragile mental health. But Bertha also stands for Rhys's creative need to write a new version of what Bertha's life might have been like. This Rhys did, in her novel *Wide Sargasso Sea* (1966). During the action of Teale's play, character, props and set combine to help tell the story of Rhys's life.

ACTIVITY 6.4
Writing

Write a set description for a stage adaptation of 'A Real Durwan' (Reading 2 on p.287). Decide which type of set – bare, split or full – best suits the story. Also, try to think of how your set establishes the location and era, as well as launching the story.

DISCUSSION

Choosing a bare set would enable you to switch locations easily using a single prop. For instance, you could switch to Boori Ma's past, to East Bengal, just by using a banana leaf or a pewter bowl from her third daughter's wedding. With a split stage this past life could be permanently represented, though you need this only if you are going to use it substantially. A full stage is ostensibly less flexible, but even with this option, switches in time and location can be achieved with lighting changes.

It is important to realise that your set can be a dynamic part of the storytelling; it reveals much detail to the audience. The way in which your characters react to their surroundings will also be revealing. Many of the opening sets you have looked at establish the era for the play, if not implicitly in the cultural detail, then in an accompanying note. Did you establish India in your set? Some sets also establish the time frame for the events of the story. Time can be a crucial detail that needs clarity, especially early on in your script.

A note on time

In the set for *Comedians* you will notice that real time and stage time are synchronised by the clock. The fictional time frame of a play and real, theatre-foyer time are rarely aligned in this way. The clock in *Comedians* has another function – it immediately sets a pace to events. The night-class comedians are due to perform at 8 pm; the clock lights a fuse of expectation and tension. The same can be achieved by placing your characters before any impending activity – waiting for a train (as in Chekhov's *The Cherry Orchard*, 1990 [1904]); waiting for an arrival (Beckett's *Waiting for Godot*, 1985 [1956]).

Establishing stage time like this (it doesn't have to be synchronised with real time) can also lend you a structure. By Act 3 in *Comedians* we return to the same set for the resolution and it is now 9.43 pm, and such night classes lock up at 10 pm. The caretaker duly comes in to close the play and clean the board again. David Storey's *The Contractor* (1970) is set in three acts, and is structured round the erection of a wedding marquee. In the first act we see the marquee being erected; in the last act we see it being taken down. This coincides with the classical time frame, as prescribed by Aristotle: if a play's action is completed in twenty-four hours, it concentrates the action and increases tension and suspense. Yet a day isn't the only time frame you can use – you could use an evening (as in *Comedians*), a weekend or a year. Brecht's *Mother Courage* (1987 [1940]) covers a period during the Thirty Years' War, from 1624 to 1636, and nearly all of Shakespeare's plays cover a much longer time frame than a day.

Stage directions and visual narrative

When first rehearsing the director will divide a play up into blocks; these are usually a scene in length, but longer scenes are divided up into multiple blocks. The initial purpose of blocking is to establish the positioning of characters on stage, with less emphasis placed on dialogue. The director is checking who is where, and that they are able to make their entrances and exits; continuity is checked, together with the audience's sight lines. At this point the director is also looking through the script to get some idea about the visual narrative – how the story can be told in pictures. He or she is finding the story and seeing what needs invention and what clues are given by the writer. If there is too much stage direction (often abbreviated to SD) in the script, then the director will be less able to engage imaginatively with the story. If there is not enough the director will not know what the story is about. The level of stage direction in the extract from Shaw's *You Never Can Tell*, read in the last chapter, is by modern standards excessive. The actors may resent being told how to say the lines, and William's stage direction about how he looks melancholic appears almost novelistic.

Using offstage

You should avoid putting in stage directions unless they are essential to the storytelling. It is better to let the actors and directors use their imaginations. Yet you should always imagine the visual narrative, even if it is not eventually made explicit in the script. You do not have to solve the performance problems of how to realise the set or how the play looks, but your conception has to embrace a visual idea of the eventual performance.

Often you can use things that are not seen by the audience but that are suggested in order to help tell the story. The offstage area can be a powerful tool. Just suggesting that a character will soon be arriving, or that the street outside is unsafe, can add to the tension, comedy and drama on stage. A stage adaptation of 'Violin Lessons', for instance, might have the character of Mr Bouillon always offstage, sometimes viewed from the workshop door by the man or boy, but never seen by the audience. Tanika Gupta's *Sanctuary*, discussed in Chapter 4, is set in an 'Eden-like graveyard' in London, yet we get the sense of danger from the streets and wider world offstage, and how the characters are all seeking refuge in some way from that imminent violence.

Dramatic action

A stage play's narrative is achieved with as much as 70 per cent visual action, to only 30 per cent dialogue. Devising a play's shape and unspoken narrative can form the major part of a play's conception. Much of the playwright's work involves hearing and imagining the voices of characters, researching those characters and getting to know their passions, desires and conflicts. Yet many playwrights attest to conceiving the shape of the dramatic action long before they are fully acquainted with their characters or have the lines of dialogue written.

The word 'drama' derives from a Greek word meaning 'to do' or 'action'. A dramatic action is a rising movement through the overall play which is echoed in the play's smaller episodes. Aristotle said that dramatic action was the most essential part of a drama, and that character was its vehicle. Walter Kerr, the Broadway critic, summed up the process of a dramatic action:

> All that is asked of the dramatist is that he show the beginnings of some one particular change, that he trace it through its natural turmoil, and that he bring the contending forces into different – though not necessarily a perfect – balance. Things were one way; now they are another; we have seen them move.
>
> (quoted in Griffiths, 1982, pp.14–15)

Of course, if this movement from one state of being to another is too straightforward an audience will not be interested. Any dramatic action is strewn with complications and reversals: things seem to be heading in one direction and then they turn. In Shakespeare's *Macbeth*, Lady Macbeth seems to be the cold instigator of Duncan's murder, urging her husband on. Then suddenly she is struck by convulsions of guilt and remorse, manifest in her obsession with the imaginary blood on her hands (Shakespeare, 2001, Act 5, Scene 1, p.795).

Dramatic action has obvious musical analogies, with its crescendos and diminuendos; some see it as symphonic, complete with introductory overture. It is also commonly compared to the tide, starting with a small surge, flowing and ebbing, with nascent peaks and small rushes, troughs and lulls, rising then falling, yet moving ineluctably forward to a crashing high, before falling back. Such analogies might seem grand and to apply only to big narratives – full three- or five-act plays – but when thinking about the narrative shape of your smaller-scale stage dramatisations, try to think of this rhythm and force of a rising action on events, of the climaxes and irresistible pull of small or large waves in each scene. Think in terms of an arc, with three parts to the action: the rise, the climax and the resolution. This will help bring the action alive in each individual section of your play as well as lending it basic structure.

By way of example, if you look back at the extract from Pinter's *The Homecoming* (Reading 14 on p.329) you can see the dramatic action. Part of the tension in this scene comes because of Ruth and Teddy's arrival – as if they are intruders in the house of the three bears, as in the fairy story. This is maybe even more apparent with a fuller knowledge of what has gone before in the play. The rising tension comes from this sense of danger, but it also comes from the contrast in the two characters on stage. Teddy is bright and keen, Ruth is tired and cynical. By the end of the scene, as we have seen, there has been something of a reversal. Ruth goes out for a walk and Teddy is perplexed and about to go to bed. This overall action is combined with a finely honed rhythm in the scene, an ebbing and flowing, connected to the schism in Ruth and Teddy's relationship, and achieved in the way the dialogue is orchestrated, punctuated with pauses and little surges. The dramatic action can be seen in the fine detail of this pacing.

The scene also acts as a reminder: dramatic action doesn't mean action in the thriller or adventure sense; there is no necessity for battles or fights. The dramatic action of a play need not be momentous. Characters do not have to die or marry, to kill or steal. But the action has to have a dramatic logic, given the circumstances facing the characters. You should always ask of your main character: What does he or she want? What is stopping them getting what they want? What do they most fear?

Stage scenes

The scene is a prime unit of drama – like a stanza in poetry, or a paragraph in prose. Each scene should act like a mini-play – containing an arc, a rising action building to a climactic point and a falling back towards resolution. The end of a scene sets up the next scene, so that, in *The Homecoming*, when Ruth goes out of the front door and Teddy stares after her there is a natural lull, during which Lenny, Teddy's brother, enters the room and watches him. Then the next scene proceeds. Some plays have numbered scenes or even titled scenes. Others are not formally divided, but as soon as you try to block such plays in rehearsal the natural scenic divisions in the action become apparent. *The Homecoming*, for instance, has no scene divisions, no numbers or titles, but is structured in two acts.

The switch from one scene to the next arises when either time or location shifts. A scene change can allow you to move to a different day, year, room or continent, without any problems of continuity in the storytelling (though there might be problems of changing the set and moving stage furniture around). However, the biggest definer of a scene is the dramatic action contained within it. What is the function of the scene within the wider action of the play and story, and how does the scene echo this wider action? The scene's action, its arc, has to be complete, to finish its function within the storytelling, and not be drawn out. As David Mamet says: 'Get into the scene late, get out early' (2004, p.112). What he is warning against is scenes that meander into their real beginning. Why create delays while the characters knock on and enter through doors? Why not have them already on stage? Why have your characters arranging to meet? Why not have them already together? His advice to 'get out early' warns against a dawdling resolution that might erode the play's momentum. The pace of continuity between scenes is as important as the pace within a scene. A quick departure lends pace to a play. The audience needs to be carried on a wave of interest in what happens next. Pace and tension are the tools by which to achieve this, not any lingering feeling that the characters should first finish their drinks or find an excuse to leave.

At the end of the Pinter scene, tension prevails even with the sight of Lenny staring at Teddy, who in turn is watching Ruth. It is a pause with teeth, and such tableaux – momentary, still and silent arrangements of characters – are a useful, occasional means by which theatre achieves its effect. The underlying action is not dramatically dull or dawdling at all – the audience has come, over the course of the preceding action, to perceive considerable differences between all these characters. The audience is, in this silence, seeing the menace and misgiving in the stares, imagining the contours of forthcoming conflict.

ACTIVITY 6.5 Reading	Read Scenes 2 and 3 from *Our Country's Good* by Timberlake Wertenbaker (Reading 16 on p.338). What do you think of the different lengths of the scenes? Can you see signs of dramatic action in them?

DISCUSSION	Compared with *The Homecoming*, Wertenbaker's play contains very different scene divisions. Each scene is numbered and titled. There is no prescription for the length of a scene. Some scenes, such as 2, seem momentary, and have obviously been influenced both by filmic methods, where you can have a very brief shot, and by Brechtian epic theatre, where short scenes can be juxtaposed, each contributing to the gathering pace of the action but none obliged to form a continuous, naturalistic narrative. Scene 4, for instance, deals with a scene between two characters a month after the hangings proposed in Scene 3 have taken place. You will see that even the brief Scene 2 has a triadic arc – a rising action, a climax and a resolution. In this instance the arc is just a simple three-sentence structure, with a magical arrival, metaphoric incredulity, followed by disenchantment.

Scenes tell stories

Our Country's Good is about the rehearsal and performance of George Farquhar's play *The Recruiting Officer* (1986 [1707]) by transported convicts and officers in newly colonised Australia. Farquhar's play is an eighteenth-century comedy about the abuse of power exercised by those who press-ganged men to enlist in the army. Notice how the characters are set up with a physical action for the duration of Scene 3 – 'The men are shooting birds'. This activity brings out the play's themes and dilemmas, which are concerned with whether or not it is possible to be civilised. It is a handy reminder. Ask this of all your own scenes: What are the characters doing physically? How does this contribute to the storytelling? The physical action here parallels the dramatic action. The scene ends with birds being shot, one convict dead and the probability of more to follow. Notice too how the scene begins in mid-conversation – cutting straight into the action of the scene – and ends with the punchline from a black joke.

The effect of the small scenes in *Our Country's Good* focuses the play's story on several characters rather than on one main character. An adaptation of 'Violin Lessons' using this method might, for instance, make the play more than just the man's story, and not focus so much on his workshop. It could have fleeting testimonies from the boy, from Mr Bouillon and from the boy's sister, perhaps even have a scene showing the violin lesson. This would be a more liberal adaptation, and some might say it would fundamentally change the original story.

The method of scene juxtaposition can be exciting but it can also dilute the dramatic focus. It is important, with small pieces especially, to ask what is holding the drama together. Quite often it is the fate of one character.

ACTIVITY 6.6 Reading and writing	Remind yourself of the story 'A Real Durwan' (Reading 2 on p.287) and review your responses to Activity 1.7 in the light of the work you have done in this chapter. You will recall that you imagined a dramatic adaptation of the story and had to pick a medium and some key elements to be dramatised. Now carry out the following steps:

- Identify a possible dramatic action in the story, as if you were going to adapt it for the stage.
- Identify small episodes of action that might form scenes. Arrange these in sequence.
- Imagine the visual narrative.
- Identify what might be your main character's fears, her wants, what is stopping her (if your main character is Boori Ma).

DISCUSSION	The individual scenes might consist of Boori Ma's initial cleaning session, culminating in her meeting with her neighbour. Or you might start with her trying but failing to sleep because of the fleas in her bedding. There are many options, each of which would change the story slightly. You might have many small scenes, with less focus on Boori Ma. Alternatively she

could be onstage all the time; it could be a one-character play, with the other characters offstage. All these are possible. Further invention – a character or event that does not feature in the original – is also possible. Perhaps Boori Ma has a friend in whom she confides. In order to write a dramatic adaptation you might find that you need such a character.

Scenarios

You have just written what is sometimes called a scenario – an annotated list of scenes in sequence, combining to outline the dramatic action. Look at this scenario from Steve Gooch:

Mister Fun: scenario

Scene One: Spring. A fairground. GIL and MARSHY are working the dodgems, discussing the girls. Meanwhile SHELLEY and her friend, WINA, are discussing GIL, who's bright and thinks he's flash, and MARSHY, who's very slow. WINA hopes GIL will come over and take their fare, but SHELLEY (whose parents run a stall) warns her he's likely to short-change her. It's MARSHY who comes over. And even when GIL does eventually come over and flirt, we feel the banter is really for SHELLEY's benefit.

Scene Two: Summer. The fair. While MARSHY packs up their gear, GIL is trying to get SHELLEY into his newly-acquired motor-caravan, but SHELLEY wants to discuss their prospects together. All GIL knows is he wants a life away from the routine. All SHELLEY knows is she wants 'something better'.

Scene Three: Autumn. The fair. MR ALSOPP, the fair manager, calls at the caravan one night when GIL and MARSHY are playing cards. He gives MARSHY his wages and gets rid of him in order to tell GIL he's laid off. The fair is in financial difficulty. It's moving to a fixed site shortly and, though he needs MARSHY's mechanical skills, he doesn't need GIL to pull the girls on the dodgems. GIL protests – particularly when ALSOPP implies he fiddles the fares – but the best he can wring out of ALSOPP is a half-promise of work on the new site.

Scene Four: Winter. A roadside. SHELLEY has found a menial job for herself, but GIL doesn't want her to work – even though they're very broke. When pressed, he reveals his fear that his sense of identity will disintegrate if the responsibility of 'bread-winner' is taken from him.

Scene Five: Spring again. The fair. GIL has persuaded a reluctant SHELLEY to return to the fair on its new, fixed site, on the off-chance of work. The fair is now much depleted and drabber, and the best ALSOPP can offer (besides asking them to move the caravan on) is a part-time job for SHELLEY on the refreshment stall. GIL is disgusted when she jumps at it, but she is astonished when he agrees to help organise a fund-raising supporters club.

(Gooch, 1990, p.39)

As you can see, the bare bones of a play's action can be laid out by plotting the scenes in this way. There is no need for embellishment. Such preparatory work gives you a unique preview of sequence and how your play's events will present themselves to an audience.

ACTIVITY 6.7 Writing	Take a small section (no more than two scenes) from your scenario of 'A Real Durwan' and adapt it for the stage. You were shown the correct layout for a stage script in Chapter 4. Use the script layout in Figure 1 on p.44, and follow the guidance in 'Stage scripts – some tips' on p.45. Use the set description written for Activity 6.4 if you wish.
DISCUSSION	One of the decisions you would have to make is whether to divide the action up into marked scenes, as with *Our Country's Good*, or use implicit divisions, as with *The Homecoming*. Always go over your scripts making sure that you have imagined a visual narrative, but also check that your stage directions and dialogue are not overwritten. There are many more decisions you may have encountered, including those about how realistic you want the action to be, and whether you want a non-naturalistic style of performance with characters talking directly to the audience. These important decisions about style have implications for all aspects of your storytelling.

Conclusion

In this chapter you have examined the importance of visual narrative and dramatic action to stage plays. You have explored ways of writing stage direction, and looked at some different notions of dramatic action. In trying to write a visual narrative, you have examined the implications of writing for different kinds of stages and looked at how sets are written. You have seen how dramatic action is spread across a whole play and through its individual scenes, and tried writing a brief scenario. In the next chapter you will discover how some of the dramatic principles you have so far encountered might be used when writing for radio.

References

Beckett, Samuel (1985 [1956]) *Waiting for Godot*, London: Faber and Faber.

Berkoff, Steven (1994 [1982]) *Greek* in *Plays 1*, London: Faber and Faber.

Bond, Edward (1969 [1966]) *Saved*, London: Methuen.

Brecht, Bertolt (1987 [1940]) *Mother Courage* (trans. John Willett), London: Methuen.

Chekhov, Anton (1990 [1904]) *The Cherry Orchard* (trans. Michael Frayn), London: Faber and Faber.

Farquhar, George (1986 [1707]) *The Recruiting Officer*, Manchester: Manchester University Press.

Friel, Brian (1996) *Philadelphia, Here I Come!* in *Plays 1*, London: Faber and Faber.

Gooch, Steve (1990) *Writing a Play*, London: A & C Black.

Griffiths, Stuart (1982) *How Plays are Made*, London: Heinemann Educational.

Griffiths, Trevor (1985) *Comedians*, London: Faber and Faber.

Ibsen, Henrik (1952 [1884]) *The Wild Duck* in *Three Plays* (trans. Una Ellis-Fermor), Harmondsworth: Penguin.

Mamet, David (2004) Interview with David Savran in *David Mamet in Conversation* (ed. Leslie Kane), Michigan: Michigan University Press.

Rhys, Jean (1966) *Wide Sargasso Sea*, London: André Deutsch.

Shakespeare, William (2001) *Macbeth* in *The Arden Shakespeare Complete Works*, London: Arden.

Sophocles (1982) *Oedipus Rex* in *The Three Theban Plays* (trans. Robert Fagles), London: Allen Lane.

Storey, David (1970) *The Contractor*, London: Cape.

Teale, Polly (2003) *After Mrs Rochester*, London: Nick Hern.

Further reading

Beckett, Samuel (1984) *Act Without Words 1* in *Collected Shorter Plays of Samuel Beckett*, London: Faber and Faber.

This is one of Beckett's voiceless short plays – a mime (there are others in this collection). It is interesting because of how he writes the movement instruction for the actor and because the action of the play refers continually to an unseen, offstage antagonist.

Keneally, Thomas (1987) *Playmaker*, London: Hodder & Stoughton.

This is the novel on which *Our Country's Good* is based. You could look at this to see how Wertenbaker has gone about the adaptation, how closely she has kept to the story, and how her arrangement of scenes relates to episodes in the novel.

Stafford-Clark, Max (1989) *Letters to George*, London: Nick Hern.

This offers a stage director's testimony about the rehearsal and performance of *Our Country's Good*. It gives an intriguing insight into the mechanics of the play and into how a script is converted into a performance.

7   Writing radio drama

Derek Neale

Radio drama is often commended above all other dramatic media because, it is suggested, 'the pictures are better'. In a radio play all elements of the storytelling have to be identified by sound alone, and this is both a constraint and a strength. Listeners, deprived of visual stimuli but prompted by the writer, are integrally involved in constructing the set and costumes, the events and the characters. The audience is not a communal entity like a theatre audience. There is no possibility of infectious laughter, for example; instead there is a powerful, one-to-one intimacy with the dramatic performance.

One of the first radio plays, *Danger* by Richard Hughes (1966), broadcast in 1924, was set in a coal mine after an explosion. This places all the characters in complete darkness. Such a device – effectively taking away the sight of the characters – usefully motivates the exposition of the play. The characters want to know the same range of information as the unsighted audience. It is an apt tactic for the medium. When looking at radio scripts in workshops, I ask the non-actors to close their eyes while the script is read aloud. Similarly, many radio producers testify that they often close their eyes in the control room during rehearsals and when playing back recordings.

As you have learned from earlier chapters, dramatic writing involves creating contrasts, because this in turn creates conflict between characters. Writing radio drama involves working specifically with aural contrasts. This chapter will capitalise on some of the work you have already done on differentiating between the voices of your characters – for instance, using idiom and idiolect – and take it a step further. You will also be able to use some of the dramatic tools of exposition explored in previous chapters – including subtext and status. Again, 'Violin Lessons' will be used as an example story for adaptation, and we will examine the specific layout required for radio scripts. You will be exploring the merits of radio monologues and the use of sound effects, while trying to adapt stories for radio, using either 'A Real Durwan' or a story of your own.

Creating pictures with sound

When a character is introduced in a drama the audience expects to learn at least some basic details about the new arrival. If more than one character is introduced, the audience will look for clues to help distinguish between them. You may recall two characters mentioned in Chapter 4: one who is tall and uses odd words; another who wears a yellow dress, has a bandage round her hand and is looking away from the other character. Imagine these same two characters at the start of a radio play. Listeners will be unable to see that one of the characters is tall, though they may hear that he uses odd words. They will not see the other character's yellow dress, her bandaged hand or the fact that she is looking away from the character using the odd words. How do you go about providing that information on radio? Similarly, where are the characters meeting? How did they get there? These are the questions listeners will be asking. The radio writer has to find ways of providing all the necessary storytelling detail. Using sound alone, the writer has to create pictures for the audience.

ACTIVITY 7.1
Reading

Read the extract from the start of *Temporary Shelter* by Rose Tremain (Reading 17 on p.341).

- How are characters established here?
- How is place established?
- What pictures do you think are conjured up for the listener?

DISCUSSION

Certain signposts are given in Trist's monologue, which means that it acts as an introduction. It offers details about location (a campsite in France) and two of the main characters – Larry and the speaker. Trist's second monologue gives a basic introduction for Jean-Louis. But many details are left out, which is important. The audience should never be given too much information too quickly. Notice how the dialogue between Marje and Larry informs, but in an unobtrusive manner. We learn of Larry's inhibitions, his ingenuous manner of 'being abroad', his regard for the French couple, and something of his relationship with his wife – he gets in her way and she offers him rather too much support and tolerance, though this is showing signs of fraying. We are also given the startling juxtaposition of a character like Larry, a salesman, meeting a character like Jean-Louis, a poet. This provides the promise of conflict.

In this opening the listener starts to get the 'picture' in terms of the different relationships on the campsite but also in terms of location. The script conjures up a campsite in France through the use of sound effects (cicadas, dogs barking, the sound of the characters getting in and out of tents) and by including particular references in their dialogue (queuing for showers, baguettes).

How to start

Trist's monologue in *Temporary Shelter* is separated in time; it is written from the perspective of the future when all the events have finished. Notice how the sound effects help to achieve transitions in time and place. They are written into the script, but are not laboured. Individual noises are initially indicated and then referred to lightly when necessary as 'campsite noises'. You should not write an instruction for every door that creaks open or shut. Write only what is necessary to the telling of the story. Notice that Tremain, for instance, gives an instruction for when the noise of the dogs barking should increase – because it is pertinent to what happens next. But she refrains from detailing every bark.

The dialogue and sound effects, especially at the start of a radio drama, should begin to give the listeners an idea of:

- specific place (campsite, pub, Peter's bedroom);
- context – time, era, more general place (evening, 1970s, Birmingham);
- who the characters are;
- why the characters are where they are;
- how the characters relate to one another;
- where the play is going next – a hint of the dramatic movement;
- what has happened before;
- how to differentiate between the characters in the play.

Because the script has to work so hard to establish so many different elements, writers can sometimes overburden radio dialogue with too much information. A common fault is to make the dialogue implausible by getting characters who know each other well (a husband and wife, for instance) to reveal things that would, in real life, go unspoken. Another fault is to repeat information in the dialogue which is already apparent in the sound effects. In your scripts, try to ensure that the action provides the producer with clues as to what sound effects might be used; make them explicit in the script only when the producer could not otherwise know that such a sound effect would be useful at that particular point; and write sound effects explicitly in the script only when they are essential to the telling of the story. You always have to respect the fact that your audience will be inventing pictures from the slightest clues, and that too much detail can spoil their pictures.

ACTIVITY 7.2 Writing	Write a scene or two which establishes a holiday destination known to you (up to 700 words). Include at least two fictional characters. If you wish, return to your characters involved with the mobile phone in Activities 6.1 and 6.2, or use characters you have created in your notebook. Remember this is for radio, so use sound only.

You may have found that you had too much information to convey in such a short script. It is always best to motivate exposition in some way, whether the exposition is about setting, backstory or character. Make sure the information is prompted by characters and events in the play and not just by the need to deliver information to the listener. Even Trist's narration in *Temporary Shelter*, for instance, is motivated by the character's reckoning of past events and specifically his relationship with Larry.

You need to provide the listener with some emotional attraction and engagement, and this is often achieved by suggesting your characters' fear, anger, yearning, annoyance, sadness and joy. But find actions within the story which demonstrate these states; beware of having characters declare their emotional state.

Early scenes in a play also have to introduce the methods you are using. If you are using a non-linear narrative, for instance, in which a character's wandering thoughts and fragmentary memories navigate the action, then this needs to be established from the start. If you choose to use an internal voice, make sure that it still generates pictures, because such images enrich and sustain intrigue. They keep your listener interested.

Radio scenes

When writing radio drama you have to be most attentive to the exact constraints of performance time. The radio soap *The Archers*, for instance, has episodes of twelve and a half minutes, each including at least one of the major story lines (these run for three months) and one of the minor story lines (running for a month). Each episode includes an optimum of seven characters and five scenes. This means that each scene should be performed in, on average, two and a half minutes. This gives some indication of the concise, mathematical ways in which radio drama can be constructed.

Scene, derived from the Greek word *skena*, meaning tent or stage, appears something of a misnomer when used in the context of radio, where there is no tangible performance space. Radio drama uses the 'theatre of the mind', but nonetheless is still made up of scenes, the primary dramatic units. As on the stage, a scene's duration is ruled by shifts in location and time, and by the culmination of a specific episode of dramatic action. Often in radio scripts the different scenes are not headed, and the division between scenes is not marked – as in *Temporary Shelter*. Whether or not you mark the scene divisions in your script is often decided by the type of story you are trying to tell.

Radio is a continuous medium. Whether the scenes are numbered and headed in the script or not, the writer and subsequently the producer have to decide how to achieve the transitions between them. This can be done through a range of tactics. You can use a well-signposted link, amounting to an introduction – as in the shift from Trist's monologue scene to the campsite at the opening of *Temporary Shelter*. In Fay Weldon's *Polaris* (1979), the two major scene locations are on board a Polaris submarine and at the home of Meg, the wife of the submarine's navigator, Tim. Weldon achieves the links between the scenes by using familiar sounds to identify each location quickly: the pinging of the submarine's echo sounder and the slobbering and barking of Meg and Tim's dog, Thompson. She also uses radio songs that are playing in both locations to effect the transition.

Another alternative is to have a stark juxtaposition – going from near silence to full volume, for instance, or vice versa. The radio adaptation of Ray Bradbury's futuristic short story 'The Veldt' by Mike Walker (2007), offers an example of this sort of link. Here, a mother and father talk about problems with their children; the father realises during the conversation that he cannot go fishing with his son as previously planned. The calm domestic scene then cuts to sounds of a loud battle, guns firing and shells falling. This plays for a while, shocking the listener, before breaking into a conversation scene between father and son. The battle is a computer game, but the jarring loudness of the juxtaposition illuminates the theme and anticipates action in the play: a violent outcome later in the story and a critical schism between the children and their parents.

Writing radio scripts
Script layout for radio

Look at Figure 6, a sample page from a radio script containing details of particular features. What do you notice about the way in which the script is laid out?

This script follows the BBC's guidance on layout for radio plays (BBC, 2008), and is a good model to use when writing your own scripts. Note, though, that other broadcasters may have specific requirements on presentation; check on these before submitting your script. In Chapter 8 you will learn about the appropriate layout for film scripts. In all the suggested script layouts, you will notice that there is clear differentiation between the spoken and the unspoken elements. Here are some further tips.

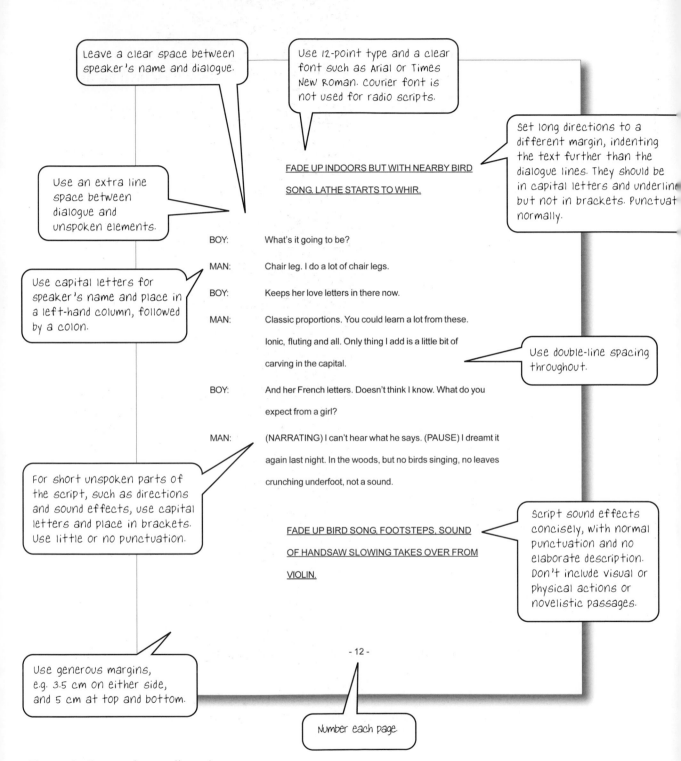

Leave a clear space between speaker's name and dialogue.

Use 12-point type and a clear font such as Arial or Times New Roman. Courier font is not used for radio scripts.

Set long directions to a different margin, indenting the text further than the dialogue lines. They should be in capital letters and underlined but not in brackets. Punctuate normally.

Use an extra line space between dialogue and unspoken elements.

FADE UP INDOORS BUT WITH NEARBY BIRD SONG. LATHE STARTS TO WHIR.

BOY: What's it going to be?

MAN: Chair leg. I do a lot of chair legs.

Use capital letters for speaker's name and place in a left-hand column, followed by a colon.

BOY: Keeps her love letters in there now.

MAN: Classic proportions. You could learn a lot from these. Ionic, fluting and all. Only thing I add is a little bit of carving in the capital.

Use double-line spacing throughout.

BOY: And her French letters. Doesn't think I know. What do you expect from a girl?

MAN: (NARRATING) I can't hear what he says. (PAUSE) I dreamt it again last night. In the woods, but no birds singing, no leaves crunching underfoot, not a sound.

For short unspoken parts of the script, such as directions and sound effects, use capital letters and place in brackets. Use little or no punctuation.

FADE UP BIRD SONG, FOOTSTEPS, SOUND OF HANDSAW SLOWING TAKES OVER FROM VIOLIN.

Script sound effects concisely, with normal punctuation and no elaborate description. Don't include visual or physical actions or novelistic passages.

- 12 -

Use generous margins, e.g. 3.5 cm on either side, and 5 cm at top and bottom.

Number each page.

Figure 6   Layout for a radio script

98

Radio scripts – some tips

- Use punctuation, pauses and silences to control the speech rhythms of monologues.
- As with stage dialogue, remember that a dash (–) at the end of a line designates that a line has been interrupted.
- Remember too that an ellipsis (...) at the end of a line designates that the line trails off.
- A pause within a line is differentiated from the speech – usually bracketed, in capitals (PAUSE). Use these cautiously.
- Notice how the man is described as (NARRATING) when he is talking, as if we are hearing his thoughts. There are several possible conventions for this: one is as I have done here; others are to put (VO) – short for 'voice-over' – or (INTERNAL) before such speeches.

Using the appropriate layout indicates to producers and script editors that your submitted script has been written specifically for radio. Notice how the layout is unambiguous; spoken and unspoken elements are clearly separated by typographic conventions. It is important to use these conventions, and not invent your own.

As an approximate measure of running time, if you use the layout advice given here, each A4 page will average out at forty-five seconds. Be aware, though, that this is an average and not an accurate gauge for individual pages, or for all scripts. The only way to gauge the running time of a script exactly is to read through it in real time, so that all the sound effects and the different pace of lines are assessed accurately.

Adaptation for radio

We will now consider some of the decisions you need to make when adapting a story for radio.

ACTIVITY 7.3 Reading	Read the following script for a radio adaptation of part of 'Violin Lessons'. The script deals with the section just after the boy and the man have met, when the boy watches the man at work. It also includes the man recalling his dream and part of the story's next passage when Mr Bouillon walks by.

Compare this version to the original section of the story. When reading, note the radio techniques used in the script.

Fade up indoors but with nearby birdsong. Lathe starts to whir, then occasional rising screeches as chisel cuts.

Man: Get off the mahogany.

Boy: What?

Man: (*louder*) The mahogany, it's seasoning, you'll warp it. Sit over there. You can still see.

Boy: What's it going to be?

Man: Chair leg. I do a lot of chair legs.

Boy: Like this one?

Man: Put it back.

Boy: Like pillars. My sister's doll's house has got pillars like that.

Man: Then your sister's a lucky girl. Put it back in the box.

Boy: Keeps her love letters in there now.

Man: Classic proportions. You could learn a lot from these. Ionic, fluting and all. Only thing I add is a little bit of carving in the capital. Doubt whether your sister's doll's house has pillars like –

Boy: And her French letters. Doesn't think I know. What do you expect from a girl?

Man: Get your foot off the mahogany.

Boy: I'm going to make an electric guitar when I'm in the fourth year.

Man: Shouldn't you be at home?

Boy: Waiting for my sister.

Man: And where is your sister?

Boy: Violin lesson. I'm supposed to sit and wait. Mr Bouillon. What a racket. Mr Bubblegum. I go down the woods.

Fade down lathe, fade up a scratching yet eventually tuneful jazz or folk violin – Stephane Grappelli perhaps, searching for coherence throughout the monologue.

Man: (*narrating*) I can't hear what he says. (*pause*) I dreamt it again last night. In the woods, but no birds singing, no leaves crunching underfoot, not a sound. Even when I see him ... the man. Standing under the silver birch. One tree, all on its own. Playing his violin. Wild. Like nothing could stop him. His hair swinging all over his face, I can't see who he is, but I know him, I think I do. Playing away but I can't hear a thing. I strain, I stop breathing, but nothing. (*silence apart from violin*) I wake up happy. Like I've been somewhere, been away. I wake up thinking there is no music. Only a picture. That's the point. I don't know what to make of it. It's like ... it's like ...

Fade up birdsong, footsteps, sound of handsaw slowly takes over from violin.

Bouillon: What a beautiful day. You work outside today?

Man: No, no, I've just got to cut these to length.

Bouillon: I see. It is ash, like my chairs?

Man: What?

Bouillon: Ash. The wood.

Man: Oh, yes. Ash. I just cut it, to length ... cut it then stack it inside.

Bouillon: This weather, it is so fine in my conservatory. They are looking very wonderful. I am pleased with them. I keep them there, you see. In my conservatory, by the reading table. (*silence*) The chairs you made for me. They are very wonderful.

Man: Oh, I see. (*pause*) Well, I better get on –

Bouillon: Everyone says how they are wonderful.

Fade up saw getting louder.

I have used a contrastive scene link here after the man's monologue – by juxtaposing the violin with the sound of birds and the handsaw. I have used music to illustrate the incoherence of the man's dream and his inarticulate grasp of what his dream might mean. All these elements amplify the aural clues that are present in the original story – for instance, the man dreams of a violinist in the woods but can never fully recall the music.

You will see that my adaptation does not include every consecutive detail of the original story. The episode with Mr Bouillon, for instance, is one particular meeting, but I have attempted to suggest the habitual nature of Mr Bouillon's walk ('He usually goes for a walk about this time'), with his line 'You work outside today?'. This implies that he has walked past the man's workshop on more than one previous occasion. I have cut the detail about the man clumsily eating a cheese sandwich, because it was an image not easily translated to radio. I decided it added little to the storytelling. I also decided not to number the scene or give it a title.

When adapting your own stories you will have to make similar decisions to those I have made in adapting 'Violin Lessons'. You need to remember at all times that you are writing for radio. As I have already pointed out, it is a medium with various constraints, but these can become strengths in your storytelling. Remember:

- the only way to establish a character's presence is to have him or her speak, or be referred to by another character;
- too many characters in a scene can confuse the listener;
- sound effects should be used sparingly;
- think in sound contrasts – different scene lengths, line lengths, volume levels, interior and exterior acoustics.

Read back over your script for Activity 7.2 and redraft it using the radio layout described above. Look at the links you made between the scenes, and at the level of sound contrast contained in your script. Rewrite if necessary.

Adaptability

Quite often in radio adaptations of long narratives such as novels there is a narrowing down of the timeline and, most probably, of the cast list too.

As Linda Hutcheon says of an adaptation of Virginia Woolf's novel *To the Lighthouse*:

> The characters who remain double as storytellers, but many are eliminated to keep the focus on the Ramsay family and Lily Briscoe. The words we hear come from the novel, but they are moved around, recontextualized, and read by different voices. These changes allow the aural version to give a sense of the novel's linguistic texture, its associative range, and its narrative rhythm.
>
> (Hutcheon, 2006, p.41)

In this way the radio adapter edits the original but can give a distinct flavour of that text and its various voices. With radio you can make listeners feel as though they are inside the head of a character. Radio also has the flexibility to shift quickly from a scene in the Himalayas to a scene in the Antarctic, and then to a house in Bermondsey, and to make such shifts plausible. Compared with film there is practically no production cost in making these shifts; compared with stage the shifts can be achieved quite naturalistically. Another strength of radio is that surreal situations can be realised more easily than in other media. In *Blossom* by Rose Tremain (1977), a widow has an affair with a younger man, but then absolves her guilt by talking to her dead husband. This internal dialogue with the character's own past would be far less intimate on film or stage. Similarly in Stephen Dunstone's *Who is Sylvia?*, the listener gets to know the pressing concerns of a family of laboratory cockroaches, at one point listening in on the mother admiring her hatching young:

Angela: (*beside herself with joy*) Darling! Oh Darling! I've waited so long ... Oh, Henry, do look, how many can you count? Aren't they adorable? So beautiful, so pale, so translucent. And so ... innocent. So defenceless without their wings. And so like you ...

(Dunstone, 1985, p.4)

Just a few seconds later in the play's running time, but a year later in the play's storyline, the listener hears the comically complex yet complacent attitude of the scientists as they look over the cockroaches:

Plackett: I want to do a transplant job on him. If we take one of the new adult males from normal conditions we can transplant its suboesophageal ganglion into old big daddy there, and we should see a revival of rhythm. Good subjects, Periplaneta, good subjects. Tried a fungus beetle once –

(p.6)

On radio everything is possible; such rapid shifts in focus are easily achieved without the need for expensive costumes, strange lighting or extravagant special effects.

The adaptation of Bradbury's 'The Veldt' offers a good example of this flexibility. The original story, written in 1952, is set in 'the future' and comments on the technological revolution happening in the 1950s home, with the advent of vacuum cleaners and televisions. In the story's world, every conceivable domestic task is performed by 'the house' rather than the occupants of the house – children are scrubbed in the bath automatically; tables serve meals that have been prepared by a fully automated stove. The biggest innovation is a children's playroom in which the walls transform into virtual 'play worlds'. During the story this room turns into the African veldt, complete with vultures and lions. In one of the scenes the family are round the dinner table. They then all walk along to the playroom and suddenly, on entering the room, they are in Africa. This is achieved instantly in the radio adaptation with the sound of a lion's roar. In future scenes, when the listeners hear the lion they know where they are. On radio the establishment of a futuristic world presents no greater technical challenge than creating a contemporary world.

ACTIVITY 7.5 Writing	Adapt for radio a five-minute section from 'A Real Durwan' or a story of your own choice. Include a monologue, more than one scene, scene links, and characters with contrasting voice patterns. This might be the start of a bigger piece but try to give this section a cohesive structure.
DISCUSSION	When adapting stories you will sometimes find that you need to invent elements that are not present in the original. You may need to find and show the reason why a character behaves in a certain way. Such invention will make the dramatic logic of the storytelling more plausible. For instance, in adapting part of 'A Real Durwan' you might have found it necessary to invent some part of Boori Ma's past, which caused her to behave in the way that she does.

Varying your voices

Switching time periods and adopting a non-linear approach can be more easily achieved in radio than in a stage play. There is no stage furniture to shift or lighting issues to address. Yet events still have to be well signposted – you have to make sure your listener knows where he or she is in time. The intimate monologue, a voice directed to the personal ear of the listener, is unique to radio drama. It creates the effect of being inside a character's head. Such radio monologues, as seen in my adaptation in the man's narration about his dream, can sometimes emulate the subtleties and variations of the first-person narrative of a novel or short story. In this way radio, more than other media, has the potential to capture the original texture, tone and flavour of a novel, short story, biography or memoir.

As in fiction, where you should always be aware and in control of point of view, so in radio drama you should keep a tight rein on the number of people who can reveal their thoughts directly in monologues. This will often be only one character. But however many you use, your method has to be established early on, otherwise you risk structural problems. In the final minutes of a play you cannot have a character revealing his or her thoughts for the first time and explaining what has happened.

A note on radio monologues

You can see from my adaptation that a radio monologue can be adept at revealing the inner thoughts of a character. But the voice still has to be dramatic. Notice the use of repetitions in the man's speech. You will recall how to dramatise a long speech from writing stage monologues, in Chapter 5. Here are some tips when writing radio monologues:

- include other voices within the monologue ('he said to me, what have you been up to, and I said to him, what do you think I've been up to');
- have an addressee implied in the speech ('you see'; 'do you understand');
- listen to the rhythm created by repetitions and variations;
- vary the pace and use punctuation to change the rhythm – having long, drawn-out lines followed by quick, short-clause lines;
- reveal a see-saw equivocation in the speaker – an internal debate;
- keep on checking as you redraft that the monologue is absolutely necessary.

You make a monologue dramatic, in short, by making it dialogic. Such speeches should be motivated by character and must move the story on. They have to serve the action of the play and cannot afford to be static, too flat or purely expositional – radio is easy to switch off!

ACTIVITY 7.6 Reading	Read the extract from *Cigarettes and Chocolate* by Anthony Minghella (Reading 18 on p.345), paying particular attention to Gail's monologue. What sort of voice do you think this is?

Minghella's play begins with a series of phone messages – on the answering machine of someone who has stopped talking to anyone. The messages contrast with one another: some are from the recipient's boyfriend, some from her friends and some from her mother. Some of the messages are short, some are long. As the script – perhaps needlessly – tells us, Gail's voice is torrential and she sounds self-obsessed; her speech is unrelenting and discursive.

Distinguishing between voices

The use of the answering machine is interesting in *Cigarettes and Chocolate*. Whereas phone scenes can be awkward on stage or film, on air any radiophonic device can offer a useful echo to the relationship between performers and listeners. Harold Pinter's play *Victoria Station* (1982), for instance, involving a long dialogue between a taxi driver and his control centre over a short-waveband transmitter, is particularly effective on radio.

As suggested earlier, aural contrast is essential to radio drama. In terms of the dialogue, such contrasts are achieved by the scriptwriter creating idiomatic differences in the way each character speaks. You can also create variety between speakers by presenting the idiosyncratic speech patterns – the idiolect – of each of your characters. It is not surprising that *The Archers* has traditionally included a vast range of voices – male, female, young, old, rural, urban, Scottish, Irish, Welsh, American, Anglo-Indian, African, middle class, working class. Rather than typifying life in rural Worcestershire, where the drama is set, this range of voices reflects the need for dramatic contrast. It is important not to go overboard in creating contrast for its own sake; such contrast must arise plausibly from your story. The simplest contrasts are often the most effective, as in my 'Violin Lessons' adaptation where a straightforward contrast is achieved by age and background.

Think of what your characters might say in public and private contexts, but also think of phrases that they use regularly. For instance, in the adaptation of 'Violin Lessons' the man uses the word 'like' frequently. Mr Bouillon's slightly odd grammar reveals he is not a native speaker, and also that he is fond of the word 'wonderful'. This is similar to creating a catchphrase for a character, but the way it works is a little more subtle. A character might say 'really' a lot, or 'quite'. You have to beware of creating stereotypes by overusing such repeated words or phrases. Mr Bouillon does not say 'what a wonderful day' as an opening line, for instance, because I gauged that would be one 'wonderful' too many. This use of repeated phrases occurs in fiction too. In 'A Real Durwan', for instance, Boori Ma often repeats the line 'Believe me, don't believe me', and Dickens's novels are full of characters with lines that typify them. In a radio play, when working well, this sort of repeated line amounts to a shorthand device, instantly establishing the character's presence and identity for the listener.

One of the keys to creating believable characters lies in being consistent in a character's use of language. As part of your editorial process, read aloud all the lines of a single character, from start to finish. Make sure the voice is consistent. Then, put your hand over the left-hand column of your script covering the names, and make sure you know who is speaking from the timbre of each line.

Look at Figure 7. Using one of the voices, write a monologue for radio on the theme of lost love, establishing your character in a place. If you need a prompt, choose from:

- a telephone booth at an airport;
- the washroom at a cinema, restaurant or theatre;
- a queue.

At first you might have found that by following and repeating one speech pattern you were not able to create a character. This can too easily become a grammatical game. But I hope that at some point the given pattern developed into something less regular and more individual. The important thing is to hear the voice; the more you listen to its rhythms and cadences, the more you will be drawn into a character. Whatever patterns a character uses there will always be modulations and variations in pace and rhythm according to content and mood. You will, of course, gain more knowledge of your character from further imaginative investigation, by inventing more details about their life, appearance and relations. You may have found you had to do this in order to write the monologue in the first place.

Using strong language

As you will have noticed, one of the voices in Figure 7 uses strong language. Cursing poses a problem on radio, where expletives are amplified by the lack of a visual counterpoint and by being broadcast into private homes. Strong language would probably not get broadcast on most stations. Generally it should be ruled out of your radio writing.

When writing for other dramatic media, use of strong language is possible and sometimes necessary. Yet even then, use it only when the drama needs and earns such language; beware of swearing gratuitously and make sure it is the character's own language, appropriate to them and the context.

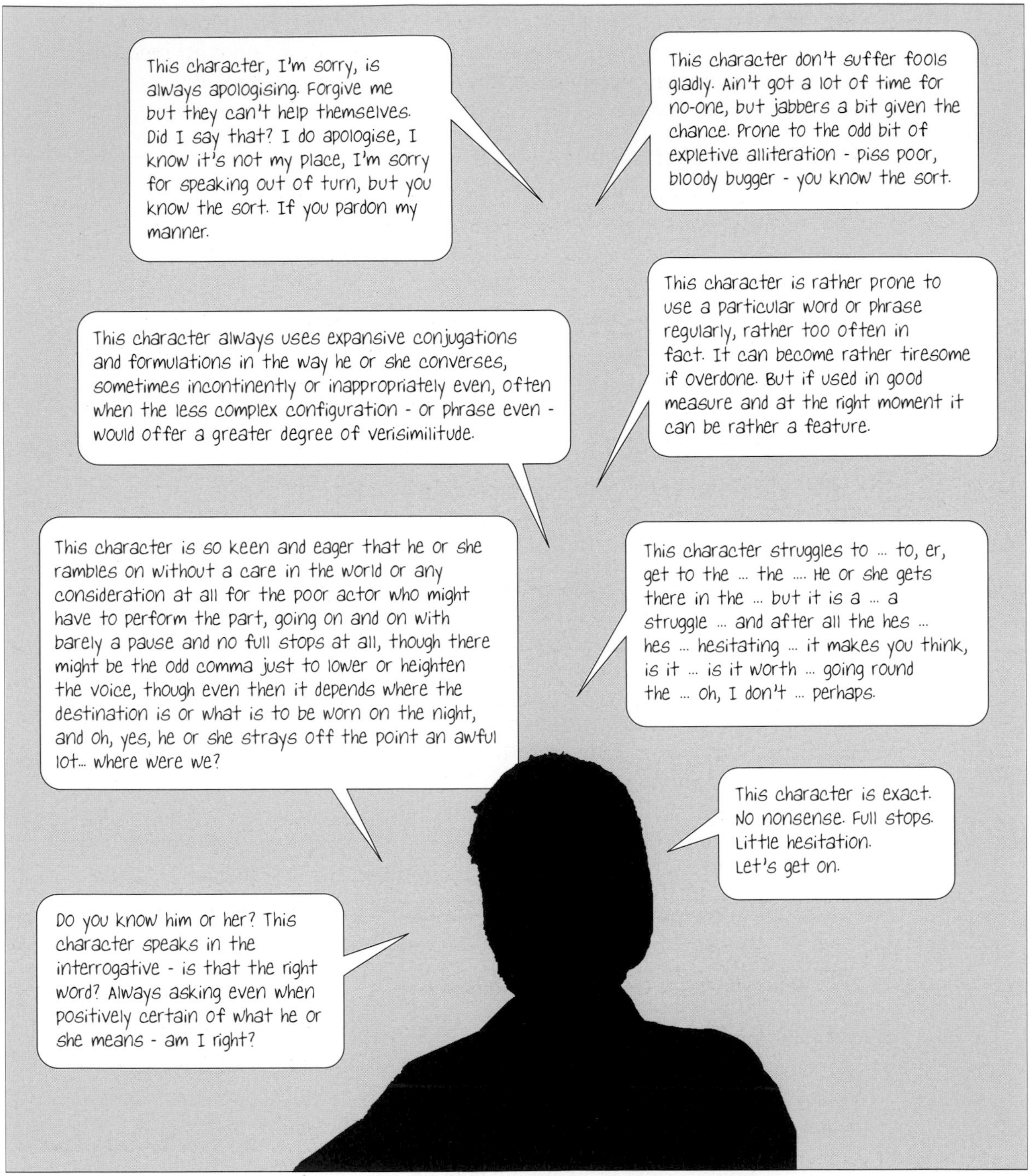

This character, I'm sorry, is always apologising. Forgive me but they can't help themselves. Did I say that? I do apologise, I know it's not my place, I'm sorry for speaking out of turn, but you know the sort. If you pardon my manner.

This character don't suffer fools gladly. Ain't got a lot of time for no-one, but jabbers a bit given the chance. Prone to the odd bit of expletive alliteration - piss poor, bloody bugger - you know the sort.

This character is rather prone to use a particular word or phrase regularly, rather too often in fact. It can become rather tiresome if overdone. But if used in good measure and at the right moment it can be rather a feature.

This character always uses expansive conjugations and formulations in the way he or she converses, sometimes incontinently or inappropriately even, often when the less complex configuration - or phrase even - would offer a greater degree of verisimilitude.

This character is so keen and eager that he or she rambles on without a care in the world or any consideration at all for the poor actor who might have to perform the part, going on and on with barely a pause and no full stops at all, though there might be the odd comma just to lower or heighten the voice, though even then it depends where the destination is or what is to be worn on the night, and oh, yes, he or she strays off the point an awful lot... where were we?

This character struggles to ... to, er, get to the ... the .... He or she gets there in the ... but it is a ... a struggle ... and after all the hes ... hes ... hesitating ... it makes you think, is it ... is it worth ... going round the ... oh, I don't ... perhaps.

This character is exact. No nonsense. Full stops. Little hesitation. Let's get on.

Do you know him or her? This character speaks in the interrogative - is that the right word? Always asking even when positively certain of what he or she means - am I right?

Figure 7

On radio, expletives usually have to be worked around. Characters can still cry and scream; they can shout and be silent, and often these forms of expression can be more violent and powerful than a curse.

Drama with less story

Some radio drama is less intent on the storyline and more intent on creating and celebrating a world through poetry and sound. Benjamin Zephaniah's *Hurricane Dub* (1988), for example, is a modern musical and poetic telling of the hurricane that hit Britain in 1987. A famous example of a radio piece which is part poem and part play is Dylan Thomas's *Under Milk Wood* (1977 [1954]), which creates an ensemble performance in which no single character dominates. It relies heavily on stock characters, presenting them through multiple narrators who, acting like a Greek chorus, echo each other in alliteratively creating the world of Llareggub, a fictional Welsh town.

In *Sunday Morning at the Centre of the World*, Louis de Bernières uses a similar method in paying homage both to Thomas and to the suburb of Earlsfield in London, where he lived for ten years:

Narrator:	Potty Ingrid throws open the sash and slings out bread that falls like rubber snow amid the dustbins and the ragged robin that grows in cracks, and the hawkweed and convolvulus and the chip-wrappers and the drying evidence of the last night's drunks.
Potty Ingrid:	Come on my darlings! My pretty ones! My sweets! My bright-eyed babies!
Narrator:	And down fly the feral doves, unbowed but battered and tattered, martyrs to mites, their guts in permanent flux from their orgies of chips and bread and burger buns, their birdseed and roadgrit and water floating with oil.
Potty Ingrid:	Come on, my darlings!
Narrator:	Potty Ingrid, her hair in knots, slams down the sash, and the three black cats of Ramillies Road spring out from behind the wall, the hedge, the bin. There used to be fifty-one pigeons, but now there's only ten.
Potty Ingrid:	I wonder where all my darlings are.

Narrator:	This is the praise and thanks of the three black cats of Ramillies Road.
The Three Black Cats:	Thanks be to Potty Ingrid, our gracious lady, Who gives us our daily birds, With crunchy bones and sweet warm blood, And feathers that stick in our teeth. Forgive us our yowlings And save us from fleabites and dogs.

(de Bernières, 2001, pp.4–5)

In this play we get characters barely developed beyond stereotypical names – Potty Ingrid, Posh Katy, Thrombotic Bert, Emphysemic Eric – yet they are all based on characters once known to de Bernières. You can also see poetic devices in this extract, particularly in the narrator's voice and use of alliteration – fly, feral; unbowed but battered, bread, burger buns, birdseed; martyrs to mites – and in Ingrid's repeated, rhythmic use of 'darlings' and the parody of the Lord's Prayer by the three cats. All the characters have contrasting voices reflecting the population of the suburb, a paradoxically real and unreal setting, in which animals speak, and sparrows form the chorus. The effect, as in *Under Milk Wood*, is like a voice orchestra, rising in crescendo but with no soloist.

ACTIVITY 7.8
Writing

Using a non-realistic narrator's voice, write the introduction to a scene. Include at least one other character. If you wish, use poetic devices. You can use one or more of the voices not yet used from Activity 7.7. Pick a hospital, a village or a school as your location.

DISCUSSION

You may have found that using a non-realistic narrator freed up your ideas and made the world you were creating less tied to mundane reality. This sort of radio drama neglects character development in favour of rhythm and sound – the celebratory mix and music of the voices. The methods common to such plays include the choric use of narrators and a focus on, and celebration of, a small, confined world. In one of the best scripts of this kind that I have seen, a student of mine produced a wonderful range of voices all focused on a slightly sinister, small-town department store. While this is a specific brand of radio drama, the methods of such plays can also inform a more story-based drama about the musical effect of enunciated language and the need for aural contrast.

Conclusion

In this chapter you have seen how important aural contrast is to radio drama. It is important to create such contrasts but not to overdo the sound effects, or to overwrite the exposition. Think musically and dramatically about the individual voice patterns and rhythms, as well as the naturalistic motivations and actions of your characters. We have also considered the importance of how to structure and link scenes, and how to go about adapting texts specifically for radio. In the next chapter we will consider film, in which sound has a very different role.

References

BBC (2008) *writersroom* [online], http://www.bbc.co.uk/writersroom/ scriptsmart/bbcradioscene.pdf (accessed 20 February 2008).

Bradbury, Ray (1962 [1952]) 'The Veldt' in *The Illustrated Man*, London: Hart-Davis.

de Bernières, Louis (2001) *Sunday Morning at the Centre of the World*, London: Vintage.

Dunstone, Stephen (1985) *Who is Sylvia?* in *Best Radio Plays of 1984*, London: Methuen/BBC.

Hughes, Richard (1966) *Danger* in *Plays*, London: Chatto and Windus.

Hutcheon, Linda (2006) *A Theory of Adaptation*, Abingdon: Routledge.

Thomas, Dylan (1977 [1954]) *Under Milk Wood*, London: Dent.

Tremain, Rose (1977) *Blossom*, broadcast on BBC Radio 4, 4 July.

Walker, Mike (2007) *The Veldt*, broadcast on BBC Radio 4, 22 May.

Weldon, Fay (1979) *Polaris* in *Best Radio Plays of 1978*, London: Eyre Methuen/BBC.

Zephaniah, Benjamin (1988) *Hurricane Dub*, broadcast on BBC Radio 4, 17 October.

Further reading

Tinniswood, Peter (1988) *The Village Fete* in *Best Radio Plays of 1987*, London: Methuen/BBC.

Tinniswood is admired as a radio dramatist. This play exhibits his idiosyncratic way of laying out the dialogue like the lines of free verse; the line lengths instruct the actors on how to say the dialogue and where to take breaths.

West, Timothy (1997) *This Gun That I Have in My Right Hand Is Loaded* in Rosemary Horstmann, *Writing for Radio*, London: A & C Black.

This is a parody of bad radio writing and offers hilarious illustrations of the effects of heavy-handed exposition and overwriting.

MacLoughlin, Shaun (1998) *Writing for Radio: How to create successful radio plays, features and short stories*, Oxford: How To Books.

This offers testimony from an experienced BBC radio drama producer. He is especially informative about script layout, time constraints and how to go about adapting a stage play for the radio.

8 Writing films

Derek Neale

When you recall films that you have liked or disliked, the chances are you will remember images of action from these films. If I try to do this I can instantly recall the smashing window at the end of *One Flew Over the Cuckoo's Nest* (1975), the lone figure on the sweeping sands in *Lawrence of Arabia* (1962), the climb up to the church tower in *Vertigo* (1958), the sheep falling over the cliff in *Far From the Madding Crowd* (1967) and the shoot-out in *High Noon* (1952). These are films I have not seen recently. Sometimes I can remember such images more easily than the name of a film or what it was about. Try this exercise yourself.

Film, whether for cinema or television, creates memorable images. This is not surprising; its main device for storytelling is pictures. This is the way in which it relays most of the necessary narrative information – details about where characters live, what they wear, how they look out of the window in the morning and what they see when they do so. The audience sees how the moods and thoughts of the characters are dramatised through their actions. If radio has to do nearly all of its narrative work through dialogue, film has to do much of its storytelling via the camera. When writing your film scripts, you need to remind yourself of this at regular intervals. Two primary units of film drama are the 'shot' and the 'cut'. A shot is the image and action that are captured by the camera. A cut is a switch from that shot to another. This chapter and the next will look at how you can use these two elements in your own scripts.

What is noticeable about my list of films above is that they are all adaptations of pre-existing texts – novels (*Far From the Madding Crowd*, *One Flew Over the Cuckoo's Nest* and *Vertigo*), autobiography (*Lawrence of Arabia*) or short stories (*High Noon*). Film narrative adapts such texts extremely well. In fact, in order to write films, many screenwriters believe the story has to be in place before you start; it is then a matter of arranging the elements of the story correctly. Chapters 8 and 9 will explore how a narrative might be 'arranged correctly' in order to tell a story in film. You will be looking at examples from cinema and television, and examining how to script sequences of images of action that tell stories. Creating visual narratives is often seen as a cinematic technique, but this method is also widely used in television drama. Rather than concentrating on the differences between television and cinema, we will be looking at these shared methods. We will also be considering the way film adaptations work and how to go about writing film adaptations of works of fiction. You will see how film scripts are laid out, again using 'A Real Durwan' and 'Violin

Lessons' as adaptation texts, as well as starting a film adaptation of one of your own stories. We will be paying less attention to dialogue and focusing more on film craft. However, dialogue is an essential part of film narrative and it is important to utilise some of the dialogue skills you have already honed in previous chapters. Although there will be no explicit mention of the dramatic techniques covered in previous chapters, you should remember that such methods – for example, those connected to subtext, status and dramatic irony – are pertinent to all dramatic media. As you will see, physical and dramatic action are particularly relevant to the storytelling methods used in film.

Creating stories with pictures

When a script is produced, part of its development involves getting the whole project storyboarded, a process comparable to blocking rehearsals for a stage performance, as discussed in Chapter 6. The story is sketched out, like a sequence of still photographs or cartoon captions, so that the director and cinematographer can see the visual sequencing of the narrative.

ACTIVITY 8.1
Reading

Look at the storyboard for *Bram Stoker's Dracula* in Figure 8 and the extract from the script printed below:

- What is present in each caption of the storyboard?
- How does this compare with what is written in the script?

> 13 INT. TRAIN TUNNEL – DAY.
>
> *Dark, a light at the end.*
>
> 14 EXT. ORIENT EXPRESS – SUNSET.
>
> *The train moves across travelling from left to right. Superimposed over this we see Harker's journal:*
>
> Harker: (VO) 25 May, Buda-Pest. Left Buda-Pest early this morning. The impression I had was that we were leaving the West and entering the East ...
>
> *As the train travels we see Harker at the train window and rails moving past strange countryside.*
>
> Harker: (VO) The district I am to enter is on the border of three states. Transylvania, Moldavia and Bukovia, in the midst of the Carpathian Mountains ...

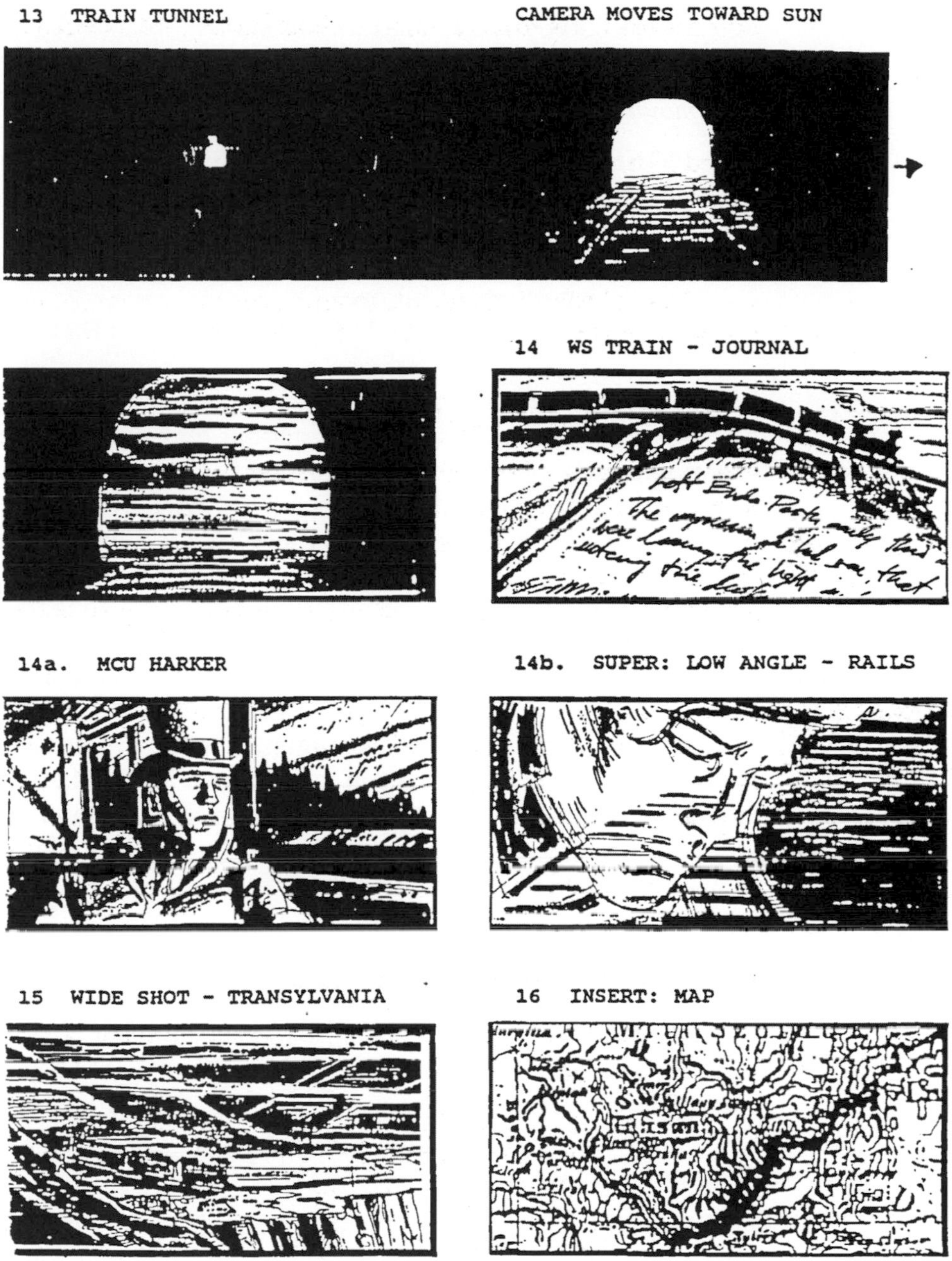

Figure 8   Storyboard for *Bram Stoker's Dracula* (The Screenwriters Store, n.d.)

15 EXT. TRANSYLVANIA FRONTIER – SUNSET.

The train travels down through the magnificent Carpathian mountains, taking us into the heart of Transylvanian darkness.

16 INSERT: MAP OF EASTERN EUROPE.

We notice the region of 'Transylvania'.

Harker: (VO cont'd) ... one of the wildest and least known portions of Europe.

(adapted from the published script, Coppola and Hart, 1992, pp.30–1)

DISCUSSION

You might recognise this section of the famous Dracula story, when the young Englishman travels into a mysterious gothic part of Europe. The storyboard goes into detail about what sort of camera shot will be used, whereas the script concentrates more on the detail of the story, describing what happens, the action of the story and what is in each scene in terms of visuals and dialogue. Each caption of the storyboard contains the characters important to that particular part of the narrative, and sometimes indicates the point of view, suggesting the camera should act as if it is the eyes of one of the characters. You will notice that the scenes are numbered and that a new scene occurs when the location or time changes. Numbering of scenes is done when a script has progressed into production – it is not a feature that you should include in your scripts. You will also notice the letters 'VO' in the script. This signifies a voice-over: an internal or narrating voice of an offscreen character. You will be looking at when and how to write voice-overs in the next chapter.

Camera shots

The storyboard for *Dracula* contains abbreviations for types of camera shot. It is useful to be aware of what the camera might be capable of, and to know what these abbreviations mean: WS – wide-angle shot; CU – close-up; MCU – medium close-up. However, you should rarely use them in your script.

Professional artists are usually employed to draw the storyboards when a film is being developed. The screenwriter is not expected to produce the drawings, though some writers do engage in preliminary sketching of the *mise en scène* – the pictorial content of each scene – for particular sections as they imagine the film. You might not produce any drawings, but much of the action of your script should be revealed through pictures. As David Mamet says: 'The story is ... carried by the shots. Basically the perfect movie doesn't have any dialogue. So you should always be striving to make a silent movie' (1991, p.72).

Watch any drama on television or DVD with the volume turned down. See if you can understand the story. In a film that is working well you will still get a strong idea of what is going on. Dialogue is only ever 'the sprinkles on top of the ice-cream cone', according to Mamet. This view is extreme and it is far less true with television drama, where the dialogue can be prominent in the storytelling. However, 'tell the story in pictures' is a very useful piece of advice when you first start to write films.

We will now examine the script of *An Angel at My Table*. The film is an adaptation of Janet Frame's three-part autobiography of the same name (1984). This extract is from the adaptation of the very start of the volume, entitled *To the Is Land*.

ACTIVITY 8.2 Reading	Read the opening to *An Angel at My Table* by Laura Jones (Reading 19 on p.347). • How much of the narrative is carried by the pictures? • How much is carried by the dialogue?
DISCUSSION	All the characters present in a scene are clearly established through their actions. Sometimes those actions consist of dialogue, yet generally very little dialogue is contained in these scenes. The information scripted for each scene gives pertinent information about location. There is no excessive detail, nothing that cannot be seen in the eventual performance. The scenes containing dialogue use it very precisely, so the audience is left to imagine the dynamic between characters. Much is made of the counterpoint between words and images, and the subtext of the exchanges is suggested in this fashion. You will also note that this is an extract from the published version of the film's script. It does not have the layout that you will need for your scripts. For instance, many of the scenes do not have scene headings. You will be learning how to write scripts using the correct submission layout, and with appropriate scene headings, later in this chapter. Most of the published scripts that you read – including the script extracts in this book – will not adhere to this submission layout.

Tightening the story

The most dramatic scene in Reading 19 – that with the teacher, Miss Botting, and the incident about the stolen money – is taken almost verbatim from Frame's book. This is a good example of how a piece of life writing can be adapted for film. Overall the script and performance are more urgently focused on Janet, losing something of the book's discursive tone and certainly the backstory about members of Frame's family. This extract of script roughly adapts 27 pages, approximately 9,000 words, of the autobiography, which illustrates how the original has to be stripped down to fit the time available on film.

Of course, if you are too concise then the events of your narrative might be lost. Yet writing with such tremendous economy appeals to many writers. John Hodge, the scriptwriter of films such as *Trainspotting* (1996) and *Shallow Grave* (1994), says that 'a screenplay is about writing as little as possible' (Hodge, 1997, p.10). He sees film's need for concision as a marvellous challenge to the writer. If you can tell your story in the fewest conceivable number of words, you will allow your viewer to use their imagination and be a part of the story's creation.

Film scenes

As with drama written for other media, the film scene, as a dramatic unit, is defined by location and/or time, together with the completion of its dramatic action. You will recall from Chapter 6 that a dramatic action has a beginning, a middle and an end; it has a rising action, a climax and a resolution. Each scene should have elements of this structure, which in turn moves the drama forward and on to the next scene. Similarly, when the action moves to a different location, or a different day, for instance, that also signifies a scene change.

A scene can be one continuous shot, but it can also be, and often is, subdivided by a number of shots. You have seen this already in the Dracula script. Scene 14, for instance, has three different shots, whereas other scenes, such as 15, have just one shot. This is not the writer's responsibility. The final arrangement of shots in a scene is the director's decision, and may not be finalised until the editing stage of film production.

You should be conscious of how the action of your story is being revealed through the camera work, but beware of falling into the trap of doing the director's work for them. Your responsibility is to give just enough information for the story to be told, and not to become preoccupied with using terms like 'close-up' and 'long shot'. Most directors will resent seeing too many explicit camera suggestions in the script. There are, however, ways of implying such shots. For instance, if you say that a character is smiling, this tells the director an important piece of story information that has to then be captured by the actor and camera, quite possibly in close-up. If you describe the sun setting behind the trees, this is a cue for a wide-angle or long shot, even though you have not explicitly written this in the script. Similarly, when you imagine the action in a scene as one continuous shot, you should keep the description of events in one paragraph.

Though you should not script the camera shots, you will produce a far better script if you fully imagine the pictures you are trying to generate, how these sit next to one another and the action of your story. In this way the major storytelling device you will be using is the shot, but in suggesting shots and in placing one scene next to another you will also be using another vital storytelling tool – the cut. We will be looking at this a little more after you have created some scenes.

ACTIVITY 8.3 Writing	Adapt for film either a section from 'A Real Durwan' or a story of your own, creating at least three scenes. Think in terms of shots that tell the story; use no dialogue.

DISCUSSION	You may have realised that in creating different scenes, making cuts between scenes and between shots, you were creating imaginative gaps in your narrative. Events cannot always be shown continuously – in fact, they rarely are. The cut is a necessary part of the storytelling. You may have found that you created longer scenes than Laura Jones does in the extract from *An Angel at My Table*, where the only substantial scene is in the classroom with Miss Botting.

Pace and rhythm

The excerpt from Jones's script consists largely of very brief scenes, so the cuts occur mainly between scenes, creating a good pace of juxtaposition. However, scenes in films can be much longer. For instance, in *Earth* (1999), Deepa Mehta's adaptation of Bapsi Sidhwa's novel *Ice-candy-man* (1988), the opening scenes are substantially longer than Jones's. Lenny, an eight-year-old girl who has had polio, is the main viewpoint in the film. The opening scenes run as follows:

1   A middle-class house in Lahore. Lenny is seen drawing a map of India fracturing at the time of partition; she then smashes a plate and is forgiven.

2   Servants are cutting flowers and preparing food, while Lenny's nanny, Shanta, eats; the servants talk about how much Lenny is spoilt.

3   A dinner party in which Lenny's parents are joined by four guests – a Sikh couple and a British couple. Lenny and her cousin are hiding under the table.

4   A park with Lenny and Shanta surrounded by Shanta's five male admirers – all of different faiths – but including Ice-candy-man.

5   Under the banyan tree. Ice-candy-man courts Shanta, but inevitably in the presence of Lenny, her ward.

6   The rooftop of Ice-candy-man's house during the spring kite festival. Shanta and Lenny come to visit and fly kites.

Some of these scenes last for several minutes, and the director (Mehta herself) uses cuts within each scene between their various visual aspects – the adults in the table scene, for instance, are juxtaposed with the children below the table. In the sixth scene the camera cuts between the kites and the characters on the roof. The director generates a rhythm of images, a multi-layered spectacle, with the brightly coloured kites against the blue sky, free but tethered. It is an image that acts as a metaphor for the characters of the story – they are of many faiths, straining for liberation at the time of India's partition, but violently tied in competition with one another. The effect is compounded by insistent music, and the scene is memorable, comparable with those film images I recalled at the start of this chapter. Single, recalled film images are invariably a composite of a number of cuts and shots combining in this way to reveal the characters and the action.

Besides the rhythm of shots, remember that there is a visual rhythm created by the duration of the scenes. Many brief, juxtaposed scenes create a fast pace, and scene length can vary enormously within a film from one minute to ten minutes. A typical two-hour feature-length film can have between forty and sixty scenes. On average a scene lasts two and a half minutes (remember the average length of a scene in *The Archers* – this is no coincidence). Obviously not every scene will be this length – as you can see in the excerpt from Jones – and for every thirty-second scene there will be one that is five minutes long. If you follow the layout advice given later in the chapter (pp.124–6), the average page of a script will run for one minute. So if you look at your script and see that your average scene length is six or seven pages, then you might have a problem with pace – it will be crawling along. If you have an average of half a page for each scene, your pace will be unrelenting; there might be a need for some variety and for your audience to pause to get to know your characters.

ACTIVITY 8.4 Writing and editing	Return to the scenes you wrote for Activity 8.3. Now enlarge or edit them so that there are three to five scenes of different length and pace, but with an overall average two to three minutes running time for each scene. You can now add dialogue if you wish.
DISCUSSION	You might have found that in creating a rhythm in your scene-making you also created visual contrasts. As you will remember from Chapter 7, aural contrasts are crucial in radio. Visual contrasts are equally important to film drama.

Visual contrasts

Robert McKee suggests that a scene has an optimum running time:

> Most directors' cameras drink up whatever is visually expressive in one location within two or three minutes. If a scene goes on longer, shots become redundant. The editor keeps coming back to the same establishing shot, same two-shot, close-up. When shots repeat, expressivity drains away; the film becomes visually dull and the eye loses interest and wanders from the screen.
>
> (McKee, 1999, p.291)

One-set films adapted from the stage, such as *Twelve Angry Men* (1957), which is located in a jury room for two continuous days, pose a problem in this respect. McKee suggests such films overcome this visual difficulty by dividing the continuous action into scenes according to who the action specifically involves at any one time and where the action takes place. For instance, in *Twelve Angry Men*, although all the action takes place in one room, one scene is by the drinking fountain, one at the main table, one by the window, and so forth.

Montage

The way the scenes in *An Angel at My Table* are placed together follows the progress of one character, but the reason one image is placed next to another is not always immediately obvious or continuous in time. We do not see the baby learning to talk, for instance, or the intermediate stages of her growing up. Nor do we see Janet going to buy chewing gum straight after stealing the money from her father's pocket (though this detail is included in Frame's book). The juxtaposition of scenes and shots gives us a cumulative, implied meaning, which is more than the explicit meaning of the action in either of the scenes (when 'Janet's hand slides into

Dad's best trousers' and when 'Janet stands at the door of the Infants room' handing out chewing gum). This implied meaning is: Janet stole the money to buy sweets, and so to buy popularity. This is concise storytelling, in which the writer trusts the audience to use its imagination and invent meaning.

It is worth pausing for a little to think about how this method of cutting between moments in the story works. The method was called 'montage' by the Russian film-maker Sergei Eisenstein in the early part of the twentieth century, though the term 'cut' is more often used nowadays. Eisenstein has a modern advocate in the films and teachings of David Mamet – an interesting commentator because he writes and directs both mainstream blockbusters and literary films (adaptations of his own stage plays, for instance). This method does not necessarily involve following the protagonist around all the time. It is 'a succession of images juxtaposed so that the contrast between the images moves the story forward in the mind of the audience'. Here is Mamet on just how important he thinks this method is:

> If you listen to the way people tell stories, you will hear that they tell them cinematically. They jump from one thing to the next, and the story is moved along by the juxtaposition of images – which is to say, by the *cut*.

> People say, 'I'm standing on the corner. It's a foggy day. A bunch of people are running around crazy. Might have been the full moon. All of a sudden, a car comes up and the guy next to me says ...'

> If you think about it, that's a shot list: (1) a guy standing on the corner; (2) shot of fog; (3) a full moon shining above; (4) a man says, 'I think people get wacky at this time of year'; (5) a car approaches.

> Juxtaposing images like this is good filmmaking. Now you're following the story. What, you wonder, is going to happen next? It's the juxtaposition of the shots that moves the film forward. The shots make up the scene. The scene is a formal essay. It is a small film; it is, one might say, a documentary.

> Documentaries take basically unrelated footage and juxtapose it in order to give the viewer the idea the filmmaker wants to convey. They take footage of birds snapping a twig. They take footage of a fawn raising his head. The two shots have nothing to do with each other. They are not a record of what the protagonist did. They are not a record of how the deer reacted to the bird. They're basically

uninflected images. But they give the viewer the idea of *alertness to danger* when they are juxtaposed. That's good filmmaking.

(Mamet, 1991, pp.2–3)

Some montage, as seen with the money and chewing gum in *An Angel at My Table*, is quite straightforward and facilitates the move from one narrative point to the next. But sometimes montage can induce wider meanings to do with theme and poetic parallels. For instance, in Eisenstein's *Strike* (1924) there is a shot of attacks on striking workers juxtaposed with a shot of a bull being slaughtered. This suggests a comparison: the workers are being treated like cattle. Similarly, during the baptism of Michael's nephew in *The Godfather* (1972), there are images of the priest performing the baptism juxtaposed with images of executions ordered by Michael. The murders initiate Michael into a life of crime, just as his nephew is being initiated into the family. These sorts of family/ murder juxtapositions are very familiar in Mafia movies, and in such television series as *The Sopranos*.

Montage sequences

Another definition of montage – and how the term is often used nowadays – describes a succession of rapidly cut, predominantly silent images (though there might be accompanying music). These facilitate a quick transition in the narrative and often condense time. Typically they occur when there is a need for the exposition of information that would otherwise take too long: for instance, in a film that has shown the lovers' first kiss, but which needs to advance the relationship quickly so we can get to the next conflict point – their divorce perhaps, or the advent of a rival. In *The Firm* (1993) the young lawyer and his wife move to Miami, and there is a montage sequence of the couple adding furniture and accoutrements to their new home. This is obviously meant to signify that several months have passed, but the sequence lasts less than a minute in the film. In Hodge's script of *Trainspotting* there is a montage sequence of London when Renton, the main character, moves there from Edinburgh:

EXT. LONDON. DAY.

A contemporary retake of all those 'Swinging London' montages: Red Routemaster/Trafalgar Square/Big Ben/Royalty/City gents in suits/Chelsea ladies/fashion victims/Piccadilly Circus at night.

Intercut with close-ups of classic street names on a street map (all the ones made famous by Monopoly).

(Hodge, 1996, p.76)

This illustrates other typical uses of this sort of montage sequence: it can establish a location quickly, and it can cover the distance of a journey. Sometimes such sequences are even titled 'montage' in the script. For a larger montage sequence, look ahead to Scene 11 in *The Hours* (Reading 20, p.350), which you will look at in Chapter 9. Such montage sequences can be seen as a lazy form of exposition if used too often, but in *The Hours* it helps to establish clearly and quickly three distinct narrative strands.

Writing film scripts
Script layout for film

Look at Figure 9, a sample page from a film script. What do you notice about the way in which the script is laid out? How does it differ from a stage or radio layout?

This script follows the BBC's guidance on layout for film scripts and television drama (BBC, 2008), and is a good model to use when writing your own. Be aware, though, that layout requirements may be different for different television slots, and also for film scripts in the USA. Though some television companies now use film layout, many studios have their own layout conventions and these can be very different from film layout, sometimes involving double spacing throughout and much larger left margins. It is best to check these requirements with individual companies before submitting scripts.

You will see that there are many differences from stage and radio scripts in this layout – not least the positioning of the names of speakers. In film scripts these sit above the dialogue, whereas in both stage and radio scripts they sit on the left. Here are some further tips.

Film scripts – some tips

- Your scene headings though brief carry very important information – for your reader and for any potential director.
- Make sure the headings contain information about where the camera will be (INTERIOR is abbreviated to INT.; EXTERIOR is abbreviated to EXT.), and details about location and time (e.g. 'INT. BEDROOM. NIGHT').
- When appropriate – and usually only in the opening scene of a sequence – give more introductory information about time. For instance, a scene heading for 'Violin Lessons' might read: 'INT. WORKSHOP. SPRING. AFTERNOON'.

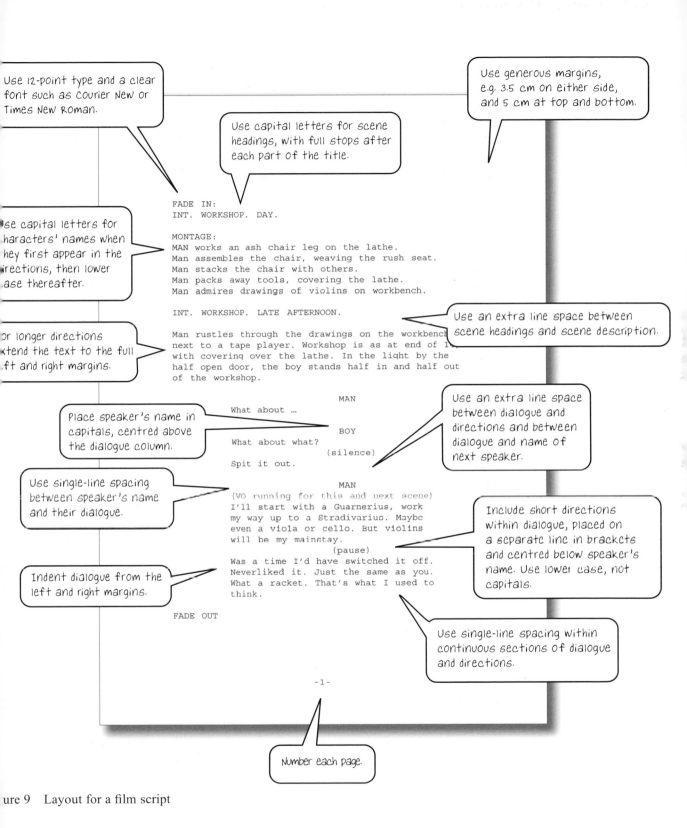

Use 12-point type and a clear font such as Courier New or Times New Roman.

Use capital letters for scene headings, with full stops after each part of the title.

Use generous margins, e.g. 3.5 cm on either side, and 5 cm at top and bottom.

Use capital letters for characters' names when they first appear in the directions, then lower case thereafter.

For longer directions extend the text to the full left and right margins.

Use an extra line space between scene headings and scene description.

Place speaker's name in capitals, centred above the dialogue column.

Use an extra line space between dialogue and directions and between dialogue and name of next speaker.

Use single-line spacing between speaker's name and their dialogue.

Include short directions within dialogue, placed on a separate line in brackets and centred below speaker's name. Use lower case, not capitals.

Indent dialogue from the left and right margins.

Use single-line spacing within continuous sections of dialogue and directions.

Number each page.

```
FADE IN:
INT. WORKSHOP. DAY.

MONTAGE:
MAN works an ash chair leg on the lathe.
Man assembles the chair, weaving the rush seat.
Man stacks the chair with others.
Man packs away tools, covering the lathe.
Man admires drawings of violins on workbench.

INT. WORKSHOP. LATE AFTERNOON.

Man rustles through the drawings on the workbench
next to a tape player. Workshop is as at end of 1
with covering over the lathe. In the light by the
half open door, the boy stands half in and half out
of the workshop.

                         MAN
          What about …

                         BOY
          What about what?
                         (silence)
          Spit it out.

                         MAN
          (VO running for this and next scene)
          I'll start with a Guarnerius, work
          my way up to a Stradivarius. Maybe
          even a viola or cello. But violins
          will be my mainstay.
                         (pause)
          Was a time I'd have switched it off.
          Neverliked it. Just the same as you.
          What a racket. That's what I used to
          think.

          FADE OUT
```

-1-

ure 9   Layout for a film script

125

- Include the names of characters that are in the scene in the directions underneath the scene heading. Announce latecomers as they arrive and not before (e.g. 'the door opens and the BOY enters').
- Describe in the directions the action of the scene, including all the movements of the characters that are relevant to the story (e.g. 'she turns, blows a kiss, before getting on the train'). Be careful not to over-direct – these are aspects of the performance for the actors and director to realise – and include only actions that are necessary for the story to be told.
- Include details about how characters should look only if this is absolutely necessary to the plot. In most instances detailed descriptions are not needed.
- The scene heading will usually give enough information about location. If you need to offer more, because it is really pertinent to the story, weave it into the direction for the scene's action. Use few adjectives in the direction and as a general rule never use more than a sentence to describe features of the location. Often even this will not be needed.

Beware of overwriting generally, and be careful not to give details that cannot be seen on the screen – such as what a character is thinking, or a hidden object like a gun in a drawer or in a pocket. This is a common pitfall with writers new to film. Part of the joy of writing films is finding other ways of revealing information, such as the thoughts of your character, to your audience. This can be done through the character's actions and behaviour, and by contrasting what is seen with what is said. The skill lies in being able to visualise a scene vividly while knowing what is going on underneath it. You have to imagine the camera at work and the visual narrative, along with the thoughts and motivations of your characters.

A film-script layout is organised so that the reader can easily visualise the story. Margins are crucial here – every section of the text with a separate function has a different margin. As suggested earlier, using the appropriate film layout gives you an average timing of one minute a page, so counting the number of pages can help you gauge how long your scenes might be. This is only an approximation though; scenes have to be enacted in real time to get a more accurate estimate.

Adaptation for film

Let's now consider a film adaptation of the final few pages of 'Violin Lessons', when the status relationship between the man and boy has reversed. This is played out in a series of scenes which reveal that the boy's sister has run away to Brighton with Mr Bouillon, and that the man is going to make violins instead of chairs.

Read the film adaptation of 'Violin Lessons' below.

- How has the adaptation kept to or altered the original story?
- Can you see any of the film techniques that we have looked at in this script?

FADE IN:

INT. WORKSHOP. DAY.

MONTAGE:

MAN works an ash chair leg on the lathe.

Man assembles the chair, weaving the rush seat.

Man stacks the chair with others of the same design.

Man packs away tools, covering the lathe.

Man admires drawings of violins laid out on workbench.

INT. WORKSHOP. LATE AFTERNOON.

Man rustles through the drawings on the workbench, next to a tape player. Workshop, as at end of last scene, with covering over the lathe. In the light by the half-open door, the BOY stands half in and half out of the workshop. Man notices him, waves him in, happy to see him, but then remembers something, falters.

Man: Haven't seen you for a ...

Boy: Been busy.

      (*silence*)

Man: What about ...

Boy: What about what?

      (*silence*)

      Spit it out.

Man: Your sister.

Boy: What about her?

      (*pause*)

Man: What happened to her?

Boy: Brighton.

Man: Brighton?

Boy: Mr Bubblegum.

EXT. BRIGHTON BEACH. DAY.

Waves crash and roll; at a distance a MAN and YOUNG WOMAN walk hand in hand, occasionally kissing, enthralled with one another. From her red hair it becomes apparent the young woman is VERONICA and then that the man is MR BOUILLON.

EXT. STREET NEAR SEA FRONT, BRIGHTON. AFTERNOON.

A man in his late forties, greying-red hair, VERONICA'S FATHER, talks in agitated fashion with a POLICEWOMAN. We don't hear the exchange. He is referring to a piece of paper with an address. We see a number on the paper:

'116'

Not far away we see on the balcony of a house, overlooking the sea, a chair, the same type as seen in the opening montage. A closed violin case rests on the chair's rush seat.

INT. WORKSHOP. EVENING.

Man rustles through the drawings on the workbench, next to a tape player. Boy removes his tie and drops it on the floor. He looks at the man as if daring him. Man doesn't respond. Boy sits on mahogany planks; again no response. Man watches the green and black tie lying on the floor as it catches a gust of wind from the door near to the violin moulds; his eyes light up when he sees the moulds, and he puts them on top of the drawings. Boy looks at him as if he is stupid, then picks up one of the violin moulds.

Boy: What are these?

      (*pause*)

Man: My next job.

Boy: What do you want to make those for?

Man switches on tape player. Beethoven's Violin Concerto starts, rising gradually in the background over following scenes, reaching crescendo in the next scene, at the knocking on the door. Man brings the drawings over to show the boy.

The following dialogue starts with man offscreen, but the scene cuts after 'way up'. The man's dialogue continues as voice-over, running over subsequent scenes until the knocking on the door.

Man: (*VO running for this and next scene*) I'll start with a Guarnerius, work my way up to a Stradivarius. Maybe even a viola or cello. But violins will be my mainstay.

(*pause*)

Was a time I'd have switched it off. Never liked it. Just the same as you. What a racket. That's what I used to think. But now ... now ... I'm learning. Doing some research. I got this out of the library. I quite like it. Surprised me. Beethoven's my favourite. The concerto. It's the sort of music that stays with you, keeps you going. Even when you're tired, it seems so, so ... it picks you up, carries you. Makes you feel at harmony with the world.

INT. ROOM ADJOINING BALCONY AT No. 116. EVENING.

The violin case on the chair is now open. Veronica reaches into the case and picks up the violin.

She and Mr Bouillon play violins. They are not playing the music that is heard and both intermittently look frustrated and stop because of Veronica's bad playing. Mr Bouillon sometimes cringes. An insistent and loud knocking on the door begins as the music reaches crescendo and the voice-over ends.

INT. WORKSHOP. EVENING.

Boy drops the violin moulds on the mahogany planks.

Man: (*shouting*) Be careful –

Boy: Okay, okay. Keep your shirt on.

Man: Stupid boy!

Boy: It was a piece of wood.

Man: If you can't behave you better take yourself home.

Boy: Wood. Just a piece of wood.

Man picks up the moulds, dusts them down and makes sure they aren't broken. Boy grabs his bag to go.

Man: You need to learn, you need to know you can't just, you can't just come in here and ...

EXT. BRIGHTON STREET, OUTSIDE No. 116. NIGHT.

Veronica in tears comes out of the door, shrugging off the supporting arm of her father. A police car is parked outside the house.

EXT. PATH FROM WORKSHOP. EVENING.

Man looks out from workshop down towards the woods. Boy walks in opposite direction, towards the village, looking over his shoulder occasionally, sticking his middle finger up at the man, who, oblivious, turns back towards the workshop. He picks up the boy's tie, folds it gently and places it on the shelf, next to the boy's drawing of an electric guitar.

FADE OUT

DISCUSSION

A problem with 'Violin Lessons' is that the story is very much a one-set narrative, located solely in the workshop. It lacks visual contrast and faces the same sort of visual problems as *Twelve Angry Men*. Because of this some might see it as a story best suited to television rather than cinema. Both cinema films and television films rely on visual narrative. Yet television has a tradition which tends to use more dialogue and more dramatic situations between people in single locations. Here I have attempted a film version. Note the tactics I use to make the visual stimulus more varied, by cutting to Brighton and the boy's sister, Veronica.

Whether for film or television, it is usually better to deliver your exposition visually rather than have big expository speeches. The exposition about what happened to Veronica here is cued just by the words 'Brighton' and 'Mr Bubblegum'. The cut from this scene to Brighton beach uses Eisenstein's montage technique. The juxtaposition of the images creates a new meaning for the viewer – Veronica has run away with Mr Bouillon. I have chosen not to use any dialogue to reveal the rest of the Brighton action, treating that strand as a subplot. However, I have brought the boy's and Veronica's father to life. In the original story he was mentioned only briefly.

Changing the original

Some of the things you have learned about dialogue in the stage and radio chapters – about subtext, aural contrasts and idiolect, for instance – are very pertinent to film and television. As a general rule, you need less dialogue, so always look over your exchanges with a scrupulous eye for any superfluous lines. If in doubt, cut the dialogue, because if you don't the director will – or he or she will turn down your script because there is too much of it.

You will see that I have a montage sequence at the start of this adaptation script, which tells the viewer immediately how the man has changed his outlook on his work. The lathe is covered because he will no longer be using it. You will see that I resisted having a flashback scene to Veronica in the workshop, even though such a scene occurs at this point in the original story. I decided this would be a distraction and potentially confusing. I used the tie in the workshop scene because, when writing the story, I saw it as a key image that linked many scenes. Its use at the end of the script could potentially provide a connection with the opening scenes. At the end the man folds the tie neatly, as if he has confidence the boy will be back. He places it next to the boy's drawing of a guitar, an invention for this film version but one that links to an early exchange in the story. The drawing could feature in an earlier scene of this script.

In this section of the adaptation the more prominent image linking the two main locations is the violin – with the instrument moulds in the workshop and the case and Veronica's and Mr Bouillon's playing in Brighton. You will explore more linking techniques in Chapter 9. The chair and the violin music also help connect the scenes. It is not always advisable to pick music to accompany your script. You can become sidetracked away from the parts of the script you should be focusing on by the emotional build-up of a great soundtrack. However, here I picked up on a clue contained in the story – 'Beethoven's my favourite, the violin concerto'. If the music is explicit and central in the original story then you can try to use it. You will also notice I used a voice-over as a linking device and as a contrast to the visual action. You will be exploring further possibilities of using voice-over in the next chapter.

ACTIVITY 8.6 Writing and editing	Go back over the script you wrote in Activity 8.4. Edit the dialogue and revise the layout in accordance with the guidance given above.

DISCUSSION	This process of looking over and revising your scripts should, of course, be a regular exercise. Make sure that the cuts and use of montage in your scripts produce new meanings and move the story along. In my 'Violin Lessons' script I regularly contrast interior and exterior scenes. Check that you have such visual contrasts, not only between but also within your scenes.

Conclusion

You have seen in this chapter how the primary building blocks of film drama work – the shot, the cut (or montage) and the scene. Imagining the visual action of your story as well as the dialogue is essential, as is an awareness of visual contrasts. The length of your scenes and the manner in which you juxtapose them will generate the pace and rhythm of your storytelling. The next chapter will deal with larger structural shapes – inciting incidents, turning points, climaxes and framing devices, as well as the use of voice-over and flashback.

References

BBC (2008) *writersroom* [online], http://www.bbc.co.uk/writersroom/ scriptsmart/screenplay.pdf (accessed 20 February 2008).

Coppola, Francis Ford and Hart, James V. (1992) *Bram Stoker's Dracula: The film and the legend*, London: Pan.

Earth (1999) film, Deepa Mehta (director and writer).

The Firm (1993) film, Sydney Pollack (director), David Rabe, Robert Towne and David Rayfiel (writers).

Frame, Janet (1984) *An Angel at My Table*, London: Women's Press.

The Godfather (1972) film, Francis Ford Coppola (director), Francis Ford Coppola and Mario Puzo (writers).

Hodge, John (1996) *Trainspotting and Shallow Grave*, London: Faber and Faber.

Hodge, John (1997) 'How to write a hit movie', *Guardian*, 25 August.

McKee, Robert (1999) *Story: Substance, structure, style and the principles of screenwriting*, London: Methuen.

Mamet, David (1991) *On Directing Film*, London: Faber and Faber.

The Screenwriters Store (n.d.) *850+ Screenplays*, CD, London: The Screenwriters Store.

Sidhwa, Bapsi (1988) *Ice-candy-man*, London: Heinemann.

Strike (1924) film, Sergei Eisenstein (director and writer).

Twelve Angry Men (1957) film, Sidney Lumet (director), Reginald Rose (writer).

Further reading

Seger, Linda (1992) *The Art of Adaptation: Turning fact and fiction into film*, New York: Owl.

This gives an inspiring insight into the techniques of many well-known film adaptations, as well as offering constructive approaches and methods for those new to adapting stories for film. It offers guidance on adaptations from works of fiction but also considers how to go about adapting real events and scripting film versions of actual incidents.

Trottier, David (1998) *The Screenwriter's Bible*, Los Angeles: Silman-James.

Parker, Philip (1999) *The Art and Science of Screenwriting*, Exeter: Intellect.

Both of the above give wonderfully detailed advice about how to lay out a film script and on developing an idea, as well as advising on the differences presented by television. Trottier is good on American conventions and Parker is comprehensive on those in the UK.

9   Film structure

Derek Neale

In the last chapter you saw how the primary units of screenwriting – the shot, the cut and the scene – combine to tell the story. In this chapter we will continue to consider adaptation techniques using 'A Real Durwan', 'Violin Lessons' and your own work. We will also examine how a film's larger structural organisation is conceived. Some writers, when constructing films, identify the climactic moment in the story's dramatic action and then work back towards the start. Doing it this way ensures that the story's dramatic focus is clear. There will be no meandering, no wondering about where the action is heading. For other writers this clarity is only possible in retrospect, as part of their editing and redrafting process. Whichever way round you work, it is imperative at some point to chart the dramatic action in each scene and gauge how this contributes to the whole action of a film's story. Charting the action in this way usually takes the form of a 'step outline', and might be part of the submission process for a script. It is very similar to the scenario for stage plays, which you looked at in Chapter 6.

Arranging the pieces

Original non-commissioned scripts are often called 'spec scripts' – because they are submitted speculatively. All new scriptwriters need to develop at least one calling-card spec script to show to prospective directors and agents. The optimum length is up to thirty minutes, because with a script of that length a prospective agent, director or production company can see that you have a grasp of structure and are able to develop the journey of your characters. Given the high cost of film-making there is a growing trend for shorter films though, and a pragmatic approach would be to develop scripts of varying lengths. A short film can be anything from three to thirty minutes long.

It is important to bear length in mind when considering the architecture of your scene arrangement. As you will recall from the discussion of dramatic action in Chapter 6, dramatised storytelling is like the dynamic of a tide, rising and ebbing in smaller surges towards a larger, irresistible forward motion. It works according to the principle of three – a rising action, a climax and a resolution. In film writing this triadic structure is often regarded as the ideal model for a whole script, as well as for the individual parts of the script. Feature-length scripts are often in three acts. Though there are many exceptions, it is wise initially to try to use a three-part structure in your scripts.

An act in a film is a section of dramatic action, a sequence of scenes in which there is a major reversal. This is very similar to a stage act. So the reversal in 'Violin Lessons' might be in the relationship between the boy and the man, or in the man's outlook. This reversal would be dramatised by the main character, the man, being placed in a series of conflict situations where he has to decide what to do. You can also see that such a series of decisions does not have to result in a reversal that is overly dramatic. There is no murder at the end of 'Violin Lessons'. The change that comes with the reversal can be subtle. It is involvement with a character's journey and the emotional force of change in a character that will engage the audience more than anything else. The reversal should be echoed in all the smaller sections of the storytelling – in each scene, or in each wave of the incoming tide, to use the analogy. Your initial scripts may not be big enough to run for longer than one act, but the principle of a three-part structure can still apply within that single act. You should create a rising action, a climax and a resolution.

You also need an 'inciting incident' to initiate the forward movement. In an adaptation of 'Violin Lessons' the obvious inciting incident would be the first meeting with the boy. After the conflict has been initiated you can chart the forward movement towards the climax – which could be the man shouting at the boy at the end, or the discovery of what has happened to the boy's sister, depending which you take as your main plotline.

ACTIVITY 9.1
Reading

Read the start of the step outline for *Chinatown* (1974) below.

What do you think is the inciting incident?

1. 'What kinda guy do you think I am' – We meet J.J. GITTES [Jake], private detective, in his office with a client, CURLY. Curly is very upset over the photographs Jake has produced documenting Curly's wife's infidelity. Jake makes an effort to temper Curly's murderous rage, and reassures him by suggesting that he can take his time paying Jake's fee.

Jake's assistants, WALSH and DUFFY, introduce him to his next client, a MRS. EVELYN MULWRAY. Mrs. Mulwray believes her husband, HOLLIS MULWRAY, the chief of the department of Water and Power, is having an affair, and she wants Jake to investigate. Jake is ambivalent, but takes the job.

2. 'Los Angeles is a desert community' – We find Jake at a public hearing concerning the construction of a new dam. Hollis Mulwray holds the unpopular opinion that the dam is unsafe, and insists that he will not build it. He alludes to a previous dam disaster built on a similar rock formation. The hearing is suddenly interrupted by the arrival of a number of disgruntled farmers who herd their sheep into the hall. They claim Mulwray is responsible for diverting water from their valley.

3. 'The mysterious presence of water' – Jake follows Mulwray to a dry river bed. In the distance, Jake watches as Mulwray talks to a young Mexican boy on a burrow. Mulwray jots some information down on a map. Jake follows Mulwray by car to the ocean. Mulwray remains there all day, Jake watching. After night falls, a torrent of water races down a run-off channel into the ocean. Jake follows Mulwray to another reservoir. When Mulwray leaves his car, Jake plants a pocket watch underneath his tire.

(The Screenwriters Store, n.d.)

DISCUSSION

Here we can see that each step has a summary title suggesting its narrative content. You can also see that we are starting in the middle of the action in step 1 – or at the end of Jake's previous case – and that the inciting incident is the meeting with the so-called Evelyn Mulwray. Jake takes on the case, but the conflict in doing so is clear. This is the key to inciting incidents: they have to foreshadow greater conflicts. The major reversal later in the act is the revelation that this was not the real Evelyn Mulwray.

Plots

Chinatown is a thriller with a private detective as the main character. The structure would seem to be relatively easy to arrange, with plenty of generically typical plot opportunities – murders, conflict with clients, love affairs with clients, corrupt police. Yet all stories, of whatever type, have to be plotted in a similar way, with events building to climaxes and then moving on.

You will see in the *Chinatown* step outline that there is a turning point in every scene. The key is to vary the degree of reversal in each of these turning points. Even in a thriller, if every turn was a murder or a mistaken identity then the audience would tire. They might even start laughing at such repetition.

Any story that you are scripting will have a whole chronology – a list of all events from start to finish. This is often referred to as the story's timeline. The plot, as reflected in your step outline, is your choice and arrangement of events to be presented in the script. It is not the same as the story's timeline. You might start at the end or halfway through the story's timeline, for instance.

Your aim in any one scene should always be to engage the audience, to move the action forward by achieving a turning point. You do this by getting your protagonist to face a problem and make a decision. In every scene ask yourself what your main character wants, and what is stopping him or her. Who or what is the antagonist – the source of conflict? If the antagonist is hard to identify then it is likely that the scene needs attention. In many of the scenes in 'Violin Lessons', for instance, the man could be seen as the protagonist and the boy as the antagonist. Yet this is not always the case. Sometimes the man seems to be his own antagonist, and the conflict is self-generated.

With all the talk of structure it is easy to forget that character is the main focal point of all films and the reason viewers want to watch. The structural points that we have made should be manifest in your main character or characters. Their journey through a story should follow an arc of movement – embodying the rising action, the climax and the resolution. For a short film it is best to keep to a small cast if possible, because of production costs (you are more likely to be produced if the costs are low) but also for dramatic clarity. The action will get muddled in shorter narratives with too many characters and you will not have enough room to develop any individual characters if the script is overcrowded.

Subplots

Your own films may never have the same range of storylines or characters as a long-running soap, but you will often have at least one subplot, besides a main plot. The great benefit of subplots is that they can interrupt the thrust of the main action, and therefore add tension and another layer of suspense. An adaptation of 'Violin Lessons', for instance, could have a main plot involving the man's relationship with the boy – the tension for an audience would lie in guessing how these meetings will end: in friendship, enmity or something worse. The subplots could be seen as:

- the man's work – his strange dream and the question of what he should make next;
- what has happened to the boy's sister, Veronica.

Any film version would have to chart main plot and subplots together, so climaxes for all three plots would be reached more or less simultaneously. There would be an interweaving and a symbiosis between main and subplots, as there is in the original story. Each plotline would need its own inciting incident, and each its own climax and resolution; yet each would contribute to the whole and complement the other strands. It is important to choreograph subplots so that they do not clash with or clutter the main plot. One of the main functions of subplots is to help the audience care more, and possibly in a more complex way, about the story. So it is important that subplots are fundamentally linked to the main plot. In 'Violin Lessons', for example, violins link all the main characters and plotlines. In adapting stories there is, of course, always the possibility of adding or subtracting a plotline. You might not have time to include a particular strand or you might be writing for a bigger time slot, and so need to add more substance to the story. Multiple plots occur in all sorts of stories. The longer your narrative – and performance time – the more likely it is that you will use subplots. It is also conceivable that when adapting you might reconfigure the original story so that a subplot becomes a main plot.

For instance, in 'Violin Lessons', the man's search for what he should make next could take precedence over his meeting with the boy. This is an important aspect of the decision making when adapting stories because some plotlines lend themselves to drama more readily than others; some are naturally fifteen minutes long, others thirty minutes. A consideration of how much performance time you have will always affect the type and number of your plotlines.

ACTIVITY 9.2 Writing	Write a three- to five-point step outline for an adaptation of the start of 'A Real Durwan' in which you try to:

- add a thriller element in the way the scenes are arranged;
- introduce a subplot to the story – either invented or taken from elements within Lahiri's tale;
- use a three-part structure within its scenes and overall action.

DISCUSSION	The most unlikely story can benefit from the writer thinking in terms of tension, suspense and the sorts of elements usually associated with the thriller genre. You want your audience to be motivated to watch more; you want them to be inquisitive and to be speculating. If your main plot revolves around the fate of your protagonist, Boori Ma, you may have picked a subplot about a mysterious phone call received by the widow, Mrs Misra, the only resident of the building with a phone. Your subplot may have been about the Dalals's intention to buy bedding for Boori Ma, or a storyline to do with Mr Chatterjee. Even in such a short episode there are many options.

Creating links

In arranging your plotlines it is important that your audience senses a connectedness between the different strands even if that link is not immediately explained. In fact, this is a strong source of tension in film drama – juxtaposing scenes from different strands and allowing the audience to speculate and imagine how these strands might be connected. You have seen how the radio scene can cut to another scene, and how there is often need for some form of linkage. This is true of film scenes too, but, as with radio, the linkage can be enigmatic and not explain itself immediately.

Robert Altman's film *Short Cuts* (1993) is an adaptation of nine short stories by Raymond Carver (including the story 'A Small Good Thing' discussed in Chapter 1) and one of his poems. Its opening sequence, introducing all the different strands, lasts for thirty minutes. It sets the stories in Los Angeles, and links them all with a pesticide helicopter flying over the locations, spraying because there has been an infestation. This acts as a linking device but also alludes to the plagues that often feature in classical dramas – something is not right in this state. This linking and allusion was the film-maker's invention, along with setting the film in Los Angeles (the stories were originally set in various locations predominantly in the American north west). Other linking devices include a television news programme playing in various homes and a jazz singer whose songs connect many of the storylines, either by playing over the openings of scenes or by characters coming to see the singer at her club. With so many strands the film is crowded and runs to well over three hours. Yet it is fascinating as an exercise in cutting between strands and using innovatory methods to create linkage between different storylines.

A film such as *The Hours* (2002) offers a three-storyline model of film-making using parallel strands. The script is an adaptation of Michael Cunningham's novel *The Hours* (1998), itself a triptych fiction which is loosely based on the writer Virginia Woolf's life, his own mother's life, and an updated and migrated version of Woolf's novel *Mrs Dalloway*. This adapts a rich blend of fiction and life writing, and offers an intriguing example of the way in which the stories of both fictional and real lives can be adapted and transformed into surprising new narratives.

ACTIVITY 9.3 Reading	Read the scenes from *The Hours* (Reading 20 on p.350). • Note how the different story strands are established. • What links them for the audience?
DISCUSSION	The three juxtaposed strands in *The Hours* are situated in Los Angeles, 1951; in England, 1923; and in New York, 2001. They are united by the fact that it is morning, though obviously not the same morning. Each is introduced with a card telling the viewer the location and date.

These strands are of equal weight. As the scriptwriter, David Hare, has suggested:

> The central, haunting problem of the adaptation was, of course, to keep the three stories equally compelling. Nothing could be more disastrous to the impact of the film than for the audience to end up regretting the time they spent with one set of characters, and wishing they had spent more with another.
>
> (Hare, 2002, p.xi)

The strength of this method is that the audience wonders how the strands will eventually converge. This is a powerful tool for creating suspense. You may have noticed that there is a montage sequence after introductory scenes for each strand. The sequence creates a significant pace to the cutting. This is carried on in subsequent scenes, culminating in all three strands providing variants of the first line from Woolf's novel, 'Mrs Dalloway said she would buy the flowers herself'. Prior to this we have seen Dan putting flowers in a vase in the Los Angeles strand; the old flowers in Clarissa's New York apartment, and the cornflowers in Virginia Woolf's house.

Leitmotifs

The link made by the flowers in the film is cemented by the climax of this treble exclamation about buying flowers – but it is not a narrative link. One character is writing *Mrs Dalloway*, one character shares Mrs Dalloway's first name, Clarissa, and one character is reading *Mrs Dalloway*. The connection is emphatic but still does not reveal any importance – they are not seen to be related by blood, friendship, time or place. The director Stephen Daldry describes this sort of linkage as establishing leitmotifs – poetic images that repeat like refrains in each strand. Another leitmotif is connected to the preparation of food occurring in each strand. There is also one connected to the cracking of eggs and, later, another to do with kissing. Each of these image systems effects an unlikely, surprising and almost subliminal connection between the apparently disparate strands. This lends the film a dramatic unity.

ACTIVITY 9.4
Writing

Look back at your step outline from Activity 9.2 and write two scenes (up to five minutes performance time in total) which are not consecutive in the storyline but which could be juxtaposed as part of a film. One strand should be concerned with the main plot, one concerned with the subplot – include some connecting element such as a leitmotif, or some of the methods discussed in films like *Short Cuts*. Don't forget to use the correct film layout.

As you have seen in *The Hours*, the connection between disparate story strands doesn't have to be conclusive in a narrative sense. The audience will be alert to any possible parallel. Sometimes the link between scenes can be extremely enigmatic. The audience will always be looking for movement in such links, so that they feel the promise, however poetic, of an eventual coming together of the strands. The more the plot and subplot are fully thought through in the first place, the more they will work as one to fulfil this promise.

Dramatic adaptations

The key elements you can change when adapting a story are period and culture. You can update, or even backdate – changing the historical era to one that suits your purpose. If placing 'Violin Lessons' in the early twenty-first century as opposed to the early 1990s when it was originally set, a mobile phone for the boy would be a realistic and useful prop (as you have seen in Chapter 6). If set in the 1930s a catapult might be more apt.

When Mike Walker adapted 'The Veldt' (2007) for radio he placed Chelsea Clinton as the president of the USA and scripted a news bulletin in which she is reported to be wearing a burkha when visiting Iran. The radio adaptation of 'The Veldt' extends the original story. It strengthens the narrative's dramatic action – adding new cultural context, new conflict, and fleshing out elements that in the original could be considered enigmatic. For instance, the children turn on their parents in the story and offer them as food to the lions in the playroom. In the adaptation this rather radical shift in events is given dramatic logic – the children are seen to witness a lioness eating one of her cubs in order to survive and are shown a history of bad relations between children and parents throughout the ages. The reason the children eventually turn on their own parents is made plausible. It is an act of vengeance for their neglect but also, in their eyes, an act of pre-emptive self-defence. In the original story this shift to malevolence is never given such extensive causality.

The audience for any drama needs to perceive a dramatic logic to events, yet at the same time it enjoys nothing better than the tension created by details and outcomes being withheld. In *The Hours*, for instance, the dramatic logic is constantly being fractured. Tension is created by the recurring narrative interruption of the criss-crossing strands and, interestingly, Daldry says that he interpreted the shape of Hare's script as that of a thriller. This involves withholding details from the viewer. For instance, the narrative information that Laura Brown is the mother of Clarissa Vaughan's best friend, Richard, is withheld until the end of the film.

Hare, speaking about what he calls 'the great mystery of adaptation', says that 'true fidelity can only be achieved through lavish promiscuity' (2002, p.ix). He suggests that if you want to adapt a fiction then it is necessary, not optional, to change something of it. You need to make it new. The technical choice not to use voice-over was one crucial way in which Hare departed from the tone of the original novel:

> anyone approaching the task of adapting Cunningham's novel and finding that so much of the defining action happens inside the characters' heads faces an awkward choice: whether or not to allow any of the three women to speak their thoughts directly to the audience.
>
> (Hare, 2002, p.x)

Hare decided not to use voice-over to capture the novel's stream-of-consciousness narratives, but instead used two primary strengths of film – images and dramatic situations. You will be looking at Cunningham's novel, on which Hare's script is based, in more detail in Chapter 11.

A note on voice-over

Voice-over is a technique that might be berated as sloppy writing by some film writers and teachers. Yet it appeals to the novelist whose work is being adapted, and who might want to see something of a novel's narrative voice retained. For this reason voice-over often proves controversial in adaptations. For instance, Bapsi Sidhwa is reputed to have wanted voice-overs in *Earth* (1999), the adaptation of her novel *Ice-candy-man* (1988), but Deepa Mehta, the film-maker, had misgivings. In the end the adaptation contains two brief voice-overs, one at the beginning and one at the end of the film. They give a personal frame to the child, Lenny's, narrative – they are the voice of the older Lenny, looking back. They also give some historical and political context about the novel's setting – the partition of India in 1947. Yet they do not reflect the powerful and intimate point of view created by the novel's first-person, present-tense voice. The film works in a different way.

Voice-overs are generally best avoided. Try not to use them for straight exposition, revealing information that might otherwise be shown visually or through dramatic scenes. Most film-writing manuals will offer the same advice. However, voice-over is useful on occasions for counterpoint – to add contrast and irony to what is being seen on the screen. If you look back at the voice-over in the 'Violin Lesson' adaptation (Activity 8.5) you can see a measure of this in the way the man's enthusiasm, combined with the rising sound of violin music, offers an earnestness, which counterpoints the potentially comic sight of Veronica and Mr Bouillon failing to play music well together. Woody Allen uses such counterpoint in films like *Hannah and Her Sisters* (1986) and *Husbands and Wives* (1992). Martin Scorsese uses it in *GoodFellas* (1990) – but only near the start. Fleetingly both the main character, Henry Hill, and his wife, Diane, narrate their thoughts, revealing a domestic normality – youthful aspirations, a young couple falling in love and building a life – to counterpoint the savagery of Henry's occupation as a murderous gangster.

Jane Campion uses voice-over at the beginning and end of *The Piano* (1993), in the same way as Mehta does in *Earth*. Topping and tailing a film like this is a useful structural device, provided that the voice-over earns its place and is not there just for the sake of structure. In *The Piano* the counterpoint is obvious – we have a mute character, Ada, who is otherwise silent in a vocal and noisy world. Yet the viewer is allowed to hear her inner voice. She is sent as an arranged bride to New Zealand. Her child and her piano accompany her; they are her main forms of communication with the world. Her early voice-over haunts and informs her ensuing silence in the rest of the film because of its directness.

In this way a voice-over should never offer what is already being illustrated by the visual narrative. It can potentially speed up the action – but remember the screen is rarely blank during a voice-over. In *The Piano* the first voice-over runs for seven contrastive scenes. The final voice-over accompanies scenes of Ada's piano underwater after it has fallen overboard, and then scenes of newfound domestic harmony. By this time she has literally refound her voice and a degree of independence; she is learning how to speak again.

Using flashbacks

There are many films in which the opening voice-over is retrospective, narrated from the temporal position of the end. In effect the whole film is a flashback, one that is being dramatised. Some films start visually at the end too. *The Hours* begins, as does Cunningham's novel, with the death of Virginia Woolf in 1941, some eighteen years after the main Woolf strand in the book and film. This form of framing hook is common in films, and provides a trace image which the viewer will retrieve and make sense of as the film nears its final scenes. *Pan's Labyrinth* (2007), set in the aftermath of the Spanish civil war, opens with the image of a young person – boy or girl, it is hard to say – with a trickle of blood coming from his or her face; the child is dying. Only in the film's penultimate scene are we reunited with this image, as the film's main character, Ofelia, is shot by her barbaric stepfather. This sort of framing can add to the emotional impact of such scenes.

Some films have complex time arrangements signalled in the opening scenes. *GoodFellas* begins with a fully retrospective voice-over but a visual of a murder which occurs two-thirds of the way through the timeline of the story. In the opening scenes of *Babel* (2007) we see two Moroccan boys given a gun by their shepherd father in order to kill jackals. They play competitively with the gun on the mountainside and aim at a passing tourist bus, with calamitous consequences. Instead of cutting to the interior of the bus or to what the boys do next, the film cuts to a phone call being received in America by the Mexican nanny of the children of the woman on the bus who has been shot. This is hard to comprehend at this moment in the film. It is a brave cut because the audience has not seen this American setting before and its connection to the action in Morocco is complex and far from consecutive. This phone call occurs nearly halfway through the timeline of the whole story; it informs the nanny that the parents will not be back as expected. The film creates a series of narrative questions. Who was on the bus? Who got shot? How did that person get to hospital? Did they die? What happened to the boys? Tension is created by these pending questions. The film is structured to fill in the backstory with gradual flashbacks, cutting between the different strands. Flashback often poses a problem because it can radically slow the forward momentum of the action. In the case of *Babel* the method succeeds because the complex structure, with six narrative strands in all, always allows the narrative to cut to another strand, giving the film a new impetus and motivating all the flashbacks. They do not seem like blatant exposition. In films with fewer strands, flashback can be much more problematic.

In the following activity, you will look at how Dennis Potter uses flashback in his television drama *The Singing Detective*. Marlow, the main character, is lying in his hospital bed suffering from psoriatic arthropathy (as Potter did). He is in pain, and has previously hallucinated that the doctors and nurses engaged in a dance routine, singing 'Dry Bones' all around him on the hospital ward.

ACTIVITY 9.5 Reading	Read the extract from Dennis Potter's *The Singing Detective* (Reading 21 on p.354). • What links the flashback to the dramatic present? • How are the different voices achieved? • What accent or dialect are the characters speaking in?

DISCUSSION	The flashback is prompted by illness and the state of mind of the character. It seems part of his illness and almost to merge naturally with his hallucinatory state.

You will notice here how music links all the various locations – the hospital, the treetop and the kitchen, the place where it is being played on the radio. This reflects the way in which Marlowe's memory is working through association. The music itself – Bing Crosby singing 'Don't Fence Me In' – illuminates the theme. It emphasises the boy Marlow's magnificently free vantage point in the trees. It contrasts starkly with the claustrophobia of his home kitchen and with the adult Marlow's confinement in hospital.

Also of interest here is the use of phonetics in the dialogue. When I have shown this dialogue in workshops, actors have had trouble reading it or knowing what dialect it is. They have guessed anything from the southern states of the USA to Newcastle, but few have guessed the exact location – the Forest of Dean in Gloucestershire. This is perhaps instructive. Such phonetic spelling can be unhelpful, and it often needs more direction, such as the young Mrs Marlow is given (she has a London accent), to enable actors to pin it down exactly.

The whole of *The Singing Detective* can be seen to be operating through flashback. It is the story of Marlow's struggle with memory. In different circumstances such methods can be overused, and you should be cautious of using flashback too much because, as suggested earlier, it can slow the forward movement of your action. If you find you need to use it frequently then you may need to look again at your structure and in particular at your starting point. If you are using flashback so much, why not start in the past, or at least earlier? Some scripts are radically improved by doing this – cutting down on the need for so much exposition of earlier parts of the story. Be wary of using large flashbacks towards the end of your stories, attempting to reveal details that should have been released earlier and more gradually.

ACTIVITY 9.6 Writing	Using 'A Real Durwan' or a story of your own, dramatise one or two flashback scenes, framed by two present scenes (up to ten minutes performance time). Also use voice-over if you wish. Either:

- use the main character of the original story, looking back at part of his or her more comfortable past;
- or write an adaptation that is 'promiscuous' with the original story, as Hare suggests, and perhaps relocate the story in time or culture.

DISCUSSION	If you chose the first option and used 'A Real Durwan', you will have found that there was plenty of resource in the way Boori Ma talks of her past in the original story: for instance, the episodes when she crossed the border and when she attended her third daughter's wedding.

If you chose the second option and took Hare at his word, you probably realised that you could move a story practically anywhere. For instance, you could relocate 'A Real Durwan' to London. The main character could be a refugee who has a job as a cleaner in an apartment block. She might suffer because of an infestation in her rented bedsit. She could be remembering a scene from her former home or even from a week earlier.

Conclusion

You have seen in this part of the book that drama depends on differentiation and contrast – in its dialogue, in the visual storytelling, in the way it is scripted, in the characterisation, in the status dynamic between characters and the voices that characters use. You have also seen that the format of your script is crucially different for each medium and that each uses its own idiosyncratic method of carrying the narrative – there is a predominance of visuals in film, dialogue in radio, and a mix of the two on stage.

Dramatic writing for any medium is an extremely concise form of writing. Adaptation, and the economy of scriptwriting, can tighten a story, as suggested by Zadie Smith talking about the television adaptation of her novel *White Teeth*:

> The cuts were necessary to make the fat and messy kid presentable, and at least one of the changes is inspired ... A cut has been made; a motivation inserted, and an artistic clarity is the result. The moment I saw it, I gasped – this section of the novel would have been so improved had I thought of the same strategy ... In a novel, one scrabbles in the dirt for motivation or stretches for decorative language to hide the lack of it. In film,

no such disguise will be tolerated by the viewer. When we watch a man do something on screen, our guts much more than our brains will tell us the truth of the gesture. It cannot be fudged.

(Smith, 2003, p.10)

Whichever medium you choose, conflict has to be central to the way you arrange each scene and each act. Conflict, from the inciting incident onwards, causes the arc of rising tension, climax and resolution. In facing this conflict your characters will engage in the arc of their own journeys. You may use particular techniques – flashback, montage, voice-over – but remember David Hare's testimony about treating the task of adaptation promiscuously, and how this can in the end be truer to the spirit of the original than trying to be too literal. Bapsi Sidhwa, though missing some of the characters that were necessarily stripped from her original novel in the film version, *Earth*, came to feel that the movie brought the story alive in an uncanny way. Hermione Lee, though critical of some historical aspects of the film version of *The Hours*, says: 'There is a tiny pause, right at the start ... that caught at my heart, but I didn't think anyone else would notice it. It took me back to the work I did on my biography of Virginia Woolf' (2003). This pause is the actor's enunciation of part of Woolf's final letter, which was written in jagged half-lines, pause-ridden, like a poem. It obviously rang true with Lee's informed perception of Woolf's last moments.

Whatever your method and however you appropriate the original story – whether it is fiction or a piece of life writing – it is important to realise that you are making it into something completely different and new. You are making something worthy in its own right. In the final part of the book you will be looking at how these dramatic methods might influence and improve your fiction, poetry and life writing.

References

Babel (2007) film, Alejandro González Iñárrittu (director), Guillermo Arriaga (writer).

Chinatown (1974) film, Roman Polanski (director), Robert Towne (writer).

Cunningham, Michael (1998) *The Hours*, New York: Farrar, Straus and Giroux.

Earth (1999) film, Deepa Mehta (director and writer).

GoodFellas (1990) film, Martin Scorsese (director), Martin Scorsese and Nicholas Pileggi (writers).

Hannah and Her Sisters (1986) film, Woody Allen (director and writer).

Hare, David (2002) *The Hours: a screenplay*, New York: Miramax.

The Hours (2002) film, Stephen Daldry (director), David Hare (writer).

Husbands and Wives (1992) film, Woody Allen (director and writer).

Lee, Hermione (2003) 'Ways of dying', *Guardian*, 8 February.

Pan's Labyrinth (2007) film, Guillermo del Torro (director and writer).

The Piano (1993) film, Jane Campion (director and writer).

The Screenwriters Store (n.d.) *850+ Screenplays*, CD, London: The Screenwriters Store.

Short Cuts (1993) film, Robert Altman (director), Robert Altman and Frank Barhydt (writers).

Sidhwa, Bapsi (1988) *Ice-candy-man*, London: Heinemann.

Smith, Zadie (2003) '"White Teeth" in the flesh', *New York Times*, 1 May, Arts and Leisures, 2:1, p.10.

Walker, Mike (2007) *The Veldt*, broadcast on BBC Radio 4, 22 May.

Further viewing and reading

Adaptation (2002) film, Spike Jonze (director), Charlie Kaufman (writer).

This film is about the process of adapting a text into a screenplay and comically contemplates some of the decisions to be made, for instance, about voice-over and endings. It comments in meta-filmic fashion on film-writing techniques and Hollywood conventions.

Vogler, Christopher (1999) *The Writer's Journey*, London: Pan.

This book analyses a number of popular films in terms of mythic archetypes and story shapes and is very informative about the arcs of the characters' journeys. Vogler applies these terms to well-known films such as *The Full Monty* and *Pulp Fiction*.

10   Film technique in fiction

Linda Anderson

Movies of the mind

As a teenager I used to make up stories in my head and would see
the actual words forming tickertape sentences in my mind's eye.
When I started to write seriously, I imagined that this knack of verbal
visualisation would be an asset to me as a fiction writer. It took me a while
to see it as an obstacle. I would often produce material where the words
were so much the point and so laboriously dazzling that they obscured the
vision I wanted to transmit. The fact is that in fiction the vision predates the
words. Stories come to us first as visions – dramatic, emotional and
shimmeringly unformed – before we set them down in actual language.

This is not to say that the words don't matter. Power of language is one
of the joys of both writing and reading, the thing that distinguishes one
story from another and makes the best ones memorable and thrilling.
We have to find precise, eloquent and fresh ways of expressing our visions.
But the words are secondary; they are there to serve the story, or as novelist
and tutor John Gardner puts it, to trigger 'the fictive dream'. Here is his
description of the kind of willed hallucination the fiction writer needs to
be able to foster – and to defend against 'hostile mental forces', such as
self-doubt or caring too much about the work's eventual outcome:

> In the writing state   the state of inspiration   the fictive dream
> springs up fully alive: the writer forgets the words he has written
> on the page and sees instead his characters moving around their
> rooms, hunting through cupboards, glancing irritably through their
> mail, setting mousetraps, loading pistols. ... This ... is the
> desperately sought and tragically fragile writer's process: in
> his imagination, he sees made-up people doing things – sees
> clearly – and in the act of wondering what they will do next, he
> sees what they will do next, and all this he writes down in the best,
> most accurate words he can find, understanding even as he writes
> that he may have to find better words later, and that a change in the
> words may mean a sharpening or deepening of the vision.
>
> (Gardner, 1983, p.120)

Once you start looking for it, it becomes easy to spot where a writer's
fictive dream has faltered and you will find incidences in published as well
as in unpublished work. You can tell when words have been chosen for
effect rather than accuracy and when writing is coming mainly from the

intellect. There will be too much explanation, simplistic cause and effect, too much generalisation and summary. You will be very familiar by now with the dynamics of showing and telling. Telling has its necessary place and its advantages – condensing time, for example, or allowing various degrees of omniscience in the narrative point of view. But it is difficult for writers to achieve the right proportion of telling, and many of the stories I see from student writers tend to rely on telling to an unnecessary degree.

ACTIVITY 10.1
Reading

Read the following start of a story that I've written to be deliberately bad, though it has some redeeming features. Make notes on what works and what doesn't. In particular, look for any disruption of the fictive dream that is being created in you as reader.

Daniel was watching from his bedroom window. The man glanced up at him before pushing the gate open. There was something eerie about his approach down the path because of the twilight and the soundlessness created by the double glazing. *Please don't let Dad answer the door*, Daniel prayed, his legs leaden at the prospect of going downstairs, entering the zone his father had commandeered for himself these last few months when they had rarely even eaten together. What on earth would his rusty-voiced father do, faced with this policeman come to tell him of his son's misdeeds? Or worse, could it be the woman's husband or partner? Daniel started to dash downstairs just as the doorbell shrilled through the house.

The stupid thing was that it had taken just one blurred glimpse to trigger his obsession with the woman. After his mother's death he had thrown himself into his studies. Already top of his class, he set about outshining himself. He visited the café every afternoon after school. It was a Starbucks in a former church and had just the right atmosphere to help him study while sipping on a series of syrupy lattes. Algebraic equations, Latin translations, historical facts – it was his alternative to grief. One day, he was gazing out of the latticed window when she came into view. There was an impression of burnished brown hair, tawny complexion, a soft green coat, graceful limbs, all etched in sunlight. He grabbed his belongings and bolted outside. He followed her down the high street, walking alongside her at one point to catch a look at her face. Stepping behind her again, he had a sudden aerial view of the situation, a schoolboy in pursuit of an elegant stranger who was probably at least thirty years old. But he couldn't stop himself and it became his daily mission to watch and wait for her and then follow her to her workplace (a lawyer's office), her lunch place (Pret A Manger), and finally, all the way home (number 9 bus, alighting at Canterbury Road). Her house was a disappointment – a dingy semi lit up like an operating theatre, not the mysterious mansion he had imagined. *You're not my type*, he thought. *Leave me alone.* He ran away when she turned off a downstairs light and peered out at him in alarm. It hadn't taken long to track him down, obviously – the purple school blazer, his stoop, his specs, his too long hair ...

DISCUSSION

You may have found that the story starts with some intriguing hooks. What has Daniel done? What is wrong with his father? Why is there no sign of a mother? We feel plunged right into a mystery and a crisis.

But the next paragraph is all backstory summarising what has led up to this point. It is heavily condensed and implies a crude cause and effect: the boy's stalking is a direct consequence of the ungrieved loss of his mother. It isn't all analysis; it contains a dramatic scene showing Daniel's pursuits of the woman, but this competes with the opening dramatic scene, which is now freeze-framed with Daniel in mid-flight rushing down the stairs and the unidentified stranger waiting on the doorstep.

I've read hundreds of stories that start like this – they pull the reader in effectively but then proceed to provide the backstory, a full history and explanation of what happened before the opening. Explanatory passages can be even more static than my example, giving detached physical descriptions of characters or places that seem like a packet of information the reader needs to know before proceeding with the story.

The writing trance described by Gardner is a kind of internal film-making, just as reading a novel with absorption is akin to recreating a movie in our inner consciousness. In the rest of this chapter, we will explore the usefulness of film techniques in fiction writing, the ways in which conscious application of film craft might help us to structure our stories dramatically, to move gracefully from one scene to another, and to avoid problems of over-explanation, abstraction and summary.

Applying film technique to fiction

Film technique and the art of writing fiction share a great deal of common ground.

At the start of the twentieth century, pioneer film-makers turned to novels and poetry for guidance on how to convey their stories in what was then a new medium. You have read in Chapter 8 about Russian director Sergei Eisenstein who developed the concept of montage. He found inspiration in the works of Pushkin, Milton and de Maupassant, among others. He learned the rudiments of 'analytical cutting', the kind of purposeful editing that creates and intensifies meaning, from Hollywood director D.W. Griffith, the 'father' of American cinema. Eisenstein has described how Griffith took his cues from the novels of Charles Dickens. He quotes an anecdote told by Griffith's wife concerning a discussion between the director and his employers about the making of the first version of *Enoch Arden*, entitled *After Many Years* (1908). The exchange shows the sheer novelty of montage at that time as well as the surprising Victorian source of the inspiration:

> When Mr Griffith suggested a scene showing Annie Lee waiting for her husband's return to be followed by a scene of Enoch cast away on a desert island, it was altogether too distracting. 'How can you tell a story jumping about like that? The people won't know what it's about.'
>
> 'Well,' said Mr Griffith, 'doesn't Dickens write that way?'
> 'Yes, but that's Dickens; that's novel writing; that's different.'
> 'Oh, not so much, these are picture stories; not so different.'
>
> (Eisenstein, 1949, pp.200–1)

Although Dickens died three decades before the invention of film, it was his novels that inspired Griffith with ideas on where to point the camera and how and when to move it; how to shoot scenes, and how to arrange stories.

Just as the early film-makers used fiction as a training ground, so we can draw on film technique to empower and dramatise our fiction and, in particular, to avoid the pitfalls of excessive 'telling'. You are already familiar with the basic film concepts of cut, shot and montage. All of these have direct analogies in fiction.

'Cuts' and 'shots' in fiction

A cut is when one image ends and is instantaneously replaced by another – this is how transitions are made from one shot to the next. In fiction, we can write a graceful equivalent, using crisp sentences as in this example: 'A faint breeze carried the sound of traffic. A thrush sang and then stopped as if wearied. She checked her mobile for the hundredth time.'

A shot is the basic unit of film-making. As you know, it is an uninterrupted flow of imagery. Shots can place their objects at varying degrees of distance depending on the desired impact. Similarly, the narrative voice in fiction is always adjusting the readers' view of the world it creates by altering our distance from its images. The equivalent in film is the range of angles from long shot, medium shot, close-up, to extreme close-up. Let's look at how these apply to the opening of Dickens's *Great Expectations*. The narrator, Pip, begins to tell his life story. He sometimes refers to himself in the first person and sometimes in the third.

> Ours was the marsh country, down by the river, within, as the river wound, twenty miles of the sea [*long shot*]. My first most vivid and broad impression of the identity of things, seems to me to have been gained on a memorable raw afternoon towards evening. At such a time I found out for certain, that this bleak place overgrown with nettles was the churchyard [*medium shot*], and that Philip Pirrip, late of this parish, and also Georgiana wife of the above, were dead and buried; and that Alexander, Bartholomew, Abraham, Tobias, and Roger, infant children of the aforesaid, were also dead and buried [*close-up of headstones*]; and that the dark flat wilderness beyond the churchyard, intersected with dykes and mounds and gates, with scattered cattle feeding on it, was the marshes; and that the low leaden line beyond was the river; and that the distant savage lair from which the wind was rushing, was the sea [*extreme long shot*]; and that the small bundle of shivers growing afraid of it all and beginning to cry, was Pip [*medium shot*].
>
> (Dickens, 1994 [1861], pp.5–6)

This passage starts with a long shot establishing the setting and time, 'a memorable raw afternoon'. It then moves into a close-up of the headstones, panning, each in turn, to the graves of Pip's father, his mother and his five brothers. Most authors might linger there, on such a desolating stack of bereavements, but Dickens goes into a gradual long shot that looks out over the mounds and gates and dykes to the marshes, then to the river, and finally beyond, to the farthest horizon, 'the distant savage lair from which the wind was rushing'. He then cuts from that far distant point to a medium shot of the orphan boy, 'the small bundle of shivers'. Dickens's strategy makes the setting take on an almost metaphysical dimension. We don't dwell on the pathos of Pip's orphanhood but on some hint of his destiny, his pitting himself against the large and threatening world.

A striking use of a long shot occurs in Ian McEwan's novella *On Chesil Beach* (2007). Set in 1962, this is the story of a young couple, Edward and Florence, just married and starting their honeymoon at a hotel in Dorset. Both sexually inexperienced, their attempt at lovemaking ends in humiliation and Florence flees from the hotel and along the beach. Here is the start of the scene where Edward comes to confront her:

> She watched him coming along the strand, his form at first no more than an indigo stain against the darkening shingle, sometimes appearing motionless, flickering and dissolving at its outlines, and at others suddenly closer, as though moved like a chess piece a few squares towards her. The last glow of daylight lay along the shore, and behind her, away to the east, there were points of light on Portland, and the cloud base reflected dully a yellowish glow of street lamps from a distant town. She watched him, willing him to go slower, for she was guiltily afraid of him, and was desperate for more time to herself.
>
> (McEwan, 2007, p.139)

The long shot reduces the familiar, beloved man to a flickering shape. It emphasises the distance that has opened up between the couple; the man is 'other' now, a stranger. His inexorable approach towards Florence like a moving 'chess piece' creates an atmosphere of extreme tension. The sober description of the fading daylight and the glimmer of lights along the coast contribute an elegiac note. The scene is set for a life-changing encounter.

Montage in fiction

In Chapter 8 you read about how montage works in films – meaning and forward action are created through juxtaposition of images or whole scenes. Such juxtaposition is dynamic. It creates a new reality out of disparate fragments, as in David Mamet's example of the footage of birds snapping a twig and of a fawn raising its head (p.122). If these shots are juxtaposed, they create a sense of alertness to danger, an idea not present in either shot in isolation.

A similar technique can be used in fiction. Let's turn again to *Great Expectations* for an example of a sequence of images that creates a new meaning and multiplies emotional impact. Pip has come to visit Miss Havisham, a jilted bride who has lived for decades in her decaying wedding finery. He takes in the details of her strange appearance with growing horror:

> But, I saw that everything within my view which ought to be white, had been white long ago, and had lost its lustre, and was faded and yellow. I saw that the bride within the bridal dress had withered like the dress, and like the flowers, and had no brightness left but the brightness of her sunken eyes. I saw that the dress had

been put upon the rounded figure of a young woman, and that the figure upon which it now hung loose, had shrunk to skin and bone. Once, I had been taken to see some ghastly waxwork at the Fair, representing I know not what impossible personage lying in state. Once, I had been taken to one of our old marsh churches to see a skeleton in the ashes of a rich dress, that had been dug out of a vault under the church pavement. Now, waxwork and skeleton seemed to have dark eyes that moved and looked at me. I should have cried out, if I could.

(Dickens, 1994 [1861], p.55)

The incantatory repetitions of 'I saw' and of 'once, I had been taken' make this a hypnotic piece of writing, concluding with the brilliant sequence of the remembered waxwork, followed by the skeleton, followed by their grotesque animation in the living dead woman in front of him. This is accomplished by two cuts leading to a terrifying new image.

Montage also deals with larger arrangements of image and scene, of course. Take a look at this extract from Antoine Wilson's first novel, *The Interloper*, where the narrator is discontented at a dinner party.

A current event absorbed, amoeba-like, all the other topics, and the small conversations became a big group conversation. There had been another suicide bombing in the Middle East. It had been all over the news that day. Dozens of people, many of them children, dead.
The talk went round and round, with expressions of sympathy for the victims, shaking heads of halfway-around-the-world impotence, a few words about the news media, early symptoms of compassion-fatigue and its cousin, compassion-fatigue-fatigue. There is no group duller than one's peers.

'I cannot understand how someone would think it's a good idea to blow themselves up,' said our host.

'And kill children,' added our hostess. Various gestures of agreement.

'It's incomprehensible.' This from a short and bearded Professor of Something.

'They're maniacs.'

I hadn't said anything. I had been trying to cut the foil from a bottle of white wine with the sharp tip of the opener's corkscrew. I had not yet learned that most foil tops can be pulled right off, sleeve-like. You have to keep your eye on that sharp metal tip if you don't want to spear your finger and give yourself tetanus. I sliced the foil and removed it successfully.

(Wilson, 2007, p.56)

The narrator's exasperation with the group's trite conversation is funny and scathing. But the juxtaposition with his focus on the trivial action of opening the wine adds even more irony. His exaggerated fear of cutting his finger and getting tetanus contrasts comically with the suicide bomber's total disregard for self-protection. The narrator's little obsession with the art of opening wine bottles seems more authentic than the group's 'concern' for bomb victims. Simply positioning these two elements together creates deeper resonances.

ACTIVITY 10.2
Editing

Look through one or two stories that you have already drafted, even ones that you may consider complete. Choose a section of about 200 words and annotate it in the way that I have done with the opening extract from *Great Expectations*. Can you identify a variety of shots or is everything seen from the same distance?

Now review your whole story, checking the arrangement of your images and scenes to see whether any new juxtapositions might benefit your story by adding richness, meaning or economy.

DISCUSSION

If you found that your story extract was all in medium shot, try using a combination of shots (long, medium, close-up) to create a dynamic rhythm in one or more scenes and to add meaning without direct explanation.

Did you find that a new arrangement of scenes in your story might intensify its drama or enable you to cut any elements? Or did you find your story effective in its existing arrangement?

When revising your story drafts, you may find it useful to imagine yourself as a writer-director and try to visualise every element of your story powerfully, applying film techniques as appropriate. Make sure that you choose each type of shot or montage for a purpose, not randomly or just for its own sake.

Writing varied scenes

A scene is an extended moment or action which seems to exist in 'real time' on the page or screen. There are two basic types of scene in fiction: dramatic and static.

Dramatic scenes are tense and often eventful; something happens – a murder, a car chase, a demand for divorce. But dramatic scenes are not always sensational. They may explore subtle conflict or muted emotion, so that nothing 'happens' but everything is highly charged. For example, two good friends meet for lunch. The man is secretly in love with the woman but dare not say so. His unspoken yearning and her lack of awareness could make for a taut, dramatic scene.

Static scenes contain more ordinary and restful moments, the lulls that occur before or after tension. But static scenes are not frozen like paintings. They should never stall the story or just fill in the moments between events. Their function is to provide verisimilitude and tension release.

Stories need both types of scene, dramatic and static, in order not to become melodramatic and implausible (with relentless drama) or dull and cosy (with too much stasis).

Here are the opening scenes of two novels, Ian McEwan's *Enduring Love* and Marguerite Alexander's *Grievance*. Both narratives begin with a picnic – but notice the differences.

> The beginning is simple to mark. We were in sunlight under a turkey oak, partly protected from a strong, gusty wind. I was kneeling on the grass with a corkscrew in my hand, and Clarissa was passing me the bottle – a 1987 Daumas Gassac. This was the moment, this was the pinprick on the time map: I was stretching out my hand, and as the cool neck and the black foil touched my palm, we heard a man's shout. We turned to look across the field and saw the danger. Next thing, I was running towards it. The transformation was absolute: I don't recall dropping the corkscrew, or getting to my feet, or making a decision, or hearing the caution Clarissa called after me. What idiocy, to be racing into this story and its labyrinths, sprinting away from our happiness among the fresh spring grasses by the oak. There was the shout again, and a child's cry, enfeebled by the wind that roared in the tall trees along the hedgerows. I ran faster. And there, suddenly, from different points around the field, four other men were converging on the scene, running like me.
>
> (McEwan, 1997, p.1)

> It is, Steve supposes, the particular quality of the September afternoon that makes the group so picturesque. The air is so still that the few leaves that are ready to fall drift to the ground with a kind of languor, their colours, in their slow descent, caught in the slanting rays of the sun. It was to enjoy the effect that Steve had lingered; otherwise he might not have noticed the young people at all. There are about half a dozen, mostly seated, one or two of the young men lying, under the handsome chestnut tree in the college quadrangle.

A picnic seems to be in progress. A woollen rug is spread on the grass, dotted with plates of food and large jugs of Pimm's, its colour harmonising with the autumnal tones of the setting. It must be somebody's birthday, or perhaps a celebration of reunion at the beginning of the new academic year.

(Alexander, 2006, p.3)

The first scene begins with brief stasis, then moves suddenly into drama. It starts by establishing the lovers' tranquil picnic with almost hallucinatory physical details – even the vintage of the wine is etched on the narrator's memory because of the life-changing event that erupts: a fatal hot-air balloon accident.

The second scene is static. It contains leisurely details about the setting. A university lecturer enjoys his college grounds and idly watches some students having a picnic. Nothing happens. This opening scene introduces the main character – older, watchful – and a campus setting at the start of a new academic year. It fulfils plenty of functions but the dramatic tension will start in later scenes.

ACTIVITY 10.3 Reading	Find a chapter in a favourite novel or use some pages from a story or chapter you are currently working on. Identify each separate scene as dramatic or static. Is there an identifiable rhythm to the scenes or does one type predominate? What is the effect on the overall mood of the piece of writing?
DISCUSSION	You may have found some scenes difficult to categorise. Sometimes there are 'quiet' scenes where dramatic or even explosive things might be happening in someone's thoughts or in unspoken dynamics between characters: for example, a man has a heartbreaking realisation at a bus stop; an interviewer keeps calm even though a job applicant resembles his missing son. Such scenes are dramatic despite, or even because of, their surface ordinariness.

Writers have a tendency to favour one type of scene. Think about what you like to read and about your own writing. Do you like to include quarrels, crises, accidents, betrayals, things that complicate and disrupt your characters' lives? Or do you like to linger over settings, to show your characters as they get out of bed, queue at the bank, go to work and get lost in thought? Recognising your preferred type will show you where you need to compensate in order to create a suitable balance. Remember that both types of scene, dramatic and static, are necessary.

Be aware of the nature of your scenes and use them in an appropriate rhythm to prevent melodrama or monotony.

Scene construction

Successful scenes in film and fiction share common principles: they rely chiefly on showing, not telling. Every element in them is carefully selected and arranged for maximum economy and meaning. Perspective and point of view are tightly controlled.

You will already be familiar with the idea of story structure – the way the most compelling stories have a definite arc: rising action/climax/falling action/resolution. This same structure applies in miniature to the individual scenes comprising the story. Every scene should have a definite beginning, middle and end: each scene needs a recognisable dramatic shape. Sometimes fiction writers are less adept than screenwriters at creating shapely scenes. They write scenes that drift and trickle into each other. The idea of *making* a story rather than just writing one can help combat this tendency. Like film-makers, we can write plans and maps of our stories. We can outline the action for each scene on notecards, listing the entry and exit points, the rising and falling action. Putting the cards together, we can check that each scene furthers the story and that we have both action moments and enough stasis moments for tension release and good pacing. It is often best to do this playing around with the story's structure when you already have the material in draft form, the fictive dream caught on the page, otherwise the story might risk being too much the product of your intellect and too 'made to order'.

Let's look at the opening scene from 'River of Names', one of the stories in Dorothy Allison's *Trash*.

> At a picnic at my aunt's farm, the only time the whole family ever gathered, my sister Billie and I chased chickens into the barn. Billie ran right through the open doors and out again, but I stopped, caught by a shadow moving over me. My Cousin Tommy, eight years old as I was, swung in the sunlight with his face as black as his shoes – the rope around his neck pulled up into the sunlit heights of the barn, fascinating, horrible. Wasn't he running ahead of us? Someone came up behind me. Someone began to scream. My mama took my head in her hands and turned my eyes away.
>
> (Allison, 2002 [1988], p.9)

This gripping scene is very filmic – intensely visual and sensual and all accomplished with tight, minimal details in just seven sentences. It has a clear arc of rising and falling action, which I will track in detail:

1 At a picnic at my aunt's farm, the only time the whole family ever gathered, my sister Billie and I chased chickens into the barn. *(Starts with static summary in the first two phrases, then moves into forward action.)*

2 Billie ran right through the open doors and out again, but I stopped, caught by a shadow moving over me. *(Action leading to a dramatic 'peak' – the narrator stops, catching sight of the shadow.)*

3 My Cousin Tommy, eight years old as I was, swung in the sunlight with his face as black as his shoes – the rope around his neck pulled up into the sunlit heights of the barn, fascinating, horrible. *(Starts with a hint of exposition, then moves into the scene's climax, the highest 'peak'. This is appropriately the longest sentence, prolonged by 'fascinating, horrible', which has the effect of slowing down time.)*

4 Wasn't he running ahead of us? *(Stasis moment while the narrator is confused or in denial. This is the beginning of the falling action.)*

5 Someone came up behind me. *(Continuing falling action.)*

6 Someone began to scream. *(Momentary reverting to rising action, delaying relief for the reader.)*

7 My mama took my head in her hands and turned my eyes away. *(Resolution and exit point: the mother's futile attempt to shield her daughter.)*

In the rest of this story, we never find out exactly what happened to the hanged boy. The story's focus is on the girl, how she survives growing up in a desperately poor family whose lives are full of drunkenness and a glut of 'death by misadventure'. So the point of view is carefully chosen here. Because we see, hear and feel what the narrator experiences, it is very intimate. The shadow of the dead boy moves over the reader too.

ACTIVITY 10.4
Writing

Take a story that you have already drafted, one that is at least 2,000 words long, and now dissect and redesign it with the help of notecards. You will need one card for each scene. Write down the bare bones of each scene's action. For example, the opening scene from 'River of Names' could be described on one card like this:

> *Family gathering at aunt's farm.*
> *Girls run into barn.*
> *Narrator finds dead cousin (main action).*
> *Mother arrives; tries in vain to protect daughter.*

Once you have listed each scene's contents, make sure that every scene has clear entry and exit points and its own mini-arc of rising and falling action, making additional notes to mark these if you want.

Lay all your cards out on a table and consider whether your scenes are in the best order and whether they all move the story forward. Do you have a good rhythm of dramatic and static (tension releasing) scenes? Does your overall story have a dramatic shape of rising action, climax, falling action and resolution?

Redraft your story. Don't be afraid to discard anything in your original draft that seems too explanatory or abstract or even superfluous.

The scope of fiction

Throughout this chapter you have learned how you might use film techniques to enhance your fiction. The two forms share common ground and a linked history, as you have seen. But they have significant differences as well and it is important to exploit the full range of fiction's possibilities. Most films can only show hints of a character's inner consciousness. In *Making Movies Work*, Jon Boorstin says: 'No matter how brilliant the characterisation, a movie can never probe the inner workings of the mind the way a good novel can' (Boorstin, 1995, p.71). Nor can a film convey a powerful narratorial voice in the sustained way that a novel does.

A comparison of the novel and film versions of *Notes on a Scandal* illustrates this point. Zoë Heller's 2003 novel was praised for its mastery of tone and language. It has an unreliable narrator, Barbara Covett, a caustic and manipulative schoolteacher who becomes fixated on her colleague, Sheba, who has a perilous sexual liaison with a young pupil. In an interview printed in the *Observer* (17 December 2006), Heller describes one way in which the film is very unlike the novel. 'The movie's Barbara is more thoroughgoingly villainous than the original, with a much more conscious and explicit mission to entrap her victim. Most audiences seem to perceive her as a closeted lesbian with a clear sexual motive for stalking Sheba – and, again, that was not the case in the book' (Thorpe, 2006).

Here is an example of the inner workings of Barbara's mind as captured in the novel:

> On the way home, I stopped in at LoPrice, the supermarket at the end of my road, to get a pint of milk and some bread for the next morning. The man in front of me at the checkout laid his purchases on the conveyor belt with a terrible, shy precision: a jar of instant coffee;

a single Kaiser roll with a smudge of dirt on its hard crust; a tin of tuna; a large jar of mayonnaise; two boxes of Kleenex. [...] [He] watched his things being rung up with careful attention. Back home, he would make his grim tuna sandwich and his cup of sawdust coffee. He would eat in front of the television, as single people do. And then he would turn to his bounteous supply of tissues ... for what? Tears? Sneezes? Masturbation?

There was a small confusion when the girl at the till mistakenly included my milk and bread as part of the man's basket. 'No, no,' the man murmured angrily. Shooting me a nasty look, he grabbed the little metal divider and slammed it down on the conveyor belt to section off my things from his. Lonely people are terrible snobs about one another, I've found. They're afraid that consorting with their own kind will compound their freakishness. The time that Jennifer and I went to Paris together, we saw an airline employee at Heathrow ask two very fat people in the check-in line where they were both off to. The fat people were not a couple as it happened, and the suggestion that they were, panicked them. Leaping apart, they both shouted in unison, 'We're not together!'

I understood their horror. Even Jennifer and I were prey on occasion to a certain self-consciousness about the impression we made as a twosome. Alone, each of us was safely unremarkable – invisible, actually – as plain women over the age of forty are to the world. Together, though, I always suspected that we were faintly comic: two screamingly unhusbanded ladies on a day out. A music-hall act of spinsterhood.

For a second, I had an impulse to shout at the man in LoPrice – to tell him that I was not like him at all, that I had friends.

(Heller, 2003, pp.113–15)

We see the unshielded core of Barbara here – how mortified and vulnerable she feels about her age and aloneness. We also see how her mercy is tinged with malice: her clairvoyance about the man's solitary evening edges into voyeurism when she speculates about masturbation. It isn't possible for the reader to fully dislike her or to sum her up easily.

This quality of 'voice' and direct access to interior world is unique to fiction. This is not to say that fiction is superior to film; just that they possess separate terrain as well as common ground. If you incorporate film techniques into your writing, your fiction will become more visual, sensual, and with more supple transitions between scenes and even between sentences. But you need never sacrifice fiction's gift of being able to render a character's inner life in all its complexity.

References

Alexander, Marguerite (2006) *Grievance,* London: Fourth Estate.

Allison, Dorothy (2002 [1988]) *Trash*, New York: Plume.

Boorstin, Jon (1995) *Making Movies Work: Think like a filmmaker*, Los Angeles: Silman-James Press.

Dickens, Charles (1994 [1861]) *Great Expectations*, London: Penguin Popular Classics.

Eisenstein, Sergei (1949) *Film Form: Essays in film theory* (ed. and trans. Jay Leyda), New York: Harcourt, Brace & World.

Gardner, John (1983) *On Becoming a Novelist*, New York: Harper & Row.

Heller, Zoë (2003) *Notes on a Scandal*, London: Penguin.

McEwan, Ian (1997) *Enduring Love*, London: Jonathan Cape.

McEwan, Ian (2007) *On Chesil Beach*, London: Jonathan Cape.

Thorpe, Vanessa (2006) 'Illicit passions and a walk on the red carpet', interview with Zoë Heller about film adaptation of *Notes on a Scandal*, *Observer*, 17 December.

Wilson, Antoine (2007) *The Interloper*, New York: The Other Press.

Further reading

Green, George (2007) 'Hanging together – structuring the longer piece' in *Wordsmithery: The writer's craft and practice* (ed. J. Steel), Basingstoke: Palgrave Macmillan, pp.36–48.

This contains advice with a particular focus on scene-building within longer narratives.

11   Splicing the strands

Derek Neale

In the last chapter you examined how film and fiction influence one another. In particular you saw how the juxtaposition of film shots and its effect – often called montage – have been influenced by fiction, and in turn how such methods can usefully influence the way in which you write your fiction. In this chapter we will look at such interweaving between narratives on a larger scale, to see how the juxtaposition and splicing of disparate strands can create tension. We will examine how characters and their associated storylines converge – how they are propelled towards one another. We will explore how structuring a piece of fiction in this way might alter its pace, sometimes speeding the reader on, sometimes making them pause. By trying these various techniques, we will also consider how they can make a narrative work in dramatic and poetic ways.

Converging characters

One of the first films to use juxtaposed shots, Edwin S. Porter's docudrama *The Life of an American Fireman* (1903), is constructed by cutting between different scenes of incomplete action – from the firemen racing towards a fire, to the studio scene of the mother and child trapped inside the building, then back to the firemen arriving at the fire, and so forth. When the two sets of characters meet – the firemen rescue the mother and child – the two spliced strands converge as one. This outcome is relatively obvious for the audience to pick up on, long before the firemen arrive at the scene.

Sometimes the point at which larger, spliced narrative strands might converge is less obvious. This uncertainty in the reader or audience is something you can use in your storytelling. It is a source of tension because the reader is always speculating about how the strands might meet. One of the most commonly used methods in film and fiction is to cut between strands involving two different characters. Peter Carey's novel *Oscar and Lucinda* (1988), which announces two narrative strands in the title, offers an example of this. Oscar Hopkins's narrative begins when he is young:

> Oscar was fifteen, an age when boys are secretive and sullen. Yet he did not question his father's views. He knew his own soul was vouched safe and when he read the Bible, aloud, by the fire, he placed no different interpretation upon it than the man who poked the little grate and fussed continually with the arrangement of the coal. They both read the Bible as if it were a report compiled by a

conscientious naturalist. If the Bible said a beast had four faces, or a man the teeth of a lion, then this is what they believed.

(Carey, 1988, p.8)

The setting is Devon, England, 1856. Oscar's naturalist father (the man who poked the little grate) is a member of the Plymouth Brethren. He is a non-conformist, as Oscar himself grows to become, though one of a rather different ilk. In fact Oscar comically rebels against his upbringing by becoming an Anglican priest.

Lucinda Lepastrier's narrative begins in the mid-nineteenth century as well, but in New South Wales, Australia:

> The doll was her ninth birthday present. It had come in a ship across the world, just as her mama and papa had. She was very pretty with bright blue eyes and corn-yellow hair. Her cheeks were as smooth as china, and cool against your neck on a hot day. The doll had been purchased by Marian Evans who had gone in a coach to a great exhibition, especially to buy it. At that time Lucinda – much impressed by what she called the 'expedition' – did not know what an exhibition really was, but it later occurred to her that the doll must have come from the building she was to so admire in her adult life – the Crystal Palace.

(p.78)

When realising that there are two separate strands, the reader weighs up all the contrary and similar facts about each of the characters   Australia, England, male, female, their ages, their depiction as solitary children with no siblings. The reader looks for ways in which these two characters might one day converge. A fantastic image of a glass church has appeared in the novel before these characters are introduced. So, given the historical setting, the aware reader will be alerted to the possibility of a connection with Crystal Palace (built in 1851 to house the Great Exhibition). From the contrast in locations the reader may also expect an antipodean journey at some point in the narrative – and they do indeed get one. The characters first meet on a voyage from England to Australia.

ACTIVITY 11.1 Writing	Write (up to 200 words) in the third person about a single day in the life of a character who lives in a village or on a particular street. This may be a historical or contemporary character. You might use a character you have already created in your notebook. Write (up to 200 words), again in the third person about the same day, but this time concerning the activities of another character in the same village or street. Your two characters should not yet meet.

You may have found that, having created one character, it was difficult to exclude him or her from the second narrative. A tension can arise between the two characters, even in the writing. The key is to communicate this tension to the reader. An awareness of it will make the reader want to carry on. You will be thinking about how you might do this shortly, and will be using these same characters in the next writing activity, so keep them in mind.

A note on genre

In *Oscar and Lucinda*, the reader's expectation of a possible romantic link between the characters is compounded by the contemporary first-person narrator. This narrator opens the novel but rarely, after the first two chapters, intervenes with any first-person pronouns, conducting most of the narrative in the third person.

The narrator is hardly present as a character in the action. Yet he implies that Lucinda is fundamental to his own genealogy and explicitly calls Oscar his great-grandfather in the book's opening paragraph. The reader is led to believe that this is a family saga, but also, more prominently, a love story. The pacing of the spliced narrative strands about one character and then the other suggests that Oscar and Lucinda will eventually fall in love and have children – giving rise to the narrator's own bloodline. Indeed, the first of these expectations is fulfilled – they fall in love. Yet in a tragic and comic series of events the usual romantic outcome – marriage and reproduction – is confounded. In this way, Carey plays with the reader's expectations about the generic content of romance narratives. He plays similarly with the reader's expectations surrounding historical narratives and family histories.

This generic play is also apparent in the odd appearance of one of the main characters. The narrator admits that he and his close family look like Oscar, who is not a conventional romantic hero: 'we had red hair, long thin necks like twisted rubber bands'. The narrator wishes his appearance were different, as does even the 'pretty' Lucinda, who longs for different-coloured hair. This is all playing against the grain of a conventional romance story. Similarly, Oscar and Lucinda are compelled not by the conventions of sexual attraction, but by their shared and often illicit obsession – gambling. You will recall from Chapter 1 the tactic of playing with genre and playing against the grain of a genre. In this respect Carey plays with the reader's generic expectations on several levels. The reader is expecting the characters to converge in a certain way; the narrative then twists slightly, which is both entertaining and more intellectually stimulating than if the convergence of the two strands was generically straightforward.

Time and length

Oscar and Lucinda is a large novel, in which there is plenty of room to include cross-cut strands like this. There is less scope in briefer narratives, but it can still sometimes prove to be a useful method. When writing and editing your stories, you should always ask: whose story is it? This is good and often-given advice. In short fiction the story invariably belongs to one character, and by thinking otherwise you risk dispersing the focus and weakening the narrative. Yet, you will encounter occasions when a story rightly belongs to two characters and you will need to structure the narrative around this double approach. The longer the story, the more likely it is that such cross-cutting will be effective. When structuring a story in this way, it is better to embark on both strands as soon as possible; beware of leaving it too long to establish the second strand. Then ensure that you maintain both strands in a balanced way.

Using a tight time frame – of a day, for instance – is a handy constraint, assisting the writer's need to shape the action. James Joyce's *Ulysses* (1960 [1922]) happens in a single day, as do numerous other novels, including Graham Swift's *Last Orders* (1996), which you will be looking at in the next chapter.

ACTIVITY 11.2
Writing

The characters you created in Activity 11.1 should now meet. Choose a time frame. For instance, the action could happen in the course of a day, a morning or even within an hour. Your characters should meet towards the end of this time frame – for instance, at the end of the day. Write about this meeting (up to 300 words). If you are struggling for a reason for them to meet, choose from the following:

- one character is looking for the other;
- one spills a drink over the other;
- they have an argument;
- they have coffee or tea together;
- they are involved in an accident.

DISCUSSION

In writing your narrative, your first decision will have been about how your characters might meet. You may have realised that the meeting did not need to be dramatic – they did not have to fight or marry – though, of course, these are possibilities. Characters can converge in a number of ways: for example, they might just pass in the street. By placing the meeting at the end of your time frame, you may have produced a rising action (as described in Chapter 6) leading up to this. You may have seen that it became the climax of your narrative. This can work well but sometimes it can present challenges, as we will now see.

Meetings

Finding the way in which two characters converge can actually define the size and genre of your narrative. Sometimes the meeting can be a relatively low-key event, if the emotional trajectory of the characters has been well enough established. It is the significance of events to the characters that is important, not the status of those events. It will be more difficult to achieve a momentous culmination of events in briefer narratives. Marriages, deaths, robberies and murders can appear melodramatic if not given enough narrative space, but they can still be achieved. Much depends on where you position such events in the narrative.

In Tobias Wolff's short story 'Bullet in the Brain' (1996), a tale of only 2,500 words, two characters converge: a book critic and a bank robber. The story is told in a third-person narrative which is closely aligned with the main character, Anders, 'known for the weary, elegant savagery with which he dispatched almost everything he reviewed' (Wolff, 1996, p.200). The narrative gives only a few lines of dialogue to the bank robber because he is really only a catalyst for the story. Yet from the title onwards the reader is aware that there is going to be a collision.

Anders is in a queue at a bank and casts a tired eye on those around him, noticing especially, and crucially, the type of language being spoken. The bank robbers enter the scene and start using the clichéd language of the street and of movies (dead meat; bright boy; *capiche*). Anders can do nothing but exclaim, and eventually laugh. This gets him into trouble – but the bullet heralded by the story's title doesn't end the story. Anders is shot in the head but Wolff arranges it so that this happens right in the centre of the narrative – Anders dies but paradoxically lives on for a few more pages. The rest of the story deals with an incident from Anders's past, recalled because a neurotransmission is sparked by the bullet entering Anders's head. This memory illuminates his personality for the reader. It is noticeably just one event, not the clichéd 'life passing before his eyes', though the narrator informs the reader of some of the events Anders is not remembering, cleverly sneaking in some backstory. The positioning of the shooting gives some emotional depth to Anders. By the last sentence, the reader better understands his sense of humour, his cynicism, and the tragedy and comedy of his life. If Wolff had put the murder right at the end, this would have been a very different story, one dominated by the melodrama of the shooting. Similarly if all of his life had appeared to him after he was shot, the method would have seemed hackneyed and the narrative would have been too crowded, the impact of individual memories would have been lost.

ACTIVITY 11.3 Writing	Cut and paste the narratives of your two characters from Activity 11.1 with the narrative of their eventual meeting from Activity 11.2, adding or editing as necessary to create a story (up to 1,000 words). Try to arrange the story so that it has juxtaposed strands, alternating between the two characters until they meet. Note that the meeting does not now need to be at the end of the time frame of your narrative. Place it where you think it works best.

DISCUSSION	This method of splicing strands can be difficult to pull off satisfactorily in a brief narrative, but attempting it may give you the incentive to use such methods on other projects. There is no right way of going about it – writing an individual character's narrative in its entirety from beginning to end, then doing the second character, or writing the narrative section by section, are both viable approaches. But try to retain your initial excitement and interest in how your characters will meet; your reader will pick up on this. Each story you write will create its own demands and will usually suggest its own methods. Obviously there is plenty of room for using this technique when writing a novel. It can offer a stimulating bonus to the writer, relieving the possible tedium of always being with one character. You can vary the voice and point of view between the strands, perhaps using the past tense in one and the present in the other, or using a stream of consciousness in one strand and an objective third-person point of view in the other.

These sorts of experiments can create structural challenges. For example, how should you unify the separate parts? How do you begin such a narrative so it appears to include, or launches, both strands? And at what point should you make the switches between the strands?

Gathering the strands
Controlling tension

What you might discover in first trying this method is that by juxtaposing the two strands you interrupt the linear progression of the action. This is useful because it can prevent some parts of your story appearing too straightforward or melodramatic. The narrative might otherwise appear too unrelenting, too full of major events, to be plausible. Also, by stopping the action at crucial points you might sometimes be able to leave the reader on a precipice, wanting to know what happens next. Switching between strands at points of finely wrought tension, rather than overplaying such scenes, is comparable to when the curtain falls at the end of an act in a stage play, or the advertisement break in a television drama. It leaves the reader, like the audience for a dramatic performance, tense and eager to continue after the interval.

You will be familiar with the importance of finding the right time to leave a scene from your work in the last chapter and in Chapter 1, as well as from your work on drama throughout Part 2. It is equally important to find the opportune moment when cutting from one narrative strand to another. The new, interloping strand will often act as a relatively calming piece of narrative, and a useful contrast in pace can be created. Splicing the different strands can prove to be a way of sustaining interest, contrast and tension. However, it is important to be cautious and balanced when using this method. You don't need a tense curtain cut, leaving a scene on a cliffhanger, for every juxtaposition. In fact it would probably make the narrative too predictable if you were to do this.

It is equally important to offer some small promises – often implicit – that this new strand will eventually link back to the previous strand. The incoming strand should have an interest and momentum of its own, and these aspects should be apparent straight away. You can't afford to include a meaningless strand which doesn't help to push the whole story along. As you will recall from Chapter 9, subplots in films should be symbiotically related to main plots. This is true also of the different narrative strands in cross-cut fiction. If your interceding strand is uninteresting and holds not even a vague promise of linking to the previous strand, then your reader is liable to desert you.

A crucial element to be gauged in how you arrange your stories is how much narrative space you give to each strand. For instance, in Carey's *Oscar and Lucinda* the first seventy pages are given over to an introduction of Oscar, then some thirty pages to Lucinda's introduction, before the splicing really commences. The film version, scripted by Laura Jones (1998), begins by splicing the two strands almost immediately, in fact starting Lucinda's story before Oscar's. There is less time to establish major characters on the screen, so it is important to launch any major players as soon as possible. This is also often the case with short stories.

Gauging how much narrative space is given over to each strand can be instinctive. As indicated earlier, *Last Orders* by Graham Swift is a novel that has a time frame of one day. Four men set off to scatter the ashes of a friend, so the narrative also benefits from the structure of a journey, with definite staging points between Bermondsey, the embarkation point, and the Kent coast, their destination. As Swift says: 'I had to get the characters from London to Margate, so I had to think, "Well, they should be getting to Chatham about now", or whatever' (quoted in Baker, 2007, p.184).

The novel also offers an example of how to use multiple narrators (that is, more than two). As the story of the day and the journey unfolds, each chapter is narrated by a different character. These narratives alternate between the dramatic present of the journey and the shared past of the group. Swift says:

> in *Last Orders*, you are jumping in time and from one character to another, and conceivably someone could take it all apart and wonder if I might have had a completely different structure at first, where I followed one character all the way through. But no, I somehow knew when it should be Ray, or Vince, and when it should be in the present or the past. I had an intuition about it.
>
> (p.177)

Addressing the balance between strands is a task that you should reassess when editing, checking to see that each narrative is in the right proportion. It is also an ongoing task as you are writing. Having slightly different proportions for different strands can fundamentally alter the nature of your story. Carey's *Oscar and Lucinda*, for instance, gives more narrative space to Oscar because the novel is more his comi-tragic tale. But it is easy to imagine a version of the story in which the textual proportions were altered slightly, and in which Lucinda might get more of the narrative, and become the major figure.

You can achieve structural unity by ensuring that each fragment is complete in itself. You will have heard this advice in various parts of the drama chapters and in the last chapter, but it is important – make sure each scene and section of your narrative has a structural shape, with a beginning, middle and end. Check that each section has a narrative purpose – taking the story forward – and a dramatic action, rising to a climax, however subtle that climax might be. This will help you create a whole, unified structure. By using this technique of cutting between strands you will be creating a useful tension in the reader – the tension of delayed narrative fulfilment. However, bear in mind when cutting that it is important to maintain the structure of beginning, middle and end in each of your scenes.

Using a linking narrative

If you decide to use a cross-cut narrative method, how do you launch it? Who do you start with? The film of *Oscar and Lucinda*, like the book, deploys the framing device of a distant, contemporary relative, relating family history using voice-over. This testimony of an ancestral witness might be termed a 'linking narrative' in the novel, because it pulls all the fragments together.

In John Berger's novel *To the Wedding* (1996), several characters are spread across Western and Eastern Europe. They travel by train, by car, by motorbike, heading towards a wedding. Yet they are all 'heard' by a male character who resembles the mythical Tiresias – blind but all-seeing. Mysteriously, he witnesses all the events of the story. The man, Tsobanakos, lives in Greece, while perceiving events in France, Italy, Poland and Czechoslovakia. His entrancing, non-realistic linking narrative cuts seamlessly between countries, between the present, the past, childhood and old age, guided by the voices in his head. He sits outside a bar in the Greek port of Piraeus: 'I could hear the cranes loading, they load all night. Then a completely silent voice spoke, and I recognised it as the railwayman's' (Berger, 1996, p.11).

The railwayman is someone to whom Tsobanakos recently sold a charm in an Athens market, a gift for the man's dying, but soon to be wed, daughter. As Tsobanakos goes on to explain:

> The railwayman is talking Italian into a telephone and standing in the kitchen of his three-roomed house in the town of Modane on the French side of the Alps. He is a signalman, Grade II, and the name on his letterbox is Jean Ferrero. His parents were emigrants from the rice town of Vercelli in Italy.
>
> The kitchen is not big and seems smaller because of a large motorbike on its stand behind the front door which gives on to the street. The way the saucepans have been left on the stove shows that the cooking is done by a man. In his room, as in mine in Athens, there's no trace of a feminine touch. A room where a man lives without a woman, and man and room are used to it.
>
> (pp.11–12)

This novel has a haunting story, made more so by this surreal linking narrative. Other methods of linking narrative strands might involve an anonymous third-person voice. You could also use a character who is more closely involved with the action. There are many different options, one of which is to choose not to have any narrative linking the spliced sections, as you will see shortly.

ACTIVITY 11.4
Writing and editing

Revisit the story you wrote using different narrative strands in Activity 11.3.

Write a linking narrative (up to 300 words) which launches the two strands, which offers occasional links between the parts, and which features in the resolution. Either use third-person voice – as seen in the extract from *To the Wedding* – or the first-person voice of a witness – as suggested in the discussion of *Oscar and Lucinda*.

DISCUSSION

The easiest choice in these circumstances is an anonymous third-person omniscient voice. Yet even with this option you will still have to decide whether to make the voice dominant or more or less invisible, merging with the other narratives. There is always a challenge in choosing to use a first-person, witness narrative. Where do you position the character who is narrating in relation to the action? This can be a stimulating problem for you to solve as a writer, and often, as with *Oscar and Lucinda*, it can add another layer of intrigue and speculation to the reading experience.

Unlinked strands

Some narratives do not use a linking narrative to unite the different parts. Instead the various sections sit side by side, the writer trusting the reader to find the points of potential connection. The film *The Hours* cross-cuts between three different story strands in three different eras (1923, 1951 and 2001), as you saw in Chapter 9. Michael Cunningham's novel *The Hours* (1999), on which the film is based, cuts between the same three strands. Here there is a complicated relationship between the strands for the reader to decipher. Apparently there are no suggestions of family saga or love story (as there are in *Oscar and Lucinda*). Neither is there an overarching narrator to pull the different parts together (as in *To the Wedding*).

In fact *The Hours* has an extra narrative strand – if you count the Woolf strand, which covers her suicide in 1941 and which opens both the film and the novel. The death is placed as a starting hook for the viewer or reader, a glimpse of what happens in the future and a moment towards which all three narratives travel, either literally or thematically. At the start of *Oscar and Lucinda* the hook is two-fold: a great-grandchild (who are the great-grandparents?) and the image of a glass church (who made it?). These various types of hook are often described as proleptic – a term that derives from the Greek word for anticipation. It is a way of foreshadowing the end of a particular story at the start. It sets up the expectation of convergence – the reader or viewer will expect all the different narrative strands to head towards this culmination.

In some strands it will be a literal culmination – as is the case with the Woolf strand and her suicide in *The Hours*. The prolepsis works in a more thematic way for the other strands in the novel. For instance, the 1949 (1951 in the film) Los Angeles strand portrays a woman, Laura Brown, in the grip of mental turmoil. She appears to be struggling desperately with the conventions of motherhood and married life. The possibility of suicide gathers menacingly over her throughout her narrative. In the 2001 New York strand the theme of suicide appears via the character of Richard, a writer and best friend of the modern day Clarissa (Clarissa Vaughan rather than Dalloway, though sometimes nicknamed 'Mrs Dalloway'). Richard has written a novel in which his heroine commits suicide. He is suffering from the effects of Aids, and eventually takes his own life.

The theme of suicide is also paralleled in Woolf's novel *Mrs Dalloway* (1996 [1925]), where the character of Peter Walsh, suffering from shell shock after the First World War, commits suicide. Of special interest in *The Hours* (which was Woolf's working title for *Mrs Dalloway* when she was writing it) is the way that Cunningham, within each of the three main strands, imitates, but also creates a variation on, Woolf's style.

ACTIVITY 11.5
Reading

Read the extract from the novel *The Hours* (Reading 22 on p.360). This is a passage from the Mrs Brown strand of the novel, set in 1949, which includes sections from Woolf's *Mrs Dalloway* (which the character Laura Brown is reading).

What do you notice about the similarities and differences between the two narratives – Cunningham's and Woolf's?

DISCUSSION

Cunningham's novel is a loving tribute to *Mrs Dalloway*. Not only does he use Woolf's novel as part of his own novel's content and thematic concern, but he also, daringly, attempts a stream-of-consciousness narrative in each of his three strands. His voices are all relatively similar, and all use the present tense, as if this gives his characters quicker access to their flights of uncertain and often associative thought. All three strands can be seen to be grappling with the past, asking questions of it, in much the same way as Woolf's narrative voice in *Mrs Dalloway*.

Different streams of consciousness

Cunningham's narrative in the passage you have just read is focused on the consciousness of Laura Brown, just as Woolf's narrative is centred on the consciousness of Clarissa Dalloway. Yet Woolf's stream soon flows a little wilder. It is freer and more omniscient; it can see into the minds of any characters it chooses, even if it is focused primarily on Clarissa's thoughts. You can see this when it gains access to the thoughts of Scrope Purvis as Clarissa is waiting for Durtnall's van to pass.

Cunningham fleetingly uses some of this more wide-ranging stream of consciousness later in his novel, when he gives the reader access to the thoughts of a character called Louis. But there is generally nothing like the omniscience of Woolf's voice. The full flow of Woolf's method is best seen in the party scene at the end of *Mrs Dalloway* where the narrative perches in the consciousness of practically all the guests. It is as if she can hear all the voices of the city. The reader witnesses their reactions to each other as they pass. Cunningham's narrative is much more controlled and focused on individual points of view. This is a far safer first step when trying out the stream-of-consciousness method – otherwise you risk blurring the focus of your story.

Poetic cutting

Like *Oscar and Lucinda*, Kiran Desai's novel *The Inheritance of Loss* (2006) contains the alternate narratives of two characters. The first is Sai, an orphan and the granddaughter of a retired judge who lives in Kalimpong, north-east India, during an uprising in the Himalayan territory. Biju is the other character, the son of the judge's cook, who, having not yet attained legal US status, works in various restaurants in New York. His many chores include stirring vats of Bolognese sauce at Pinocchio's and delivering Szechuan wings with French fries on a bicycle when working for Freddy's Wok. The novel cuts between Indian and US narrative strands, but cutting is also an integral method within each strand. The narratives often don't contain consecutive action, but jump between moments and places. This is a section from Biju's narrative which gives a flavour of his cut-up, fragmentary life:

> *Biju at the Baby Bistro.*
> Above, the restaurant was French, but below in the kitchen it was Mexican and Indian. ...

> ———————

> Biju at Le Colonial for the authentic colonial experience.
> On top, rich colonial, and down below, poor native. Colombian, Tunisian, Ecuadorian, Gambian.

> ———————

On to the Stars and Stripes Diner. All American flag on top, all Guatemalan flag below.

Plus one Indian flag when Biju arrived.

(Desai, 2006, p.21)

From this fast-moving catalogue of kitchens in which Biju has worked the reader sees how much he has learned about politics and population distribution. The significant thing about Desai's narrative is that she uses such brief sections and deploys this device so freely. This is not a cutting between strands or distinct characters but between brief episodes in time and action – and sometimes just between images.

Sai's narrative is generally more consecutive than this example but it nonetheless often cuts back and forth in time, and splices the present with strands about the cook's and the judge's respective pasts, as well as Sai's initial journey to Kalimpong.

ACTIVITY 11.6
Reading

Read the following passage from *The Inheritance of Loss*. It is set at a time not long after the death of Sai's parents, when she has just come to live in the house. The cook has just presented the judge and Sai with bowls of peppery tomato soup.

What effect do you think the section breaks have on the narrative?

The judge took a spoon from a bowl of cream and thwacked a white blob into the red.

'Well,' he said to his granddaughter, 'one must not disturb one another. One's had to hire a tutor for you – a lady down the hill, can't afford a convent school – why should one be in the business of fattening the church ...? Too far, anyway, and one doesn't have the luxury of transport anymore, does one? Can't send you to a government school, I suppose ... you'd come out speaking with the wrong accent and picking your nose. ...'

The light diminished now, to a filament, tender as Edison's first miracle held between delicate pincers of wire in the glass globe of the bulb. It glowed a last blue crescent, then failed.

'Damn it!' said the judge.

In her bed later that evening, Sai lay under a tablecloth, for the last sheets had long worn out. She could sense the swollen presence of the forest, hear the hollow-knuckled knocking of the bamboo, the sound of the *jhora* that ran deep in the décolleté of the mountain.

Batted down by household sounds during the day, it rose at dusk, to sing pure-voiced into the windows. The structure of the house seemed fragile in the balance of this night – just a husk. The tin roof rattled in the wind. When Sai moved her foot, her toes went silently through the rotted fabric. She had a fearful feeling of having entered a space so big it reached both backward and forward.

Suddenly, as if a secret door had opened in her hearing, she became aware of the sound of microscopic jaws slow-milling the house to sawdust, a sound hard to detect for being so closely knit unto the air, but once identified, it grew monumental. In this climate, she would learn, untreated wood could be chewed up in a season.

(Desai, 2006, p.34)

DISCUSSION

These breaks in the storytelling are not like cuts as the curtain falls; the method is more poetic than theatrical. The arrangement of sections resembles the arrangement of stanzas within a poem and the level of development between parts of the narrative is prompted more by the sort of memory association you get in a poem than the chronology of events you get in a narrative. Similarly, it gives a primacy to images, as a poem might. Though the unreliable electricity supply is a mundane and tedious fact of life for the inhabitants of Kalimpong, the image of the bulb fading is paradoxically magnified and made distinct by putting it in its own section. It symbolises the faded grandeur and rottenness of this world, as do the worn sheets replaced by toe-pierced and equally rotten tablecloths and the microscopic jaws reducing the house to sawdust.

The Eisenstein method of film montage is often spoken of as the 'poetry of cinema' and narratives such as Desai's offer a similar hybrid method of storytelling. The novel's narrative is preoccupied with personal and cultural memory, yet the strands of past and present entwine without any conspicuous or intrusive blocks of backstory. By highlighting the imagery, the writing style enables such imagery to work on many levels, creating a poetic effect. And while the spliced strands in this method are often about different characters in different locations, they can also be about the past and the present; they can be about different facets of just one character.

ACTIVITY 11.7 Writing	Look back over the work you have done for Activities 11.1–11.4. Write the opening of a new version of the story you have already written or the opening of a new scenario with two new characters (up to 500 words). Whichever you choose, proceed by:

- *either* using a stream-of-consciousness style (as seen in *The Hours* or *Mrs Dalloway*);
- *or* using a method like Desai's, concentrating on certain images, and using section breaks freely.

DISCUSSION

Desai's use of lines to mark the division between sections is unusual. Other writers might denote a break with an asterisk, or row of asterisks. More commonly many writers just insert an extra line space to mark the difference between sections. Whatever typographic device you choose, the danger of structuring your story in such quickly spliced strands is that the narrative can become fragmentary or static. You have to remember that a story written in this style still has to carry the reader forward and to offer certain signposts to tell the reader where they are and which characters they are with. A key editorial aid in checking that such a narrative is working in the basic way in which a narrative should is to ask a draft reader specifically if they can pinpoint any places in the narrative where they get lost.

Similarly, if you used a stream-of-consciousness style, ask a reader to tell you if they found it confusing. Stream of consciousness is an easy style to write in a loose way – a way that can render it incoherent for your reader. The challenge with Woolf's method is that if it is badly done the reader can easily get lost and misunderstand the narrative. You need to give the reader proper signposts to distinguish between characters and to show who is thinking what thoughts at any particular time. Cunningham's more restricted type of stream of consciousness is a little easier to pull off. It is important to establish the method early on in your story – whether you are going to stick with one character's consciousness or have a degree of omniscience – and to be consistent in this method.

Conclusion

In this chapter you have seen how the storylines for major characters can be developed by splicing narrative strands. Characters can be written so that they converge, and the expectation of them heading towards one another can create tension for your reader. By trying the methods of switching between narrative strands you have explored the possibility of delaying narrative fulfilment, and creating contrasts in pace. The position of events within a narrative can be all-important. You have seen how narrative hooks might launch your story, and considered using linking narratives to unite the different strands, as well as the alternative of just sitting the strands side by side.

Finally, you have seen how the idea of splicing narrative strands can be poetic and empower images to work on a symbolic as well as a literal level. In *The Inheritance of Loss*, images of rottenness accumulate to realise the fading, postcolonial world of Kalimpong. One of the features of this decay, not yet discussed, is the voice of the judge and his particular idiolect. We will look at such voices in more detail in the next chapter.

References

Baker, Barbara (ed.) (2007) *The Way We Write: Interviews with award-winning writers*, London: Continuum.

Berger, John (1996) *To the Wedding*, London: Bloomsbury.

Carey, Peter (1988) *Oscar and Lucinda*, London: Faber and Faber.

Cunningham, Michael (1999) *The Hours*, London: Fourth Estate.

Desai, Kiran (2006) *The Inheritance of Loss*, London: Hamish Hamilton.

Jones, Laura (1998) *Oscar and Lucinda* (screenplay), London: Faber and Faber.

Joyce, James (1960 [1922]) *Ulysses*, London: Minerva.

Swift, Graham (1996) *Last Orders*, London: Picador.

Wolff, Tobias (1996) 'Bullet in the Brain' in *The Night in Question*, London: Bloomsbury.

Woolf, Virginia (1996 [1925]) *Mrs Dalloway*, London: Penguin.

Further reading

Crace, Jim (1999) *Being Dead*, London: Penguin.

This novel is a fiction which, like 'Bullet in the Brain', positions its potentially melodramatic event early on. The two main characters are murdered in the opening of the narrative. The rest of the novel traces their life histories, the emotional journeys of both characters, while their unfound bodies decompose.

Ondaatje, Michael (1992) *The English Patient*, London: Picador.

Michaels, Anne (1998) *Fugitive Pieces*, London: Bloomsbury.

Both these novels use poetic stanza-like splicing between strands, like Desai's method (though they don't use line separators). They are novels that work less chronologically, or at least are less linear in their way of presenting the story's chronology, in comparison to a story like *Oscar and Lucinda*.

12   Voices in fiction

Derek Neale

The fiction writer is often seen as an impersonator, mimicking the various voices that speak in the dialogue of the story but also manufacturing a voice to carry the narrative of his or her fiction. It is important to remember that a fiction's narrative voice is never quite that of its author – it is an invented voice in which the author's sensibility can be sometimes more and sometimes less easily discerned. John Mullan (2007) suggests that there was an eighteenth-century split between types of fiction writers which has prevailed to the modern day: those who follow Fielding, in whose fiction the author's voice is prominent, and those who follow Richardson, by including 'other' voices in their storytelling. This chapter will concentrate on the latter definition of fiction as a form of impersonation. We will examine how writing fiction might connect with some of the techniques for writing dialogue and monologues looked at in Part 2 when exploring writing for stage, radio and film.

Dramatic monologues

As you will recall from Chapters 5 and 7, dramatic monologues are made interesting for the audience in a variety of ways. They can't afford to be clogged with unpronounceable clauses, no matter how grammatically correct such clauses might be. It is important that the actor is able to energise the monologue and bring it alive in performance. Monologues and dialogue should have an aural rather than a written quality. Narrations in novels and stories can work in similar ways. It is sometimes useful to view a narrative voice as a dramatic monologue, and the act of reading as a performance of that voice.

We will now examine an extract from a dramatic monologue by Alan Bennett which was performed as part of a series of television monologues called *Talking Heads*.

ACTIVITY 12.1 Reading	Read the start of Bennett's play *Her Big Chance* (Reading 23 on p.364). • What are the elements that make this writing dramatic? • What makes it interesting? • What do you learn of the character?
DISCUSSION	This drama is unusual because monologues are rarely used in television, especially not for a whole play as was the case in this series. More commonly in plays, for all media, monologues contribute a small part of the action. Some plays will not contain any monologues.

The key to writing a dramatic monologue, one that entertains and engages its audience, is to make it dialogic in some way, so that more than one voice and character is suggested in the speech's single oration. This is achieved here by the exchanges with Rex and later with Spud. There also seems to be a comic and ironic difference – a dialogue if you like – between what Lesley says and what actually happens. There is a dramatic hook at the start ('I shot a man last week') which is eventually explained when it transpires that Lesley is an actress. The voice interests the reader and the audience because the important information about acting is delayed.

Lesley's speech is typified by hyperbole and overstatement ('I must must must get involved, right up to the hilt') and by the strangely complicated diction which often reveals Lesley's aspirations. Sometimes it reveals that she is pretentious (the motel ambience; veneer of civilisation). It often sits comically against the reality of her dealings with dubious characters with names like Spud.

Narrative voice

The strength of Bennett's monologue as a narrative is that it offers a concerted point of view, but one in which the audience – and even the reader – also gets an ironic glimpse of a viewpoint other than the narrator's. In this sense the audience/reader has to work hard, as Bennett says:

> there is a single point of view, that of the speaker alone with the camera, and with the rest of the story pictured and peopled by the viewer more effort is demanded of the imagination. In this sense to watch a monologue on the screen is closer to reading a short story than watching a play.
>
> (Bennett, 1988, p.7)

Bennett goes on to suggest that the narrative in such monologues offers 'a stripped-down version of a short story' and that the style of the storytelling is 'necessarily austere'. Any literary stylistics ('he exclaimed' instead of 'he said', for instance) would appear too self-conscious in performance. He also suggests that adverbs 'over-egg the pudding or else acquire undue weight in the mouth of a supposedly artless narrator' (p.7). This is useful advice, not only when hearing and composing dramatic monologues, but also when creating the voices of narrators in your fiction.

We will now explore how such monologue voices might be used in a short story.

ACTIVITY 12.2 Writing	You will remember the different types of voices in Figure 7 on p.108. Pick one of the voices you have not yet used and write a short passage of fiction (up to 400 words) using that voice.

DISCUSSION	This discipline of keeping to the voice of a narrator – keeping within the idiolect, keeping to the diction, keeping to the perspective – is an important skill when writing fiction. At first it may seem 'austere', as Bennett calls it, but if done well it can allow the reader to see around and between the words, to imagine the full and complex world surrounding the narrator. It can be rewarding to apply some of the methods used on idiom and idiolect from Chapters 4, 5 and 7 to your narrators' voices, specifically when the narrator is the first-person voice of a character situated inside the world of the story.
	As part of your editing process you should always read your narratives out loud, as if you were enacting them. This will often give you a different insight into how well the voice is working in terms of consistency, rhythm and pace.

Voices from work

Lesley's voice in Bennett's monologue is very much a product of the work she does – acting. You will recall in *The Inheritance of Loss*, looked at in the last chapter, how the judge uses the word 'one' instead of 'you' or 'I' or 'we' ('one's had to hire a tutor'; 'one must not disturb one another'). It reveals much about him as a character, illustrating the sort of work he once did before retiring but also revealing how he now relates to the world around him. It is a symptom of decay, and symbolic of how he has become isolated and divorced from normal modes of communication. You will recall also my professor (in Chapter 4, p.54) using repeated, oratorical turns of phrase in a public situation: 'it seems to me'; 'that is to say'; 'as it were'. Such features of language can bring a narrator's voice alive, because they reveal much about the context in which the character is speaking.

ACTIVITY 12.3 Reading	Read the extract from Graham Swift's novel *Last Orders* (Reading 24 on p.366). • What typifies the way in which the character-narrator speaks? • What idiom or dialect do the characters use?

DISCUSSION	The narrator here uses the present tense as if he is reporting events, with no interpretation. There is a predominance of short sentences and brief clauses. Yet there are no hesitations, no meaningless lines of dialogue, as there might well be in such a real-life exchange. Nothing is included which does

not add to the narrative. Certain parts of speech are repeated to characterise the narrator, but these also typify the idiom (South London) that is used by all the characters – 'aint' instead of 'is not' and 'don't' instead of 'doesn't'. You will notice that there are small variations between characters. Vic, for instance, the undertaker and a slightly more formal character, says 'isn't' and not 'aint'. Many of the phrases and sentences in both the narration and the dialogue are elided, with little opening words lopped off – 'went a treat' instead of 'it went a treat'; 'managing' instead of 'she is managing'. And some clauses, which might ordinarily be attached to sentences with a comma, sit in their own sentences ('Like he's building up steam.'), the punctuation arranged as if Swift is directing an actor how to say the lines.

Stylising voices

The voices in *Last Orders* could be seen to exemplify 'poor English' and to contain clichés – 'building up steam', for instance. The voices use language in a way that may seem over-familiar, and in these types of narrative the important and much repeated creative writing advice – that you should always avoid cliché – is put in a different perspective. Such voices can often rely on the use of cliché. But the writer still has to be in full control of how such figures of speech are used. Many of the characters in the novel have lines with double negatives – 'they didn't have no honeymoon' (Swift, 1996, p.29) and sometimes triple negatives – 'aint never gone nowhere' (p.6). Such features of language are modulated by Swift, so that they reflect the idiom and idiolect of his characters. They appear consistent with the world he is creating.

Swift says that *Last Orders* was different from his other books:

> something happened which made the language different. I think it was to do with trusting, more than I ever had done, so-called ordinary language – the language of people who you could say, wrongly, aren't so articulate. I was using a sort of language of the street; not directly, in that it was not like a tape-recording, but I was using it, and found it very liberating. I found all the apparent limitations of it not to be limitations at all, and this language could be very eloquent, just as more articulate language can be a barrier. So I got interested in simpler words, simpler phrases, shorter and more economic sentences, which might be more transparent and might get you more quickly to the things that matter.
>
> (quoted in Baker, 2007, pp.183–4)

Interestingly Swift emphasises, as Bennett does, the economy of the voice. Yet he says it is not like verbatim, recorded speech. There is a degree of stylisation involved and the conciseness of the speech leaves a great deal unsaid. In these exchanges the subtext – as explored in Chapter 5 – is crucial, making the reader work hard in imagining the dynamics between the various characters. For instance, throughout the early part of the novel you realise that Lenny is often sniping at Vince (the driver of the car in the chapter you have just read), often ironically calling him 'big boy'. This dynamic is well established between the two characters by the time, later in the narrative, the reason for it is revealed – Vince was going out with Lenny's daughter but stopped seeing her after she fell pregnant.

The characters in *Last Orders* are clearly differentiated. One of the devices that separates them is the nature of their different jobs – Jack, the dead character, was a butcher; Vince is a car salesman; Ray, a fruit and vegetable seller; Vic, an undertaker.

ACTIVITY 12.4 Writing	Think of a character in a particular profession in which you have never worked. If you need a prompt, choose from one of these: judge, waitress, waiter, professor, nurse, bricklayer or journalist.

Write a short passage (up to 400 words) in the voice of your character in which he or she recounts to work colleagues a meeting with either a friend or an associate.

DISCUSSION	In order to write this voice you probably needed to do some imaginative research on the vocabulary such a character might use – as Swift had to. When creating character voices it is also helpful to think of word order and particular grammatical formations and abbreviations, and the formalities and informalities that might be appropriate to the character. It can be helpful to collect the features of language that a character uses and which might encapsulate that character. You may have found that the context was crucial. Where was your character situated – were they in familiar or unfamiliar surroundings? This can have an important effect on the type of language they might use.

It is important when getting your narrator to, in effect, 'tell a story', that the voice is made dramatic in some way. Try to avoid a flat recounting of events. You can include direct speech of other characters (as Swift does) or you can make the exchanges more reported and less direct (as Bennett does).

You can return to this activity to try some other professions, and also try one which you know. Writing the voices of a familiar workplace offers rich possibilities for impersonation and stories, but it can sometimes be more difficult to objectify and imitate in a stylised fashion the voices closest to you.

Phonetics

In Activity 12.4, you may have tried to write some sort of dialect or attempted to establish the idiolect for your character. You have seen the dangers of using too many apostrophes and offering complicated phonetic spelling when writing voices for the stage, film and radio. You will recall, for instance, the script of *The Singing Detective* in Chapter 9 – 'Lovely bit o' plum, yunnit? Thou costn't byut plum' (Reading 21, p.356). If this featured in a novel it could present a serious difficulty for your reader. But you will also recall one of the passages from *Cloud Atlas* in Activity 1.4 of Chapter 1: 'Old Georgie's path an' mine crossed more times'n I'm comfy mem'ryin' (Mitchell, 2004, p.249). This passage is written phonetically and quickly establishes the narrator's way of speaking. In the space of just a few lines the reader is able to tune into and read the voice. Phonetics can work remarkably well in a narrative. However, it is important to strike a balance when picking the phonetic features of the voice for your reader. If you have a voice which you represent as 'I wa' goin' to wor' whe' I sa' 'im comin' ou' of 'is 'ouse', you will see how difficult it is to understand and read – partly because in this instance the apostrophe has been overused. Such a voice would be especially problematic over an extended narrative. It is also very difficult to maintain consistency when stylising a voice by using so many elided words.

It is always important to hear such voices as you write them. Yet it is often better to stylise the imitation by using word choice and word order rather than relying too heavily on apostrophes to mark pronunciation. Pick key features of the language being used rather than attempt to achieve a total phonetic imitation. It is imperative that you are consistent in the way that you stylise an idiom and a character's voice. Often the use of one or two words on a fairly regular basis can engender a dialect. For instance, 'mind' when used at the end of a clause – 'I was going down the road mind' – suggests a Geordie accent; 'didnae' instead of 'didn't' suggests a Scottish voice. Make sure you use the same kinds of word choices and turns of phrase throughout. You will find it easier to be consistent if you deploy fewer key features to represent the voice. This will also give your reader a clearer sound for a voice. For instance, compare the apostrophe-filled sentence above with this version: 'I was going to work, wasn't I, and that's when I saw him. Coming out his house, wasn't he.' The simple repetitions – 'wasn't I', 'wasn't he' – give a quick idea of the rhythm of the voice and give the first clues to the psychology of the character.

Fictional communities

The level of imaginative yet consistent impersonation in *Last Orders* has the effect of inviting the reader into a community of characters. In many ways this is the trick that all fiction is trying to pull off. The narrator's voice, and how convincing it might appear to the reader, is the key to this invitation. It needs to be consistent with itself and with its surroundings. If it fails on either of these counts then the reader will not believe in it. Joshua Ferris's novel *Then We Came to the End* (2007) creates a fictional world which is a workplace community. It is narrated unusually in the first-person plural. It is set in the offices of an advertising agency in Chicago:

> Things got very quiet, until Joe himself finally broke the ice. 'By the way,' he said. 'How are you all doing with the cold sore spots?'
>
> We were in the process of coming up with a series of TV spots for one of our clients who manufactured an analgesic to reduce cold sore pain and swelling. We took in Joe's question kind of slowly, without any immediate response. We might have even exchanged a look or two. This wasn't long after his second promotion. Doing okay, more or less, we said, in effect. And then we probably nodded, you know, noncommittal half nods. The thing was, his question – 'How are you all doing with the cold sore spots?' – didn't seem a simple question in search of a simple answer. So soon after his promotion, it seemed more like a shrewd, highly evolved assertion of his new entitlement. We didn't think it was actual concern or curiosity for how we were progressing on the cold sore spots so much as a pretense to prod our asses.
>
> (Ferris, 2007, p.93)

The 'we' is the communal group that works in the office. Even though the novel is written in the first-person plural, different individual voices frequently enter into the narrative, such as Joe's at the start of this extract. The use of 'we' holds two immediate connotations – the royal 'we', which implies a dominant, incontestable opinion (we think this is good and that is bad and will not be contradicted); the slightly spooky 'we', which often evokes a childlike but potentially threatening confederacy (we don't like you). Both of these are suggested to the reader by the use of 'we' in Ferris's novel. The use of 'we' also seems most appropriate because the novel is concerned with the way in which office life erodes individual sensibility, creating mythical groupings – the community of workers, the bosses, those who are too capable, those who are less capable – and feelings of paranoia and resentment, feelings of inclusion and exclusion.

Voice register

Ferris's method – explicitly using 'we' – is an unusual tactic. Fictions like Swift's *Last Orders* are in effect doing the same thing, inviting the reader into a world with set boundaries and long-standing relationships, in which exchanges between characters were going on long before the reader first engages with the narrative. Swift impersonates the particular voices of his characters by portraying their register – their idiosyncratic syntax, word choice and general use of language. In your own fiction the key is to locate the register of your characters' voices. The most effective writing doesn't use unnecessarily complicated or erudite language but rather uses words and turns of phrase that are appropriate for the character and the particular fictional community that the character inhabits. This is still the main task for the writer – identifying the community and finding the right register – even when the narrator is ostensibly presenting the world of a solitary character, as you will now see.

ACTIVITY 12.5 Reading	Read the following extract from 'Prelude to an Autobiography: A fragment' by Amit Chaudhuri.

- What characterises the voice of the narrator and the depicted fictional community?
- What do you think of the writing?

> I felt the urge to write this after I began to read Shobha De's memoirs. If she can write her memoir, I thought, so can I. For who would have thought, Shohba De least of all, that one day she would write her life story for other people to read? She had been an ordinary, if beautiful, girl who got recruited (as she says) from a middle-class home into modelling, never particularly interested in studies (I was the same at her age), and then, through accident and ambition, got married into one of Bombay's richest families, started her own magazine and began writing her own gossip column, got divorced, reinvented herself as a writer of middles for Bombay newspapers, married again, became India's first successful pulp novelist, and now has written her memoirs. Through what a strange chain of events people arrive at the world of writing – and Shobha De's transformation has been one of the most unexpected in my lifetime. It shows me the endless possibilities of the society we have lived in. And I ask myself the question: if she can be a writer, and inscribe her thoughts and impressions in language, why not I?
>
> There's the question, of course, of who would want to read my memoirs, or whatever it is I'm setting out to write – because I'm not altogether sure what it is. But (although I've never seen myself as a writer before) these are questions, I'm certain, that preoccupy

(inasmuch as I can enter the mind of a writer) all who write (it's an area I know little about). And it consoles me to think that at one time every writer must have done what I'm doing now, starting out and not knowing where it was leading to. It's not a feeling you can communicate to someone who's never tried it. Some people, I'm sure, end up taking this route by intention and dedication, after years of preparation – my daughter has a friend who, at thirteen, is already writing lovely poems that have been published in *Femina* and her school magazine; I'm sure she'll be a fine writer one day, and she looks set for that course. Others, like myself, and probably Shobha De, arrive at that route by chance (although Shobha De very differently from me), and it's from her that I take a kind of courage, that she should have ended up a writer, although it makes me smile even as I say it.

(Chaudhuri, 2002, pp.70–1)

DISCUSSION	This is a piece of writing which exemplifies the challenge to the author when imitating character voices. If necessary the writer must write as if he or she is just learning to write, as if unable to write very well at all. This is what Chaudhuri is doing here in what is, in effect, an imitation of a new writer's first attempts at a memoir or diary. The female narrator is well-educated and verbose. In this fictional world she is ambivalently affected by a character – Shobha De. She is impressed by her former friend's success, and prone to deride it. Schoolgirl rivalry has carried on into adulthood. The narrator does not have a problem producing words – she is the opposite type of character to Swift's reticent men in *Last Orders*. Her problem lies in arranging those words. She is far more naive about literary style and eloquence than Chaudhuri himself, yet the story is true to this character. All writers might recognise the struggle of the narrator as she articulates the mixed emotions involved with 'trying to frame a sentence', as she later terms it. The sentencing is in fact often grotesquely protracted, with added clauses, digressive thoughts, and an over-use of brackets.

Writing in different registers

Chaudhuri's story offers an important lesson because it illustrates how you may sometimes have to write a less coherent narrative than you are really capable of. With such narrators you will have to quell your urge to put the verb in the right place, to make the sentence succinct, to cut the excess or rearrange the phrasing – because if you did so it would betray the voice of your narrator. In fact, the craft of creating such a voice consists largely of getting words in the wrong place, and allowing them to stay there because this reveals a truth about the character. This is the supreme test of fictional ventriloquism – writing a voice that is true to the story you are trying to tell – and this is what Swift was talking about when he talked of finding a natural eloquence in the voices of his characters.

Jane Rogers's novel *Mr Wroe's Virgins* (1991) tells the story of a nineteenth-century prophet who declares God to have told him to take seven virgins into his house. The novel, partly based on historical fact, is narrated from the viewpoint of four of the women, offering perspectives often of the same events, spliced together in alternating versions. We get religious virtue and a zealot's belief from Joanna:

> 'The Lord has instructed me to take of your number, seven virgins for comfort and succour.'
> Praise God. This is the sign the women are not forgot. My heart leaps to his words, as the instrument to the hand of the craftsman.
>
> The joy of that moment will never leave me – nor, I think, will it be easily forgotten by any of those blessed enough to be present. God was indeed among us, He spoke to our hearts, He called us to join His glorious service.
>
> (Rogers, 1991, p.6)

We get a knowing disbelief from Leah, a character who, unknown to everyone, has an illegitimate child:

> Seven? They say his wife is sickly, but seven? Judith touches my elbow, I know, I am trying not to giggle. It is so quiet, it seems no one breathes in the whole of Sanctuary. I must not laugh. I must not. Will he really? Will they let him? Who?
>
> Once Abigail Whitehead said to me, 'Can you imagine doing it with the Prophet?' We laughed with our heads beneath our quilt work, for fear God might have overheard.
>
> (p.3)

And we get the non-believer, Hannah, who feels incredulous and betrayed:

> My aunt and uncle have given me to a prophet.
> Given – handed over – with less heartsearching than they would undergo in parting with a crust to a beggar.
>
> It is a Christian Israelite: I have been once to their meeting place, which they call Sanctuary. The prophet is a small crazed

hunch-back with the manners of a bear, who foretells the end of the world.

(p.10)

These contrastive voices reveal the differing responses of the narrators. Each voice has its typical stylistic features: Joanna with her biblical analogy; Leah with her quick repetitions and insistent questioning; Hannah with the use of dashes and her oral emphasis on certain phrases. Each voice also offers some clues to the historical era (the 1830s), but this again is done in a stylised fashion. So, in Leah's voice, for instance, we get the word 'sickly' rather than 'ill', but the historical features of the language are not overdone.

The fourth narrative voice does not appear until later in the novel because Martha, a brutalised woman who is mute, having been raised almost as an animal, initially has no language with which to speak. Her senses are heightened and she knows all the other characters by their smell. Rogers eventually introduces Martha's voice as she gradually becomes aware of language:

Eat. Eat. Stuff hot cold sharp sweet. Much. Cram it in. Tear bread crust eat. Dough soft mouth filling. Yellow cheese crumbling sour. Hard egg slippy white. Dry inside. Eat. Shove in mouth.

(p.104)

This barely coherent, primitive voice grows as Martha becomes educated and she awakens to human interaction. Her voice, as it develops, typically omits definite and indefinite articles and sometimes talks in a rambling fashion. But by the end of the book she can reveal her sensory perceptions in language and reflect on her bleak past:

It is dark, speechless. This life is its opposite. All that this life is, it was not. This life is hot sweet bright smooth gold. Has water fruit skin eyes breath dreams singing voices the flight of birds. All these were absent.

I who was a stone am now tree and bird, I who was blind am sighted. I am a living woman.

(p.251)

When talking about the novel, Rogers (2008) has revealed that this journey of Martha's into language was a real challenge to write, and was more easily realised in the television dramatisation (an adaptation written by Rogers), where Martha could be seen in action. In the novel the pre-language Martha could only be revealed through narration about her by the other characters.

Researching registers

Rogers's novel offers a strange fictional community – a hunchback prophet and seven young women. It is a *tour de force* of ventriloquism, in that it imitates historical voices and the voice of someone who has barely got a voice. Compared to the character of Martha, the narrator of Andrew O'Hagan's novel *Be Near Me* (2006) is at the other extreme of the linguistic scale.

ACTIVITY 12.6
Reading

Read the extracts from *Be Near Me* and O'Hagan talking about how his character and book came into being (Readings 25 and 26 on pp.368 and 369).

- How do the different voices in the passage contrast?
- What do you learn of the narrator from his voice?
- Are the fictional community and characters in the novel close to O'Hagan's own life experience?

DISCUSSION

Be Near Me is written in the voice of a present day Catholic priest, Father David, a highly educated aesthete who often appears more concerned about the quality of his wine than he does about mundane reality or indeed about matters of right and wrong. The story is set in a contemporary community – a small Scottish town on the Ayrshire coast. Mrs Poole, the narrator's housekeeper, is gradually seen as Father David's moral critic and the book's conscience.

The voice of the narrator, Father David, is interesting because his life history is so different from O'Hagan's – as the author admits. The problem of impersonation was one of imagining what it was like to attend a privileged public school, to read history at Balliol College, Oxford, to be a member of an elite clique which talked in Proustian quotes, and to study to be a priest in the English College in Rome. Yet O'Hagan's impersonating imagination – and his research – rose to the challenge. Father David's is a voice that is self-consciously well written. It is the opposite of the voice in the Chaudhuri story; there is an aesthetic aspect to the way in which each sentence is formed. Yet this aestheticism is also the narrator's weakness, a preoccupation which blinds him to the best way to behave in many different circumstances. Here there is a stark contrast between the postman's bleak small-mindedness and the way Father David can only respond by musing on Liszt and Chopin.

O'Hagan testifies to how 'acting' is involved when he writes. This is most apparent in the way the different voices are realised. In terms of idiolect and idiom all three voices are distinct. The postman's variety of Scottish dialect is rendered simply with features such as 'ae' replacing 'of', and 'didnae' replacing 'didn't'. Apostrophes are sometimes deployed but there isn't a profusion of them. Mrs Poole uses 'aye' and 'yer' instead of 'yes' and 'your', but is slightly more English than the postman, using 'of' not 'ae'. The novel tells the story of how Father David becomes involved in a court case after kissing a fifteen-year-old boy. This dangerous material is handled subtly and humanely, resisting the sensationalist extremes of such a topical storyline. Key to this subtlety is the narrative voice.

Unreliable narrators

You can see from the extract that the narrator in *Be Near Me* is consistent throughout in portraying a character who speaks in a certain register. Yet there is also something untrustworthy about the voice and the information it conveys. Father David is an unreliable narrator. It is as if the priest does not really hear, understand or want to give prominence to what the postman says.

Yet Father David is relatively understated in his unreliability. He is not like Dostoevsky's narrator in *Notes from Underground* (1961 [1864]), giving one set of information to the reader and then contradicting himself in the next sentence. Neither is his unreliability announced by the title of the story, as is Felix, the narrator in Thomas Mann's *Confessions of Felix Krull, Confidence Man* (1955). Instead, the sophistication of the voice acts like a mask, concealing vital details behind the narrative. Investigating the fuller story is a task for the hard-working and imaginative reader.

ACTIVITY 12.7 Writing	Write a story (up to 1,000 words) which includes a contrast between the voice of your narrator and the voices of the story's other characters. Your characters should speak in different registers; use the extracts from Rogers and O'Hagan as models. You can use characters and scenarios that you have previously thought of and sketched in your notebook. You may choose to make your narrator unreliable.
DISCUSSION	It is important that you establish a distinction between the various voices you use in any one narrative. As you progress to write larger fictions you may choose to separate different strands with different narrative voices. Always try to differentiate between such narrators by using language in slightly different ways in each voice. Make the voices in themselves distinct – rather than using italics or bold in order to distinguish them.

Conclusion

This chapter has focused on first-person narrators and the dialogue voices in your fiction. You have seen how using some of the methods associated with dramatic monologues might be of use in creating a narrative voice, and how important it is to stylise the voice using diction and syntax, in order to achieve the mimicry of idiom and idiolect. The voices you create are located in a fictional community and it is important to identify and use the appropriate register for your narrative voice, and for your dialogue voices, in order to articulate the story.

You will now go on to explore how rhetoric, the use of language as a tool of persuasion, can help to develop the style of your poetic and fictional voices.

References

Baker, Barbara (ed.) (2007) *The Way We Write: Interviews with award-winning writers*, London: Continuum, pp.183–4.

Bennett, Alan (1988) *Talking Heads*, London: BBC Books.

Chaudhuri, Amit (2002) 'Prelude to an Autobiography: A fragment' in *Real Time*, Picador: Oxford.

Desai, Kiran (2006) *The Inheritance of Loss*, London: Hamish Hamilton.

Dostoevsky, Fyodor (1961 [1864]) *Notes from Underground* (trans. Andrew MacAndrew), New York: Signet.

Ferris, Joshua (2007) *Then We Came to the End*, London: Viking.

Mann, Thomas (1955) *Confessions of Felix Krull, Confidence Man* (trans. Denver Lindley), London: Secker & Warburg.

Mitchell, David (2004) *Cloud Atlas*, London: Sceptre.

Mullan, John (2007) 'Andrew O'Hagan talks to John Mullan', *Guardian*, July podcast [online], http://books.guardian.co.uk/bookclub/ 0,,1549565,00.html (accessed 25 January 2008).

Potter, Dennis (1986) *The Singing Detective*, London: Faber and Faber.

Rogers, Jane (1991) *Mr Wroe's Virgins*, London: Faber and Faber.

Rogers, Jane (2008) Interview, A363 *Advanced creative writing*, Audio CD2, Milton Keynes: The Open University.

Swift, Graham (1996) *Last Orders*, London: Picador.

Further reading

Smith, Ali (2005) *The Accidental*, London: Hamish Hamilton.

This novel offers an example of a story told through five different stream-of-consciousness voices, each gaining the language features of individual characters. It offers a rich example of a narrative with multiple cross-cutting strands and one that contrasts radically with *Last Orders*.

Eugenides, Jeffrey (2002) *The Virgin Suicides*, London: Bloomsbury.

This is another example of a novel that uses a first-person plural narrative. A group of teenage boys narrate the story and create an effect which is sometimes like a Greek chorus, sometimes like the communal voice of intrigued neighbours.

13   Rhetoric and style

Bill Greenwell

In Chapters 10 and 11, you have looked at the influence of film techniques on narrative, and in Chapter 12, at the creation of voice. In this chapter, you will be exploring ways of developing your style, and looking in the first instance at what we can learn from the techniques used by orators – at what is called 'rhetoric'. (The word *rhetor* means 'orator'.) Around 2,500 years ago, Aristotle set out to identify the attributes a good orator needs. He insisted that the art of rhetoric is not simply that of persuasion, but 'the detection of the persuasive aspects of each matter' (Aristotle, 1991, p.70). In other words, a speaker has to make the most of the material available.

A public speech deploys, with a certain ostentation, a number of stylistic devices – devices that are important because the speech is designed to be heard at the time of its delivery, and must make its full impact then and there. These devices are subtly transferable to the page, whether in fiction, non-fiction or poetry. After all, a writer seeks to persuade readers, and to use the most persuasive aspects of style to make them read on. In this chapter, we will look at a variety of features used by writers to be persuasive in this way – features such as repetition, rhythm, qualification, parenthesis, antithesis and tone.

Persuading the reader

Rhetoric is about making the best possible use of words. It is about clarity of purpose and of meaning. Whatever you write, it has to have maximum impact, all of the time.

<table>
<tr>
<td>

ACTIVITY 13.1
Reading

</td>
<td>

Read the following extracts from John F. Kennedy's inaugural address as President, 20 January 1961, and identify what strategies Kennedy uses to hold his audience.

</td>
</tr>
</table>

> 3 ... Let the word go forth from this time and place, to friend and foe alike, that the torch has been passed to a new generation of Americans, born in this century, tempered by war, disciplined by a hard and bitter peace, proud of our ancient heritage, and unwilling to witness or permit the slow undoing of those human rights to which this nation has always been committed, and to which we are committed today at home and around the world.

> 4 Let every nation know, whether it wishes us well or ill, that we shall pay any price, bear any burden, meet any hardship, support

any friend, oppose any foe to assure the survival and the
success of liberty.

...

14   So let us begin anew, remembering on both sides that civility
is not a sign of weakness, and sincerity is always subject to proof.
Let us never negotiate out of fear, but let us never fear to negotiate.

15   Let both sides explore what problems unite us instead of
belaboring those problems which divide us.

16   Let both sides, for the first time, formulate serious and precise
proposals for the inspection and control of arms, and bring the
absolute power to destroy other nations under the absolute control
of all nations.

17   Let both sides seek to invoke the wonders of science instead of
its terrors. Together let us explore the stars, conquer the deserts,
eradicate disease, tap the ocean depths and encourage the arts and
commerce.

...

19   And if a beachhead of co-operation may push back the jungle
of suspicion, let both sides join in creating a new endeavor, not a
new balance of power, but a new world of law, where the strong
are just and the weak secure and the peace preserved.

20   All this will not be finished in the first one hundred days.
Nor will it be finished in the first one thousand days, nor in the life
of this Administration, nor even perhaps in our lifetime on this
planet. But let us begin.

...

25   And so, my fellow Americans, ask not what your country can
do for you; ask what you can do for your country.

(quoted in Corbett and Connors, 1999, pp.459–61)

DISCUSSION   Kennedy's speech was co-written with his speech-writer Ted Sorensen, and
it is often used as an example of eloquence – although you will probably
find it quite high-flown from your twenty-first-century vantage point, and
sometimes self-consciously archaic. The words 'anew' and 'heed' are
obvious examples of this kind of archaism, as is the biblical phrase
'go forth'.

However, Kennedy uses several other powerful devices in the speech, of which the most noticeable is his use of repetition (the classical term for this type of literary or rhetorical repetition is 'anaphora'). The most obvious instance of this is in the instruction 'Let both sides', which opens paragraphs 15, 16 and 17. But there are many other echoes, very often used in developing a cumulative drive: 'human rights *to which* this nation has always been *committed*, and *to which* we are *committed* today' (para.3; my italics).

Kennedy also welds together opposing ideas, so that the sentences have a symmetry, a device called 'antithesis': '*a new* endeavor, not *a new* balance of power, but *a new* world of law' (para.19; my italics).

A political speech like this, especially perhaps a formal one, depends upon repetition, not just of phrases, but of rhythms, helping the listeners to grasp the point easily and immediately. The rhythmical repetition in Kennedy's speech sometimes occurs when he develops an idea, as when the phrases have the same pattern: 'we shall pay *any* price, bear *any* burden, meet *any* hardship, support *any* friend, oppose *any* foe ...' (para.4; my italics).

If you strip the political content out of Kennedy's speech, you will discover that he is using, in a more ostentatious way, the same techniques as many powerful writers. This is as true of antithesis as it is of anaphora.

Repetition, qualification and antithesis

In Chapter 12, you saw how voices in dramatic monologues are related to voices in fiction. In a similar way, the style of an orator's speech is mirrored in the style of fiction. The task of an orator is to make the content of a speech clear, fresh, and memorable. We can see the same process at work in fiction and non-fiction, sometimes more subtly, but at other times with almost as much ostentation as in a speech. Here is a passage from Maggie Gee's novel *Grace*:

> *It was* what Bruno had wanted all along: *to be part of* them, *to be part of* it all, the easy laughter, the brotherhood. *It wasn't* just selfish, all the same. The thing he was *part of* now was *bigger than* Bruno, *bigger than* both of them. His mind ran over it again and again, *the best day* of all, *the best day* of his life.
>
> (Gee, 1988, p.53; my italics)

The repetitions here are as clear as in Kennedy's rhetoric. The difference is in the tone, which is more ruminative. An equally clear example can be found in the following excerpt from Wilson Harris's novel *Jonestown*:

> That fortune *would unfold* in Dreams long before it was conferred upon me. It *would unfold* in absurd, even humiliating, ribaldry, when Deacon taunted me in San Francisco. It *would unfold* by unforeseen stages into a honeymoon with bliss. *I would be appointed* – when Deacon vanished after Jonestown – to return in Memory theatre to his wedding feast. *I would be appointed* to read or scan the intricate, terrifying seed gestating in the womb of the Virgin of the Wilderness. *I would be appointed* to play the role of her bridegroom.
>
> (Harris, 1996, p.85; my italics)

And here is an excerpt from Zadie Smith's *On Beauty*. This time, the writing is more complex, but the techniques are still visible:

> It was bright when the service began; now the sky was overcast. The congregation were more talkative departing from the church than they had been before – sharing anecdotes and memories – but still did not know *how to* end conversations respectfully; *how to* turn the talk from the invisibles of the earth – love and death and what comes after – to its practicalities: *how to* get a cab and whether one was going to the cemetery, or the wake, or both.
>
> (Smith, 2005, p.288; my italics)

In Smith's case, she makes, as does John F. Kennedy, the second sentence repeat a pattern – the parenthetical phrases mirroring each other in phrasing, shape and rhythm. She also uses antithesis. The first sentence sets 'bright' against 'overcast'; the second sentence sets 'more talkative' against 'than before', 'invisibles' against 'practicalities'. Importantly, she also sets up a forward movement by qualifying and re-qualifying the options of the congregation: 'the cemetery, the wake, or both'.

We can see the same patterning of language at the opening of A.L. Kennedy's novel *Day*:

> Alfred was growing a moustache.
>
> An untrained observer might think he was idling, at a loose end in the countryside, but this wasn't the case. In fact, he was concentrating, thinking his way through every bristle, making sure they would align and be all right.
>
> His progress so far was quite impressive: a respectable growth which already suggested reliability and calm. There were disadvantages to him, certain defects: the shortness, inelegant hands,

possible thinning at his crown, habit of swallowing words before they could leave him, habit of looking mainly at the ground – and those few extra pounds at his waist, a lack of condition – but he wasn't so terribly ugly, not such a bad lot.

(Kennedy, 2008, p.1)

We can see the writer qualifying 'idling', 'concentrating', 'impressive' and, incrementally, 'defects', before finally qualifying Alfred not being 'terribly ugly'. We can also see how crucial her use of punctuation – comma, colon, dash – is to the movement of the prose.

ACTIVITY 13.2
Reading and writing

Read the extract from L.R. Dunne's official report on the 1943 Bethnal Green disaster (Reading 27 on p.371). The writing here is quite stilted – deliberately so, because it is a government-commissioned report. Use this as the basis for a piece of fiction (up to 400 words) in which you concentrate on using the rhetorical devices of repetition, antithesis and qualification discussed above. Don't be afraid to use them in an exaggerated way to start with. You can always cut them back.

DISCUSSION

In your rewriting you should find that you dwell a little longer on the description of the action, that you are re-focusing what you describe more consciously for your reader. Your reader will also be encouraged to pause, as you will intensify their experience with each successive qualification. Qualifying and developing an image, an action, or an idea will also help tug your reader forward, and will also help your reader to focus on the movement of the words and help to draw your reader into your writing.

Refining the focus

In this passage from Sandra Cisneros's *The House on Mango Street*, the narrator uses repetition not only to summon up a memory of her aunt, but also constantly to refine that memory:

But I knew her sick from the disease that would not go, her legs bunched under the yellow sheets, the bones gone limp as worms. The yellow pillow, the yellow smell, the bottles and spoons. Her head thrown back like a thirsty lady. My aunt, the swimmer.

Hard to imagine her legs once strong, the bones hard and parting water, clean sharp strokes, not bent and wrinkled like a baby, not drowning under the sticky yellow light. Second-floor rear apartment. The naked light bulb. The high ceilings. The light bulb always burning.

(Cisneros, 1991 [1984], pp.58–9)

Cisneros is using a more fractured sentence structure than Gee, Harris or Smith, but the techniques of repetition, antithesis and qualification are all in use. The qualification is achieved not only by the accretion of detail, but also by the clarification of one phrase in another: 'the bones hard and parting water, clean sharp strokes'. The antithesis is in the use of contrast – 'not bent', 'not drowning'. When you write like this, you are refining an image, taking the reader more deeply into what you want them to picture. This isn't the same as telling the reader what to think, but is an invitation to the reader to come closer. You might notice also that Cisneros uses another technique. When she describes what is not imagined – 'not bent and wrinkled like a baby, not drowning under the sticky yellow light' – she makes the reader visualise them just the same. The contrast or antithesis between what is imagined and not imagined makes each image come alive.

ACTIVITY 13.3 Reading	Read the extracts from the opening chapter of Chimamanda Ngozi Adichie's novel *Half of a Yellow Sun* (Reading 28 on p.372). • What do you notice about its style? • How does Adichie persuade you to read on? • What rhetorical devices are being used?
DISCUSSION	We can see some repetitions and qualifications from the outset. In the second paragraph, Ugwu 'did not believe ... did not disagree' and is 'too choked with expectation, too busy imagining'. He cannot imagine telling his sister *how* the bungalows are painted, *how* the hedges are trimmed. He marvels at *how* the bulb is bright, *how* it does not cast shadows as at home. He knows that, if he touches Anulika, she will slap his hand, perhaps slap his face. An equally important kind of repetition occurs when Ugwu is exploring the bungalow over a period of weeks: 'In the following weeks, the weeks when he examined ... when he discovered that a beehive ... and that the butterflies ...'.

Adichie could have written 'In the following weeks, when he examined ...'. Instead, she repeats the word 'weeks', to ease us into the sentence. Read any literary fiction, and you will find that the rhythm of your reading is being controlled, quietly, or even assertively, by this kind of repetition.

A similar technique is used here when Adichie has Ugwu think of evil spirits. We see from Ugwu's point of view: 'Evil spirits, that was it. The evil spirits had made him do it ... The evil spirits would not win'. An idea is introduced, developed and established. The same is true of the palm tree Ugwu sees at this stage: he sees 'a thin palm tree', and realises he has never seen 'a palm tree that short ... It did not look strong enough to bear fruit, did not look useful at all'. We are shown the palm tree. We are invited, with Ugwu, to reflect on it, and we have our view of it clarified and refined. As a writer the temptation might be to show us a palm tree, and then to move on. It might also be tempting – many new writers are tempted like this – to avoid repetition, or to use synonyms. Do not be afraid to use the same phrase more than once.

Adichie arranges her sentences so that they bring together what is, and what is not, creating a constant contrast between one feeling or place and another. She makes Ugwu look back to his old home, and around him in his new surroundings. She makes him check and then verify detail: 'He looked up at the ceiling, so high up, so piercingly white ...'. Adichie does the same when she has Ugwu conjure up his mother's making of the meal, gradually refining the act of preparation into the actions of pounding and grasping. This kind of slow, patient unfolding of information (whether of setting, character or action) will help your readers focus and re-focus, rather as if you were leading them into a succession of dark rooms, in which they had slowly to acclimatise themselves to the level of light.

Parenthesis

Adichie also uses a harder technique to master: parenthesis. Parenthesis involves interrupting a sentence, to qualify what is happening or to create the effect of an aside. When thinking of Jomo's stories, Ugwu interrupts his memory to be more precise about the details of Jomo's stories: 'he did not believe Jomo's stories – of fighting off a leopard barehanded, of killing two baboons with a single shot – but he liked listening to them'.

Virginia Woolf, as in this example from *To the Lighthouse*, frequently deploys parenthesis to elaborate a line of thought:

> They had rooms in the village, and so, walking in, walking out, parting late on door-mats, had said little things about the soup, about the children, about one thing and another which made them allies; so that when he stood beside her now in his judicial way (he was old enough to be her father too, a botanist, a widower, smelling of soap, very scrupulous and clean) she just stood there. He just stood there.
>
> (Woolf, 1971 [1927], p.22)

One of the many advantages of adding parenthesis is that it gives the writing a slightly conversational edge, because as talkers, we are naturally prone to digression. Using it will help your reader to feel just a little like a listener – and help the act of reading to involve the ear as well as the eye.

Find an instruction manual for an electrical appliance. Try rewriting an extract from it so that, instead of being – or attempting to be – scrupulously helpful, you use the conversational technique of parenthesis.

You may have found that the exercise with the instruction manual makes the text absurd or comic, because you have tested parenthesis on a non-literary form. But what you've written will seem thoughtful, even quizzical. You will doubtless feel that the parenthesis has been overdone; and, like any stylistic effect, parenthesis can certainly be over-used. You can lose your reader in a distracting sequence of asides.

Notice here that I have asked you to apply parenthesis not to direct speech, but to another kind of prose. Essentially, parenthesis will strengthen the sense of a speaker, whether the narrative is in the first person, as with Cisneros and Harris, or uses the third person, as with Gee, Smith, A.L. Kennedy and Adichie.

Variation and rhythm

Adichie also uses variation, in the lengths of her sentences and in the balance of interior monologue, explanation and dialogue. This kind of variation is important to you as a writer. A sequence of sentences of identical lengths, or with identical structures, will make the prose seem predictable and dull. As with all the techniques noted in this chapter, a little goes a long way. The aim is not to have you repeat and refine obsessively, or to count the words in every sentence to ensure that you balance longer and shorter sentences. But the rhythms *do* matter. Adichie subtly interrupts the pattern of her chapter with dialogue, just as she introduces some very short sentences. Sentences here, like 'He scrubbed the floors daily' or 'But he did not mind' or 'He froze', prevent the reader from drifting away. They re-energise the prose, because they are sudden, plain and sharp. Kennedy's speech does much the same thing. ('But let us begin' is the shortest sentence in the full speech, but there are others which contain over sixty words. Kennedy has constructed the piece so that the sentences are more often below the average sentence length rather than above it.)

Euphony

Prose writers use many poetic techniques, as you have seen in the descriptions of cutting and using imagery in Chapter 11. The techniques also include assonance, alliteration and even rhyme. In the earlier extract from Harris's *Jonestown*, 'absurd' rhymes with 'conferred'; in the Cisneros extract, the phrase 'yellow smell' occurs – an internal rhyme. These echoes, although occasional in prose, are part of rhetorical technique. They make the prose melodious – pleasant to 'hear'. The word for this is 'euphony'. There may, of course, be times when the content of what you write requires a rough, discordant or staccato sound. It is worth reading your prose aloud to see if it has appropriate, poetic qualities.

In Adichie's piece, there are several examples of euphony. For instance, in the sentence 'He heard Master's raised voice, *excited* and *childlike*, followed by a long silence and he imagined their *hug*, and her *ugly* body pressed to Master's' (Reading 28, pp.376–7; my italics), the assonance in 'excited and childlike' and the rhyme on 'hug' in 'ugly' help the sentence to move smoothly along. There is a danger that you can start to think too hard about this, and an excess of full rhyme would create an off-putting jingle, but practising euphony will help you to use it naturally. Aristotle noted the need for the musicality of prose, but was careful to issue a health warning – advising speakers not to drop into metrical rhythms, but to avoid being flat. Good prose is never flat. In fact, curiously enough, it is often reasonably easy to make good poetry out of sections of prose, whereas it is generally hard to make good prose out of passages of poetry. Prose borrows on occasion from the more pronounced rhythms of poetry; poetry tends to be denser, more compressed.

ACTIVITY 13.5 Writing	Using the third person, write two passages (each up to 250 words) about the sea, or a stretch of water. You could write a descriptive piece in which there are no people, or a passage involving a journey undertaken by two people – although, once again, avoid dialogue. In the first piece, make the water tranquil; in the second, depict the water in a storm. Use these two passages to try out different patterns of variation and rhythm, and even of rhyme.
DISCUSSION	Your second piece of writing might have had more variation in it, and a more pronounced rhythm, especially if each piece was purely descriptive. If you introduced characters and viewpoints, however, the rhythms might well have followed patterns of thought as well as the motion of tide and swell. You might also have found that, in trying to introduce verbal echoes like rhyme, you produced too rich a mixture. Some writers prefer to write prose that is more direct. Sometimes this is an issue of genre; mid-twentieth century 'pulp' writers like James M. Cain and Erle Stanley Gardner, for instance, took pains to focus the reader on the action, and to cut away long or complex sentences. The richer the mixture, the more intensely you will be expecting your readers to linger over the language. You will often also find that early chapters, in which the writer lures the

reader in, luxuriate in language a little longer. This is a question not only of preference, but of tactics.

Tone

The tone of a piece of writing is a key aspect of its style. It is a way of influencing the way your reader reads, or, as I am encouraging you to think, 'hears' the piece. Kennedy's speech is intended to be firm, judicious and weighty, but accessible. The accessibility comes from the fact that over 70 per cent of the words in the complete speech are monosyllables; the 'weight' comes from the use of formal, often slightly archaic, phrases. The Adichie extract is much more expansive, and has a leisurely, generous rhythm, so that the tone is attractive and sympathetic to Ugwu.

However, it may suit you to make the tone of your writing more excitable, more fastidious, more subdued, more hurried, more lurid, more abrupt (and so on). You may wish to make the tone relatively calm, and allow the events to carry the force of the narrative.

It is often wise to keep much of the tone of the piece understated, however colourful the language, and especially when you are not using speech. (Understatement is a matter of degree, of course.) It is exceptionally hard to sustain a narrative if it is permanently excitable – although it can be done, perhaps if you are using a voluble narrator.

The next two activities ask you to think about contrasts in tone.

ACTIVITY 13.6
Reading

Read the following extracts from Liz Jensen's *My Dirty Little Book of Stolen Time* and Hilary Mantel's *Fludd*. What do you notice about their respective techniques?

It was a Wednesday, & I had eaten little since Sunday, Fru Schleswig & I having been well-nigh broke all winter due to the sudden absence of my two most lucrative clients – Herr Fabricius, jailed for fraud ('a temporary hitch, I assure you, *skat*: I will be rogering you again within the twelvemonth'), & Herr Haboe, more permanently vanished, indeed now lying one metre below ground, cause of death one bad oyster. Our shortage of ready cash, exacerbated by my recent medical indisposition & Fru Schleswig's habitual schnapps-induced torpor, meant that this morning I was in a sorry state, half hallucinating from hunger, & Lord, I do believe that I had not even applied lipstick, perfume or rouge! The snow flurried around my head like cruel confetti, & a lone crow cawed in what remained of a tree, then – mid-croak – dropped suddenly dead with a candid little thud on to the cobbles. The snow was now thickening to a white whirr, so I ran the last stretch, & burst through the door of Herr Møller's bakery, panting. The bell clanged as I entered – O, yes, the sweet smell of sugar & yeast & hot buns! – & my fate was all but sealed.

But before I pull you with me into the dizzying whirlpool of events that innocent-looking moment sucked me – ignorant! innocent! – into, let me beg a shred of your time to say an important, nay crucial word on the subject of trust. Trust, which lies at the heart of the pact we shall make together, you & I, dear (& beloved already – yes!) reader, in the sharing of these tear-stained confessions, the grubby dog-eared journal that charts the topography of my adventures.

(Jensen, 2006, pp.5–6)

In the House there would be a coal fire, no heating in any other room, though there might be a single-bar electric fire kept, to be used in some ill-defined emergency. In the kitchen, a deep sink and a cold-water tap, and a very steep staircase, rising to the first floor. Two bedrooms, a garrett: outside, a cobbled yard shared between some ten houses. A row of coalsheds, and a row of lavatories: to each house its own coalshed, but lavatories one between two. These were the usual domestic arrangements in Fetherhoughton and the surrounding districts.

Consider the women of Fetherhoughton, as a stranger might see them; a stranger might have the opportunity, because while the men were shut away in the mills the women liked to stand on their doorsteps. This standing was what they did. Recreational pursuits were for men: football, billiards, keeping hens. Treats were doled out to men, as a reward for good behaviour: cigarettes, beer at the Arundel Arms. Religion, and the public library, were for children. Women only talked. They analysed motive, discussed the serious business, carried life forward. Between the schoolroom and their present state came the weaving sheds; deafened by the noise of the machines, they spoke too loudly now, their voices scattering through the gritty streets like the cries of displaced gulls.

(Mantel, 1990, p.13)

DISCUSSION

Jensen's narrator is plainly very excitable. In this passage, she is upbeat, scatterbrained, intimate. The tone is established by the length of the sentences, usually between thirty and forty words long – although the first sentence has over seventy words. The sense of chatter is also brought about by the frequency of parenthesis, the repeated use of questions, the exclamations, the digressions and the elaborations. Sentences are also repeatedly embroidered with additional adjectives, and the writing contains little tricks like the unusual use of ampersands, and the mixture of archaic phrasing and contemporary imagery. (The logic for this is that the speaker is a time-traveller who has experience of the nineteenth and twenty-first centuries.) Jensen's speaker is also a good example of the creation of idiolect, which was discussed in Chapter 4 (see pp.49–52).

The contrast with Mantel's passage is considerable. The tone is understated, wry and controlled. In fact, the wry tone comes entirely from the contradiction between the formality of the narrator, who, like Jensen's narrator, addresses us directly ('Consider ...'), and the bizarre lifestyle attributed to the people Mantel is describing. Mantel's narrator, however, is omniscient. As with Jensen's passage, Mantel's passage is partly a parody, in this case of social history. The comedy in this extract comes from the poker face of Mantel's narrator, who does not question what is being explained.

ACTIVITY 13.7
Writing

Write two passages (each up to 250 words), one of them in as relentlessly upbeat a tone as you can manage, the other wry and understated. What do you notice about the tactics you have employed and the choices you made?

DISCUSSION

In the upbeat piece you may have used: longer sentences, but ones containing frequent and irregular pauses; more variation of sentences; more flamboyant vocabulary; digressions and parentheses; denser clusters of consonants; questions and exclamations. Questions have a tendency to increase the pace of a piece because of the rising inflections they imply. Exclamations are particularly hard to handle: if you want your reader to smile, or even to laugh out loud, and to cause these reactions through your use of style, then an exclamation mark is often the last thing you want. It is the literary equivalent of writing 'joke' in the margin.

Understatement can take many forms. You probably varied the sentences to a lesser degree in your second piece, and it is likely that the pauses within the sentences were more regular, making the pace more steady. If you look at the opening of V.S. Pritchett's 'The Fly in the Ointment' (Reading 3, p.296), you will see that the first paragraph moves at a steady pace, and has sentences of roughly equal length (after the brief, opening, nine-word sentence, they have twenty-six, thirty and thirty-seven words respectively). Not until the fifth paragraph do the sentences repeatedly shorten, as Pritchett focuses on the son's anxiety.

I also asked you make the writing 'wry'. There is a very particular kind of understatement you can use if the events are surreal or absurd. A deadpan narrator (omniscient or otherwise) can bring out the comedy of a piece, by treating the events with almost preternatural calm. The contrast between what is said, and how it is said, will create an irony which will draw your reader in.

Conclusion

This chapter has explored a range of stylistic techniques, starting with how an orator's rhetorical style is transferable to writing prose. Not all an orator's tricks are transferable. For instance, it is rare to find in fiction the technique called 'antimetabole' – the repetition of words in successive clauses, but in transposed grammatical order, as in the line most often quoted from Kennedy's speech ('Ask not what your country can do for you – ask what you can do for your country'). Rare: but not impossible. There is an example in the passage used as a reading for the next chapter, from Annie Proulx's story 'In the Pit': she writes of 'the place where land without water was worthless, and there was a lot of worthless land' (Reading 29, p.378).

In this chapter we have considered the importance of tone. Style and tone are not subjects about which it is wise to be dogmatic, and over-use of some of the techniques outlined above – examples of which have been selected – could create mannered writing. However, the kinds of techniques illustrated here are far from incidental, and it is quite likely that noticing their use will, for a time, affect your reading. The main aim of all such techniques is to make your reader stay with you, to persuade your reader that it is worth moving on. In the next chapter, you will look at the potential of analogy and figurative language to enrich your writing.

References

Aristotle (1991) *The Art of Rhetoric* (trans. Hugh Lawson-Tancred), Harmondsworth: Penguin.

Cisneros, Sandra (1991 [1984]) *The House on Mango Street*, New York: Vintage.

Corbett, Edward P.J. and Connors, Robert J. (1999) *Classical Rhetoric for the Modern Student*, Oxford: Oxford University Press.

Gee, Maggie (1988) *Grace*, London: Heinemann.

Harris, Wilson (1996) *Jonestown*, London: Faber and Faber.

Jensen, Liz (2006) *My Dirty Little Book of Stolen Time*, London: Bloomsbury.

Kennedy, A.L. (2008) *Day*, London: Vintage.

Mantel, Hilary (1990) *Fludd*, Harmondsworth: Penguin.

Smith, Zadie (2005) *On Beauty*, Harmondsworth: Penguin.

Woolf, Virginia (1971 [1927]) *To the Lighthouse*, Harmondsworth: Penguin.

Further reading

Corbett, Edward P.J. and Connors, Robert J. (1999) *Classical Rhetoric for the Modern Student*, Oxford: Oxford University Press.

This is a compendious textbook on rhetoric, with a wide range of readings and analyses, including a very much more detailed study of John F. Kennedy's speech, and of many extracts from fiction and non-fiction. The audio recording of Kennedy's inaugural speech on 20 January 1961 is widely available on the internet.

Booth, Wayne C. (1961) *The Rhetoric of Fiction*, Chicago: University of Chicago Press.

This is a highly accessible exploration of the way in which writers persuade readers to read fiction.

14   Using analogy

Bill Greenwell

In his poem 'Brassneck', Simon Armitage refers to a pickpocket 'fishing a prial of credit cards out of [the] britches' of a football fan (Armitage, 1992, p.5). The most unusual word in that line is the 250-year-old word 'prial', a corruption of 'pair royal', which means a set of three playing cards of the same denomination. What Armitage has done is to refresh an obscure word and, in the process, to give a line in his poem an unusual new flavour.

In this chapter, we will look at how the power of analogy can transform your writing. We will also look at the potential pitfalls of analogy, and read a contrary view, that writing should shy away from being so expressive.

What is analogy?

An analogy is any word or phrase that expresses a similarity between one object, event or quality, and another. We usually divide analogies into similes (in which the comparison is explicit) and metaphors (in which the comparison is implied). Armitage's use of 'prial' is a metaphor – he doesn't prefix the term with 'like' or 'as' to compare the credit cards with a prial, as a simile would. (Notice that a simile does not always need to start with 'like' or 'as' – it can, for instance, use a phrase such as 'the shape of', or 'the colour of'.) Sometimes a single, metaphorical word has been used so frequently that it is really no longer figurative – for example, in Armitage's poem the pickpocket is 'fishing' the cards out. This use of 'fishing' is now common – although it is also slang – which makes its proximity to 'prial' all the more striking.

Surprising analogies, whether single words, phrases, metaphors or similes, can make your writing come alive. The challenge is to use the words or phrases sufficiently sparingly to give them maximum impact – a piece of writing full of these kinds of words would become unreadable, or at any rate, hard to read. However, as shown in Armitage's poem, a startling effect can be brought about by using an unusual word, especially one that is rarely seen.

ACTIVITY 14.1
Writing

Try writing a sentence or a phrase using the following words in a modern context:

- maculate (as an adjective; it means 'stained', as in the opposite of 'immaculate');

- scumbled (this is the past tense of a verb meaning to blur the outline or shape in painting, either by adding a thin, opaque film or by rubbing the surface);
- gangrel (a noun meaning a vagabond or drifter).

You can add to this list by hunting through a decent-sized dictionary for unfamiliar words.

At first, using these three words out of their original context might seem hard. But you could, for example, use all three of them to describe eyes. An image of tearfulness would give you an idea of stained, red-rimmed eyes ('maculate eyes'), or of eyes being covered by a thin film and blurred ('scumbled eyes'). Shifty eyes might be called 'gangrel eyes' (in this case, you would be re-using a noun as an adjective).

You may have found all sorts of other possibilities. Essentially what you are doing is startling your reader, momentarily, by making your writing distinctive.

Startling the reader

Startling the reader isn't a matter of applying the verbal equivalent of electric shocks – although, as we will see, there are writers who take pleasure in maintaining a very high frequency of stylistic surprises. You can startle readers in a number of ways which may be quite unobtrusive, but which will help you draw them in. You will have seen from your own reading that it is often an idiosyncratic element in the writing that engages you and makes the writing special. What form that idiosyncrasy takes will vary, but the oddity will be there, in any genre, and in any kind of writing. The oddity may occur in the situation, in the depiction of character, in the subject, or in the setting. It may also come from the use of language.

Try this puzzle. Can you spot any connections between the following items? Fog; Australia; Atlas (the figure represented in mythology as holding the world on his shoulders); a turnip; an owl; a loaf; a basket full of wriggling eels; a loaf rising in an oven; a clown; a Mexican bean.

At first sight, you may be hard pressed to find any connections between them. You may spot, perhaps, that Mexican beans and eels make surprising movements. But a turnip doesn't. It's a stolid root vegetable. It seems to be keeping odd company here. Nevertheless, there is a piece of writing which brings a turnip and a Mexican bean together (and, for good measure, brings in all the other items as well – and more). It's a poem by Sylvia Plath called 'You're'.

Read 'You're' (notice that the title is also the opening line), and see if you can work out how the images converge.

You're

Clownlike, happiest on your hands,
Feet to the stars, and moon-skulled,
Gilled like a fish. A common-sense
Thumbs-down on the dodo's mode.
Wrapped up in yourself like a spool,
Trawling your dark as owls do.
Mute as a turnip from the Fourth
Of July to All Fools' Day,
O high-riser, my little loaf.

Vague as fog and looked for like mail.
Farther off than Australia.
Bent-backed Atlas, our travelled prawn.
Snug as a bud and at home
Like a sprat in a pickle jug.
A creel of eels, all ripples.
Jumpy as a Mexican bean.
Right, like a well-done sum.
A clean slate, with your own face on.

(Plath, 1965, p.57)

DISCUSSION

Once you have spotted the clue (there are nine months from the Fourth of July to All Fools' Day on 1 April), this riddle of a poem neatly solves itself. It is a poem to an unborn child. Successively, Plath has compared her unborn child to a surprising variety of different objects and experiences. You don't have a clear idea where you are in fog, or what things look like, any more than you can 'understand' an unborn child. Your understanding is even more remote than Australia (this image would have been even more forceful in 1962, when the poem was written and when long haul flights were less common). A turnip doesn't speak and neither does an unborn child; by using the word 'mute', Plath half-animates the turnip.

This poem is unusual in that its riddle form allows it to bring together such a wide range of analogies, and I don't suggest that you should pepper your prose, poetry or drama with as many analogies as you can. 'You're' is an extreme example of using analogy to bring an idea alive – but it is useful to look at an extreme example. Even a single one of the analogies would be striking in a speech, a passage or a poem: 'The child inside her felt like a sprat in a pickle jug', for instance, would be an arresting phrase on its own.

The density or frequency of analogies is a matter of taste and judgment, and some readers and writers enjoy analogy more than others, as we shall see. Poetry usually licenses you to use analogy more frequently than if you are writing prose. But you should not neglect the potential of analogy in prose as well.

Nor should you neglect the way that Plath is using other techniques here as well as analogy. There are her signature internal rhymes: 'a creel of eels', for instance (a creel is a basket), and 'the dodo's mode'. There is some striking assonance (echo of a vowel), as in 'Gilled like a fish' or 'Bent-backed Atlas, our travelled prawn'. There is a pattern of echo ('Fools' picks up 'spool', and 'Jumpy' picks up 'jug').

Developing analogies

Most strikingly, in Plath's poem there is the use in the sixth line of 'trawling' applied to owls. Normally we think of 'trawling' as something fishermen and boats do. Of course, 'trawl' is sometimes used as an ordinary verb as well, to the extent that we might not think of it as metaphor. We might trawl through a box of objects, looking for something, for instance. But Plath is using 'trawling' here in its sense of hunting, which is what fishermen do when they are trawling. The surprise factor – the dramatic use of the word – comes in its application to a bird looking for prey. In describing an unborn child as an owl 'trawling the dark', Plath is blending two metaphors into one.

ACTIVITY 14.3
Writing

Find a picture of someone involved in an unusual occupation, or one that has been superseded by contemporary technology: for example, a telephone switchboard operator, someone ploughing by hand, a basket-weaver or a blacksmith. Look at the details of the picture. What analogies can you find for what is happening or for the details you can see? (The switchboard operator might look as if he or she was knitting, for instance.) Come up with a list of ten analogies, noting whether they are similes or metaphors.

DISCUSSION

A good analogy is one that is fresh, arresting – and not too complicated. A simile such as 'roared like a lion', or 'laughed like a hyena', is too commonplace to have any effect. It's a cliché. A simile such as 'opening the door like a moon-faced stranger holding a briefcase containing suspicious sheaves of classified documents' – presumably indicating that the action is shifty – is over-developed and unwieldy. The word 'suspicious' will cancel out most of the point of the simile. The action of 'opening the door' will be lost in the process.

One-word analogies

Analogies can be created by the subtle use of a single word, a word in which there is sudden and suggestive force. In Fleur Adcock's poem 'Incident', she refers to 'the grovelling sea' (Adcock, 1991, p.6). The word 'grovelling' is a genuine surprise, and seems to imply not only that the sea is low, perhaps at a low ebb, but is also creeping to the shore in a manner that suggests humiliation. The actual sound of the word – perhaps by sound-association with 'gravel' or 'growl' – also suggests a low-pitched, desultory motion. The analogical force of an individual word can be seen in prose as well as poetry.

ACTIVITY 14.4
Reading

Read the passage below, which is the opening of the short story 'The Wheelbarrow' by V.S. Pritchett. Which words carry particular analogical force?

> 'Robert,' Miss Freshwater's niece called down from the window of the dismantled bedroom, 'when you have finished that, would you mind coming upstairs a minute? I want you to move a trunk.'
>
> And when Evans waved back from the far side of the rumpled lawn where he was standing by the bonfire, she closed the window to keep out the smoke of slow-burning rubbish – old carpeting, clothes, magazines, papers, boxes – which hung about the waists of the fir trees and blew towards the house. For three days the fire had been burning, and Evans, red-armed in his shirt-sleeves and sweating along the seams of his brow, was prodding it with a garden fork. A sudden silly tongue of yellow flame wagged out: some inflammable piece of family history – who knew what? Perhaps one of her aunt's absurd summer hats or a shocking year of her father's daydream accountancy was having its last fling. She saw Evans pick up a bit of paper from the outskirts of the fire and read it. What was it? Miss Freshwater's niece drew back her lips and opened her mouth expectantly. At this stage all family privacy had gone. Thirty, forty, fifty years of life were going up in smoke.
>
> (Pritchett, 1984, p.113)

DISCUSSION

There are at least six examples of analogy in this passage. In the first paragraph, the bedroom is described as having been 'dismantled'. When we dismantle something (usually a piece of furniture or equipment, although the original sense is of taking off a cloak – a mantle) we take it apart. Here, the bedroom has been packed up, not taken to pieces. The word 'dismantled' is a more dramatic and expressive way of describing the process. A little later the lawn is described as 'rumpled', a word we would usually associate with fabric (it originally meant 'wrinkled'), but here it is used of grass. The fir trees are brought alive by being provided with 'waists'. In the next sentence, Evans is sweating along 'the seams' of his brow: a neat analogy for the lines on his forehead, taken from embroidery or possibly from geology, as in seams of coal.

The most obvious use of analogy is in the reference to the fire: 'a sudden silly tongue of flame wagged out'. Describing the flicker of a flame as a tongue is quite commonplace; it is the use of 'silly' and 'wagged out' which makes the image come alive, and not only describes the fire, but hints at the absurdity either of the contents of the papers that are burning or of their authors. Finally, there is the use of 'outskirts' to describe the edge of the fire. The word is taken from its more familiar role in describing the edge of a town. You might notice here, incidentally, that when we use 'outskirts' of a town, we're using what must once have been a striking metaphor, since 'outskirts' referred originally to the lower part of a woman's dress, although it has been used of the fringe of a town since the late sixteenth century. Metaphors are often absorbed into the language; as writers, our task is to keep refreshing the ways in which a word can be used.

ACTIVITY 14.5
Reading

Read the following extracts from *Into the Heart of Borneo* by Redmond O'Hanlon, in which he describes an evening meal in the jungle, and an attempt at going to sleep. Look for any surprising analogies used by O'Hanlon to make this piece of life writing more dramatic, and consider how they work:

> it had dawned on me that the fish and rice in my mess-tin would need all the attention I could give it. The sebarau was tasteless, which did not matter, and full of bones, which did. It was like a hair-brush caked in lard. ...
>
> Slipping under the mosquito net, I fastened myself into the dark-green camouflage SAS tube. It seemed luxuriously comfortable. You had to sleep straight out like a rifle; but the ants, swarming along the poles, rearing up on their back legs to look for an entry, and the mosquitoes, whining and singing outside the various tunes of their species in black shifting clouds, could not get in.
>
> 'Eeeeeee – ai – yack yack yack yack yack!' Something screamed in my ear, with brain-shredding force. And then everyone joined in.
>
> 'Eeeeeee – ai – yack yack yack yack yack te yooo!' answered every other giant male cicada, maniacally vibrating the tymbals, drumskin membranes in their cavity amplifiers, the megaphones built into their bodies.

'Shut up!' I shouted.

'Wah Wah Wah Wah Wah!' said four thousand frogs. ...

I switched off the torch and tried to sleep. But it was no good. The decibel-level was way over the limit allowed in discotheques. And, besides, the fire-flies kept flicking their own torches on and off; and some kind of phosphorescent fungus glowed in the dark like a forty-watt bulb.

(O'Hanlon, 1985 [1984], pp.39–40)

DISCUSSION

O'Hanlon's piece works because it consistently uses a pattern of images related to domestic British activities in order to bring the experience of a jungle in Asia into the reader's frame of reference. We do not expect to find discotheque noises in Borneo, or amplifiers or light bulbs. It also works because the oddity of the allusions is comic, to the point of being surreal. The ants are depicted as 'rear[ing] up' like horses, and the analogy of the fish and rice to a lard-caked hairbrush is both peculiarly domestic (lard, hairbrush) as well as pleasurably appalling. The analogy of sleeping 'straight out like a rifle' creates an impression of extreme rigidity and discomfort, which playfully and ironically undercuts the preceding suggestion that the sleeping arrangements are 'luxurious'.

How far can you go?

To a certain extent, the use of analogy can be related to genre; some writers also use analogy as a signature. The most famous simile addict (he even kept a notebook of them) was Raymond Chandler, whose private detective, Philip Marlowe, is prone to come out with show-stoppers. In *Farewell, My Lovely*, a large, extravagantly-dressed man is described as being 'about as inconspicuous as a tarantula on a slice of angel food' (Chandler, 1975 [1940], p.7). In *The Long Goodbye*, Marlowe admits, in similar vein, to being out of place himself: 'I belonged in Idle Valley like a pearl onion on a banana split' (Chandler, 1978 [1953], p.85). These are paradoxical similes, defining their subjects by sardonic example of what they cannot be; but Chandler was equally good at strange, new and sideways expressions. In *Trouble Is My Business*, Marlowe (generally under the weather) remarks, 'I felt like an amputated leg' (Chandler, 1976 [1946], p.28). Other writers (Kathy Lette and Clive James, for example) use outrageous similes as trademarks:

Wielding a cotton bud like a miniature police truncheon, she pointed to one small black hair I'd never noticed sprouting from my chin. It looked, in the magnified looking glass, like a sequoia tree.

(Lette, 1998, p.45)

Heat focused by a nacreous sky like the lining of a silver tureen dissolved the surface of the water into a storm of sparks, which were projected as wobbling bracelets of pure light on the otherwise maculate façades of crumbling plaster and rotting marble.

(James, 1990, p.132)

In these cases, as in Chandler's case, the similes are functioning partly as parodies. They draw attention to themselves as similes (we might give James due credit, however, for using 'maculate'!).

The degree of analogy in a piece of writing is a matter of taste, too, for writer and reader. It is important to spot that the hyperbolic analogies of James and Lette are designed to be comic, and that their respective styles of writing depend upon the frequent use of exaggerated analogies. The more extravagant the analogy, the more likely it will be to have a comic effect – and as a writer you need to ask yourself whether laughter is the dominant reaction you wish to elicit. More often, analogy is designed to draw readers in, to make them feel that the world of the written word is an exciting and dramatic place to be. In her physical descriptions, Zadie Smith often uses analogy to make her characters distinctive, as in this simile in *On Beauty*: 'His sentimental eyebrows made the shape of two separated sides of a steeple, always gently perplexed' (Smith, 2005, p.65). Hilary Mantel also frequently conjures up extraordinary analogies, as in this example from *The Giant, O'Brien*: 'The month was now November, and the moon small and peevish: a copper coin lightly silvered, a counterfeit light' (Mantel, 1998, p.130). In her memoir *Giving Up the Ghost*, Mantel refers ironically to Orwell's advice about plain writing:

> This is what I recommend to people who ask me how to get published ... Remember what Orwell says, that good prose is like a window-pane. Concentrate on sharpening your memory and peeling your sensibility. Cut every page you write by at least one-third. Stop constructing those piffling little similes of yours. Work out what it is you want to say. Then say it in the most direct and vigorous way you can ... But do I take my own advice? Not a bit ... I stray away from the beaten path of plain words into the meadows of extravagant simile: angels, ogres, doughnut-shaped holes. And as for transparency ... window-pane prose is no

guarantee of truthfulness. Some deceptive sights are seen through glass, and the best liars tell lies in plain words.

(Mantel, 2003, pp.4–5)

Of course, one difficulty you might run into is becoming addicted to analogy (explicit or implicit), or creating a piece of writing too dense and various for the reader to follow. The effect of constantly clashing analogy, or of a complex sequence of unrelated analogies, can be damaging, because it can distract the reader into absorbing the analogies at the expense of the narrative. Suppose, for instance, that I wrote:

> The bird sailed overhead like an arrow fired at Crècy, and landed in some branches which seemed to be strangling the life out of each other. Karen watched it like a miser, and lit the fuse of her fifth cigarette. She looked at the imbroglio of the tree, and tapped her foot as if ready to conduct a down-at-heel cha-cha band. In the distance she heard the tinnitus of passing cars, on the ring road which looped towards the inland like flat black ribbon. She felt vulture-hungry.

I'm confident that the reader would be screaming for some simple prose.

ACTIVITY 14.6 Reading	Read the passage from Annie Proulx's story 'In the Pit' (Reading 29 on p.377). Proulx is fond of using analogies, as you will see. Ask yourself whether they add to, or detract from, your pleasure in reading.

DISCUSSION	It will certainly be a matter of taste as to whether you are impressed by the sheer frequency of Proulx's analogies, or whether you find them more absorbing than the story.

In the complete story, which is only 4,000 words long, there are over forty explicit comparisons (using 'as', 'as if', 'as though', 'like', and phrases such as 'the colour of') of one thing to another: one every 180 words or so. There is even one ('that damn little sink the size of a sardine can') in a piece of dialogue, but you should notice that even Proulx steers clear of filling speech with analogies. We see and think and therefore write, using analogies, but we rarely use them in speech, and when and if we do, we tend to use fairly well-worn ones. Be wary of filling dialogue with figurative language, unless you are using a consciously poetic genre – as in Dylan Thomas's use of figurative language in *Under Milk Wood* (1954).

Proulx uses explicit analogy in 'In the Pit' to describe light, colour and shade; shape, arrangement and size; movement; sound; smell; texture – as well as the appearance of people and objects. Some of them could be said to demand some knowledge on the part of the reader. For instance, I don't know anything about alder trees, but I will have to take it on trust that they are 'hard and corded'. The opening simile, in which the mother is described as looking 'like Charles Laughton in a flowered wrapper', depends upon knowing who Laughton was (a famously skilful actor, whose looks were the opposite of a conventional screen idol's, and who is best remembered for playing Captain Bligh in *Mutiny on the Bounty*, and the title role of *The Hunchback of Notre Dame*). The idea of Laughton in drag is a comic insult.

However, almost all the other explicit analogies are highly accessible, expressive, and would be equally at home in a poem (the limousine being 'mocha-coloured', for instance). There may well be a question about the effectiveness of so many analogies in a piece, but if you use images sparingly in your own writing, they may add great power to your prose.

Explicit analogy is only one of the writer's weapons in 'In the Pit'. Proulx also uses implicit analogy many times. The mother 'shuffled a deck' of envelopes; the sky is filled with 'raw, bunched clouds'. Sometimes, Proulx simply livens up the prose with unusual words, as in 'a frowsty bed, a table with bulbous legs'. The word 'frowsty' (an old British word for 'stale') is rare. I only know it from its use in Philip Larkin's poem 'Church Going' (Larkin, 1964). It might send a reader to a dictionary, as with 'prial', the word I noted at the start of this chapter. Do not be afraid of this – but use analogy in moderation if you want your reader to stay with you.

Developing analogies

Fiction and non-fiction can be given particular zest by using unusual and provocative vocabulary and imagery, even if Proulx is more given to its use than most. It is a good idea to keep a record of the kind of minor or major analogies which you come across, and to note down ideas as they come to you. If you see yourself principally as a writer of prose, it is a good idea to read poetry; and it follows that the reverse is true as well. Here, for instance, is a particularly rich and complex sequence of similes used by William Faulkner in his novel *Light in August*. It is about watching a wagon come into view:

> the vehicle does not seem to progress. It seems to hang suspended in the middle distance forever and forever, so infinitesimal is its progress, like a shabby bead upon the mild red string of road. So much is this so that in the watching of it the eye loses it as sight and sound drowsily merge and blend, like the road itself, with all the peaceful and monotonous changes between darkness and day,

like already measured thread being rewound onto a spool. So that at last, as though out of some trivial and unimportant region beyond even distance, the sound of it seems to come slow and terrific and without meaning, as though it were a ghost travelling a half mile ahead of its own shape.

(Faulkner, 1971 [1932], p.8)

You can see here that the rhythm of the sentences themselves, their clauses, their internal rhymes, their use of long vowels, all add to the analogies being used. Analogies cannot be used in a vacuum.

ACTIVITY 14.7
Writing

Write a description of three characters (up to 100 words each), one aged sixteen, one aged fifty and one aged ninety, in which you use metaphors or similes. What are their sources? Which senses are they using – touch, scent, hearing? Are you using texture, colour, shape? How exaggerated do you feel that they are? Don't hold back in this activity, but create wild and freewheeling analogies.

DISCUSSION

Allowing yourself to let your imagination take flight is an important part of the process. Go back to your descriptions a day later and see if they are still fresh, or if they need to be edited and made more subtle. Consider how frequently you are using analogy, how ostentatious your analogies are, and whether they work better as explicit or implicit comparisons. You may also find that you have been able to create an analogy which develops and extends in the way that Faulkner's description moves restlessly onwards.

Poetry and analogy

In a poem, as in prose, analogies can exist as single and sudden sideways looks which bring the world dramatically alive, or they can exist as continuous, controlled and related metaphors. So, for instance, you might describe a river ferry – as Les Murray does in his poem 'Machine Portraits with Pendant Spaceman' – like this:

Not a high studded ship boiling cauliflower under her keel
nor a ghost in bootlaced canvas – just a length of country road
afloat between two shores, winding wet rope reel-to-reel,
dismissing romance sternwards. ...

(Murray, 1986, p.101)

Murray uses three distinct analogies, two of them interestingly negative (the ferry is not an impressive steamer, or an eerie sailing-boat, but something very mundane).

Or you might wish to create an extended analogy, as here in Ian McMillan's poem 'Branwell Brontë is Reincarnated as a Vest':

Branwell Brontë is Reincarnated as a Vest

I hang here like a ghost
on the midnight line;

frost hardens me, hardens the frocks
I hang with.

Irony to hang here on
a night crashing with the loud moon,

the moon only I can hear.

I hang here like a ghost
on the midnight line;

if you stand by the garden shed,
there, that side of the garden shed

and look at me from that angle,
look towards the washing machine from that angle,

I'm almost invisible behind the frocks.

I hang here like a ghost.
The frost hardens
and dawn is dark years away.

(McMillan, 2000, p.12)

What McMillan has done is beguilingly subtle. The familiar Charlotte, Emily and Anne Brontë are known to us through their writings, but also because of a portrait by their brother Branwell, in which he has erased his own image, much as he has been erased from history. Our view of him is obscured – rather as a vest might be obscured by three frocks, unless seen at an angle (the use of 'frocks' reminds us that this apparently old-fashioned word is still in common use in Yorkshire, where the poem is set). By making the setting contemporary, McMillan has made it a poem, not only about Branwell Brontë, but about loneliness and self-effacement. It's a poem that manages to be melancholy and comic at the same time.

ACTIVITY 14.8
Writing

Imagine a group of people – any number from three to several thousand. Here are some suggestions:

- The Beatles;
- a crowd at a Wimbledon tennis final;
- a family portrait from the Edwardian era or earlier;
- the people in the extract from Plath's journal (see Reading 10 on p.312).

Freeze-frame them, and focus on one of them, an 'odd-one-out', as in McMillan's poem. Think of analogies you could use which describe the relationship between the 'odd-one-out' and the rest of the group. You might like to use inanimate objects, as McMillan does with the vest and the frocks. For instance, a down-hearted person in a group of enthusiasts could be seen as a dowdy umbrella in a group of bright parasols.

Draft a poem (up to 10 lines) or a passage of fiction or life writing (up to 250 words) based on your image.

DISCUSSION

There are many ways in which you could create an 'odd-one-out'. Perhaps the solitary figure was a ghostly presence beside living figures, or shunning the limelight on a stage, while the others were active. Perhaps they were cowed, like a captured fugitive surrounded by warders. Perhaps they were like a private soldier, standing among officers, or someone wealthy, surrounded by thieves. The way to take this forward would be to play with the analogy, so that the point was made, but not overstretched.

More complex patterns

Sometimes it is possible to sustain more than one line of analogy – especially in poetry – so that there are, for instance, three or four threads interwoven. This is harder to manage, because there is a risk of the extended analogies becoming confused with one another.

ACTIVITY 14.9
Reading

Read Linda France's poem 'Little Dogs Laugh', below. What patterns of metaphor can you distinguish?

Little Dogs Laugh

Dog was mongrel smile, stray and small as me,
pleated gums stitched with teeth. Kiss and lick
grew a bite, ripped open my playground lips.

Tears. Running red and mad barking
were muzzled by my sister's handkerchief,
a double-deck ride to the infirmary.

I blinked like a falling star, and sky
was the howl in my mouth. I wanted swings.
I wanted a cow to jump over the moon.

But little dogs laughing pinned me to a bed,
its whiskery blanket, with their crisp elbows,
a silver needle sewing the ragged corners.

I kicked. Back at home, I bared my baby
canines for Mam and Dad, showing off
the black embroidery, a tickle of stunned flies.

(France, 1994, p.11)

DISCUSSION

There are three strands woven together in France's poem, which depicts a child being treated after being bitten by a dog. She has had to have stitches in her mouth. France uses recurrent points of metaphorical reference to enrich the poem. The poem is underpinned (because the speaker is a child) by extracts from the nursery rhyme 'Hey diddle diddle' ('Hey diddle diddle/The cat and the fiddle/The cow jumped over the moon/The little dogs laughed to see such fun/And the dish ran away with the spoon'). The nonsensical jingle of this is set against the way everything takes on the property of a small dog – not only the 'little dogs' (medical staff) who stitch her mouth on a 'whiskery' blanket, but also the girl herself. Her 'barking' is 'muzzled' by her sister; she 'howl[s]'; she 'bared ...[her] canines' (teeth) for her parents. In the last stanza, she has come to resemble the dog that bit her. The poem also uses repeated metaphors of fabric and cloth to allow France to bring out the image of the stitches in the skin. The dog's gums are 'pleated'; the child's lips are 'ripped'; we see a handkerchief and a blanket (which could have 'corners' like the mouth); her teeth look as if they have been embroidered.

What makes 'Little Dogs Laugh' work is the almost surreptitious use of recurrent, triple analogy. As a writer, you have to work and rework this kind of material, so that – as here – the images coalesce, rather than collide.

Cutting out analogies

In a well-known and much-cited interview, the Belgian author Georges Simenon (the creator of Maigret, and author of about 400 novels or novellas) told his interviewer about an exchange he had with his literary editor, the novelist Colette:

Simenon: I remember I gave [Colette] two short stories and she
              returned them and I tried again and tried again.

Finally she said, 'Look, it is too literary, always too literary.' So I followed her advice. It's what I do when I write, the main job when I rewrite.

Interviewer: What do you mean by 'too literary'? What do you cut out, certain kinds of words?

Simenon: Adjectives, adverbs, and every word which is there just to make an effect. Every sentence which is there just for the sentence. You know, you have a beautiful sentence – cut it. Every time I find such a thing in one of my novels it is to be cut.

(quoted in Cowley, 1977 [1958], p.146)

Simenon saw, in effect, the art of the analogy, and its potential for colour, as almost entirely wasteful. He claimed never to change the plot during revision; only to pare down the language. As a writer, what you have to decide is what you like or dislike about words: whether you would rather have the spare, uncomplicated style advocated by Simenon, or the rich mixture favoured by writers like Proulx.

ACTIVITY 14.10
Reading and writing

Read the passage below from Simenon's novel *Maigret and the Wine-merchant*.

Then experiment with the passage to see if it will bear the weight of additional adjectives, adverbs and analogies.

He slept heavily. If he had had any dreams that night, he had forgotten them by the morning. The wind must have changed during the night and, with it, the weather. It was much less cold. Rain was falling in a steady downpour, and the windows were streaked with it.

'Aren't you going to take your temperature?'

'No, I can tell it's normal.'

He was feeling better. He drank two cups of coffee with relish, and, once again, Madame Maigret rang for a taxi.

'Don't forget your umbrella.'

When he got to his office, he glanced quickly through the pile of mail on his desk. This was a long-established habit of his. He liked to see if there were any envelopes addressed in a hand he recognized, a letter from a friend, perhaps, or one containing some information that he was waiting for.

Today, there was an envelope addressed in block capitals, and marked 'Personal' in the top left-hand corner. The word 'Personal' was underlined three times.

Chief Inspector Maigret,
Officer In Charge of Criminal Investigations,
38, Quai des Orfèvres.

He opened this letter first. It contained two sheets of paper of the kind normally to be found in cafés and brasseries. The headings had been cut off. The sheets were covered with very neat handwriting, with regular spacing between the words, suggesting that the writer had an orderly mind, and was a stickler for detail.

(Simenon, 1973 [1970], pp.84–5)

DISCUSSION

As you will have noted, Simenon uses only three adverbs, and indeed only five adjectives in this passage. It would be wrong to say that he never uses analogies in his work, but he uses them very rarely, and never extravagantly. With Simenon, the focus is always on the action, and he never lets the language detract from this. You may have found that adding the colour and force of analogy looked distracting, even pyrotechnic. The character Maigret is himself a downbeat and methodical detective, and Simenon's style matches the character. Nevertheless, Simenon's distaste for excessive verbal play is a good reminder of the need to think through the use of analogy. The pleasure of using analogy, and of reading pieces that use analogy, is interestingly subjective.

Conclusion

This chapter is about what it is possible to do with analogies and language to make your writing richer and more verbally stimulating. As the difference between Proulx and Simenon shows, the extent to which you might use comparisons is a matter for you to consider. Analogy is a tool, but it is not compulsory to use it. There are no firm rules, but you should understand that analogy has as much potential to confuse readers as to delight them. When badly used, analogies can seem like mannerisms; when well used, they can add interest, excitement and precision to a narrative. They are often used to create settings, and you will find a greater incidence of them at the openings of stories or chapters. Although you will find them more frequently in poetry, they are not poetry's sole province. Whatever Simenon says, they are often what will make your prose both lively and entertaining.

References

Adcock, Fleur (1991) *Selected Poems*, Oxford: Oxford University Press.

Armitage, Simon (1992) *Kid*, London: Faber and Faber.

Chandler, Raymond (1975 [1940]) *Farewell, My Lovely*, Harmondsworth: Penguin.

Chandler, Raymond (1976 [1946]) *Trouble Is My Business*, Harmondsworth: Penguin.

Chandler, Raymond (1978 [1953]) *The Long Goodbye*, Harmondsworth: Penguin.

Cowley, Malcolm (ed.) (1977 [1958]) *Writers at Work, The Paris Review Interviews, First Series*, Harmondsworth: Penguin.

Faulkner, William (1971 [1932]) *Light in August*, Harmondsworth: Penguin.

France, Linda (1994) *The Gentleness of the Very Tall*, Newcastle upon Tyne: Bloodaxe.

James, Clive (1990) *May Week Was in June*, London: Picador.

Larkin, Philip (1964) *The Whitsun Weddings*, London: Faber and Faber.

Lette, Kathy (1998) *Altar Ego*, London: Picador.

McMillan, Ian (2000) *Perfect Catch: Poems, collaborations and scripts*, Manchester: Carcanet.

Mantel, Hilary (1998) *The Giant, O'Brien*, London: Fourth Estate.

Mantel, Hilary (2003) *Giving Up the Ghost*, London: Fourth Estate.

Murray, Les A. (1986) *Selected Poems*, Manchester: Carcanet.

O'Hanlon, Redmond (1985 [1984]) *Into the Heart of Borneo*, Harmondsworth: Penguin.

Plath, Sylvia (1965) *Ariel*, London: Faber and Faber.

Pritchett, V.S. (1984) *Collected Stories*, Harmondsworth: Penguin.

Simenon, Georges (1973 [1970]) *Maigret and the Wine-merchant* in *The Sixth Simenon Omnibus* (trans. Eileen Ellenbogen), Harmondsworth: Penguin.

Smith, Zadie (2005) *On Beauty*, Harmondsworth: Penguin.

Thomas, Dylan (1954) *Under Milk Wood*, London: J.M. Dent.

Further reading

Sommer, Elyse and Sommer, Mike (1991) *Falser Than a Weeping Crocodile and Other Similes*, Detroit: Visible Ink Press.

Sommer, Elyse with Weiss, Dorrie (1995) *Metaphors Dictionary*, Detroit: Visible Ink Press.

These two collections are the fullest dictionaries of similes and metaphors, although there are other shorter collections.

15 Poetry: the freedom of form

Bill Greenwell

Constraint and potential

In the last chapter, we looked at the considerable potential of analogy, and the opposing possibility that cutting analogy can also have virtues. In this chapter we are going to look at the energy that the constraint of poetic forms provides – and also the energy that comes from adapting and subverting those very same forms. When you work on these forms, you will also find that you are made more aware of the need to create rhythm in prose, as discussed in Chapter 13.

Form is a constraint, but constraints are very often what make writing take flight. At first, trying out new forms might seem a little like limbering up, and that is perfectly appropriate. You learn how to cook, to ride a bicycle, to throw pots, to sail, by practice. It's the same with poetic forms, of which there are thousands if you include all of their variants. In this chapter we are going to look at four forms: the villanelle, the pantoum, the sestina and the sonnet. What they have in common is a quality we considered in Chapter 13 – the force of repetition.

Repetition

Poetic forms originally used repetition because they were sung forms. Repetition was a feature designed to help the listener and to hold the listener's attention. Prose style can be seen to borrow from orators' patterns of repetition, as you saw in John F. Kennedy's speech in Chapter 13, and poetry can also be seen to borrow from the repetitions of songs and chants. In both cases, new uses are made of repetition. Repetition suits the writer's concentration on an image or idea. Formal schemes help the writer and reader to focus on similarities and parallels – to bring out analogies, as we saw in Linda France's poem 'Little Dogs Laugh' in the last chapter. Repetition means that readers are forced to think through the different facets of the poem's subject, and formal poems are like well-designed echo-chambers.

ACTIVITY 15.1
Reading

Read these two lines, and suggest ways in which they are related to each other:

> From bitter searching of the heart
> We rise to play a greater part.

It isn't only the 'heart/part' rhyme that connects the lines. The rhyme signals to the reader that there is a relationship between the two lines; that the positive consequence of looking at our emotions is that we move on to understand and to participate in the world more fully. These lines, if repeated at intervals, would form a constant reminder of the need to be positive. And that is exactly how the lines are used – as a sort of refrain in a villanelle by Frank R. Scott. The relationship between sung forms and repetitive poetic forms is illustrated in this case by the fact that Leonard Cohen set this villanelle ('Villanelle For Our Time') to music on his 2004 album, *Dear Heather*.

The villanelle

A villanelle depends on the repeated use of two lines, initially the first and third, throughout its nineteen lines. These two lines each make four appearances and are the closing two lines, so the sense of a refrain is very powerful indeed. Here are the rules for a villanelle:

- There is no set pattern for the rhythm, although each line uses the same rhythm (commonly three, four or five beats to the line).
- It uses only two rhymes (**a** and **b**) and is nineteen lines long.
- In its most exacting form, the first line recurs with the same words in the sixth, twelfth and eighteenth line; the third line reappears as the ninth, fifteenth and final line.
- The first and third lines use the **a** rhyme, and the overall scheme is arranged in five tercets (three-line stanzas) and a quatrain (a four-line stanza), as follows:

aba aba aba aba aba abaa.

As you can see, there is some working backwards involved in attempting a villanelle. The moment you have chosen the first line, you have chosen the penultimate line, and the moment you have chosen the third line, you have the final line. You are always going to be working towards that final refrain.

Here are two suggested first lines for a villanelle. Use one of them to write a three-line opening for a villanelle – or invent your own – bearing in mind that this is a line you will have to use again.

- **a** There is a current moving to the shore (*five beats*)
- **b** I heard a footstep at my gate (*four beats*)

If you look at my two opening lines, you will see that I have done two things. The first is to choose rhymes ('-ore' and '-ate') for which there are many matches, allowing me more freedom. The second is that I have written lines which could be broken up – like this, for instance:

> There is a current. Moving to the shore, ...
>
> There is a current, moving. To the shore ...
>
> I heard a footstep. At my gate ...
>
> I heard. A footstep at my gate ...

It is useful to write key lines which are susceptible to this kind of alteration.

Thus, there are two paramount features. First, you need powerful, adaptable refrains; second, you need to think about the rhymes. After all, you have to find six **b** rhymes, and seven **a** rhymes. It's no use deciding to use, for instance, 'pilgrim', as one of your rhyme words, because there just aren't six or seven satisfactory rhymes.

Starting a villanelle

One way to start writing a villanelle is to have a strong idea of the refrains and to work with them. Unless you are very familiar with the form, it's best at first to get a sense of what even an indifferent one would look and sound like. To do this, we'll look initially for rhymes and refrains. The result is bound, at first, to be artificial, and even nonsensical. Don't worry.

I'm going to start with a (slightly modernised) famous iambic pentameter: Shakespeare's 'Shall I compare you to a summer's day?', which I have chosen because the '-ay' rhyme is one of the easiest in the English language. I have to find an answering refrain if I am to make sense of the final pair of lines. I'll try 'Perhaps it's best to drive the blues away'. I've already set myself up for a trick ending, as you'll see. I now know that the poem will look like this:

```
1   Shall I compare you to a summer's day?
2
3   Perhaps it's best to drive the blues away.

4                                           -ay.
5
6   Shall I compare you to a summer's day?

7                                           -ay.
8
9   Perhaps it's best to drive the blues away.
```

```
10                              -ay.
11
12  Shall I compare you to a summer's day?

13                              -ay.
14
15  Perhaps it's best to drive the blues away.

16                              -ay.
17
18  Shall I compare you to a summer's day?
19  Perhaps it's best to drive the blues away.
```

Suppose you were to experiment with an apparently easy **b** rhyme: 'sun'. Here's what I've come up with:

```
1   Shall I compare you to a summer's day?
2   I'll claim you have the properties of sun.
3   Perhaps it's best to drive the blues away,

4   To cheer you with a simile, to say
5   How bright you are. I'll shout when I've begun,
6   Shall I? Compare you to a summer's day?

7   Agreed? It is a simple game to play,
8   And you'll feel better, surely, when I'm done.
9   Perhaps it's best to drive the blues away.

10  I must do something: you seem (if I may)
11  Depressed. Besides, analogies are fun:
12  Shall I compare you to a summer's day –

13  Or would that only emphasise how grey
14  You feel? – Life's got you somewhere on the run,
15  Perhaps. It's best to drive the blues away.

16  I promise only that I won't betray
17  Your truths. Am I the company you'd shun?
18  Shall I compare you to a summer's day?
19  Perhaps it's best to. Drive the blues away!
```

When I put this together, I found – and this is often the case with a villanelle – that I had to anticipate some problems. Any time you practise writing a villanelle, you'll find your eyes glued to the rhyme words. I expected '-un' to provide me with a reasonably easy rhyme, but I have to admit that 'shun' was something of a compromise. What I didn't determine here at all was the subject, and the idea of a cheerful person annoying a cheerless one emerged out of the lines I'd set myself. So, a form can often produce an unexpected subject.

The potential problems you need to consider in writing a villanelle are these:

- There is a natural tendency to write in monosyllables, which you should try to avoid over-using.
- Be wary of end-stopping all the lines – look for some enjambment, to give the poem forward movement.
- Unless the final line is capable of being broken up in different ways, it will not allow you any variation.

If you're going to write a good villanelle, you have to go through this process of familiarising yourself with the form first. Anything other than a comic villanelle (in which the rhymes will be ostentatiously part of the fun) really needs you to work first on the potential content of the poem, and then on finding ways in which content and form might work together.

One of the best-known examples of working on the content initially is the villanelle 'One Art' by Elizabeth Bishop, of which this is the nineteenth and final draft:

One Art

The art of losing isn't hard to master;
so many things seem filled with the intent
to be lost that their loss is no disaster.

Lose something every day. Accept the fluster
of lost door keys, the hour badly spent.
The art of losing isn't hard to master.

Then practice losing farther, losing faster:
places, and names, and where it was you meant
to travel. None of these will bring disaster.

I lost my mother's watch. And look! my last, or
next-to-last, of three loved houses went.
The art of losing isn't hard to master.

I lost two cities, lovely ones. And, vaster,
some realms I owned, two rivers, a continent.
I miss them, but it wasn't a disaster.

– Even losing you (the joking voice, a gesture
I love) I shan't have lied. It's evident
the art of losing's not too hard to master
though it may look like (*Write* it!) like disaster.

(Bishop, 1984, p.178)

Notice here how Bishop has varied the conventional pattern. She has chosen a formally less rigorous option, which requires the refrain lines to be similar, rather than exactly the same. She repeats the first refrain line precisely ('The art of losing isn't hard to master'), until its final appearance, when she quietly varies it, changing 'hard' to 'not too hard'. But she varies the second refrain throughout so that, although each line ends with the word 'disaster', the phrasing is otherwise different, most emphatically in the final line. She also allows herself half-rhymes in the body of the poem (she rhymes 'gesture' with 'disaster' and 'master').

We know from the availability of her drafts, however, that Bishop approached 'One Art' in a way less likely to lead to a dominance of form over content. She started with a sketch or draft of the poem, and turned it slowly into a villanelle. Her first full draft, after two false starts, begins:

> Mostly, one begins by 'mislaying':
> keys, reading-glasses, fountain pens
> – these are almost too easy to be mentioned,
> and 'mislaying' means that they usually turn up
> in the most obvious places, although when one
> is making progress, the places grow more unlikely

and later

> I've lost smaller bits of geography, like
> a splendid beach, and a good-sized bay

and later

> One might think this would have prepared me
> for losing one average-sized not ~~especially~~   exceptionally
> beautiful or dazzlingly intelligent person
>
> (quoted in Quinn, 2006, p.225)

In other words, she moves from the mundane image of losing objects to the powerful theme of losing love. In the margin she noted some potential rhymes – a good practice to get into as you write. What Bishop is doing with the villanelle is far more important than mastering the form. She is matching the villanelle to a repetitive but deeply felt experience, working on her subject before transmuting it.

Forms generate ideas

As you have seen, forms will generate ideas, but the best poems which use formal structures will be rooted in the ideas and feelings themselves. Notice how the constraint of the villanelle helps Bishop to write about the impossibility of escaping the idea of loss, no matter how her speaker considers it. In other words, Bishop's poem uses repetition to dwell on her subject. One of the most famous villanelles is Dylan Thomas's 'Do Not Go Gentle Into That Good Night'. The reason it works so well is that its subject is a repeated invocation to resist death, as if the readers need to have the command dinned into them.

ACTIVITY 15.3 **Writing**	Think of a subject that suits the villanelle form, a subject in which the repetition has a developing, important and meaningful function. Practise writing a villanelle. You might begin with two refrains and the resulting rhymes; or, if you prefer, use Bishop's greater freedom with the second refrain. Remember: it doesn't have to be in iambic pentameter.
DISCUSSION	If this is your first attempt at a villanelle, you will probably find that it sounds a little stilted, like an exercise. That's fine. Keep working on your first attempt, or try another one. Learning the form is the only way to become confident enough to experiment with it, as Bishop did. The most important thing is to find a subject that suits its repetitions. Later, you can graduate to the method Bishop used in 'One Art' – sketching an idea with only a rough sense of the form, and then moulding the language so that form and content are brought together.

The pantoum

In one of her letters, Elizabeth Bishop wrote:

> I don't think one should stick to the old forms, of course, but just by having them in one's head they seem to start the machinery going ... And I think it makes it easier to get the effects one wants, perhaps and also not to waste time doing what's been superbly done already. (Another of my ambitions is a *PANTOUM*.)
>
> (quoted in Quinn, 2006, p.261)

A pantoum is Malay in origin. It has a very exacting form and an even more pronounced pattern of repetition than a villanelle. Unlike the villanelle, the pantoum has no specified length, only a specified pattern.

ACTIVITY 15.4 **Reading**	Here is a (very short) pantoum. See if you can identify the rules of the form. Think about the pattern of the stanzas.

They say

They say my mother fell asleep
beneath the flurries of the sea,
to lie there, drowning, in the deep
illusion: what was not to be.

Beneath the flurries of the sea,
she vanished, like an empty thought,
illusion. What was not to be
possessed her, held her. She was caught.

She vanished, like an empty thought;
she drifted as the currents cooled,
possessed her, held her. She was caught,
and, by these means, her dreams were fooled.

She drifted as the currents cooled,
to lie there, drowning, in the deep,
and, by these means, her dreams were fooled.
They say my mother fell asleep.

DISCUSSION

A traditional pantoum has three rules:
- The stanzas have four lines.
- The basic rhyme scheme is **abab**.
- The second and fourth lines of the first stanza turn into the first and third lines of the second stanza, and so on – until the last stanza, in which the original **a** lines become the **b** lines (ideally, the first line becomes the last line, too).

So the rhyme scheme of the pantoum above is:

abab bcbc cdcd dada.

Adapting the pantoum

Remember: the example in Activity 15.4 is a strictly rhymed, octosyllabic pantoum. Traditionally, the pantoum has only eight syllables in a line, but you can vary this. No one says that you can't break loose from the pantoum: when you are working with a form, and it starts working against what you want to write, adapt the form or ditch it. You could, for instance, avoid using rhyme and simply work with the repetition of the lines. You could loosen the metre. And you could also make the repeated lines similar to, rather than replicas of, the original lines.

As with the villanelle, it is best to practise the scheme first, and then to work on making something of the pantoum's potential. In particular, you need a good first line.

ACTIVITY 15.5 Writing	Write a sixteen-line pantoum, either rhymed or unrhymed, on a subject of your choice. Think first about whether rhyming suits the content best.
DISCUSSION	The pantoum is full of echoes, and since it has to be devised so that it returns to the beginning, it suits subjects such as obsession, searching and finding, comparing the present with the past. If you use rhyme, you will find that the pantoum finishes emphatically, and that it is more likely to make a decisive statement to resolve any conundrum you may have set yourself and the reader. An unrhymed pantoum, without the assertiveness that rhyme provides, will have a more meditative air.

Sestinas: last words

Sestinas have been highly popular in writing workshops, and increasingly in print, since about 1990 (they were rarer before 1990, although the form is Italian in origin, and has an 800-year history). They have one great advantage, and present one great difficulty. The advantage is that they use no particular rhythmic scheme, though it's true that most English sestinas use iambic pentameter; the difficulty is that they use only six end-words, all of which appear seven times, and in a specified order. Make one mistake with this order and you have to undertake considerable revision to get the poem straight.

In a sestina, there are six sestets (six-line stanzas) and a tercet, usually called an 'envoi', which uses the six end-words again:

Stanza 1:	**1** 2 3 4 5 **6**
Stanza 2:	**6** 1 5 2 4 **3**
Stanza 3:	**3** 6 4 1 2 **5**
Stanza 4:	**5** 3 2 6 1 **4**
Stanza 5:	**4** 5 1 3 6 **2**
Stanza 6:	**2** 4 6 5 3 **1**
Envoi:	usually 1 and 2, 3 and 4, 5 and 6 *or* 1 and 4, 2 and 5, 3 and 6 (although other combinations are possible).

Thus, if you choose the end-words 'broken', 'hands', 'hours', 'subside', 'weeping' and 'welcome' in the first stanza, they will appear in different orders in each of the successive stanzas. In the three-line envoi, three of the words will occur during the lines, and three at the end of the lines.

Choose six end-words for a sestina. What advantages do they offer you? How susceptible are they to repetition and variation?

DISCUSSION

The last word of each stanza is the last word of the first line of the next stanza. This means that you are going to have to choose six words of which some at least have special properties – perhaps they will have more than one meaning, or even occur as different parts of speech. For instance, if you use, say, 'restful', 'devil', 'conscience', 'open', 'guilt' and 'exotic', you will almost certainly find that the only really adaptable word is 'open', because it has different meanings, contexts, and can be a verb as well as an adjective. You have to control the words or they will start to control you.

Experimenting with sestinas

The sestina lends itself to a meditation or debate, to turning an idea over with the aim of resolving it (hence the envoi). I think that the sestina has a troubled or melancholy air, and that it suits spiritual subjects. This is because of the way its echoes seem to have an air of doubt about them.

Read the sestina below, once again by Elizabeth Bishop. See if you can work out how she has given herself some freedom from the form's technical prescription.

A Miracle for Breakfast

At six o'clock we were waiting for coffee,
waiting for coffee and the charitable crumb
that was going to be served from a certain balcony,
– like kings of old, or like a miracle.
It was still dark. One foot of the sun
steadied itself on a long ripple in the river.

The first ferry of the day had just crossed the river.
It was so cold we hoped that the coffee
would be very hot, seeing that the sun
was not going to warm us; and that the crumb
would be a loaf each, buttered, by a miracle.
At seven a man stepped out on the balcony.

He stood for a minute alone on the balcony
looking over our heads toward the river.
A servant handed him the makings of a miracle,
consisting of one lone cup of coffee
and one roll, which he proceeded to crumb,
his head, so to speak, in the clouds – along with the sun.

Was the man crazy? What under the sun
was he trying to do, up there on his balcony!
Each man received one rather hard crumb,
which some flicked scornfully into the river,
and, in a cup, one drop of the coffee.
Some of us stood around, waiting for the miracle.

I can tell what I saw next; it was not a miracle.
A beautiful villa stood in the sun
and from its doors came the smell of hot coffee.
In front, a baroque white plaster balcony
added by birds, who nest along the river,
– I saw it with one eye close to the crumb –

and galleries and marble chambers. My crumb
my mansion, made for me by a miracle,
through ages, by insects, birds, and the river
working the stone. Every day, in the sun,
at breakfast time I sit on my balcony
with my feet up, and drink gallons of coffee.

We licked up the crumb and swallowed the coffee.
A window across the river caught the sun
as if the miracle were working, on the wrong balcony.

(Bishop, 1984, pp.18–19)

You can see in the poem how Bishop varies the sentence-lengths, crosses line-endings, diverts the reader's attention with a question. She also succeeds in using the words in a simple, unambiguous sense – although she does use 'crumb' as a noun and as a verb. Her particular technique is to change the way she approaches the end-words, so that we have 'a certain balcony', 'my balcony', 'on the balcony', 'the wrong balcony'. This sestina has a slightly surreal air, and makes the ordinary seem extraordinary.

ACTIVITY 15.7
Writing

Now try writing your own sestina. Don't hold back from experimenting. You could, for instance, vary the line-lengths and play with proper nouns ('Susan'/'lazy susan'; 'Harry'/'to harry'). You also have the option of splitting words across lines, so that, for instance, 'night' could become 'night-/ingale'. But splitting words might look like trickery, and ostentation is what a sestina has to avoid.

DISCUSSION	Because a sestina works a little like a mathematical puzzle, you will always have to be careful not to make your struggle with the mathematics seem too obvious. In a really good sestina, your reader will hardly notice – perhaps *not* notice – the end-words. A good way of doing this is by using the disguise that enjambment offers. If you keep end-stopping lines, the six words will drown out the sound of the rest of the poem. One technique to avoid unless you are in a very bold mood is end-rhyme. Although there are rhymed sestinas, they tend to draw attention to the end-words, the very words that you should distract the reader from noticing.

Experimental sonnets

You are probably more familiar with the sonnet than with the forms I have discussed up to now. To remind you, a sonnet is, conventionally, fourteen lines in length. It uses iambic pentameter. It develops an idea, and then moves to resolve it, after a shift (a 'volta'), often at the end of the eighth line. It rhymes, and there are several given models for rhyming – Petrarchan, Miltonic, and so on. Shakespearean sonnets finish neatly with a couplet. Trying out traditional sonnet forms is the only way to get a feel for their formal possibilities. But there are many variations of the sonnet, and trying these, or even creating new variations, may move you from experimenting to creating original pieces. Rupert Brooke wrote a Shakespearean sonnet in reverse, starting with the couplet, a comic poem which describes the descent of a marriage from passion to bathos:

Sonnet Reversed
Hand trembling towards hand; the amazing lights
Of heart and eye. They stood on supreme heights.

Ah, the delirious weeks of honeymoon!
Soon they returned, and, after strange adventures,
Settled at Balham by the end of June.
    Their money was in Can. Pacs. B. Debentures,
And in Antofagastas. Still he went
    Cityward daily; still she did abide

At home. And both were really quite content
    With work and social pleasures. Then they died.
They left three children (besides George, who drank):
    The eldest Jane, who married Mr Bell,
William, the head-clerk in the County Bank,
    And Henry, a stock-broker, doing well.

(Brooke, 1932, p.161)

Brooke's poem raises two important points about experimenting with established forms, and about rhyming forms in general. The first is that, in varying a form, you need to think about whether the variation is for its own sake. If it is, you will learn something; but it won't be a poem you're likely to keep, because the actual experiment will be the subject of the poem. The second is that it is all too easy to use strict forms, ones that use rhyme in particular, to create comic poems. Brooke's poem varies the form appropriately because it's about a reversal of a romantic mood – although it does have one clunking phrase, in my opinion: 'still she did abide'.

Testing the sonnet

I'm going to take a well-known sonnet, Wordsworth's 'Lines Composed upon Westminster Bridge' (1802), and edit it so that it still adheres in some ways to the form.

Lines Composed upon Westminster Bridge, September 3, 1802

Earth has not anything to show more fair:
Dull would he be of soul who could pass by
A sight so touching in its majesty:
This City now doth, like a garment, wear
The beauty of the morning; silent, bare,
Ships, towers, domes, theatres, and temples lie
Open unto the fields, and to the sky;
All bright and glittering in the smokeless air.
Never did sun more beautifully steep
In his first splendour, valley, rock, or hill;
Ne'er saw I, never felt, a calm so deep!
The river glideth at his own sweet will:
Dear God! the very houses seem asleep;
And all that mighty heart is lying still!

(Wordsworth, 1969 [1802], p.214)

Here's my variation on it:

> Earth has not anything more fair:
>   who could pass by
> a sight so touching in its majesty?
>   See this city wear
> the morning; silent, bare.
>
> Ships, towers, domes, theatres, and temples lie
>   open to fields and sky,
> bright and glittering in the smokeless air.
> I never saw the sunlight steep
>   valley, rock, or hill
> like this, never felt a calm so deep.
> The river glides at will.
> The houses seem asleep;
>   and all that heart is still.

As you will see, I have tried to modernise the language ('steep' and 'majesty' are the words that have caused me the greatest difficulty). I have removed some inversions which sound awkward to a contemporary ear. I haven't changed the rhyme scheme or rhymes, but I have varied the rhythm considerably, so that it is more irregular, less determinedly iambic. I have also quietened the poem, by removing some of the exclamations and more extravagant phrases.

You can choose any well-known sonnet and experiment with it in any way you think fit. You might like to edit one, as I have done, but feel free to try out ideas of your own. The idea is to test yourself and the structure. Using an already existing poem is a good way to push yourself, since the original poem is another constraint with which to struggle. Struggle is essential to writing poetry. With stricter forms, you have to be prepared to manoeuvre so that you say what you want to say, rather than being controlled by the form. In the exercise above, I might have gone on to change rhymes, or to remove rhymes, or to make the rhymes internal.

Variations

There are many well-known sonnets – including Shelley's 'Ozymandias' – with experimental rhyme patterns. There is also a sixteen-line sonnet (used for a sequence, *Modern Love*, by George Meredith in the nineteenth century, and used by Tony Harrison in his 'School of Eloquence' sequence in the late twentieth century). Some writers have also experimented with unrhymed sonnets.

Read the following unrhymed poems by Robert Graves and Beth Ann Fennelly.

- In what way are they sonnets?
- In what way are they different from one another?
- What advantages might there be to removing the rhymes from a sonnet?

With Her Lips Only

This honest wife, challenged at dusk
At the garden gate, under a moon perhaps,
In scent of honeysuckle, dared to deny
Love to an urgent lover: with her lips only,
Not with her heart. It was no assignation;
Taken aback, what could she say else?
For the children's sake, the lie was venial;
'For the children's sake', she argued with her conscience.

Yet a mortal lie must follow before dawn:
Challenged as usual in her own bed,
She protests love to an urgent husband,
Not with her heart but with her lips only;
'For the children's sake', she argues with her conscience,
'For the children'– turning suddenly cold towards them.

(Graves, 1966, p.102)

Poem Not to Be Read at Your Wedding

You ask me for a poem about love
in lieu of a wedding present, trying to save me
money. For three nights I've lain under
glow-in-the-dark stars I've stuck to the ceiling
over my bed. I've listened to the songs
of the galaxy. Well Carmen, I would rather
give you your third set of steak knives
than tell you what I know. Let me find you
some other store-bought present. Don't
make me warn you of stars, how they see us
from that distance as miniature and breakable,
from the bride who tops the wedding cake
to the Mary on Pinto dashboards
holding her ripe red heart in her hands.

(Fennelly, 1996, p.65)

Pinto: a make of car.

If you are working on unrhymed sonnets, you have to compensate for the absence of rhyme in a number of ways – that is, if you still want to leave it as a sonnet. Graves and Fennelly show you two ways of doing this. Graves divides his poem into an octet and a sestet, and makes the sestet resolve the octet in an echoing way. Choosing your subject for an unrhymed sonnet is important. The absence of rhyme, especially where it's expected, lends itself to ideas or subjects which are partly or even wholly unresolved, whereas conventional sonnets – often about love – tend to resolve any opening debate, and finish on a note of harmony or elation. Graves's poem is about disappointment, frustration and dissatisfaction – and the absence of rhyme helps this, as does the sometimes uneasy iambic pentameter.

Fennelly's sonnet is much looser than that of Graves because there is not such an obvious division between one part and another. However, there is a turn in the poem, a shift, a 'volta', during the eighth line; and the last three lines have the same summary force as a closing couplet. In Fennelly's case, notice that the subject is also disappointment (even if the tone is upbeat). That is to say, each poem is dissonant: it is full of discordance or disagreement. Dissonance lends itself to un-rhyming, and to uncertain or inexact rhyming – and Fennelly shifts in and out of iambic pentameter throughout.

Changing sonnet rhythms

You can vary the rhythm and line-length of a sonnet to mirror your subject. The fourteen-line convention, and the sonnet's underlying pattern, can still be visible, and can form the superstructure of the poem. But within that, you can achieve considerable movement.

Read the experimental sonnet 'Fly' by Christopher Reid. Why is it shaped as it is?

Think about the following subjects, and draft suggestions about how you might subvert the sonnet form to accommodate them: a memory-lapse; acrobats; a flock of sheep being herded by a dog; being drunk.

Fly
A fat fly fuddles for an exit
at the window-pane.
Bluntly, stubbornly, it inspects it,
like a brain
nonplussed by a seemingly simple sentence
in a book,
which the glaze of unduly protracted acquaintance
has turned to gobbledygook.

A few inches above where the fly fizzes
a gap of air
waits, but this has
not yet been vouchsafed to the fly.
Only retreat and a loop or swoop of despair
will give it the sky.

(Reid, 1996, p.28)

DISCUSSION

Christopher Reid's poem 'Fly' mirrors a fly's movement. You can see from this poem that Reid is also varying the rhythm to mimic the rhythm of the speaker's thoughts. A sonnet about a memory-lapse might be achieved by missing out some of the lines, or parts of lines, to mimic the gaps in thought. A sonnet about acrobats might involve turning some of the lines upside down. A sonnet about a flock of sheep might move in an eccentric fashion across a page, mimicking obedience to the dog. A drunk sonnet – assuming it has the energy to finish – might become progressively less sure of its rhyme, line-length, even its hold on the form.

A different kind of variation occurs in the following sonnet written by Keith Douglas. His speaker's vantage point is from above a battlefield, but, as we are told, it looks very much as if the speaker is looking ahead, as if at a stage (hence the many disturbing theatrical images):

Landscape with Figures 2

On scrub and sand the dead men wriggle
in their dowdy clothes. They are mimes
who express silence and futile aims
enacting this prone and motionless struggle
at a queer angle to the scenery
crawling on the boards of the stage like walls
deaf to the one who opens his mouth and calls
silently. The décor is terrible tracery
of iron. The eye and mouth of each figure
bear the cosmetic blood and hectic
colours death has the only list of.
A yard more, and my little finger
could trace the maquillage of these stony actors.
I am the figure writhing on the backcloth.

(Douglas, 1990 [1978], p.103)

Maquillage: theatrical make-up.

This is a subversive sonnet, because it is using four beats (tetrameter), and because its rhyme scheme is disguised in most places by slant rhymes, some of which are on the penultimate syllable. The rhyme scheme is as follows:

abbacddcdefdef.

There is a twist on this, too: the **e** rhyme, a slant rhyme, is 'hectic/actors'; but there is also the sense of a final couplet, because of the 'ac' echo in 'actors/backcloth'. The use of these jarring devices fits the subject well: this is a Second World War sonnet about the ironic theatricality of death.

Shifting the beat

You can write sonnets that shift the beat from line to line, and sonnets that use an interesting mixture of colloquial and figurative language. It is also feasible to create a series of sonnets with its own interlocking structure. One such series is called 'a crown of sonnets'. In a crown, the last line of each sonnet becomes the first line of the next sonnet; and the last line of the last sonnet is the same as the first line of the first sonnet.

In Paul Muldoon's crown of sonnets, 'The Old Country', in *Horse Latitudes* (2006), there are particularly good examples of shifting the beat. Here is the third of the thirteen sonnets:

> Every resort was a last resort
> with a harbor that harbored an old grudge.
> Every sale was a selling short.
> There were those who simply wouldn't budge
>
> from the *Dandy* to the *Rover*.
> That shouting was the shouting
> but for which it was all over –
> the weekend, I mean, we set off on an outing
>
> with the weekday train timetable.
> Every tower was a tower of Babel
> that graced each corner of a bawn
>
> where every lookout was a poor lookout.
> Every rill had its unflashy trout.
> Every runnel was a Rubicon.

(Muldoon, 2006, p.39)

Bawn: a large house.

Muldoon's sonnet is conversational, varying the number of beats to the line, and shifting between stronger rhymes, like 'over'/'Rover', to weaker rhymes, like 'lookout'/'trout' (the stress falls on 'look', not 'out'). He also uses slant rhyme ('bawn'/'Rubicon'). What is also striking is the way he has increased the repetitive force of the sonnet, even though he has loosened the rhythm and understated some of the rhymes. Six lines begin with 'Every' or 'where every'; five lines repeat a word ('resort', 'harbor', 'shouting', 'tower', 'lookout'); and there are other verbal echoes – 'weekend'/'weekday', 'corner'/'bawn'. Muldoon also revels in paradox – the poem has a strong, forward movement, and a flip, playful tone, even though the sonnet consists of a litany of frustrations, dead ends, arguments and an anticlimax.

There is a further, more complex development of a crown, sometimes known as a 'wreath of sonnets', in which there are fifteen sonnets, and the fifteenth consists of the first lines, in order, of the preceding fourteen. Crowns and wreaths are forms of sequence; we will look at sequences further in Chapter 17.

ACTIVITY 15.10
Writing

Write an experimental sonnet, playing with the original form. Make sure in each case that you justify to yourself why you have altered a traditional form. Here are some suggestions:

- a sonnet that uses only one or two rhymes;
- a sonnet that uses hexameters or heptameters (respectively, six or seven beats to the line);
- a sonnet in which there are only one, two or three syllables in the line;
- an unrhymed sonnet.

DISCUSSION

Do not be afraid to move away from the sonnet form if the poem's logic takes you in that direction. There is a satisfaction in meeting the demands of a set of rules, but a poem can escape the rules if it needs to, and you can manipulate the rules to make the poem fit your subject. In other words, the exercise will be good for you, but you may want to test the form to develop your theme.

Conclusion

Although we have dealt with only four forms here – villanelle, pantoum, sestina, sonnet – the aim has been both to explore formal techniques, and to encourage moving on from strict adherence to them. To repeat Elizabeth Bishop's comment, 'They seem to start the machinery going'. Trying all or any of them out will give you an insight into how to turn a constraint into an opportunity, and confidence with a form will also give you confidence to adapt it to your own ends.

In this chapter, you have seen that poetic forms work within the security of a structure. You have also seen how rules can be subverted and structures can be experimental. In Chapter 16, you will consider ways in which you can use time to provide fiction with structure, and ways in which you can experiment with time in your narratives.

References

Bishop, Elizabeth (1984) *The Complete Poems 1927–1979*, London: The Hogarth Press.

Brooke, Rupert (1932) *The Complete Poems*, London: Sidgwick & Jackson.

Cohen, Leonard (2004) 'Villanelle For Our Time' on *Dear Heather*, Columbia Records CD B0002XK4FG (includes the text of the villanelle by Frank R. Scott).

Douglas, Keith (1990 [1978]) *Complete Poems*, Oxford: Oxford University Press.

Fennelly, Beth Ann (1996) 'Poem Not to Be Read at Your Wedding' in *The Best American Poetry 1996* (ed. Adrienne Rich), New York: Scribner.

Graves, Robert (1966) *Poems Selected by Himself*, Harmondsworth: Penguin.

Muldoon, Paul (2006) *Horse Latitudes*, London: Faber and Faber.

Quinn, Alice (ed.) (2006) *Elizabeth Bishop: Edgar Allan Poe & The Juke-Box – Uncollected poems, drafts, and fragments*, New York: Farrar, Straus and Giroux.

Reid, Christopher (1996) *Expanded Universes*, London: Faber and Faber.

Wordsworth, William (1969 [1802]) *Poetical Works*, Oxford: Oxford University Press.

Further reading

Strand, Mark and Boland, Eavan (eds) (2000) *The Making of a Poem*, New York: Norton.

This is an excellent introduction to the major forms and to 'open' forms of writing poetry, and it also contains a well-selected anthology.

Bishop, Wendy (1999) *Thirteen Ways of Looking for a Poem*, New York: Longman.

This is a large anthology of forms, with examples of how they can be written and also subverted. It also contains a series of accessible introductions and exercises. The forms include those explored in this chapter and others, such as the ghazal, the compound form called the terzanelle, and syllabic poetry.

16   Time and timing

Bill Greenwell

Time in narrative

This chapter discusses four different aspects of time: the difference between the time used in a story and the time used in a plot; the tempo or pace of a narrative; the order in which events are disclosed; and the extent to which a writer can affect the time a reader takes to read a text. Note the difference in the two terms, 'story' and 'plot'. A story consists of all the events that happen. A plot is the arrangement of those events to form a narrative. You have already seen this in the context of film narratives in Chapter 9, when looking at story timelines and step outlines.

In any narrative, time is a crucial and surprisingly complex factor. It is complex because it is not always something over which you have total control. If you are going to make the most effective use of time in your writing, it will help if you put yourself in the place of your reader.

ACTIVITY 16.1 Research	You can discover the implications of time for your writing in a simple way. Choose a piece of fiction or life writing (yours or someone else's, published or unpublished) of about 1,000 words. Write down what you discover about: • the period of time taken by all the events referred to in the narrative, including any backstory; • the period of time in which the narrative is set; • how much of that time is described, and how much of that time is not described, in the narrative.
DISCUSSION	You may have found that 'time' means very different things. You might find, for instance, that the narrative is set over one week, but that it gives the reader knowledge of what has taken place – or will take place – over a much longer period of time. A narrative that lasts a week will not show every minute of that week – indeed, it will include only moments from it, and will dwell on some parts of it for longer than others. Almost invariably, the time shown by the writer will be only a fraction of the total time in which the action of the narrative takes place. A narrative may refer to actions that have taken place in the past without resorting to the formal device of flashback. Thus, for instance, the action may take place over a few days, although we may learn in those few days about the events of many years, or even decades.

Real time and fictional time

Sometimes you may find that years, or even centuries, are covered in only a few sentences; at other times, you may find that the time covered by the writing is roughly equivalent to 'real time'. The most obvious example of this is when dialogue is being used: there is a presumption that the dialogue is taking place 'as it happens', particularly if there are no accompanying descriptions of gesture, manner or setting. It is possible to slow down time so that what is written takes longer than 'real time' – for instance, if you describe what is happening in a character's thoughts as he or she listens to others talking. Effectively, you are going over the same time twice.

| ACTIVITY 16.2 Reading | Read the following passages. I have composed the first two; the third passage is from Thomas Hardy's *The Return of the Native*. |

What do you notice about the time involved?

Passage 1

It took thirty thousand years for the empire to control the outer wastes of the galaxy. And now, after the storms had subsided, and the frozen and livid satellites at the edge of the universe had been conquered, it only remained for the commander to deal with his new prisoners.

Passage 2

'If you want my advice,' she said sulkily, 'you'll give this evening a wide berth.' He hardly heard her, gazing (as he was) so intently at the movement of her mouth.

Passage 3

Her presence brought memories of such things as Bourbon roses, rubies, and tropical midnight; her moods recalled lotus-eaters and the march in *Athalie*; her motions, the ebb and flow of the sea; her voice, the viola. In a dim light, and with a slight rearrangement of her hair, her general figure might have stood for that of either of the higher female deities.

(Hardy, 1994 [1895], p.58)

| DISCUSSION | The first passage takes us through thirty millennia in the first sentence, before settling into an unspecified present time (where the commander has to deal with his prisoners). These huge tracts of time are uncommon outside science fiction and fantasy novels. |

The second passage actually uses more time than the telling. It duplicates the time, partly because of the brief explanation 'she said sulkily', and partly because the action of the second character takes place at the same time as she is speaking.

The third passage could be said to use no time at all, because Hardy has stopped the narrative to comment on a character. This kind of pause can be used to describe a setting as well as a character.

ACTIVITY 16.3 Writing	Compose a short piece of fiction (up to 300 words), and note down how long you think the action takes. Then rewrite it, so that it uses either more or less time than your original. Does one version have an advantage over the other?

DISCUSSION	What this exercise asks you to consider is whether your writing is moving at the right pace. Did speeding it up or slowing it down cause the writing to be more engrossing? Did you want the reader to dwell on the detail you added or subtracted? If you added dialogue, did you do it in a way that accelerated the pace? The use of time in this way is going to affect the extent to which your readers dwell on action. You might want the readers to be moving at a leisurely pace, or you might want to have them turning the pages energetically.

Reading time

The average reading speed for university students is thought to be between 200 and 350 words a minute when reading for pleasure (Rayner and Pollatsek, 1989, p.182). This is three or four times as fast as an average typist can type, and about twice as fast as an audio-book is read. Of course, people's reading times are not as constant as this average speed suggests. Some readers classify themselves as 'slow' or 'fast', and many readers are mercurial. They skip. They read a page more than once. They lose their places and have to start again. They fail to finish. They read several books, piece by piece, over a protracted period of time. Although the audience of a stage play cannot alter the speed of a play – other than by applauding – radio listeners and film and television viewers can now halt proceedings. They can do this either by recording a play or story, or by deciding to listen online, pausing as they go. You will not be able to control your readers, but it will help you to construct a narrative if you try to anticipate their reading time.

|  **ACTIVITY 16.4** Writing | What can you do to influence reading time? Make some notes on tactics you could use to affect how your writing will be read – how you will maintain and sustain the interest of your readers. |

DISCUSSION

There are at least two ways in which you can exert some control over reading time, and both are important to how effective your writing might be. Both involve playing with time when devising the order and structure of your sections or chapters.

The first is to withhold information from the reader, so that he or she needs to read on, uninterruptedly, to find out the desired information. The second, which is related, is to fail to provide the information when the reader wants it. The most obvious place where this might happen is at the end of a chapter, but it can also happen, in a subtler way, within a chapter.

This is not to say that every piece of writing has to consist of cliff-hangers, nor that a piece of writing should be solely involved with action. That would cause considerable dizziness. But sleight of hand and a ruthless form of teasing are important to you as a writer, no matter what your genre. You can see this form of teasing in soap opera, which has to hold its audience over commercial breaks as well as from one day to the next. Soap opera is a speeded-up form of serialisation (the readers of a Dickens novel had to wait a month for the next instalment).

Withholding information

As I've suggested, one way to influence reading time is to deny the readers what they want. The following exercise will help you to practise withholding information.

| **ACTIVITY 16.5** Writing | Imagine three episodes at three different locations:
• a fully dressed man walking towards a stretch of water;
• a woman opening a window quickly;
• a telephone ringing in an empty room.
Devise the outline for a story in which these three episodes occur, and connect them together. For instance, the man could be discovering something owned by the woman who is opening the window. The phone may be ringing with a message about the man. The man may be the father of the woman. |

Once you have your outline planned, write some brief notes about each episode. This will include what has led up to it, and what will happen next. Now look in each set of notes for a moment at which to interrupt the episode, a point at which you aim to leave the reader uncertain of what happens next. What you should now have are three parts of a larger story, each part interrupted at a crucial moment.

The aim here is to force you to think about how to tantalise readers. They will have to concentrate not only on what is about to happen, but also on the relationship between the successive episodes – or chapters, as they might become. You will have much more hold over the way in which they read on. A chapter that resolves events before it ends is likely to give some satisfaction – but it will not propel the reader forwards. A chapter that follows immediately on from the preceding chapter may solve the problem you have set the reader, but it will often provide too speedy a gratification. It is sometimes better to change time, location, focus, character – even voice – so that the novel becomes richer in texture. As you have seen in Chapter 11, the process of separating strands, and setting up a tension as to where they will converge, is a means of keeping your readers in a state of uncertainty, an uncertainty that will encourage them to read on.

Time and order

It is impossible to consider the use of time without also considering the order of the events. Here is a summary of the events of a short story, which you will be asked to read later in the chapter. The events in this summary are in chronological order, not in the order in which they are given by the writer. In other words, this is not a summary of the plot.

As a student in 1988, a man meets and falls in love with a woman. She is his first lover. In the early days of their relationship, they separate briefly, and in the interval, he has a casual one-night relationship with another woman (he is her first lover). He resists any further communication with her, and is soon back with his original girlfriend, whom he goes on to marry. The rejected woman never forgets her first lover. However, she too subsequently marries, and becomes a lawyer. She has a close female friend and they are constantly in each other's company.

After about a decade and a half, the man's marriage breaks down (because of his infidelity), and divorce proceedings begin. At about the same time, unknown to him, the woman with whom he has had the brief fling dies of cancer, during which she is nursed by her constant friend. As the divorce is being finalised, he receives an email from this friend, telling him of the other woman's death. At first he does not recognise the name, nor that of the informant.

He contacts her. She explains that the dying woman wanted him to know. This stirs up in him memories, not only dim memories of the one night, but also of his wife as a young woman. He contacts the informant again, and meets her. She shows him photos, and is apparently angry with him. With so many memories stirred up, he visits his wife, feeling he still loves her. She rejects him, and he returns to meet the informant again.

It transpires that the informant has herself been in love, secretly, with the woman who died, and is envious of his brief physical contact with her. She asks him to describe it. Unable to recall much of it, he describes instead his sexual encounter when he got back with the woman who became his wife. His listener is rapt with vicarious pleasure at hearing what she believes to be a description of an encounter with the woman she has loved.

We could express the use of time in this chronological sequence in a chart, as set out below. The numbering of the years in the left-hand column is approximate; the middle column focuses on the man; the right-hand column focuses on the woman with whom he had a brief affair and her close female friend.

1988	Man meets wife-to-be. Splits up with her. Has one-night stand. Reunites with and marries first girlfriend.	Woman has one-night stand. She confides in a girlfriend.
1989		After distress, woman meets and marries another man. She remains close to girlfriend.
	About thirteen years pass	
2002	Man has first extra-marital affair.	
2004	Marriage breaks up; divorce set in motion.	Woman diagnosed with cancer; nursed by friend; dies.
2005	Man contacted by woman's friend. Meets friend, thinks of events in 1988. Sees wife again.	Friend contacts man. Meets man, tells him what happened.
	Friend of dead woman reveals she loved her, and asks man to tell her what sexual encounter in 1988 was like.	

ACTIVITY 16.6 Writing	Plot a story using the summary of events given above. To do this, you need to decide how you would tell the story, how you would order it, and how you would distribute and manage time in the story. You will find it helpful to draw up a chart, but this time put the events in the order in which they would occur in your story. What further decisions do you need to make in order to plot the story?
DISCUSSION	In planning how you would create the plot, you will need to have considered at what point to start the narrative. You will also have to decide how much time to give to each incident, each element of the narrative. There are seventeen or eighteen years involved in the story, and six characters: the man; his wife; the man's lover; the lover's eventual husband; the lover's close friend; and the woman with whom the man has the second affair. Who will be the focal character? How will you deal with the thirteen years of the marriage? How will the characters be brought together? What proportion of the story will deal with each period of time within it? You might like to add the approximate number of words to the chart you have already drawn up (you could also use percentages).

In the next activity, you are asked to read the actual short story from which I drew the summary of events. You should find it interesting to compare your suggested use of time and order with how the author uses them.

ACTIVITY 16.7 Reading	Read the story 'That First Time' by Christopher Coake (Reading 30 on p.380). Compare your suggested use of time and order with Coake's.
DISCUSSION	We can see from the story, and from the chart below, that at least three-quarters of the narrative is set in the 'present' of the story, and that it occurs within a very short space of time. The day of the first email and conversation is followed a week later by a single night, a Tuesday, in which Bob meets Vicky, goes to see Yvonne, comes home, and then goes to Vicky's house. About half the narrative occurs in the space of about nine hours (at most), and a further quarter of the narrative is flashback which occurs *within* these nine hours. In other words, although the story itself seems to cover about seventeen or eighteen years, Coake has contrived the telling so that it takes place, with appropriate flashbacks, in one session of about an hour, and another continuous sequence, a week later, of nine hours. This story is made dramatic by economy of time. Being economical with time is as important as being economical with place and character, as here: Coake concentrates on only four characters (Bob, Vicky, Annie, Yvonne).

The flashbacks are gently assisted by the device of using old photographs. But what gives the story its dramatic strength is its dynamic and simple use of time.

In the chart below, I've added in the right-hand column the approximate word count for the events in Coake's story.

	Event in 'That First Time'	Focus of time	Number of words (approx.)
1	Bob receives email and ponders it	2005	400
2	Vicky tells Bob about Annie's death	2005	400
3	Bob thinks about Annie	Shifts between 2005 and 1988	400
4	Bob looks at old pictures	2005	400
5	Bob reconstructs meeting Annie	1988	400
One week passes			
6	Bob talks to Vicky on phone; agrees to meet	2005	1,000
7	Bob meets Vicky in the restaurant	2005 with two shifts to 1988	1,000
8	Bob reconstructs meeting Annie, rejecting her, reuniting with Yvonne	1988	800
9	Bob remembers first cheating on Yvonne	2002	200
10	Bob goes to see Yvonne	2005	800
11	Bob thinks back to student days	1988	200

	Event in 'That First Time'	Focus of time	Number of words (approx.)
12	Bob talks to Vicky on phone; agrees to meet	2005	400
13	Bob meets Vicky, and looks through the album, recollects student days, is told about Annie	Mainly 2005, intercut with memories from different times	2,000

Concentrating time

Novelist William Styron, best known for *Sophie's Choice* (1979), once described how he solved a problem with his first novel, *Lie Down in Darkness* (1951):

> the book started with the man, Loftis, standing at the station with the hearse, waiting for the body of his daughter to arrive from up North. I wanted to give him density, but all the tragedy in his life had happened in the past ... It stumped me for a whole year. Then it finally occurred to me to use separate moments in time, four or five long dramatic scenes revolving around the daughter, Peyton, at different stages in her life. The business of the progression of time seems to me one of the most difficult problems a novelist has to cope with.
>
> (quoted in Cowley, 1977 [1958], p.275)

Novels and short stories hold the reader by concentrating action, and by using key moments in time. The illusion of several years passing is usually achieved by restricting events to short, intense bursts of time. A novel or memoir which lurches at speed from one time to another is likely to confuse the reader, and to lose the reader too. There are some famous examples of concentrating time. Barry Hines's *A Kestrel for a Knave* (1969 [1968]) – later filmed and better known as *Kes* – takes place in a single day, as does Ian McEwan's *Saturday* (2003). Malcolm Lowry's *Under the Volcano* (1946) sets eleven of its twelve chapters on a single day (the exception being the first chapter, which is a year earlier). The critical moment in Emily Brontë's *Wuthering Heights* (2007 [1847]), from the moment when Cathy and Heathcliff argue over an almanac to the moment of Heathcliff's leaving after overhearing Cathy says it would 'degrade her' to marry him, lasts nine hours, but occupies about a tenth of the entire novel. In McEwan's short novel *On Chesil Beach* (2006) there is an interesting contrast between different chapters in the use of time. The third chapter covers perhaps half an hour, including a short flashback, but occupies nearly thirty of the novel's 164 pages. The final seven pages of the novel cover about four decades, making the point that a single calamitous incident can affect an entire lifetime.

Holding the reader

As Coake's story demonstrates, keeping the action reasonably simple, and time under control, is one way to intensify a story, and therefore encourage the capricious reader to remain absorbed. However, 'That First Time' is a short story, and the expectation of a short story is that it will be read at one sitting. This is also true of most poetry, although this genre often depends upon rereading (or re-hearing). You might wish to see a play or film more than once, especially in a new production or interpretation, although usually, the experience is intended to be a single one.

ACTIVITY 16.8 Reading	Reread the opening eleven paragraphs of V.S. Pritchett's 'The Fly in the Ointment' (Reading 3 on p.296), up to 'the firm was becoming a ghost'. • How is time being used at the opening of this story? • How does Pritchett use time to move the reader on?
DISCUSSION	In Pritchett's story we start at a sort of standstill ('the dead hour of the afternoon'), in which a few snapshots are taken to establish the mood. In the second, third, fourth and fifth paragraphs, about five minutes elapse (the son walks a quarter of a mile). However, during these five minutes we are encouraged to shift back thirty years, and forwards again, pausing on 'a few years of prosperity'. In the sixth paragraph, the one that opens 'It was a shock', we are held up for a while – 'it was a long time before he heard footsteps' – although time is here edited down until the conversation that ensues, which takes us close to real time. In the last paragraph in the extract, we are moved suddenly backwards and forwards, so that we see the father and the factory as it once was, and as it is now. If you now look over the rest of the story, you will see that it consists almost entirely of dialogue, and that the whole incident is compressed into perhaps half an hour in all. You will see that Pritchett uses time in three ways:

• time moves forwards, at different speeds, creating variety;
• time is allowed to move backwards briefly, creating interest;
• time is edited out so that the action is more dramatic.

Time, in other words, has been deployed so that we, as readers, are constantly kept on our mettle. A writer needs to be able to influence reading time for a straightforward reason: to make sure that the reader does not make a conscious decision to set your writing aside out of either frustration or boredom. One of the ways in which to do this is to vary the tempo of what is written, so that the story moves between 'real time' and a more accelerated time. This means developing a piece so that, for instance, dialogue is not overly protracted, and so that both action and focus shift.

ACTIVITY 16.9 Writing	Write an account (up to 750 words) of an evening spent in one location, reminiscing with a friend, which may be either fictional or autobiographical. It can be set anywhere, and should take place over a period of no more than two hours. When you have written the piece, include some actual or approximate times in the margin (for instance, '10.32 p.m.' or 'between 10.00 and 10.30 p.m.'). If you omit sections of time, note this as well as any kind of flashback or foreshadowing.
DISCUSSION	Two hours may now strike you as a long period of time in which to set a piece of fiction or life writing, since the process of reminiscence – coexisting in this case with the present, or interwoven with the present – takes space. You may have found that the focus on one location and a short period of time gave you the freedom to control the writing. The time over which the writing was set is a way of anchoring the writing so that it is more focused, and more absorbing to a reader.

Altering sequence

All fiction and non-fiction could be said to experiment with time, using methods such as acceleration, deceleration, omission and pause. It is common enough to begin near the end of the time-span of a novel or film. The 'whodunnit' genre is based on the idea of moving back in time to find out the cause of a crime. There are several examples of moving 'backwards' through a narrative. For example, Martin Amis's *Time's Arrow* (1991) moves backwards from the death of its central character to his birth. The aim is to move from the nature of the character's life towards its cause. Harold Pinter's play *Betrayal* (1978) moves back in time in each act, helping us to understand why and how the characters' relationships have developed. In Sarah Waters's *The Night Watch* (2006a, see Reading 6 on p.305), she took the decision to open the action in 1947, and then successively to move it back to 1944 and 1941, so that we understand what has brought the characters to the position they are in, in 1947. In this, she was influenced by Pinter's *Betrayal* (Waters, 2006b).

Something similar happens in the novel *A Good Man in Africa* (1981) by William Boyd. The second half of the novel takes place before the first half, clarifying the reason for the events we are first shown. Similarly, Simon Moss's play *Cock-Ups* (1984) dramatises the death of the playwright Joe Orton at the hands of his partner Kenneth Halliwell, who then committed suicide. In the first act of the play, Orton and Halliwell are dead (and the 'crime' is being investigated by one of Orton's most famous characters, Inspector Truscott); the second act reconstructs the last forty-five minutes of Orton's and Halliwell's lives. The last act of Caryl Churchill's play *Top Girls* (1982), which is discussed in Chapters 2 and 5, takes place a year before the events of the first two acts. Writer-director Christopher Nolan's film *Memento* (2000) is a thriller which jumps backwards in stages – its central character suffers from short-term memory loss, and the film reconstructs what has happened to him. When repackaged as a DVD, a version was included which edited events into chronological order – a reminder of the demands that experiments with time can make on, in this case, viewers.

Readers and viewers are increasingly prepared for shifts in time: what is important is that there is a logic for the shifts. Formal experiment with time is only important if it is used to delay a revelation, especially by inviting readers and viewers to speculate about earlier events which have led to what we are presented with at the outset. Fiction, as with drama, as we saw in Chapter 5, is about revealing secrets.

Conclusion

In this chapter we have explored a variety of ways in which time can be used: the organisation of time around one or two central events; the use of devices to manipulate the pace of the reader's experience; and the restructuring of time-frames at a minor and major level to make a narrative come alive. We have also seen that time does not exist on its own as a stylistic device, and that it can amplify a theme. In the next chapter we will look at the use of theme and sequence in narratives and poetry.

References

Amis, Martin (1991) *Time's Arrow*, Harmondsworth: Penguin.

Boyd, William (1981) *A Good Man in Africa*, London: Hamish Hamilton.

Brontë, Emily (2007 [1847]) *Wuthering Heights*, Harmondsworth: Penguin.

Churchill, Caryl (1982) *Top Girls*, London: Methuen.

Cowley, Malcolm (ed.) (1977 [1958]) *Writers at Work, The Paris Review Interviews, First Series*, Harmondsworth: Penguin.

Hardy, Thomas (1994 [1895]) *The Return of the Native*, Harmondsworth: Penguin.

Hines, Barry (1969 [1968]) *A Kestrel for a Knave*, Harmondsworth: Penguin.

Lowry, Malcolm (1946) *Under the Volcano*, London: Jonathan Cape.

McEwan, Ian (2003) *Saturday*, London: Jonathan Cape.

McEwan, Ian (2006) *On Chesil Beach*, London: Jonathan Cape.

Memento (2000) film, Christopher Nolan (director and writer).

Moss, Simon (1984) *Cock-Ups*, London: Faber and Faber.

Pinter, Harold (1978) *Betrayal*, London: Eyre Methuen.

Rayner, Keith and Pollatsek, Raymond (1989) *The Psychology of Reading*, London: Prentice-Hall International.

Styron, William (1951) *Lie Down in Darkness*, London: Corgi.

Styron, William (1979) *Sophie's Choice*, London: Jonathan Cape.

Waters, Sarah (2006a) *The Night Watch*, London: Virago.

Waters, Sarah (2006b) Interview, RTÉ [online], http://www.rte.ie/arts/2006/0519/waterss_av.html?2120710,null,209 (accessed 27 February 2008).

Further reading

Ford, Ford Madox (1995 [1915]) *The Good Soldier: Norton Critical Edition* (ed. Martin Stannard), New York: W.W. Norton.

This modernist classic has a narrator, Dowell, who ranges freely back and forth across ten years, telling a tale in which he hardly realises he has been involved (its celebrated first line is 'This is the saddest story I have ever heard'). Ford was one of the first to experiment with time and time-shift.

Thirteen Conversations About One Thing (2001) film, Jill Sprecher (director) and Karen Sprecher (writer).

This film plays cleverly with time by moving backwards and forwards between four parallel, different stories, which sometimes overlap, and meditating on the themes of destiny, coincidence, chance and luck (hence the 'Thirteen' of the title, although the film is also divided into thirteen sections). It uses images based on Edward Hopper's paintings to give the film unity.

17 Theme and sequence

Bill Greenwell

The short-story writer Frank O'Connor was once asked what the greatest essential of a story was. He replied

> You have to have a theme, a story to tell. ... A theme is something that is worth something to everybody. ... The moment you grab somebody by the lapels and you've got something to tell, that's a real story. *It means you want to tell him and think the story is interesting in itself.* If you start describing your own personal experiences, something that's only of interest to yourself, then you can't express yourself, you cannot say, ultimately, what you think about human beings.
>
> (quoted in Cowley, 1977 [1958], p.181; my italics)

This chapter will look at the importance of theme and how it might hold together a sequence of shorter pieces of writing. O'Connor's definition of a theme – 'what you think about human beings' – is a good one to hold on to: a theme is an exploration of how humans behave, of their values, their predilections. This is what lifts a story above the level of an account.

Writers do not think in themes when they begin to write; they tend to think in images, as Michael Ondaatje commented of his novel *The English Patient* (1992):

> Then there was a nurse and there was a patient, there was a man who was stealing back a photograph of himself. It was those three images. I did not know who they were, or how they were connected. So I sat down, I started to write and try to discover what the story was. And build from those three germs, really. I tend not to know what the plot is or the story is or even the theme. Those things come later, for me.
>
> (Ondaatje, 1996)

In other words, themes develop during the course of writing, emerge during or after the germination of story, plot and character. In previous chapters you have looked at the way in which voices, images, editing, style, analogy and the manipulation of time can strengthen a story. You have looked at the ways in which fiction and non-fiction borrow from drama and film to give a narrative its maximum impact. All these techniques have one purpose: to develop your story's theme.

As readers, you encounter a theme through reverberations and echoes in the writing, through a sense of a repeated preoccupation with particular ideas or debates. As writers, you have to establish those echoes, and to develop ways of signalling the ideas and debates beneath the surface of your stories – not in a stark and obvious way, but in as subtle a way as can be managed.

Imagine two different, contemporary characters who are jealous or envious, of someone or something else. One might be jealous of a colleague's success at work; another might be jealous of a friend's happy marriage. Write two short, separate passages of prose (up to 200 words each), one about the first character, and the other about the second.

If you placed these two pieces in a longer narrative they would have some resonance perhaps, especially if the characters were brought together by the plot. You would be encouraging your reader or audience to think of the causes and the nature of jealousy. At some level you would be creating a theme. The dominance of the theme would depend on the extent to which you persisted with it. Asking readers to compare the attitudes of two or more characters would give your work additional focus. In Ian McEwan's novel *Enduring Love* (1997), for instance, one character (Joe) becomes obsessed by the attention given to him by a stalker (Jed). Joe's obsession is rational; Jed's is caused by a psychiatric disorder. Nevertheless, their mutual obsession leads us to dwell on the nature of obsession, and this theme acts as a gateway to other recurring ideas in the novel.

Telling parallel stories

One way in which to develop a theme is to create separate narratives and to allow the reader to see the connections between them. We can see this in Michael Cunningham's novel *The Hours* and its film adaptation, scripted by David Hare, which were discussed in Chapters 11 and 9 respectively. Only once does a character from one of the three narratives meet one from another, but the stories are held together by comparisons, echoes and similarities. The writer encourages the audience to link the stories by using visual devices – the flowers in the film of *The Hours*, for instance. The repeated images encourage the viewer to speculate on what brings the three stories together.

Another device you can use to bring out a theme is the setting, or place, as in Adam Thorpe's rural environment in his novel *Ulverton* (1992), which we will look at later. Hotels (as well as hospitals, boarding-houses, aeroplanes, stations and so on) are often used in fiction because they bring strangers together under one roof, and thereby give them an odd equality of status. William Trevor's *The Boarding-House* (1965), Emma Tennant's

Hotel de Dream (1976) and Ali Smith's *Hotel World* (2001) are just three examples among many.

ACTIVITY 17.2
Writing

Imagine two rooms in the same hotel, in each of which there is a character. These two characters do not know each other. Write a passage (up to 200 words) for each character, in which you reveal their thoughts. You might choose to do this in the first person, or to use another form of interior monologue. Work on making the characters dwell on similar subjects.

DISCUSSION

You might have found that the characters' thoughts you described were about being away from home temporarily, about the strange freedoms and constraints that hotel rooms possess. Hotels lend themselves to themes of alienation and separation. If you were to work both characters into the same fiction, you might choose to keep the respective occupants of each room separated, or you might have them meet and amplify their themes.

A more radical example of using a hotel occurs in Terence Rattigan's pair of linked one-act plays *Separate Tables* (1955). Each is set in the same location (a Bournemouth hotel), and with the same minor characters. However, the protagonists of each play, in each case a woman and a man, have no direct connection with the protagonists of the other. What the two couples have in common is loneliness. Placing the plays side by side helps the writer to emphasise his theme: the private, uncertain worlds of the characters in each of them. In other words, place and structure help the writer to bring out the theme.

A more complex example is Geoff Ryman's hypertext and print novel *253* (1998). Two years before its publication in print, *253* – which tells the stories of 252 passengers, and the driver, on a tube train, and links them together – was available online as an interactive text, allowing readers to choose the order in which they read the fictions, each of which is 253 words long. The individual, private aspirations of each character are described as they sit in close proximity, but in a confined space. The place (the tube train) and the structure lend themselves to the novel's theme – the articulation of private frustrations and aspirations. We see into people's heads; but they cannot communicate with each other, even though they are, ironically, in a public space.

Bringing characters together by using place is also a staple of popular fiction, such as Maeve Binchy's *Evening Class* (1996), in which the overlapping aspirations of a large cast of characters are brought together by their attendance at an evening class in Italian. Television and radio soap operas, from *The Archers* to *Coronation Street*, also depend upon location to develop storylines which sometimes run in parallel.

Time and theme

Rattigan's plays *Separate Tables* are set over time: a year and a half separates the two plays, and the two meetings in the hotel. Thorpe's *Ulverton* contains twelve chapters which range over more than 350 years, but each chapter is set in the same rural community. As Thorpe testified, his theme became the rural world of England, its

> secret history, the hidden history. And I think part of the political programme of *Ulverton* was bound up with allowing voices that have been suppressed or are suppressed even now, when you look at history, to have their say.

> (Thorpe, 1996)

ACTIVITY 17.3 **Writing**	Either use any research about place you might have done for Activity 3.1 (relocating a story in the past) or find an account of the place in which you live as it was fifty years ago ('place' here can be taken to mean house, village or town). Write a passage (up to 200 words) on what it would have looked like, smelled like, and what it would have felt like to be there, assuming yourself to be the same age then as you are now. When you have finished, write another passage (up to 200 words), set fifty years in the future, in which a character imagines what it would have been like to live where you are now. It is up to you whether or not your character is correct in what he or she imagines.
DISCUSSION	If you place the two passages side by side you will find that, inevitably, you have created a piece which is about the nature of memory of place. Memory, as noted in Chapter 3, can be unreliable even memories of the same incident, as in the passages from Raban and Theroux (see Readings 4 and 5 on pp. 303 and 304). By seeing the same place from two perspectives you are already launching into an interesting theme – the way in which we view the past. It can be useful, in developing any theme, to have more than one 'take' on the same place or time.

Theme and the reader

Developing a theme does not mean that you need to explain it to the reader. Thorpe did not set out with a theme for *Ulverton*, or even with a novel in mind: he began with a single short story. As his theme came to him, he developed it through a succession of styles, from stream of consciousness to letters, to the final chapter which is a film script. It is, in fact, perfectly possible to read *Ulverton* as a succession of short stories. Thorpe testified that he wanted the reader to have to work hard because 'I don't see much point in writing a novel unless the reader works because there's so much in life and in culture at the moment that's just for easy consumption' (Thorpe, 1996).

One of the decisions you need to make is how ostentatious your themes will be. Leaving space for the reader is vital.

ACTIVITY 17.4 Reading	Read the extracts from Julian Barnes's novel *A History of the World in 10½ Chapters* (Reading 31 on p.399). They come from the seventh chapter, from the first two of what he calls 'Three Simple Stories'. What connections do you think Barnes wishes you to make between the two passages?
DISCUSSION	In the two passages, Barnes's theme of the relationship between myth and reality, and between art and reality, is examined through looking at alternative versions of history. The story of Lawrence Beesley (who did indeed exist, and whom Barnes met) makes us look at the way the *Titanic* is represented in fiction, whether on film, in a novel or in life writing. The revisiting of Bartley's story (which is a piece of late Victorian hokum) strengthens the discussion and amplifies Barnes's theme, which he repeats throughout the book. Only two chapters have any characters in common. But all the chapters explore the process of 'alternative' histories, whether through looking at a relationship between a man and a woman from two points of view, or looking at political action from two points of view, or interpreting history and religion in different ways.

If you are writing a sequence of pieces, it is important to let images resonate and to assist the echoes you are creating. Both the Beesley and Bartley stories involve disaster at sea. Many of Barnes's chapters involve disastrous journeys by water (and Barnes extends this to astronauts travelling on a 'ship' through space to land on the moon, as well as to the biblical Noah's Ark). The stronger the pattern of images, the greater the resonance of your theme. What you can learn from Barnes is how to weld a longer piece of writing together by allowing the reader to undertake much of the process of connection.

With a sequence like this, you can also blur and blend genre. *A History of the World in 10½ Chapters* – although published as a novel – is an interesting blend of life writing and fiction, including as it does autobiographical and myth-making sections like the ones in the readings, and works of 'purer' fiction.

Threads and echoes

Short-story collections are often linked by the tone of the writer as well as by the writer's preoccupations. For instance, we could say that Raymond Carver's stories focus on the dysfunctional or isolated lives of ordinary men and women in small-town America, and that this is his theme. However, there are interesting ways in which you can create a more closely linked, themed sequence of stories. One of these is to introduce echoes between them, sometimes by using location, sometimes by using recurrent characters, sometimes by repeating major incidents in one story as minor incidents in others.

In Kate Atkinson's collection of twelve short stories, *Not the End of the World* (2002), the underlying theme is of transformation, or the desire for it, but this theme is built up only through subtle echoes in the structure. A car crash on the M9 is incidental in the fifth story, but central to the tenth and glimpsed in the eleventh. In the third story, an incidental character is referred to as having died during dental surgery, but this incident resurfaces more centrally in the ninth story (this pattern is repeated with many characters). A television script proposed in one story resurfaces as a programme watched in a later story. The collection is like a sound-chamber, in which there are constant reverberations, often of Ovid's *Metamorphoses*. Each story remains readable as a separate entity; together, they encourage the reader to meditate on Atkinson's theme.

Another way to forge a close relationship between two stories is to connect the plot and subplot, as you saw in Chapter 9 when looking at film structure. Similarly, in Shakespeare's *King Lear*, the king is an old man who treats his three children as pawns. This could be seen as his fault alone, were it not that, in the same play, his closest adviser, Gloucester, also treats his own two children as pawns. The echo of the plot in the subplot means that the theme is strengthened. Lear abuses his power; so, too, does Gloucester's younger son, Edmund. Yet Lear and Edmund never exchange a word in the play, and are only briefly on stage together. The audience draws the parallels.

Blending two or more stories is a perfect way of developing a theme. Liz Jensen's novel *Ark Baby* (1998) began life as two separate, abandoned novels, one about a vet in the twenty-first century, the other about a nineteenth-century foundling. Rescuing both narratives, she wove them into a single novel which plays on the themes of heredity, and the way that ideas of creation have developed from Darwinism into scientific experiment (Jensen, 2008). *Ark Baby* is a 250-page novel – but even in a short story, the interplay between two incidents is what will often bring out its theme.

Theme and life writing

It might be thought that life writing is not concerned with theme – and it is true that conventional full-length autobiography and biography are less interested in theme than fiction, drama or poetry. However, there are occasionally biographies which take a particular line on their subject, or which concentrate on particular aspects. For instance, Claire Tomalin's *Thomas Hardy: The time-torn man* (2006) depicts her subject as a poet whose response to his first wife's death, as a man and as a writer, reveals an energetic, romantic and lyrical individual – a man steeped in the music of his childhood. Significantly, she starts her biography with Emma Hardy's death, not with Hardy's birth.

In food writer Nigel Slater's *Toast: The story of a boy's hunger* (2003), the structure is based on Proustian associations with particular meals or tastes. Little attempt is made to link the events chronologically, and the book focuses specifically on childhood and adolescence – for instance, on the 'hunger', as here, for sexual attraction.

> The kitchen looked out on to the gravel car park and then to the wide field that led down to the river. 'No children in the bar' meant exactly that and they would often sit in the car park with pint glasses of lemonade while their parents drank in the lounge bar with its wood panels and hunting prints. There was one girl, older than the others, with piercing violet eyes and dark hair that straggled down over her shoulders, who would sit in the passenger seat of her parents' Humber Hawk for hours, sometimes reading, other times just staring out at the other kids. No one ever brought a drink out to her. Whenever the smoke of the grill ... became unbearable I would stand in the car park with a lime and lemonade, or sometimes a shandy, and she would look up from her book and smile.
>
> Whenever drinks were poured by mistake they were brought into the kitchen for the staff. ...
>
> One night a tray of drinks arrived in the kitchen – the result of someone doing a 'runner' – with only Diane and me to drink them. I took a couple of them out to the girl in the Humber, who received them with a smile that was cheeky, quizzical. She knocked them back like I had only ever seen anyone do on television. Later, when I overcooked a steak and I hadn't got time to eat the evidence, I ran out into the car park with it, wrapped up in napkin, and gave her that too.
>
> I started to watch out for Julia, at least I knew her name now if nothing else, and started cooking bits of fillet specially for her; the

tail end perhaps, or a slice that had been cut too thin. 'Don't cook it so much next time,' she would say, with the same cheeky grin.

(Slater, 2003, pp.195–6)

When life writing focuses, especially in snapshots and extracts, on aspects of a life, it can easily build up the kind of strength of theme to be found in fiction. Short passages of life writing have more power to focus, because they are not obliged to deal with a complete life.

ACTIVITY 17.5
Writing

Choose some incidents in either your life or someone else's which have to do with one of the following themes: regret, desire, escape, guilt or money. Write a short piece (up to 300 words) on one of the incidents, and make notes on the others, focusing on one of the suggested themes.

DISCUSSION

At first, these projected pieces may seem separated, but because you are writing about the same life, and on the same subjects, you may see a theme emerging. The words themselves do not constitute themes. 'Money', for instance, is a subject, rather than a theme. What matters is how you explore the impact, effect, importance (and so on) of money. As you saw from the extracts from Barnes, you can leave the reader to draw conclusions, or you can blend the pieces so that you provide, or even lead, a debate for the reader.

You can explore this in a longer piece of work, perhaps particularly in longer fiction or in a poetry sequence, through repeated or recurrent images. One of my favourite examples of this is in Dickens's novel *Our Mutual Friend* (1997 [1865]), in which he uses two dominant sequences of images to suggest the corruption of money: dust-heaps and dolls. One character, Mr Venus, runs a shop selling bones, artificial limbs and stuffed animals. This alerts us to the many doll-like features of the characters, to the shallowness and artificiality of their attitudes, and to a recurring theme of Dickens – that people are often treated like so many commodities.

Theme in poetry sequences

Writing a sequence of poetry invariably involves the use of echo and resonance, sometimes with more emphasis on the structural similarity of the poems which the sequence contains. A sequence is designed to develop a theme and to explore ideas through images, often by shifting and altering the perspective of each successive poem.

In Chapter 2, we looked at Carol Ann Duffy's poem 'We Remember Your Childhood Well' (see pp.17–18). Although it can be read in isolation, it is the sixteenth poem in a sequence of forty-four poems published as *The Other Country* (1990). Here are two poems, 'Ape' and 'Boy', from the same point of the sequence. What would you say their relationship is to 'We Remember Your Childhood Well', and to each other?

Ape

There is a male silverback on the calendar.
Behind him the jungle is defocused,
except in one corner, where trees gargle the sun.

After you have numbered the days, you tear off
the page. His eyes hold your eyes
as you crumple a forest in your fist.

(Duffy, 1990, p.20)

Boy

I liked being small. When I'm on my own
I'm small. I put my pyjamas on
and hum to myself. I like doing that.

What I don't like is being large, you know,
grown up. Just like that. Whoosh. Hairy.
I think of myself as a boy. Safe slippers.

The world is terror. Small you can go *As I
lay down my head to sleep, I pray* ... I remember
my three wishes sucked up a chimney of flame.

I can do it though. There was an older woman
who gave me a bath. She was joking, of course,
but I wasn't. I said *Mummy* to her. Off-guard.

Now it's a question of getting the wording right
for the Lonely Hearts verse. There must be someone
out there who's kind to boys. Even if they grew.

(p.29)

DISCUSSION

Duffy's method of organisation in *The Other Country* is to take her theme of 'otherness' and gradually to shift and amend its context. In 'Ape', a human ('you') stares at a photograph of another primate, only to discard the paper on which it is printed in the same way that humans destroy forests. The ape of the calendar is in every sense in another 'country' from the calendar owner. This tension and separation is picked up in the two views of the world discussed in Chapter 2 – the differing views of a childhood memory in 'We Remember Your Childhood Well'. By the time the reader has reached 'Boy', there is a tension of a different sort between childhood and adulthood. The speaker is helpless, unable to 'grow up'. The three poems are very different in style, length and voice. But there are links between all three poems: the parents in 'We Remember Your Childhood Well' won't allow the child to grow up, to be independent; the man in 'Boy' is trapped by feeling 'hairy' – just as the silverback is hairy. In all three, 'the world is terror'; in all three, the central figure is oppressed.

Structuring a sequence

In Duffy's collection, the poems hold a kind of restless conversation with the reader. Having found her theme, she seems to have shuffled her pack of poems until they were in the most interesting and suggestive order. However, there are many other ways of creating a themed sequence, and one is to take a set of characters, or a group of naturally related phenomena or objects. The pressure of the structure will help you locate your ideas. For instance, Frieda Hughes bases a sequence, *Waxworks* (2002), on wax models at Madame Tussaud's. It presents over fifty figures from myth and history, ordered to imply a growing darkness, finishing as it does with images of apocalypse and hell. The order of a sequence will help determine the theme, whether the theme is developed incrementally, as with Hughes, or improvised upon, as with Duffy's *The Other Country*.

ACTIVITY 17.7
Writing

Think of four herbs and research their properties. For instance, fennel is said to suppress appetite and thyme is said to stop nightmares (both herbs are said to have many other properties). Draft some ideas for poems based on your four herbs.

DISCUSSION

It would be possible to plan quite literal poems, for instance, about the medicinal or symbolic meaning of herbs. However, a sequence can have a great deal of power if it foils the reader's expectation – if, instead of seeing from an expected point of view, the poet were to write in this case, for instance, about what the herbs cure. For fennel and thyme, I would be tempted to write about appetite and nightmare. You could connect the poems in at least two possible ways, apart from their herbal origins: you could create the same voice for both poems, and have the voice speak about the effect of appetite and nightmare (the nightmare poem could be about an insatiable appetite). You could also use the same structure for each poem (say, a sonnet), so that the relationship was kept intact.

Letting themes emerge

Subjects of poems in sequences should be allowed to fire your imagination, not to control it. It is best to write about related subjects and to see what theme emerges – to break away from the starting points. You can experiment by writing poems that are linked to a series of related paintings or photographs. For instance, in Anne Ryland's *Autumnologist* (2006), there is a seven-poem sequence, 'After Vermeer', based on seven of the Dutch artist's paintings. You could plan a sequence of poems linked to a series of paintings which are similar, or which are based on an existing, ordered sequence, such as William Hogarth's *The Rake's Progress*. (*The Rake's Progress* is a sequence of eight paintings published as engravings in 1735. It chronicles the moral decline of the spendthrift Tom Rakewell, who descends by degrees from good fortune to debt, and finally incarceration in an asylum.) Were you to choose a series like *The Rake's Progress*, its order would structure your sequence for you.

However, there are many other ways to arrange a sequence. In Carol Ann Duffy's collection *The World's Wife* (1999), she explores gender in a sequence of monologues, spoken by the imaginary or imagined wives of famous mythological, literary or historical men (Mrs Midas, Mrs Darwin, Queen Kong, and so on). Order is far less important here than in Duffy's *The Other Country*; unity of approach is what binds the monologues in *The World's Wife*. Incidentally, mythological and historical figures give a writer great scope for theme and invention. Jane Griffiths's poem 'Icarus on Earth', in her collection of the same name (2005), uses Icarus not as a mythological character, but as the controlling idea behind eleven poems about a contemporary young man's aspirations. The sequence is spoken by six voices, and includes both a pantoum and an experimental sestina (the envoi is between the fourth and fifth stanza).

Narrative sequences

C.S. Lewis wrote that poetic sequences were 'not a way of telling a story'. Instead, Lewis likened a sequence to an 'archipelago of narrative' and referred to its 'meditative' quality (Lewis, 1954, pp.327–8). Lewis was referring to sonnet sequences, and this quality of meditation is specifically given shape and control by the sonnet form. In this form, you can explore the subject from very different angles, while maintaining the unity which the sonnets provide. The same meditative quality is also present in contemporary free-verse sequences which use a degree of chronology.

ACTIVITY 17.8 Writing	From your notebook – or from a published journal – pick seven days in chronological order (they do not need to be one week). Make notes towards a projected sequence which follows those days, picking a fragment or detail of image from each. Connect the days by theme, even though you are following a given order.

DISCUSSION	In describing a succession of days it is important to shape them into more than a mere sequence of events. Constructing a sequence of poems brings into sharp focus the need not to tell your reader too much – perhaps more clearly, but just as importantly, as in fiction, drama, and the kinds of life writing described in this chapter. Your sequence will start to work once it provides glimpses and snapshots and, as in the process of screenwriting described in Chapter 9, and echoed in Chapter 11, your poems will only work if they leave space for the reader's imagination to move at liberty. The principle of a fugue is used in Ciaran Carson's sequence *For All We Know* (2008). Its general epigraph cites these words by the pianist and composer Glenn Gould: 'Fugue must perform its frequent stealthy work with continuously shifting melodic fragments that remain, in the "tune" sense, perpetually unfinished.'

ACTIVITY 17.9 Reading	Read the four poems below. They are consecutive poems from Selima Hill's eighty-poem sequence *Bunny* (2001a). • In what way are they connected? • How much does a reader have to supply?

Blancmange

First of all everything goes thick.
Her hands and face are coated in thick glue.

And then she sinks; and then the word *blancmange*
fills the flooded woods with wobbly blue.

Angora

The soothing blob of wobbly blue
turns indigo

and calmly explodes
in tiny angora stars

where coloured pets
collapsing with a puff

are congratulating themselves
on dying happy.

Budgie

They offer her a bowl of warm Bemax
and wrap her in a blanket like a clock

and put her in a room with a budgie
and let her cry until the doctor comes.

Doctor

The doctor says
the lodger says I'm sorry.

But it isn't enough.
It isn't enough, I'm sorry.

(Hill, 2001a, pp.62–5)
Bemax: A commonly prescribed vitamin drink in the 1950s.

DISCUSSION

A great deal of the disturbing strength of these poems comes from what we are forced to imagine. All we have are four very short glimpses, curious and emotive, but connected thematically by the image of thick liquid and of coating. The related images of glue, blancmange and Bemax suggest that the main figure is retreating into herself, and also that she is being sedated. She is certainly being treated as less than human, and sees herself as less than human too: she is like a budgie, like a wrapped-up clock. We get the sense of the adolescent girl retreating from the known world, being institutionalised. These poems come at a transitional stage in the narrative. They are, until the last line of 'Doctor', strange and subdued. Nothing is explicit. If you write a narrative sequence in poetry you need to be ruthless about making it sparse, about letting the reader do the work of connecting the events.

Hill began her sequence originally with the idea of creating a positive sequence of images of a young woman growing up in the 1950s (Hill, 2001b). But she found that her material was darker, and she let it take a new course, a course that she developed by visiting her childhood home. *Bunny* became a strong narrative sequence consisting, principally but not exclusively, of short poems (four to eight lines). They chronicle an unnamed teenage girl's experience of solitude, abuse, depression and recovery – her trauma at the hands of adults. A key figure in the narrative is a lodger (also nameless), whose desire for the girl is horribly overpowering.

Bunny is a poetry sequence, but you could equally create a sequence out of short pieces of prose. One of the novels from which an extract is taken in Chapter 13 – Sandra Cisneros's *The House on Mango Street* – consists of short passages of between 400 and 800 words. Cisneros said of it that:

> I recall I wanted to write stories that were a cross between poetry and fiction. I was greatly impressed by Jorge Luis Borges' *Dream Tigers* stories for their form. I liked how he could fit so much into a page and that the last line of each story was important to the whole in much the same way that the final lines in poems resonate. Except I wanted to write a collection which could be read at any random point without having any knowledge of what came before or after. Or that could be read in a series to tell one big story.
> I wanted stories like poems, compact and lyrical and ending with a reverberation.
>
> (quoted in Olivares, 1988, p.160)

Conclusion

This chapter has explored the subterranean nature of theme in fiction, non-fiction, drama and poetry sequences. The novelist Nigel Watts compares theme to 'a unifying thread, a line of thought that leads through a story upon which the plot events are strung like beads' (Watts, 1996, p.115). The thread, no matter what the genre, should not be too visible. If, like me, you prefer a musical metaphor in describing theme, then it is important that its echoes are not too loud. A sequence of chapters, a sequence of stories, a sequence of dramatic scenes and a sequence of poems need to be connected in a surreptitious and imaginative way, so that the reader can delight in glimpsing the thread, sensing the echo. Whether you are writing a novel or a play, or compiling collections of stories, dramatic episodes, or poems which are united by theme, take great pleasure in finding the best order – the richest, most tantalising and most powerful order or sequence. Laying the trail of your theme, as you discover it, is one of the most enjoyable experiences for any writer – and following the trail will engross your reader.

References

Atkinson, Kate (2002) *Not the End of the World*, London: Doubleday.

Binchy, Maeve (1996) *Evening Class*, London: Orion.

Cowley, Malcolm (ed.) (1977 [1958]) *Writers at Work, The Paris Review Interviews, First Series*, Harmondsworth: Penguin.

Cunningham, Michael (1999) *The Hours*, New York: Farrar, Straus and Giroux.

Carson, Ciaran (2008) *For All We Know*, Oldcastle: The Gallery Press.

Dickens, Charles (1997 [1865]) *Our Mutual Friend*, Harmondsworth: Penguin.

Duffy, Carol Ann (1990) *The Other Country*, London: Anvil.

Duffy, Carol Ann (1999) *The World's Wife*, London: Picador.

Griffiths, Jane (2005) *Icarus on Earth*, Tarset: Bloodaxe.

Hill, Selima (2001a) *Bunny*, Tarset: Bloodaxe.

Hill, Selima (2001b) Interview, *Woman's Hour*, BBC Radio 4 [online], http://www.bbc.co.uk/radio4/womanshour/2001_39_tue_03.shtml (accessed 2 March 2008).

Hughes, Frieda (2002) *Waxworks*, Tarset: Bloodaxe.

Jensen, Liz (1998) *Ark Baby*, London: Bloomsbury.

Jensen, Liz (2008) Interview, A363 *Advanced creative writing*, Audio CD3, Milton Keynes: The Open University.

Lewis, C.S. (1954) *English Literature in the Sixteenth Century*, Oxford: Clarendon Press.

McEwan, Ian (1997) *Enduring Love*, London: Jonathan Cape.

Olivares, Julian (1988) 'Sandra Cisneros' *The House on Mango Street* and the Poetics of Space' in *Chicana Creativity and Criticism: Charting new frontiers in American literature* (ed. Maria Herrera-Sobek and Helena Maria Viramontes), Houston: Arte Publico Press.

Ondaatje, Michael (1992) *The English Patient*, London: Bloomsbury.

Ondaatje, Michael (1996) Interview, *Salon.com*, November 1996 [online], http://www.salon.com/nov96/ondaatje961118.html (accessed: 2 March 2008).

Rattigan, Terence (1955) *Separate Tables*, London: Hamish Hamilton.

Ryland, Anne (2006) *Autumnologist*, Darlington: Arrowhead.

Ryman, Geoff (1998) *253: The print remix*, London: Flamingo; *253* is available online at http://www.ryman-novel.com/ (accessed 2 March 2008).

Slater, Nigel (2003) *Toast: The story of a boy's hunger*, London: Fourth Estate.

Smith, Ali (2001) *Hotel World*, London: Hamish Hamilton.

Tennant, Emma (1976) *Hotel de Dream*, London: Gollancz.

Thorpe, Adam (1992) *Ulverton*, London: Secker & Warburg.

Thorpe, Adam (1996) Interview, *Erfurt Electronic Studies in English* [online], http://www.uni-erfurt.de/eestudies/eese/artic96/hagenau/3_96.html (accessed 2 March 2008).

Tomalin, Claire (2006) *Thomas Hardy: The time-torn man*, London: Viking.

Trevor, William (1965) *The Boarding-House*, London: The Bodley Head.

Watts, Nigel (1996) *Writing a Novel and Getting It Published*, London: Hodder & Stoughton.

Further reading

Rabinowitz, Anna (2001) *Darkling*, Dorset, Vermont: Tupelo Press.

Darkling is an experimental narrative sequence of fragmented poetry about the Holocaust, filled with voices and images, and held together by an unusual 'armature'   it is an acrostic sequence in which each line successively spells out every letter of Thomas Hardy's end-of-the-century poem 'The Darkling Thrush'. As a sequence, it opens up unusual new ways of organisation.

Buford, Bill (ed.) (1984) *Granta 14: Autobiography*, London: Granta Publications.

Buford, Bill (ed.) (1992) *Granta 41: Biography*, London: Granta Publications.

These are two excellent anthologies of biographical and autobiographical writing, both of which include short memoirs with strong and particular themes.

1   'Violin Lessons'

Derek Neale

1

'What do you think you're doing?' I say. He just stands there leaning over the split door; doesn't run away, doesn't say anything. Kids are always snooping around, coming down the lane on their way to the woods. They run off when they see me. They look at me as if I'd eat them alive. This one's wearing his school uniform. Eleven, I'd say, twelve at the outside; his green and black tie flapping in the wind. I press the red button and the lump of oak on the lathe whirs and slows. Still on the threshold, I'll say that for him; waiting until he's invited.

'What do you do in here?' he says. His voice echoes around the rafters. It's not often I get a visitor; not here, not in the workshop.

'Come in, if you like. Have a look.' I say, 'Have to take that tie off though.' If there's a rule worth having it's that one: no loose clothing of any description. 'Before you know it the circular saw will have it,' I tell him. 'Or else it'll get wrapped around the lathe. And you'll go with it.'

I let him press the green button; click and whir, the oak starts to spin. He wants to see me in action. I tell him not to sit on the mahogany; it's still seasoning and might warp. He stands and watches.

'What's it going to be?' he says.

'A chair leg,' I tell him. 'My speciality legs.' I point to the pile I've done that week. He picks one up and says it looks like a pillar:

'My sister's old dolls' house has got pillars just like that.'

'Then your sister's a lucky girl,' I say. I don't believe him. Dolls' houses don't have proper pillars. My legs have all the right proportions; Ionic chair legs of the classic order, fluting and all. The only thing I add are the carvings in the capital.

'Keeps her love letters in there now. And her French letters.'

'What?' I say. I don't know what he's talking about.

'In the dolls' house, doesn't think I know. What do you expect from a girl!' I reach for the half inch chisel and tell him not to rest his foot on the mahogany.

'I'm going to make an electric guitar when I'm in the fourth year.'

I pretend not to hear him. 'Shouldn't you be at home?' I say.

'I'm waiting for my sister.'

'And where's your sister?'

'Violin lesson, down the lane with Mr. Bouillon. I'm supposed to sit and listen to that racket! I usually go down the woods.'

He searches in his pockets, pulling out his rolled up tie. It unravels like an escaped snake onto the floor. He looks at me and picks it up before I can say anything, but I'm thinking of the dream; the violin and the woods. I dreamt it again last night:

I'm walking in the woods, but there are no leaves crackling under foot, no birds singing or branches creaking. Not a whisper. There's a man standing under a silver birch, playing a violin as if his life depended on it. I don't see his face but I feel as if I know him. He seems possessed by the music but I can't hear it. I strain, I stop breathing, but I can't hear it. I have this dream regularly. I wake up happy, like I've been on a long journey. I've come to think there is no music. Only a picture, that's all.

I press the red button, staring at the mahogany; a ball of green and black springing to life, rolling off the wood into the shavings on the floor.
I realise it's the boy's tie. I look down and see him staring at me defiantly, dangling something wrinkled and wet in the air between us.

'Want a French letter?' he says. 'I found it in the woods. Hasn't been used.'

He pushes it towards my face and I tell him to go.

2

Mr. Bouillon walks past the door. He nods and smiles. My mouth is full of cheese sandwich; some of it falls out as I try to smile back. He's about my age, young for a violin teacher. They say he lives alone but once I saw him walking down the lane with a young woman. She had ginger hair. I made him a set of rush chairs last year. They were in ash, simple things; he didn't want any carving on them. I throw the rest of my sandwich out for the birds and watch Mr. Bouillon walking under the ash tree at the edge of the woods. He usually goes for a walk about this time.

I prefer mornings. In the morning the woods are empty, save for the blackbirds and thrushes rustling in the undergrowth. I could go to work in the van, drive round, but I like to walk. It's a habit of mine; I like kicking through the dew, breaking the spiders' webs across the path. I always stick to the path, but my eyes wander through the mist rising over the pond, up to the glowing red pine bark, and down through the dappled grey lines of beech. I get my ideas there, for the carvings. I gather the shapes like kindling; twigs of light, branches of shadow. I bring it all back here and then I set to work; drawing, measuring, planning. That's where all the hard work's done, the construction. Shapes and ideas are nothing without hard work, and a solid framework. It's table legs this month; Doric. They have

to be sturdier, less ornate: but the bevel in the shaft presents a challenge.
One slip either way and I've had it.

*

The boy lets himself in and goes straight over to the circular saw.
He touches the still blade with his finger tips.

'Dad doesn't think Mr. Bouillon's a very good teacher,' he says.
'He's going to send her somewhere else.'

The boy comes every Wednesday now, while his sister has her violin
lesson. He says he wants to be my apprentice, but he's got a long way to
go. He does some sanding and a little hand sawing. Most of the time he
stands watching; making me think out loud, asking what wood I'm using,
and nagging me to split some plinths on the circular saw. That's his
favourite; watching it slice through, straight as a die. Sometimes he sits on
the mahogany and I tell him to get off. He laughs about it but he gets up.

I look up and see the boy's hand is still on the blade.

'Get your hand off that saw!' I say. He gets a comb from his pocket.
Using the saw blade as a mirror he combs his hair.

'Why are all your legs like pillars?' he says. 'Why don't they ever
have curves in them?'

'They do have curves,' I say. 'Of course they have curves.' But the
boy has put his comb away and is swaying backwards and forwards,
outlining a figure of eight with his hands:

'A bit of ... you know.'

I don't know what he means but something is nagging; at the back of
my head, something to do with the legs. The man in the dream flashes
through my mind. I know there's a curve in the picture, the sort of curve
the boy's talking about, but I can't make it out. I can't remember.

The boy is staring at me. I'm hot and sticky. I pull at his tie and he
says 'okay'. He unties the knot slowly and slides it off. He stuffs it in his
pocket without rolling it.

'How do you do this?' he says. I have to think for a moment.

'Well,' I say, 'first of all you decide on materials, which wood and
what size. Then there's the shape and style to consider.'

'No,' he says, 'I mean, why do you do it?'

'Why? Because I get satisfaction from it, of course, from getting a
lump of rough old wood and seeing it grow into something new, something
that I've ...'

'Carved up,' he interrupts. 'That's what you do isn't it? Just carve it
up.' My mouth is dry, I can't talk. I look around at the table legs stacked
against the wall, and the table tops and cross-members next to them. I feel
trapped. I want to put all the parts together, to stack them up and burn them.

The boy sits on the mahogany picking his nose. I tell myself it's almost over. A few more Doric legs and it will all be done. That's what I always tell myself: I just pick a new job, a new horizon, and aim for it. It doesn't matter how difficult it is, doesn't matter if it never gets made. But I've got to have the next job somewhere, I've got to be thinking about it. I wave my chisel at the boy but he doesn't get up off the mahogany. He's not looking. He's scowling over towards the door. I turn and see a white blouse and a mass of ginger hair. I can't see a face.

'Who's that?' I say, before I can stop myself.

'Verruca with the big bazookas,' says the boy.

'Veronica, if you don't mind,' she says. 'I've come to get my baby brother.'

She raises her head and sweeps her hair back. I don't understand. I thought his sister would be younger. She looks too old for a school uniform, too old for violin lessons. She looks down at her tie; she's trying to put it on but hasn't fastened the top buttons of her blouse.

'Can I come in?' she says.

'You'll have to take that off,' says the boy, pointing over to the tie.

'Why?' she says, guarding the unfastened part of her blouse with her hands. She looks at me as if I might hurt her.

'Safety,' I say, trying to sound reassuring. 'Machine tools you see. I make it a general rule, no loose fitting clothing.'

'You heard him,' says the boy. 'Get 'em off!'

I turn back to the lathe and pretend to look for another chisel.

'Shut up you ...' she says but I press the green button. The lathe starts whirring and I can't hear what they shout at each other, only the tone of their voices. I feel as though I shouldn't be there. The pine leg spins faster and my chisel cuts deep, ringing the wood below the capital. This one's almost finished, spinning on its side like a fallen ballerina. I think of new shapes, of curves and twists; the next job. But I don't know what it is.

I press the red button. While the leg slows and stops I put the chisels away. The boy sits on the mahogany, sorting through his pockets. I look at him and feel helpless. His sister has let herself in. She leaves her violin by the door and wanders around touching things. She holds her tie by her side and leans over the pine leg on the lathe, sniffing at the uncut wood on the bench.

'Beautiful smell,' she says. 'What is it?'

'Damson,' I say. 'Does it smell nice?'

'Can't you smell it?' She picks it up and holds it up to my nose. I can smell nothing. She puts the wood back on the bench and leans over it again:

'Mm ... you don't know what you're missing.'

My stomach's rolling and I feel hot. I'm looking at her. She's holding her hair back. A silver cross, a crucifix on a chain, hangs out of her blouse. It dangles onto the lathe. In my mind the lathe starts turning and I want to tear the chain from her neck. I look at the green and red buttons, start and stop, side by side, then back at the crucifix; the face, and the thorns sticking into the head. I imagine the blood, the weight of the body, sagging. I feel my lips curl but I don't know why I'm smiling.

She looks up and sees me staring. She smiles but seems uneasy. Her hand snatches at her blouse and she fastens the buttons up to the neck. She glances over at the boy then smiles at me in a different way. She's sure of herself now.

'Could you teach me how to use this?' she says, putting her hand on the lathe.

'Veronica!' says the boy.

'I'd really like to learn. Why not?'

I don't know what to say, but she doesn't seem to expect me to say anything. She puts her foot up on the bench, smoothing down her black tights. She pulls at the lace of her shoe.

'I'm going,' says the boy. He gets up but waits at the door. She ties her lace slowly. I feel angry, I want to get back to work. I pick up a chisel, but her leg is too close; I can't reach the green button. I don't try. I think she's going to tie her other shoelace but she wanders off round the mahogany to the door. She smiles at me when she picks up her violin, but she's smiling through me, as if I'm not there. The boy looks at her as though he hates her and walks off. I hear her shout down the lane: 'What's the matter with you?' I press the green button and see a school tie, curled out on the mahogany.

3

It's Wednesday but I don't expect the boy to come. He hasn't been for three weeks now, not since his sister saw me staring at her crucifix. But the boy's tie has helped me with the next job. It lies on the mahogany, a green and black snake, curling and swerving, slinking round. Twisting. It's alive. The mahogany's beginning to warp but I'm not too worried; I don't think I'll be needing it. I'm ordering the new wood tomorrow.

I'm drawing curves. It's a new experience for me, I've no means of measuring them. It's the next job, the early stages. I wrecked the bevel on two legs this morning; it was no use carrying on. I kept going too far, cutting too deep or using the wrong chisel. I wasn't myself; I kept thinking about the crucifix, that and the dream. The dream has changed. There's usually a storm now. I stand in the woods, the branches whipping all around me. The rain pours into my eyes so I can't see, but I feel as if the man's still there, playing his violin. I want more than ever to hear the music, I want him to be playing one of those hymns; 'To be a Pilgrim', or 'Onward Christian Soldier Marching as to War'. Sometimes I hear a screech, like violin strings being scratched and stretched. Most of the time all I can hear is the wind whipping the branches. I try to look, but the rain drives into my eyes so I have to turn away.

*

The boy reaches over and unlatches the bottom half of the door. He lets himself in. He looks different, he's unsure; he's wearing jeans and a sweater. I offer him one of my cheese sandwiches. He stands, stiff as a board, not wanting to look me in the eye.

'Have you seen Veronica?' he says.

'No, I haven't,' I say. But I feel strangely guilty, as if I'm lying. I think of the crucifix dangling over the lathe.

'She's gone missing,' he says. 'She went to her new violin class on Monday. No one's seen her since.'

I feel clumsy, I don't know what to say. I look at the tie, curled up on the mahogany. Before I can stop myself I tell him: 'You left your tie.' He picks it up and examines it.

'It's not mine,' he says, and looks up at me. The tie hangs from his hand down to the ground, the curves all straightened out. I wish I hadn't mentioned it.

'It's hers,' he says. He's looking hard into my eyes, searching but drawing back at the same time, as if he's scared, as if I might eat him alive.

'Sh ... She must have left it,' I stutter, 'last time you were here.' His eyes scan from one side of my face to the other, looking for something, looking as if he might run at any moment.

'Has she been here?' he says.

'No,' I say. 'Not since that last time, the last time you were here.'

He still looks at me but he's not searching anymore, at least I don't think so. I wait to make sure but the silence is more than I can bear. 'Your mother and father must be worried,' I say, but I realise straight away that they must be more than worried. Much more. I cover my mouth with my hand. I don't know why I'm smiling, I know that it's wrong. He looks up to the rafters, and I see he's grabbing at something, something that he's heard.

'She was going to go to college next year,' he says. Did he hear his parents say it? Did he hear their voices crack? His voice doesn't crack. It's just serious. He looks at me as if I know something.

4

When I drove past Mr. Bouillon's house this morning I saw them putting up a For Sale sign just inside the gate. They say he's already gone. I wonder whether he took the rush chairs with him. I drive round in the van every morning now. After the boy came and told me about his sister

I started seeing faces everywhere; hanging in the honeysuckle, nestling in the branches, even in the mud around the pond. The faces were all smiling; her smile. They stayed with me even when I got here. I shut the door, top and bottom, trying to keep them out. But they kept coming and I kept seeing the crucifix dangling over the lathe as it span round, thorns wrapped around the pale white wood, blood splashing everywhere. It's just as well I managed to finish the table legs when I did.

It put a bit of a shadow over things. But I won't be needing the lathe or the circular saw half as much with the new job. I picked up a bending iron yesterday, now all I've got to do is teach myself how to use it. I made the moulds out of some beech that I've had for years, it's well seasoned. I decided on a Guarnerius, it seems the easiest to start with. I'm picking up the wood this afternoon, after I've been to the record library.

I stopped having the dream. Well, I stopped remembering it. I still wake up some days with the same feeling, as if I've been on a long journey. I still want to hear the music. That's why I joined the record library. Beethoven's my favourite, the violin concerto. It's the sort of music that stays with you, keeps you going.

*

I feel a tap on my back as I'm bending into the van to get the last piece of sycamore.

'What have you got there?' says the boy, but he walks off into the workshop before I can tell him. He sits down on the mahogany, leaning forward, with his elbows on his knees. His tie hangs in a straight green and black line, down to the floor.

'What is it?' he says, as I bring the last load in.

'Well,' I say, 'this is sycamore for the back, ribs, head and neck. And this is Swiss pine for the belly.' I pick up a piece of each to show him: I want to show him how pleased I am with it.

'What are you making, a body?' he says. 'What's this?' He jumps up and grabs the ebony from the dust sheet covering the circular saw. 'Bloody hell, it's like lead.' I start to explain but he puts it down on the mahogany and peeps under the sheet covering the lathe. 'What happened to your legs?' he says. 'I liked your legs.' I pick up the ebony and take it over to the bench, out of his reach. I feel as if I should guard it. 'Well, what happened to the legs?' he says. My fingers stroke the smooth black surface of the wood, and I remember her tying her shoelace, her foot up on the bench where the ebony sits.

'I've got a new job on now,' I say, trying to pull myself out of it. But I've started thinking: the crucifix dangling down over the lathe.

'Suppose you want me to take this off,' he says, starting to undo this tie.

'No,' I say. 'There's no need.' He's not listening and takes it off anyway. He puts his feet up on the mahogany, so he's almost lying down. He looks at me as if he wants me to say something.

'It's alright,' I say. 'You can sit on there now. I've got no use for it.'

He stretches out, looking at me all the time, as if he's waiting for me to say something else. But I'm watching the tie. It's alive; green and black, next to him on the mahogany, curled out and twisting.

'What about ...' I say, but he gets up slowly from the mahogany and walks away. 'No,' I say, 'What about the ... What about your sister?' I feel guilty about asking.

'Her?' he says, his voice rising as if he's just smelt something rotten. He looks like he doesn't want to talk about it. I don't understand. I see the crucifix catching on the lathe and pulling her down, the chain cutting into her neck, pulling her down.

'But what happened?' I say, I can't help myself.

'What happened?'

'She's in Brighton,' he mumbles, 'with Mr. Bubblegum.'

'What?'

'Mr. Bouillon, the violin teacher,' he says. 'Ran off with him. What a slut!'

'I thought ...' but I don't know anymore what I thought.

'She rang,' he says, 'but not before half the country was out looking for her. Dad went berserk. He's going down there next weekend to try and find them.'

I think of his sister and Mr. Bouillon round a table drinking tea, sitting on rush seats. My chairs in Brighton, by the sea. The boy looks up and asks me what I'm smiling about. He kneels down, picking up the moulds from the floor: 'What are these?'

'The next job,' I say. 'Moulds for the next job.' I can't stop smiling, I want to tell him.

'Violins?' he says, his voice cracking. 'What do you want to make violins for?'

I tell him I'm going to start with a Guarnerius, just to see how it goes; I'll work my way up to a Stradivarius. Then I might even try the odd viola or even a cello, who knows. But violins will be my mainstay, violins are what I want to make. I rush to the shelves at the back of the workshop, to get the drawings to show him, but as I'm coming back with them the boy drops the moulds down onto the mahogany. They bounce off onto the floor and I run over to pick them up.

'You stupid boy!' I shout, 'Be careful with them!' And I brush the shavings off them, shouting at him all the time, 'You stupid, stupid boy!' They're not broken but I'm still shouting at him, I can't stop. He turns to the door and grabs his tie, looking up at me as if I'm in the rafters, his eyes wide, as if I fill the whole workshop.

I watch him run down the lane. I'm not shouting now, just staring off into the branches of the ash tree on the edge of the woods. The wind curls the leaves silver-side up, and I think of the rush chairs tucked under the table, down there in Brighton. It makes me think; I wonder if his sister and Mr. Bouillon ... I want to call out to the boy and stop him but he's already passed the ash tree. I think of the rush seats, down there by the sea, and I see two violins resting on them.

Two new Guarnerius.

Source: Derek Neale (1993) 'Violin Lessons' in *Mafia! An Anthology of New Fiction*, Norwich: Centre for Creative and Performing Arts, University of East Anglia, pp.31–49.

2 'A Real Durwan'

Jhumpa Lahiri

Boori Ma, sweeper of the stairwell, had not slept in two nights. So the morning before the third night she shook the mites out of her bedding. She shook the quilts once underneath the letter boxes where she lived, then once again at the mouth of the alley, causing the crows who were feeding on vegetable peels to scatter in several directions.

As she started up the four flights to the roof, Boori Ma kept one hand placed over the knee that swelled at the start of every rainy season. That meant that her bucket, quilts, and the bundle of reeds which served as her broom all had to be braced under one arm. Lately Boori Ma had been thinking that the stairs were getting steeper; climbing them felt more like climbing a ladder than a staircase. She was sixty-four years old, with hair in a knot no larger than a walnut, and she looked almost as narrow from the front as she did from the side.

In fact, the only thing that appeared three-dimensional about Boori Ma was her voice: brittle with sorrows, as tart as curds, and shrill enough to grate meat from a coconut. It was with this voice that she enumerated, twice a day as she swept the stairwell, the details of her plight and losses suffered since her deportation to Calcutta after Partition. At that time, she maintained, the turmoil had separated her from a husband, four daughters, a two-story brick house, a rosewood *almari*, and a number of coffer boxes whose skeleton keys she still wore, along with her life savings, tied to the free end of her sari.

Aside from her hardships, the other thing Boori Ma liked to chronicle was easier times. And so, by the time she reached the second-floor landing, she had already drawn to the whole building's attention the menu of her third daughter's wedding night. 'We married her to a school principal. The rice was cooked in rosewater. The mayor was invited. Everybody washed their fingers in pewter bowls.' Here she paused, evened out her breath, and readjusted the supplies under her arm. She took the opportunity also to chase a cockroach out of the banister poles, then continued: 'Mustard prawns were steamed in banana leaves. Not a delicacy was spared. Not that this was an extravagance for us. At our house, we ate goat twice a week. We had a pond on our property, full of fish.'

By now Boori Ma could see some light from the roof spilling into the stairwell. And though it was only eight o'clock, the sun was already strong enough to warm the last of the cement steps under her feet. It was a very old building, the kind with bathwater that still had to be stored in drums, windows without glass, and privy scaffolds made of bricks.

'A man came to pick our dates and guavas. Another clipped hibiscus. Yes, there I tasted life. Here I eat my dinner from a rice pot.' At this point in the recital Boori Ma's ears started to burn; a pain chewed through her swollen knee. 'Have I mentioned that I crossed the border with just two bracelets on my wrist? Yet there was a day when my feet touched nothing but marble. Believe me, don't believe me, such comforts you cannot even dream them.'

Whether there was any truth to Boori Ma's litanies no one could be sure. For one thing, every day, the perimeters of her former estate seemed to double, as did the contents of her *almari* and coffer boxes. No one doubted she was a refugee; the accent in her Bengali made that clear. Still, the residents of this particular flat-building could not reconcile Boori Ma's claims to prior wealth alongside the more likely account of how she had crossed the East Bengal border, with the thousands of others, on the back of a truck, between sacks of hemp. And yet there were days when Boori Ma insisted that she had come to Calcutta on a bullock cart.

'Which was it, by truck or by cart?' the children sometimes asked her on their way to play cops and robbers in the alley. To which Boori Ma would reply, shaking the free end of her sari so that the skeleton keys rattled, 'Why demand specifics? Why scrape lime from a betel leaf? Believe me, don't believe me. My life is composed of such griefs you cannot even dream them.'

So she garbled facts. She contradicted herself. She embellished almost everything. But her rants were so persuasive, her fretting so vivid, that it was not so easy to dismiss her.

What kind of landowner ended up sweeping stairs? That was what Mr. Dalal of the third floor always wondered as he passed Boori Ma on his way to and from the office, where he filed receipts for a wholesale distributor of rubber tubes, pipes, and valve fittings in the plumbing district of College Street.

Bechareh, she probably constructs tales as a way of mourning the loss of her family, was the collective surmise of most of the wives.

And 'Boori Ma's mouth is full of ashes, but she is the victim of changing times' was the refrain of old Mr. Chatterjee. He had neither strayed from his balcony nor opened a newspaper since Independence, but in spite of this fact, or maybe because of it, his opinions were always highly esteemed.

The theory eventually circulated that Boori Ma had once worked as hired help for a prosperous *zamindar* back east, and was therefore capable of exaggerating her past at such elaborate lengths and heights. Her throaty impostures hurt no one. All agreed that she was a superb entertainer. In exchange for her lodging below the letter boxes, Boori Ma kept their crooked stairwell spotlessly clean. Most of all, the residents liked that Boori Ma, who slept each night behind the collapsible gate, stood guard between them and the outside world.

No one in this particular flat-building owned much worth stealing. The second-floor widow, Mrs. Misra, was the only one with a telephone. Still, the residents were thankful that Boori Ma patrolled activities in the alley, screened the itinerant peddlers who came to sell combs and shawls from door to door, was able to summon a rickshaw at a moment's calling, and could, with a few slaps of her broom, rout any suspicious character who strayed into the area in order to spit, urinate, or cause some other trouble.

In short, over the years, Boori Ma's services came to resemble those of a real *durwan*. Though under normal circumstances this was no job for a woman, she honored the responsibility, and maintained a vigil no less punctilious than if she were the gatekeeper of a house on Lower Circular Road, or Jodhpur Park, or any other fancy neighborhood.

On the rooftop Boori Ma hung her quilts over the clothesline. The wire, strung diagonally from one corner of the parapet to the other, stretched across her view of television antennas, billboards, and the distant arches of Howrah Bridge. Boori Ma consulted the horizon on all four sides. Then she ran the tap at the base of the cistern. She washed her face, rinsed her feet, and rubbed two fingers over her teeth. After this she started to beat the quilts on each side with her broom. Every now and then she stopped and squinted at the cement, hoping to identify the culprit of her sleepless nights. She was so absorbed in this process that it was some moments before she noticed Mrs. Dalal of the third floor, who had come to set a tray of salted lemon peels out to dry in the sun.

'Whatever is inside this quilt is keeping me awake at night,' Boori Ma said. 'Tell me, where do you see them?'

Mrs. Dalal had a soft spot for Boori Ma; occasionally she gave the old woman some ginger paste with which to flavor her stews. 'I don't see anything,' Mrs. Dalal said after a while. She had diaphanous eyelids and very slender toes with rings on them.

'Then they must have wings,' Boori Ma concluded. She put down her broom and observed one cloud passing behind another. 'They fly away before I can squash them. But just see my back. I must be purple from their bites.'

Mrs. Dalal lifted the drape of Boori Ma's sari, a cheap white weave with a border the color of a dirty pond. She examined the skin above and below her blouse, cut in a style no longer sold in shops. Then she said, 'Boori Ma, you are imagining things.'

'I tell you, these mites are eating me alive.'

'It could be a case of prickly heat,' Mrs. Dalal suggested.

At this Boori Ma shook the free end of her sari and made her skeleton keys rattle. She said, 'I know prickly heat. This is not prickly heat. I haven't slept in three, perhaps four days. Who can count? I used to keep a clean bed. Our linens were muslin. Believe me, don't believe me, our mosquito nets were as soft as silk. Such comforts you cannot even dream them.'

'I cannot dream them,' Mrs. Dalal echoed. She lowered her diaphanous eyelids and sighed. 'I cannot dream them, Boori Ma. I live in two broken rooms, married to a man who sells toilet parts.' Mrs. Dalal turned away and looked at one of the quilts. She ran a finger over part of the stitching. Then she asked:

'Boori Ma, how long have you slept on this bedding?'

Boori Ma put a finger to her lips before replying that she could not remember.

'Then why no mention of it until today? Do you think it's beyond us to provide you with clean quilts? An oilcloth, for that matter?' She looked insulted.

'There is no need', Boori Ma said. 'They are clean now. I beat them with my broom.'

'I am hearing no arguments,' Mrs. Dalal said. 'You need a new bed. Quilts, a pillow. A blanket when winter comes.' As she spoke Mrs. Dalal kept track of the necessary items by touching her thumb to the pads of her fingers.

'On festival days the poor came to our house to be fed,' Boori Ma said. She was filling her bucket from the coal heap on the other side of the roof.

'I will have a word with Mr. Dalal when he returns from the office,' Mrs. Dalal called back as she headed down the stairs. 'Come in the afternoon. I will give you some pickles and some powder for your back.'

'It's not prickly heat,' Boori Ma said.

It was true that prickly heat was common during the rainy season. But Boori Ma preferred to think that what irritated her bed, what stole her sleep, what burned like peppers across her thinning scalp and skin, was of a less mundane origin.

She was ruminating on these things as she swept the stairwell – she always worked from top to bottom – when it started to rain. It came slapping across the roof like a boy in slippers too big for him and washed Mrs. Dalal's lemon peels into the gutter. Before pedestrians could open their umbrellas, it rushed down collars, pockets, and shoes. In that particular flat-building and all the neighboring buildings, creaky shutters were closed and tied with petticoat strings to the window bars.

At the time, Boori Ma was working all the way down on the second-floor landing. She looked up the ladderlike stairs, and as the sound of falling water tightened around her she knew her quilts were turning into yogurt.

But then she recalled her conversation with Mrs. Dalal. And so she continued, at the same pace, to sweep the dust, cigarette ends, and lozenge wrappers from the rest of the steps, until she reached the letter boxes at the bottom. To keep out the wind, she rummaged through her baskets for some newspapers and crammed them into the diamond-shaped openings of the collapsible gate. Then on her bucket of coals she set her lunch to boil, and monitored the flame with a plaited palm fan.

That afternoon, as was her habit, Boori Ma reknotted her hair, united the loose end of her sari, and counted out her life savings. She had just woken from a nap of twenty minutes, which she had taken on a temporary bed made from newspapers. The rain had stopped and now the sour smell that rises from wet mango leaves was hanging low over the alley.

On certain afternoons Boori Ma visited her fellow residents. She enjoyed drifting in and out of various households. The residents, for their part, assured Boori Ma that she was always welcome; they never drew the latch bars across their doors except at night. They went about their business, scolding children or adding up expenses or picking stones out of the evening rice. From time to time she was handed a glass of tea, the cracker tin was passed in her direction, and she helped children shoot chips across the carom board. Knowing not to sit on the furniture, she crouched, instead, in doorways and hallways, and observed gestures and manners in the same way a person tends to watch traffic in a foreign city.

On this particular afternoon Boori Ma decided to accept Mrs. Dalal's invitation. Her back still ached, even after napping on the newspapers, and she was beginning to want some prickly-heat powder after all. She picked up her broom – she never felt quite herself without it – and was about to climb upstairs, when a rickshaw pulled up to the collapsible gate.

It was Mr. Dalal. The years he had spent filing receipts had left him with purple crescents under his eyes. But today his gaze was bright. The tip of his tongue played between his teeth, and in the clamp of his thighs he held two small ceramic basins.

'Boori Ma, I have a job for you. Help me carry these basins upstairs.' He pressed a folded handkerchief to his forehead and throat and gave the rickshaw driver a coin. Then he and Boori Ma carried the basins all the way up to the third floor. It wasn't until they were inside the flat that he finally announced, to Mrs. Dalal, to Boori Ma, and to a few other residents who had followed them out of curiosity, the following things: That his hours filing receipts for a distributor of rubber tubes, pipes, and valve fittings had ended. That the distributor himself, who craved fresher air, and whose profits had doubled, was opening a second branch in Burdwan. And that, following an assessment of his sedulous performance over the years, the distributor was promoting Mr. Dalal to manage the College Street branch. In his excitement on his way home through the plumbing district, Mr. Dalal had bought two basins.

'What are we supposed to do with two basins in a tworoom flat?' Mrs. Dalal demanded. She had already been sulking over her lemon peels. 'Who ever heard of it? I still cook on kerosene. You refuse to apply for a phone. And I have yet to see the fridge you promised when we married. You expect two basins to make up for all that?'

The argument that followed was loud enough to be heard all the way down to the letter boxes. It was loud enough, and long enough, to rise above a second spell of rain that fell after dark. It was loud enough even to distract Boori Ma as she swept the stairwell from top to bottom for the second time that day, and for this reason she spoke neither of her hardships, nor of easier times. She spent the night on a bed of newspapers.

The argument between Mr. and Mrs. Dalal was still more or less in effect early the next morning, when a barefoot team of workmen came to install the basins. After a night of tossing and pacing, Mr. Dalal had decided to install one basin in the sitting room of their flat, and the other one on the stairwell of the building, on the first-floor landing. 'This way everyone can use it,' he explained from door to door. The residents were delighted; for years they had all brushed their teeth with stored water poured from mugs.

Mr. Dalal, meanwhile, was thinking: A sink on the stairwell is sure to impress visitors. Now that he was a company manager, who could say who might visit the building?

The workmen toiled for several hours. They ran up and down the stairs and ate their lunches squatting against the banister poles. They hammered, shouted, spat, and cursed. They wiped their sweat with the ends of their turbans. In general, they made it impossible for Boori Ma to sweep the stairwell that day.

To occupy the time, Boori Ma retired to the rooftop. She shuffled along the parapets, but her hips were sore from sleeping on newspapers. After consulting the horizon on all four sides, she tore what was left of her quilts into several strips and resolved to polish the banister poles at a later time.

By early evening the residents gathered to admire the day's labours. Even Boori Ma was urged to rinse her hands under the clear running water. She sniffed. 'Our bathwater was scented with petals and attars. Believe me, don't believe me, it was a luxury you cannot dream.'

Mr. Dalal proceeded to demonstrate the basin's various features. He turned each faucet completely on and completely off. Then he turned on both faucets at the same time, to illustrate the difference in water pressure. Lifting a small lever between the faucets allowed water to collect in the basin, if desired.

'The last word in elegance,' Mr. Dalal concluded.

'A sure sign of changing times,' Mr. Chatterjee reputedly admitted from his balcony.

Among the wives, however, resentment quickly brewed. Standing in line to brush their teeth in the mornings, each grew frustrated with having to wait her turn, for having to wipe the faucets after every use, and for not being able to leave her own soap and toothpaste tube on the basin's narrow periphery. The Dalals had their own sink; why did the rest of them have to share?

'Is it beyond us to buy sinks of our own?' one of them finally burst out one morning.

'Are the Dalals the only ones who can improve the conditions of this building?' asked another.

Rumors began spreading: that, following their argument, Mr. Dalal had consoled his wife by buying her two kilos of mustard oil, a Kashmiri shawl, a dozen cakes of sandalwood soap; that Mr. Dalal had filed an application for a telephone line; that Mrs. Dalal did nothing but wash her hands in her basin all day. As if this weren't enough, the next morning, a taxi bound for Howrah Station crammed its wheels into the alley; the Dalals were going to Simla for ten days.

'Boori Ma, I haven't forgotten. We will bring you back a sheep's-hair blanket made in the mountains,' Mrs. Dalal said through the open window of the taxi. She was holding a leather purse in her lap which matched the turquoise border of her sari.

'We will bring two!' cried Mr. Dalal, who was sitting beside his wife, checking his pockets to make sure his wallet was in place.

Of all the people who lived in that particular flat-building, Boori Ma was the only one who stood by the collapsible gate and wished them a safe journey.

As soon as the Dalals were gone, the other wives began planning renovations of their own. One decided to barter a stack of her wedding bracelets and commissioned a white-washer to freshen the walls of the stairwell. Another pawned her sewing machine and summoned an exterminator. A third went to the silversmith and sold back a set of pudding bowls; she intended to have the shutters painted yellow.

Workers began to occupy this particular flat-building night and day. To avoid the traffic, Boori Ma took to sleeping on the rooftop. So many people passed in and out of the collapsible gate, so many others clogged the alley at all times, that there was no point in keeping track of them.

After a few days Boori Ma moved her baskets and her cooking bucket to the rooftop as well. There was no need to use the basin downstairs, for she could just as easily wash, as she always had, from the cistern tap. She still planned to polish the banister poles with the strips she had torn from her quilts. She continued to sleep on her newspapers.

More rains came. Below the dripping awning, a newspaper pressed over her head, Boori Ma squatted and watched the monsoon ants as they marched along the clothesline, carrying eggs in their mouths. Damper winds soothed her back. Her newspapers were running low.

Her mornings were long, her afternoons longer. She could not remember her last glass of tea. Thinking neither of her hardships nor of earlier times, she wondered when the Dalals would return with her new bedding.

She grew restless on the roof, and so for some exercise, Boori Ma started circling the neighbourhood in the afternoons. Red broom in hand, sari smeared with newsprint ink, she wandered through markets and began spending her life savings on small treats: today a packet of puffed rice, tomorrow some cashews, the day after that, a cup of sugarcane juice. One day she walked as far as the bookstalls on College Street. The next day she walked even farther, to the produce markets in Bow Bazaar. It was there, while she was standing in a shopping arcade surveying jackfruits and persimmons, that she felt something tugging on the free end of her sari. When she looked, the rest of her life savings and her skeleton keys were gone.

The residents were waiting for Boori Ma when she returned that afternoon at the collapsible gate. Baleful cries rang up and down the stairwell, all echoing the same news: the basin on the stairwell had been stolen. There was a big hole in the recently whitewashed wall, and a tangle of rubber tubes and pipes was sticking out of it. Chunks of plaster littered the landing. Boori Ma gripped her reed broom and said nothing.

In their haste the residents practically carried Boori Ma up the stairs to the roof, where they planted her on one side of the clothesline and started screaming at her from the other.

'This is all her doing,' one of them hollered, pointing at Boori Ma. 'She informed the robbers. Where was she when she was supposed to guard the gate?'

'For days she has been wandering the streets, speaking to strangers,' another reported.

'We shared our coal, gave her a place to sleep. How could she betray us this way?' a third wanted to know.

Though none of them spoke directly to Boori Ma, she replied, 'Believe me, believe me. I did not inform the robbers.'

'For years we have put up with your lies,' they retorted.

'You expect us, now, to believe you?'

Their recriminations persisted. How would they explain it to the Dalals? Eventually they sought the advice of Mr. Chatterjee. They found him sitting on his balcony, watching a traffic jam.

One of the second-floor residents said, 'Boori Ma has endangered the security of this building. We have valuables. The widow Mrs. Misra lives alone with her phone. What should we do?'

Mr. Chatterjee considered their arguments. As he thought things over, he adjusted the shawl that was wrapped around his shoulders and gazed at the bamboo scaffolding that now surrounded his balcony. The shutters behind him, colorless for as long as he could remember, had been painted yellow. Finally he said:

'Boori Ma's mouth is full of ashes. But that is nothing new. What is new is the face of this building. What a building like this needs is a real *durwan.*'

So the residents tossed her bucket and rags, her baskets and reed broom, down the stairwell, past the letter boxes, through the collapsible gate, and into the alley. Then they tossed out Boori Ma. All were eager to begin their search for a real *durwan*.

From the pile of belongings Boori Ma kept only her broom. 'Believe me, believe me,' she said once more as her figure began to recede. She shook the free end of her sari, but nothing rattled.

Source: Jhumpa Lahiri (1999) *Interpreter of Maladies: Stories*, London: Flamingo, pp.70–82.

3 'The Fly in the Ointment'

V.S. Pritchett

It was the dead hour of a November afternoon. Under the ceiling of level mud-coloured cloud, the latest office buildings of the city stood out alarmingly like new tombstones, among the mass of older buildings. And along the streets the few cars and the few people appeared and disappeared slowly as if they were not following the roadway or the pavement but some inner, personal route. Along the road to the main station, at intervals of two hundred yards or so, unemployed men and one or two beggars were dribbling slowly past the desert of public buildings to the next patch of shop fronts.

Presently a taxi stopped outside one of the underground stations and a man of thirty-five paid his fare and made off down one of the small streets.

Better not arrive in a taxi, he was thinking. The old man will wonder where I got the money.

He was going to see his father. It was his father's last day at his factory, the last day of thirty years' work and life among these streets, building a business out of nothing, and then, after a few years of prosperity, letting it go to pieces in a chafer of rumour, idleness, quarrels, accusations and, at last, bankruptcy.

Suddenly all the money quarrels of the family, which nagged in the young man's mind, had been dissolved. His dread of being involved in them vanished. He was overcome by the sadness of his father's situation. Thirty years of your life come to an end. I must see him. I must help him. All the same, knowing his father, he had paid off the taxi and walked the last quarter of a mile.

It was a shock to see the name of the firm, newly painted too, on the sign outside the factory and on the brass of the office entrance, newly polished. He pressed the bell at the office window inside and it was a long time before he heard footsteps cross the empty room and saw a shadow cloud the frosted glass of the window.

'It's Harold, Father,' the young man said. The door was opened.

'Hullo, old chap. This is very nice of you, Harold,' said the old man shyly, stepping back from the door to let his son in, and lowering his pleased, blue eyes for a second's modesty.

'Naturally I had to come,' said the son, shyly also. And then the father, filled out with assurance again and taking his son's arm, walked him across the floor of the empty work-room.

'Hardly recognize it, do you? When were you here last?' said the father.

This had been the machine-room, before the machines had gone. Through another door was what had been the showroom, where the son remembered seeing his father, then a dark-haired man, talking in a voice he had never heard before, a quick, bland voice, to his customers. Now there were only dust-lines left by the shelves on the white brick walls, and the marks of the showroom cupboards on the floor. The place looked large and light. There was no throb of machines, no hum of voices, no sound at all, now, but the echo of their steps on the empty floors. Already, though only a month bankrupt, the firm was becoming a ghost.

The two men walked towards the glass door of the office. They were both short. The father was well-dressed in an excellent navy-blue suit. He was a vigorous, broad man with a pleased impish smile. The sunburn shone through the clipped white hair of his head and he had the simple, trim, open-air look of a snow-man. The son beside him was round-shouldered and shabby, a keen but anxious fellow in need of a hair-cut and going bald.

'Come in, Professor,' said the father. This was an old family joke. He despised his son, who was, in fact, not a professor but a poorly paid lecturer at a provincial university.

'Come in,' said the father, repeating himself, not with the impatience he used to have, but with the habit of age. 'Come inside, into my office. If you can call it an office now,' he apologized. 'This used to be my room, do you remember, it used to be my office. Take a chair. We've still got a chair. The desk's gone, yes, that's gone, it was sold, fetched a good price – what was I saying?' He turned a bewildered look to his son. 'The chair. I was saying they have to leave you a table and a chair. I was just going to have a cup of tea, old boy, but – pardon me,' he apologized again, 'I've only one cup. Things have been sold for the liquidators and they've cleaned out nearly everything. I found this cup and teapot upstairs in the foreman's room. Of course, he's gone, all the hands have gone, and when I looked around just now to lock up before taking the keys to the agent when I hand over today, I saw this cup. Well, there it is. I've made it. Have a cup?'

'No thanks,' said the son, listening patiently to his father. 'I have had my tea.'

'You've had your tea? Go on. Why not have another?'

'No, really, thanks,' said the son. 'You drink it.'

'Well,' said the father, pouring out the tea and lifting the cup to his soft rosy face and blinking his eyes as he drank, 'I feel badly about this. This is terrible. I feel really awful drinking this tea and you standing there watching me, but you say you've had yours – well, how are things with you? How are you? And how is Alice? Is she better? And the children? You know I've been thinking about you – you look worried. Haven't lost sixpence and found a shilling have you, because I wouldn't mind doing that?'

'I'm all right,' the son said, smiling to hide his irritation. 'I'm not worried about anything. I'm just worried about you. This' – he nodded with embarrassment to the dismantled showroom, the office from which even the calendars and wastepaper-basket had gone – 'this' – what was the most tactful and sympathetic word to use? – 'this is bad luck,' he said.

'Bad luck?' said the old man sternly.

'I mean,' stammered his son, 'I heard about the creditors' meeting. I knew it was your last day – I thought I'd come along, I ... To see how you were.'

'Very sweet of you, old boy,' said the old man with zest. 'Very sweet. We've cleared everything up. They got most of the machines out today. I'm just locking up and handing over. Locking up is quite a business. There are so many keys. It's tiring, really. How many keys do you think there are to a place like this? You wouldn't believe it, if I told you.'

'It must have been worrying,' the son said.

'Worrying? You keep on using that word. I'm not worrying. Things are fine,' said the old man, smiling aggressively. 'I feel they're fine. I *know* they're fine.'

'Well, you always were an optimist,' smiled his son.

'Listen to me a moment. I want you to get this idea,' said his father, his warm voice going dead and rancorous and his nostrils fidgeting. His eyes went hard, too. A different man was speaking, and even a different face; the son noticed for the first time that like all big-faced men his father had two faces. There was the outer face like a soft warm and careless daub of innocent sealing-wax and inside it, as if thumbed there by a seal, was a much smaller one, babyish, shrewd, scared and hard. Now this little inner face had gone greenish and pale and dozens of little veins were broken on the nose and cheeks. The small, drained, purplish lips of this little face were speaking. The son leaned back instinctively to get just another inch away from this little face.

'Listen to this,' the father said and leaned forward on the table as his son leaned back, holding his right fist up as if he had a hammer in his hand and was auctioning his life. 'I am sixty-five. I don't know how long I shall live, but let me make this clear: if I were not an optimist I wouldn't be here. I wouldn't stay another minute.' He paused, fixing his son's half-averted eyes to let the full meaning of his words bite home. 'I've worked hard,' the father went on. 'For thirty years I built up this business from nothing. You wouldn't know it, you were a child, but many's the time coming down from the North I've slept in this office to be on the job early the next morning.' He looked decided and experienced like a man of forty, but now he softened to sixty again. The ring in the hard voice began to soften into a faint whine and his thick nose sniffed. 'I don't say I've always done right,' he said. 'You can't live your life from A to Z like that. And now I haven't a penny in the world. Not a cent. It's not easy at my time of life to begin again. What do you think I've got to live for? There's nothing holding me back. My boy, if I wasn't an optimist I'd go right out. I'd finish it.' Suddenly the father smiled and the little face was drowned in a warm flood of triumphant smiles from the bigger face. He rested his hands on his waistcoat and that seemed to be smiling too, his easy coat smiling, his legs smiling and even winks of light on the shining shoes. Then he frowned.

'You hair's going thin,' he said. 'You oughtn't to be losing your hair at your age. I don't want you to think I'm criticizing you, you're old enough to live your own life, but your hair you know – you ought to do something about it. If you used oil every day and rubbed it in with both hands, the thumbs and forefingers is what you want to use, it would be better. I'm often thinking about you and I don't want you to think I'm lecturing you, because I'm not, so don't get the idea this is a lecture, but I was thinking, what you want, what we all want, I say this for myself as well as you, what we all want is ideas – big ideas. We go worrying along but you just want bigger and better ideas. You ought to think big. Take your case. You're a lecturer. I wouldn't be satisfied with lecturing to a small batch of people in a university town. I'd lecture the world. You know, you're always doing yourself injustice. We all do. Think big.'

'Well,' said his son, still smiling, but sharply. He was very angry. 'One's enough in the family. You've thought big till you bust.'

He didn't mean to say this, because he hadn't really the courage, but his pride was touched.

'I mean,' said the son, hurriedly covering it up in a panic, 'I'm not like you ... I ...'

'What did you say?' said the old man. 'Don't say that.' It was the smaller of the two faces speaking in a panic. 'Don't say that. Don't use that expression. That's not a right idea. Don't you get a wrong idea about me. We paid sixpence in the pound,' said the old man proudly.

The son began again, but his father stopped him.

'Do you know,' said the bigger of his two faces, getting bigger as it spoke, 'some of the oldest houses in the city are in Queer Street, some of the biggest firms in the country? I came up this morning with Mr Higgins, you remember Higgins? They're in liquidation. They are. Oh yes. And Moore, he's lost everything. He's got his chauffeur, but it's his wife's money. Did you see Beltman in the trade papers? Quarter of a million deficit. And how long are Prestons going to last?'

The big face smiled and overflowed on the smaller one. The whole train, the old man said, was practically packed with bankrupts every morning. Thousands had gone. Thousands? Tens of thousands. Some of the biggest men in the City were broke.

A small man himself, he was proud to be bankrupt with the big ones; it made him feel rich.

'You've got to realize, old boy,' he said gravely, 'the world's changing. You've got to move with the times.'

The son was silent. The November sun put a few strains of light through the frosted window and the shadow of its bars and panes was weakly placed on the wall behind his father's head. Some of the light caught the tanned scalp that showed between the white hair. So short the hair was that the father's ears protruded and, framed against that reflection of the window bars, the father suddenly took (to his son's fancy) the likeness of a convict in his cell and the son, startled, found himself asking: Were they telling the truth when they said the old man was a crook and that his balance sheets were cooked? What about that man they had to shut up at the meeting, the little man from Birmingham, in a mackintosh ...?

'There's a fly in this room,' said the old man suddenly, looking up in the air and getting to his feet. 'I'm sorry to interrupt what you were saying, but I can hear a fly. I must get it out.'

'A fly?' said his son, listening.

'Yes, can't you hear it? It's peculiar how you can hear everything now the machines have stopped. It took me quite a time to get used to the silence. Can you see it, old chap? I can't stand flies, you never know where they've been. Excuse me one moment.'

The old man pulled a duster out of a drawer.

'Forgive this interruption. I can't sit in a room with a fly in it,' he said apologetically. They both stood up and listened. Certainly in the office was the small dying fizz of a fly, deceived beyond its strength by the autumn sun.

'Open the door, will you, old boy,' said the old man with embarrassment. 'I hate them.'

The son opened the door and the fly flew into the light. The old man struck at it but it sailed away higher.

'There it is,' he said, getting up on the chair. He struck again and the son struck too as the fly came down. The old man got on top of his table. An expression of disgust and fear was curled on his smaller face; and an expression of apology and weakness.

'Excuse me,' he said again, looking up at the ceiling.

'If we leave the door open or open the window it will go,' said the son.

'It may seem a fad to you,' said the old man shyly. 'I don't like flies. Ah, here it comes.'

They missed it. They stood helplessly gaping up at the ceiling where the fly was buzzing in small circles round the cord of the electric light.

'I don't like them,' the old man said.

The table creaked under his weight. The fly went on to the ceiling and stayed there. Unavailingly the old man snapped the duster at it.

'Be careful,' said the son. 'Don't lose your balance.'

The old man looked down. Suddenly he looked tired and old, his body began to sag and a look of weakness came on to his face.

'Give me a hand, old boy,' the old man said in a shaky voice. He put a heavy hand on his son's shoulder and the son felt the great helpless weight of his father's body.

'Lean on me.'

Very heavily and slowly the old man got cautiously down from the table to the chair. 'Just a moment, old boy,' said the old man. Then, after getting his breath, he got down from the chair to the floor.

'You all right?' his son asked.

'Yes, yes,' said the old man out of breath. 'It was only that fly. Do you know, you're actually more bald at the back than I thought. There's a patch there as big as my hand. I saw it just then. It gave me quite a shock. You really must do something about it. How are your teeth? Do you have any trouble with your teeth? That may have something to do with it. Hasn't Alice told you how bald you are?'

'You've been doing too much. You're worried,' said the son, soft with repentance and sympathy. 'Sit down. You've had a bad time.'

'No, nothing,' said the old man shyly, breathing rather hard. 'A bit. Everyone's been very nice. They came in and shook hands. The staff came in. They all came in just to shake hands. They said, "We wish you good luck."'

The old man turned his head away. He actually wiped a tear from his eye. A glow of sympathy transported the younger man. He felt as though a sun had risen.

'You know –' the father said uneasily, flitting a glance at the fly on the ceiling as if he wanted the fly as well as his son to listen to what he was going to say – 'you know,' he said, 'the world's all wrong. I've made my mistakes. I was thinking about it before you came. You know where I went wrong? You know where I made my mistake?'

The son's heart started to a panic of embarrassment. For heaven's sake, he wanted to shout, don't! Don't stir up the whole business. Don't humiliate yourself before me. Don't start telling the truth. Don't oblige me to say we know all about it, that we have known for years the mess you've been in, that we've seen through the plausible stories you've spread, that we've known the people you've swindled.

'Money's been my trouble,' said the old man. 'I thought I needed money. That's one thing it's taught me. I've done with money. Absolutely done and finished with it. I never want to see another penny as long as I live. I don't want to see or hear of it. If you came in now and offered me a thousand pounds I should laugh at you. We deceive ourselves. We don't want the stuff. All I want now is just to go to a nice little cottage by the sea,' the old man said. 'I feel I need air, sun, life.'

The son was appalled.

'You want money even for that,' the son said irritably. 'You want quite a lot of money to do that.'

'Don't say I want money,' the old man said vehemently. 'Don't say it. When I walk out of this place tonight I'm going to walk into freedom. I am not going to think of money. You never know where it will come from. You may see something. You may meet a man. You never know. Did the children of Israel worry about money? No, they just went out and collected the manna. That's what I want to do.'

The son was about to speak. The father stopped him.

'Money,' the father said, 'isn't necessary at all.'

Now, like the harvest moon in full glow, the father's face shone up at his son.

'What I came round about was this,' said the son awkwardly and dryly. 'I'm not rich. None of us is. In fact, with things as they are we're all pretty shaky and we can't do anything. I wish I could, but I can't. But' – after the assured beginning he began to stammer and to crinkle his eyes timidly – 'but the idea of your being – you know, well short of some immediate necessity, I mean – well, if it is ever a question of – well, to be frank, *cash*, I'd raise it somehow.'

He coloured. He hated to admit his own poverty, he hated to offer charity to his father. He hated to sit there knowing the things he knew about him. He was ashamed to think how he, how they all dreaded having the gregarious, optimistic, extravagant, uncontrollable, disingenuous old man on their hands. The son hated to feel he was being in some peculiar way which he could not understand, mean, cowardly and dishonest.

The father's sailing eyes came down and looked at his son's nervous, frowning face and slowly the dreaming look went from the father's face. Slowly the harvest moon came down from its rosy voyage. The little face suddenly became dominant within the outer folds of skin like a fox looking out of a hole of clay. He leaned forward brusquely on the table and somehow a silver-topped pencil was in his hand preparing to note something briskly on a writing-pad.

'Raise it?' said the old man sharply. 'Why didn't you tell me before you could raise money? How can you raise it? Where? By when?'

Source: V.S. Pritchett (1967) 'The Fly in the Ointment' in Christopher Dolley (ed.) *The Penguin Book of English Short Stories*, Harmondsworth: Penguin, pp.283–92.

4   from *The Kingdom by the Sea*

Paul Theroux

Jonathan Raban was there on his boat, the *Gosfield Maid*, moored at Brighton Marina, just beyond Kemp Town and the nudist beach ('Bathing Costumes Are Not Required to Be Worn Past This Sign'). Jonathan had said that he was taking a trip around the British coast and was planning to write a book about it. This interested me. All trips are different, and even two people travelling together have vastly different versions of their journey. Jonathan was doing his coastal tour anti-clockwise, stopping at likely ports in his boat.

He seemed contented on his boat. He had framed prints and engravings on the walls, and Kinglake's *Eothen* was open on a table under a porthole. It was strange to see a typewriter and a TV set on board, but that was the sort of boat it was, very comfy and literary, with bookshelves and curios.

'This must be your log,' I said, glancing down. The entries were sketchy ('... light rain, wind ESE ...') – nothing very literary here, no dialogue, no exclamation marks.

He said, 'I keep planning to make notes, but I never seem to get round to it. What about you?'

'I fiddle around,' I said. It was a lie. I did nothing but make notes, scribbling from the moment I arrived in a hotel or a guest house and often missing my dinner. I hated doing it. It was a burden. But if I had been in Afghanistan I would have kept a detailed diary. Why should I travel differently in Britain?

I said, 'I hate Brighton. I think there's a kind of wisdom in that – the British person, or even the foreigner, who says simply, *I hate Brighton*. What's there to like here? It's a mess.'

'Yes, it's a mess,' Jonathan said. 'That's one of the things I like about it.'

'I've never seen so many dubious-looking people,' I said.

He said, 'It's full of tramps,' and he smiled again. Then he said that the most unexpected things happened in Brighton. He would be walking along and he would see someone dressed up as Cardinal Wolsey or Robin Hood, or musicians, or people singing and having a grand time.

I said I saw only bums and day-trippers and people trying to, um, extricate from the long day the grain of pleasure.

We decided to have lunch in the centre of Brighton, and so took the little train that rattled from the Marina, past the nudist beach, to the Aquarium. The nudist beach was mostly naked men staring hard at each other. This created heavy traffic on that part of the Front. We were pestered by a man with a monkey when we got off the train. I kept wanting to say, 'See what I mean?'

Source: Paul Theroux (1983) *The Kingdom by the Sea: A journey around the coast of Great Britain*, London: Hamish Hamilton, pp.46–7.

5   from *Coasting*

Jonathan Raban

In his Papa Doc tinted spectacles, an L.L. Bean duckhunter's camouflage shirt, with a little brown backpack hoisted on his shoulders, Paul Theroux was on his travels.

'Hi – how you doing?'

Ten years before, Paul and I had been friends and allies, but the friendship had somewhat soured and thinned since. Nor had either of us been best pleased when each had discovered that the other was planning a journey, and a book, about the British coast. It was too close a coincidence for comfort. Paul was working his way round clockwise, by train and on foot, while I was going counterclockwise by sea. At Brighton the two plots intersected briefly and uneasily aboard *Gosfield Maid*.

It took Paul less than five minutes to sum up the boat. He hunted through the saloon, inspecting pictures, books, the charcoal stove, the gimballed oil-lamps, the new, lavender-smelling gleam of the woodwork.

'Yeah,' he said; 'it's kind of ... *tubby* and ... *bookish*.'

The phrase rattled me. I rather thought that somewhere I had written it down myself.

'You making a lot of notes?'

'No,' I lied. 'I seem too busy with things like weather and navigation to notice anything on land. What about you?'

'No,' Paul lied. 'There's nothing to write about, is there? I don't know whether there's a book in this at all. I may turn out to have just spent the summer walking. Still, it keeps you fit –'

He came up into the wheelhouse, where he looked over the open pages of the log. They were innocent of any small talk except for details of courses steered, winds, compass bearings, barometric pressures and a crinkly, tongue-shaped spill of red wine.

'What's that?'

'The depth sounder.'

'Okay.'

Wary, protective of our separate books, we dealt with each other at strained arm's length. For a moment, I saw us as Britain and Argentina meeting on neutral ground in Peru.

'Lunch?'

'Yeah,' Paul looked at his watch. 'But I've got to be getting along this afternoon.'

'Where are you heading?'

'Oh ...' Paul was evidently wondering if this was going to give too much away, and deciding that it wasn't. 'Bognor Regis. Know Bognor?'

'We lived just outside, when I was nine, ten. When my father was at theological college at Chichester.'

'Ah huh.' He didn't pursue the matter of Bognor.

We took the miniature railway from the marina to the pier. Passing the nudist beach, Paul made a rapid note in his book, which he quickly tucked away. I thought, I'd better take a closer look at the nudist beach on my way back, I may have missed something apart from the obvious goose-pimples and sagging bums.

At the pier, we pushed our way through the lazy crowd; two men at work, impeded by idlers. As we waited for the traffic to give us an opening on the promenade, a lean and dingy man in a flapping Oxfam overcoat detached himself from the crowd. He had a camera and a monkey, and there was a helplessly eager look in his eye as he made a beeline for Paul in his hiking gear. After hours of searching, at last he'd found an American Tourist, he was shovelling his monkey on to Paul's shoulder and fiddling with the controls on his camera.

'Take your picture, sir?'

The monkey was scrawny and grey, the size of a rat. It was clinging to Paul's hair and grinning with fright.

'Get that monkey off my back,' Paul said. It was a clipped and military instruction. The man responded with a monkey grin and raised the viewfinder to his eye. 'Get that monkey off my back! Will you get that goddam monkey off my back?'

Source: Jonathan Raban (1986) *Coasting*, London: Collins Harvill, pp.196–7.

6   from *The Night Watch*

Sarah Waters

Kay stretched again. She looked at the clock, then glanced around for something to do: wanting to keep herself alert, and take her mind off the waiting. She found a deck of greasy playing cards, picked them up and gave them a shuffle. The cards were meant for servicemen, and had pictures of glamour girls on them. Over the years, ambulance people had given the girls beards and moustaches, spectacles and missing teeth.

She called to Hughes, another driver. 'Fancy a game?'

He was darning a sock, and looked up, squinting. 'What's your stake?'

'Penny a pop?'

'All right.'

She shuffled her chair over to his. He was sitting right beside the oil-stove, and could never be persuaded away from it, for the room – which was part of the complex of garages under Dolphin Square, close to the Thames – had a concrete floor and walls of whitewashed brick, and was always chilly. Hughes wore a black astrakhan coat over his uniform and had turned up the collar. His hands and wrists, where they projected from his long, voluminous sleeves, looked pale and waxy. His face was slender as a ghost's, his teeth very stained from cigarettes. He wore glasses with dark tortoiseshell frames.

Kay dealt him a hand, and watched him sorting delicately through his cards. She shook her head. 'It's like gaming with Death,' she said.

He held her gaze, and extended a hand – pointed a finger, then turned and crooked it. '*Tonight*,' he whispered in horror-film tones.

She threw a penny at him. 'Stop it.' The coin bounced to the floor.

'Hey, what's the idea?' said someone – a woman called Partridge. She was kneeling on the concrete, cutting out a dress from paper patterns.

Kay said, 'Hughes was giving me the creeps.'

'Hughes gives everyone the creeps.'

'This time he was actually meaning to.'

Hughes did his Death-act, then, for Partridge. 'That's not funny, Hughes,' she said. When two more drivers passed through the room, he did it for them. One of them shrieked. Hughes got up and went to the mirror and did it for himself. He came back looking quite unnerved.

'I've had a whiff of my own grave,' he said, picking up his cards.

Presently Mickey came back in.

'Any sense of what it's like out there?' they asked her.

She was rubbing her cold hands. 'A few wallops over Marylebone way, according to R and D. Station 39 are out already.'

Kay caught her eye. She said quietly, 'Rathbone Place all right, d'you think?'

Mickey took off her coat. 'I think so.' She blew on her fingers. 'What's the game?'

For a time there was relative silence. A new girl, O'Neil, got out a First Aid manual and started testing herself on procedure. Drivers and attendants drifted in and out. A woman who by day was tutor in a dancing-school changed into a pair of woollen knickerbockers and started exercising: bending, stretching, lifting her legs.

At quarter to eleven they heard the first close explosion. Shortly after that, the ack-ack started up in Hyde Park. Their station was a couple of miles away from the guns: even so, the booms seemed to rise up from the concrete into their shoes, and the crockery and cutlery, out in the kitchen, began to rattle.

But only O'Neil, the new girl, exclaimed at the sound. Everyone else simply got on with what they were doing without looking up – Partridge pinning her paper patterns a little more swiftly, perhaps; the dancing-tutor, after a moment, going off to change back into her trousers. Mickey had taken off her boots; now, lazily, she pulled them on again and began to lace them. Kay lit a cigarette, from the stub of an old one. It was worth smoking more cigarettes than you really wanted, she felt, at this stage, to make up for the frantic time to come, when you might have to go without for hours at a stretch.

There was the rumble of another explosion. It seemed closer than the last. A teaspoon which had been travelling eerily across a table, as if pushed by spirits, now flew right off.

Somebody laughed. Somebody else said, 'We're in for it tonight, kids!'

'Could be nuisance raiders,' said Kay.

Hughes snorted. 'Could be my Aunt Fanny. They dropped photograph flares last night, I swear it. They'll be back for the railway lines, if nothing else – '

He turned his head. The telephone, in Binkie's office, had started to ring. Everyone grew still. Kay felt a quick, sharp stab of anxiety, deep in her breast. The phone was silenced, as Binkie picked it up. They heard her voice, very clearly: 'Yes. I see. Yes, at once.'

Source: Sarah Waters (2006) *The Night Watch*, London: Virago, pp.176–8.

7   from *War Crimes for the Home*

Liz Jensen

It's that night, the same day Iris gets blown up, that I begin to learn more about maiming. But it's not munitions this time. It's love.

I was never the brightest. But I wasn't stupid neither. I was middling.

– I hope he's not too clever for you, says Marjorie helping me get ready, going pish pish at my neck with the phoney black-market Chanel that don't even begin to smell like the real McCoy but it's better than nothing, ain't it. She's still shivering and shaking a bit from Iris, and so am I, but I'm not pulling out of my date, not on your nelly. Life goes on.

– A girl like you doesn't want to hang around with someone too clever, says Marje. – Know what I mean, Gloria? (Full of instructions, she is, the war's made her bossy.) – Don't let him French-kiss you the first time or he'll take you for a loose woman. You know what they say about the GIs and English girls' knickers, one Yank and they're –

– Ha blinking ha, I snap at her. She knows how to try and spoil your fun, she does.

Me and Marje've helped ourselves to a few nips of Dad's brandy to swallow down Iris, so I'm ready to escape into the air and leave it behind now. I'm impatient for my date, I need some laughs after seeing that arm getting blown off, and wouldn't say no to getting blotto. His name is Ron, but the way he says it, it's Raan.

– I hope he's a gentleman anyway, she says, yawning like a cat, with Mum's mouth.

Meaning she can't wait to look him over and see if she can nick him – Bobby or no Bobby. My sis wants the best for me but she wants the best for herself too, so she has what you'd call dilemmas. But I'm prettier than her, always have been. Very similar, but better-looking, because my features is regular and hers is a tiny bit conked. Except her mouth. I would like to do swaps for that mouth.

– Now sit still while I fix that hairpin. Stop wriggling, for heaven's sake. You got ants in your pants or what?

– No. Butterflies.

– In your pants? Coo-er.

Silly cow, she is. White blouse and a pink skirt, I'm wearing, with a roll-on underneath and my best undies just in case I do turn out to be loose and Marje has done my hair up lovely coiled around a sanitary towel, it's the latest gimmick she's heard of from her Wren friend, gorgeous it looks, like a doughnut, and you'd never guess what's padding it, handy too if you find you've got the curse. She sticks the last pin in and then I do the lipstick. Red lips scarlet woman, our Dad always says when he sees a girl who's no better than she should be. Putting on powder in the mirror she lets me have another squirt of the fake Chanel. Pish pish.

Ding dong.

And I'm flying to open it like I have wings, with Marje yelling after me. –Where's your bloody poise, girl? You ain't got none, is where!

But I ain't listening to nothing about poise – Marje is the world's biggest bloody expert on poise according to her – because there he is, tall on the doorstep in his airman's uniform and his blue eyes smiling at me. Off comes the little beret cap.

– Hiya, cutie! Boy, you look a million dollars, he says.

Well, of course I do. I might even be the prettiest girl in Bristol, mightn't I.

We met last week at the Red Cross dance. I spotted him right at the beginning, and he spotted me. I turned away, flirty-flirty. Then looked back. You can't help thinking Clark Gable when you see them, no matter how hard you try. No wonder the local boys are in a sulk because they can't cut the mustard next to GI Joe, one Yank and they're off, and no wonder the girls is buzzing at the factory, buzzing with the glamour. He was taller than the others and of course the best-looking, with his good-shaped head.

I was watching him while he was jitterbugging with Moira Farney's little sister. And then he was watching me doing Hands Knees Boompsadaisy.

Hands knees and boompsadaisy,
I like a bustle that bends.
Hands knees and boompasadaisy,
What is a boomp between friends?

And every time you did the boomp you had to twist your hip and boomp your bum against the other one's bum, it was like the hokey cokey but sexy-like, and he said much later on, It was your ass that attracted me first, hon. You sure had a way of twisting that butt of yours.

Hands knees and boompsadaisy,
Let's make the party a wow.
Hands knees and boompsadaisy,
Turn to your partner and bow.

And when it's over I look across and he starts making his way over to me, in his uniform, with his cocky way of walking, knows he'll get me. He doesn't hang about.

– I sure like the look of you, babe. You wanna date next week? My name's Ron.

Except he said Raan. Deep gravelly voice he's got, makes you melt.

He was right to walk like that, because I said yes, didn't I.

We did some jitterbugging together and he bought me two gin and limes, but then I had to go, I was doing the early shift.

– See ya soon, hon, he says. – I'll come pick you up Friday.

And he was all ready to kiss me smack on the lips but I wriggled away because there was a rumour going round that the GIs thought we were easy lays and we had rounded heels from getting on our backs, and I didn't want him thinking I was one of them, did I? He looked like a speedy operator to me.

But I couldn't stop thinking about him all week, and now here he is, and my heart won't let up banging, and I'm standing there gaping at him like a speechless twat, all breathless and collywobbled.

Source: Liz Jensen (2002) *War Crimes for the Home*, London: Bloomsbury, pp.10–13.

8   from *Nella Last's War*

Saturday, 24 January, 1942

I opened a tin of pineapple, and one of sliced peaches, and made a jelly. After taking enough to make a nice helping with custard for tea, I set the fruit in the jelly, and I'll open a tin of cream tomorrow. It's only a small tin, which I saved for last Christmas, but there will be a wee dab for us all. I feel quite excited at a full table again, with laughing people round it.

All was so happy and gay; and then when Cliff went out, my husband and I had one of our rare quarrels. A chance remark started it. He gets such ideas, and worries over them. He said suddenly, 'Has Cliff volunteered to go abroad?' I replied, 'I don't know – all that was said was said in front of you, with the exception that I asked him if he *was* on embarkation leave.' He went on and on about Cliff 'being a fool' and 'if he had stuck to being a P.T. Instructor he might *never* have had to go'. Perhaps I was a bit over-excited, but I said more than I should – I know I did. I said, 'Tell me, would you cling so tightly to Cliff that you killed all that was fine and grand in him as long as he stayed in England? What about honour and duty?' He said, 'You always did talk damned daft – I want MY boy to be safe.' Oh dear me! That did it. I remember things like 'only your own selfishness', and '*never* thinking of anyone's point of view but your own', and that I thanked God that I was a fool, was reared by a fool Gran and had tried to teach my lads to be fools, and if he had been a bit more of a fool he would have been more of a man. *His* boy, indeed! He has never taught, cared for, spanked or tried to understand either of them – or *ever* thinks of writing to them – and is not always interested enough in their letters to listen if I read them.

Pent-up feelings and 'wrongs' rushed over me, and before I could get hold of myself again, I'd got in a few punches below the belt. If I knew my baby was going to his death, I'd not hold him back – even if I could. We must all play our own game as the cards are dealt, no trying to sneak aces from another. Cliff must LIVE – *not* shun life, and always be afraid of things and people and ideas, and be an old man before he has had the fire and endeavour of youth. I shook with rage, and felt a wonder that anyone but a timid girl could be so silly, childish and immature as my husband. I *may* be hard – but I've had to be, hard and resolute. Boys need a firm hand, as well as a 'mother's hand'.

When Cliff came in, the storm had blown over. But I said, 'Cliff, will you tell your father exactly how things stand – did you volunteer to go overseas?' Cliff looked calmly down at his father and said, 'Well, not exactly, but I've tried other times to get in a draft, and they knew if an odd one was wanted I was willing.' He went on, 'Anyway, it's what is to be expected.' He was a bit taken back at his father's face working with emotion, his tear-filled eyes and cry of 'I want you to be SAFE'. I said, 'Safe for what? Till his soul dies in his body, and even his body goes back on him, with repeated nervous breakdowns, and bitter inward thoughts turn his blood sour and cripple and torment him?' All he could say was, 'I want you to be *safe*, Cliff.' Cliff was embarrassed – but he is twenty-three and must see things as they are.

Source: Richard Broad and Suzie Fleming (eds) (2006) *Nella Last's War: the second world war diaries of Housewife, 49*, London: Profile, pp.183–4.

9 from *Housewife, 49*

Victoria Wood

Exterior. The Lasts' house at night.

Interior. The hallway of the Lasts' house.

WILL LAST is walking out from the kitchen. NELLA LAST is following him, and calling out.

Nella: What do you mean I should have put a stop to it? What should I have done – written to them? 'Please excuse Clifford from the machine gun corps. He hasn't got his machine-gun.'

Will: He thinks nothing of me. But you could stop him.

Nella: He's twenty-three. He's made his mind up he wants to go.

Will: I want him to be safe.

Nella: But there's no 'safe'. Michael Hockey's just been blown out of the sky. Evelyn – crushed to death. My heart grows cold when I think what might happen. But it's nothing to do with what you or I feel. It's what he wants.

Will: He's my boy.

Nella: Is he? What have you done to make him your boy? Either of them? Read to them, played with them, spanked them? No – that was all me. When Clifford was in the cubs, you didn't even do his woodwork badge with him. A master carpenter! I had to ask the man next door.

WILL is now walking up the stairs. He turns.

Will: Do you want him killed?

Nella: No, of course I don't want him killed. But if something happens, I want him to have had a life. A proper life, not some stifled, fearful existence. I don't want him smothering every spark of feeling just to suit other people.

Pause.

Will: You don't know what you're talking about.

WILL walks up the stairs.

Nella: Oh I do. I don't want it to happen to him.

WILL pauses at the top of the stairs, with his back to NELLA.

Will: Are you coming to bed?

Nella: No. I think I'll sleep in the Morrison.

WILL continues up the stairs, while NELLA walks back towards the kitchen.

Source: Victoria Wood (2007) *Housewife, 49*, © Victoria Wood 2007.

10   from *The Journals of Sylvia Plath*

June 7: The midwife stopped up to see Ted at noon to remind him that the Devon beekeepers were having a meeting at 6 at Charlie Pollard's. We were interested in starting a hive, so dumped the babies in bed and jumped in the car and dashed down the hill past the old factory to Mill Lane, a row of pale orange stucco cottages on the Taw, which gets flooded whenever the river rises. We drove into the dusty, ugly paved parking lot under the grey peaks of the factory buildings, unused since 1928 and now only used for wool storage. We felt very new and shy, I hugging my bare arms in the cool of the evening for I had not thought to bring a sweater. We crossed a little bridge to the yard where a group of miscellaneous Devonians were standing – an assortment of shapeless men in brown speckled bulgy tweeds, Mr. Pollard in white shirtsleeves, with his dark, nice brown eyes and oddly Jewy head, tan, balding, dark-haired. I saw two women, one very large, tall, stout, in a glistening aqua-blue raincoat, the other cadaverous as a librarian in a dun raincoat. Mr. Pollard glided toward us & stood for a moment on the bridge-end, talking. He indicated a pile of hives, like white and green blocks of wood with little gables & said we could have one, if we would like to fix it up. A small pale blue car pulled into the yard: the midwife. Her moony beam came at us through the windscreen. Then the rector came pontificating across the bridge & there was a silence that grew round him. He carried a curious contraption – a dark felt hat with a screen box built on under it, and cloth for a neckpiece under that. I thought the hat a clerical bee-keeping hat, and that he must have made it for himself. Then I saw, on the grass, and in hands, everybody was holding a bee-hat, some with netting of nylon, most with box screening, some with khaki round hats, I felt barer & barer. People became concerned. Have you no hat? Have you no coat? Then a dry little woman came up, Mrs. Jenkins, the secretary of the society, with tired, short blond hair. 'I have a boiler suit.' She went to her car and came back with a small, white silk button-down smock, the sort pharmacist's assistants use. I put it on and buttoned it & felt more protected. Last year, said the midwife, Charlie's Pollard's bees were bad-tempered and made everybody run. Everyone seemed to be waiting for someone. But then we all slowly filed after Charlie Pollard to his beehives. We threaded our way through neatly weeded allotment gardens, one with bits of tinfoil and a fan of black and white feathers on a string, very decorative, to scare the birds, and twiggy leantos over the plants. Black-eyed sweetpea-like blooms: broadbeans, somebody said. The grey ugly backs of the factory. Then we came to a clearing, roughly scythed, with one hive, a double-brood hive, two layers. From this hive Charlie Pollard wanted to make three hives. I understood very little. The men gathered round the hive. Charlie Pollard started squirting smoke from a little funnel with hand-bellows attached to it round the entry at the bottom of the hive. 'Too much smoke,' hissed the large blue-raincoated woman next to me. 'What do you do if they sting?' I whispered, as the bees, now Charlie had lifted the top off the hive, were zinging out and dancing round as at the end of long elastics. (Charlie had produced a fashionable white straw Italian hat for me with a black nylon veil that collapsed perilously in to my face in the least wind. The rector had tucked it in to my collar, much to my surprise. 'Bees always crawl up, never down,' he said. I had drawn it down loose over my shoulders.) The woman said: 'Stand behind me, I'll protect you.' I did. (I had spoken to her husband earlier, a handsome, rather sarcastic man standing apart, silver-hair, a military blue eye. Plaid tie, checked shirt, plaid vest, all different. Tweedy suit, navy-blue beret. His wife, he had said, kept 12 hives & was the expert. The bees always stung him. His nose & lips, his wife later said.) ...

Noticed: a surround of tall white cow-parsley, pursy yellow gorse-bloom, an old Christmas tree, white hawthorn, strong-smelling.

The donning of the hats had been an odd ceremony. Their ugliness & anonymity very compelling, as if we were all party to a rite. They were brown or grey or faded green felt, mostly, but there was one white straw boater with a ribbon. All faces, shaded, became alike. Commerce became possible with complete strangers.

The men were lifting slides, Charlie Pollard squirting smoke, into another box. They were looking for queen cells – long, pendulous honeycolored cells from which the new queens would come. The blue-coated woman pointed them out. She was from British Guiana, had lived alone in the jungle for 18 years, lost £25 pounds on her first bees there – there had been no honey for them to eat. I was aware of bees buzzing and stalling before my face. The veil seemed hallucinatory. I could not see it for moments at a time. Then I became aware I was in a bone-stiff trance, intolerably tense, and shifted round to where I could see better. 'Spirit of my dead father, protect me!' I arrogantly prayed. A dark, rather nice 'unruly' looking man came up through the cut grasses. Everyone turned, murmured 'O Mr. Jenner, we didn't think you were coming.'

This, then, the awaited expert, the 'government man' from Exeter. An hour late. He donned a white boiler suit and a very expert bee-hat – a vivid green dome, square black screen box for head, joined with yellow cloth at the corners, and a white neckpiece. The men muttered, told what had been done. They began looking for the old queen. Slide after slide was lifted, examined on both sides. To no avail. Myriads of crawling, creeping bees. As I understood it from my blue bee-lady, the first new queen out would kill the old ones, so the new queencells were moved to different hives. The old queen would be left in hers. But they couldn't find her.

Source: Sylvia Plath (2006) *The Journals of Sylvia Plath 1950–1962* (ed. Karen V. Kukil), London: Faber and Faber, pp.656–8.

11 'The Bee Meeting'

Sylvia Plath

Who are these people at the bridge to meet me? They are the villagers.
The rector, the midwife, the sexton, the agent for bees.
In my sleeveless summery dress I have no protection,
And they are all gloved and covered, why did nobody tell me?
They are smiling and taking out veils tacked to ancient hats.

I am nude as a chicken neck, does nobody love me?
Yes, here is the secretary of bees with her white shop smock,
Buttoning the cuffs at my wrists and the slit from my neck to my knees.
Now I am milkweed silk, the bees will not notice.
They will not smell my fear, my fear, my fear.

Which is the rector now, is it that man in black?
Which is the midwife, is that her blue coat?
Everybody is nodding a square black head, they are knights in visors,
Breastplates of cheesecloth knotted under the armpits.
Their smiles and their voices are changing. I am led through a
                                            beanfield.

Strips of tinfoil winking like people,
Feather dusters fanning their hands in a sea of bean flowers,
Creamy bean flowers with black eyes and leaves like bored hearts.
Is it blood clots the tendrils are dragging up that string?
No, no, it is scarlet flowers that will one day be edible.

Now they are giving me a fashionable white straw Italian hat
And a black veil that moulds to my face, they are making me one of
                                            them.

They are leading me to the shorn grove, the circle of hives.
Is it the hawthorn that smells so sick?
The barren body of hawthorn, etherizing its children.

Is it some operation that is taking place?
It is the surgeon my neighbours are waiting for,
This apparition in a green helmet,
Shining gloves and white suit.
Is it the butcher, the grocer, the postman, someone I know?

I cannot run, I am rooted, and the gorse hurts me
With its yellow purses, its spiky armoury.
I could not run without having to run forever.

The white hive is snug as a virgin,
Sealing off her brood cells, her honey, and quietly humming.

Smoke rolls and scarves in the grove.
The mind of the hive thinks this is the end of everything.
Here they come, the outriders, on their hysterical elastics.
If I stand very still, they will think I am cow parsley,
A gullible head untouched by their animosity.

Not even nodding, a personage in a hedgerow.
The villagers open the chambers, they are hunting the queen.
Is she hiding, is she eating honey? She is very clever.
She is old, old, old, she must live another year, and she knows it.
While in their fingerjoint cells the new virgins

Dream of a duel they will win inevitably,
A curtain of wax dividing them from the bride flight,
The upflight of the murderess into a heaven that loves her.
The villagers are moving the virgins, there will be no killing.
The old queen does not show herself, is she so ungrateful?

I am exhausted, I am exhausted –
Pillar of white in a blackout of knives.
I am the magician's girl who does not flinch.
The villagers are untying their disguises, they are shaking hands.
Whose is that long white box in the grove, what have they
                              accomplished, why am I cold.

Source: Sylvia Plath (2006 [1962]) 'The Bee Meeting' in *Ariel*, London: Faber and Faber,
pp.60–2.

12   from *Sanctuary*

Tanika Gupta

Act 1, Scene 1

*We are outdoors in the corner of a graveyard – a small Eden-like,
neat patch of luscious green packed with shrubbery, ornate
flowering plants (orchids) and small tubs of herbs etc. There is a
wall to one side and a large tree, which overhangs the wall into the
road outside. There is a shed to the other side and an old bench
under the tree. The shed is covered in rambling roses and clematis,
all in bloom. In the background we can see row upon row of*

gravestones, which stretch into the distance. A few bits of rubbish litter the otherwise beautiful garden.

It is a bright day. MICHAEL enters and sits on the bench beneath the tree, fashioning a piece of wood into a spoon. He works diligently whilst listening to the cricket commentary on the radio. MICHAEL is casually but smartly dressed. He looks completely engrossed in his work. SEBASTIAN wanders in and sits next to MICHAEL. He is shabbily dressed and dishevelled looking.

At first, he simply sits there in silence. Then he takes interest in what MICHAEL is doing.

Sebastian: What're you working on?

Michael: (*African accent*) It is going to be a spoon.

Sebastian: Ahhh...

SEBASTIAN watches him attentively.

You're good with your hands.

Michael: My father was a carpenter.

Sebastian: Family trade?

Michael: Not really. He was good. He made all the furniture in our village. I just do it to pass the time.

SEBASTIAN looks around.

Sebastian: I like it here.

Michael: Yes.

Sebastian: You like it here?

Michael: Yes.

Sebastian: Lots of dead people. Makes you feel lucky.

Michael: Eh?

Sebastian: That we're alive, man! However bad things are out there, at least we're not fucking six feet under. Know what I mean?

Michael: (*Polite*) I certainly know what you mean.

Sebastian: Too right. Especially when you look at all those gravestones. Young people – half my age. Cut off in the prime of their lives.

MICHAEL continues with his work.

It's the baby ones that always get me. Tiny little coffins.

Michael: Yes, that is sad.

Sebastian: Sad? It's fucking tragic.

Michael: Yes. Tragic. That is what I meant.

Sebastian: Still, like I said. Makes me feel lucky to be drawing breath. The Good Lord up there saw it fit to spare my life.

SEBASTIAN looks heavenward.

(*Shouts*) Thank you God. Not that I'm any fucking good to anyone.

The two men sit in silence.

What's your name again?

Michael: Michael.

Sebastian: Pleased to meet you, Michael. Put it there brother –

MICHAEL gingerly slaps palms with SEBASTIAN.

The name's Seb.

MICHAEL smiles a greeting. SEBASTIAN gets up and staggers around. He looks at the plants.

Very pretty.

We hear voices. A woman vicar wearing a dog collar, JENNY, and an Asian man, KABIR, enter. KABIR is pushing a wheelbarrow full of fresh rolls of turf.

Kabir: They are having the petition in their hands?

Jenny: Yes. I delivered it myself.

Kabir: They will be seeing sense.

Jenny: Yes, I'm sure they will.

Kabir: It is still being beyond all reasoning. They converted St Mary's into luxury apartments.

Jenny: Can't imagine the yuppies moving in round here. I'm going to speak to the bishop this afternoon. He's on our side. Oh – and don't forget, that journalist's coming in on Friday.

Kabir: Eh?

Jenny: You know, from *The Post*. Said she'd be here for most of the afternoon. (*Preoccupied*) Hello Michael. Seb.

SEBASTIAN grunts.

Michael: It is a beautiful morning.

Kabir: Hey, Mikey – what's the score?

Michael: Pakistan are still batting. 223 for three wickets.

Kabir: Good. Have you seen Mumtaz this morning?

Michael: No.

Jenny: She's probably hiding in her nest somewhere.

Kabir: She is always coming to greet me in the mornings – quackety – quack – but only silence today.

Jenny: She'll turn up. She usually does.

MICHAEL continues with his work.

Anyway, this journalist's going to be interviewing people – maybe even you.

Kabir: I will be telling her. This place, it is being a community asset – yes?

Jenny: Very good.

Kabir: People are coming here to pray, to mourn, to grieve and to be with their loved ones. I will be introducing her to people to speak with. Mikey?

Michael: Please Kabir – leave me out of it.

Jenny: Your testament would be useful.

Kabir: You must be helping us, Mikey.

A mobile phone rings.

Jenny: This is important. The coverage would be good for us. The more people read about this place, the better our case.

JENNY answers the phone.

> Jenny Catchpole? Edith ... of course ... he's gone into that nursing home ... I took him there myself last week. Coming here? Shit.

JENNY moves aside to have a more private conversation.

SEBASTIAN undoes his flies to have a pee. KABIR spots him.

Kabir: Oy, oy, oy ... don't you dare be pissing on my plants. And in front of a lady! (*He points at JENNY*) Shame on you! Put it away.

SEBASTIAN hesitates and then puts it away.

JENNY comes off the phone.

Sebastian: Sorry man. I wasn't thinking.

SEBASTIAN looks a bit shame-faced and staggers off. The others watch him go.

Kabir: Jenny – did you see what he was doing? People are thinking this is being a public toilet! The whole place always smelling of piss.

Michael: (*To JENNY*) He's a bit of a mess.

Jenny: But the kids love him and his classes at the church hall are very popular.

Kabir: I would not be trusting him with the charge of my children. In his last lesson he was having them all wondering around the graveyard taking photographs of baby graves. Isn't that being a little bit odd?

Jenny: He's an artist. Probably just being creative.

Kabir: Artist – my foot.

Jenny: What's the new turf for?

Kabir: The area by the pond. Especially for your baby photographers and my ducks.

Jenny: Wonderful. I thought that patch was looking a bit rough.

Kabir: Too many people stepping around there. Churning it up into mud – especially you ladies, with your thin pin like heels.

Jenny: Don't blame me. I don't wear shoes like that.

Source: Tanika Gupta (2002) *Sanctuary*, London: Oberon, pp.15–20.

13   from *Top Girls*

Caryl Churchill

Note on characters

Isabella Bird (1831–1904) lived in Edinburgh, travelled extensively between the ages of 40 and 70.

Lady Nijo (b.1258) Japanese, was an Emperor's courtesan and later a Buddhist nun who travelled on foot through Japan.

Dull Gret is the subject of the Brueghel painting, Dulle Griet, in which a woman in an apron and armour leads a crowd of women charging through hell and fighting the devils.

Pope Joan, disguised as a man, is thought to have been Pope between 854–856.

Patient Griselda is the obedient wife whose story is told by Chaucer in The Clerk's Tale of *The Canterbury Tales*.

Note on layout

A speech usually follows the one immediately before it BUT:

1: when one character starts speaking before the other has finished, the point of interruption is marked / .

e.g. Isabella: This is the Emperor of Japan? / I once met the Emperor of Morocco.

Nijo: In fact he was the ex-Emperor.

2: a character sometimes continues speaking right through another's speech:

e.g. Isabella: When I was forty I thought my life was over. / Oh I was pitiful. I was

Nijo:	I didn't say I felt it for twenty years. Not every minute.
Isabella:	sent on a cruise for my health and I felt even worse. Pains in my bones, pins and needles ... etc.

3: sometimes a speech follows on from a speech earlier than the one immediately before it, and continuity is marked *.

e.g. Griselda:	I'd seen him riding by, we all had. And he'd seen me in the fields with the sheep*.
Isabella:	I would have been well suited to minding sheep.
Nijo:	And Mr Nugent riding by.
Isabella:	Of course not, Nijo, I mean a healthy life in the open air.
Joan:	*He just rode up while you were minding the sheep and asked you to marry him?

where 'in the fields with the sheep' is the cue to both 'I would have been' and 'He just rode up'.

Act 1

[MARLENE, GRET, JOAN, NIJO and ISABELLA are already round the restaurant table.]

They are quite drunk. They get the giggles.

MARLENE notices GRISELDA entering.

Marlene:	Griselda! / There you are. Do you want to eat?
Griselda:	I'm sorry I'm so late. No, no, don't bother.
Marlene:	Of course it's no bother. / Have you eaten?
Griselda:	No really, I'm not hungry.
Marlene:	Well have some pudding.
Griselda:	I never eat pudding.
Marlene:	Griselda, I hope you're not anorexic. We're having pudding, I am, and getting nice and fat.
Griselda:	Oh if everyone is. I don't mind.
Marlene:	Now who do you know? This is Joan who was Pope in the ninth century, and Isabella Bird, the Victorian

traveller, and Lady Nijo from Japan, Emperor's concubine and Buddhist nun, thirteenth century, nearer your own time, and Gret who was painted by Brueghel. Griselda's in Boccaccio and Petrarch and Chaucer because of her extraordinary marriage. I'd like profiteroles because they're disgusting.

Joan: Zabaglione, please.

Isabella: Apple pie / and cream.

Nijo: What's this?

Marlene: Zabaglione, it's Italian, it's what Joan's having, / it's delicious.

Nijo: A Roman Catholic / dessert? Yes please.

Marlene: Gret?

Gret: Cake.

Griselda: Just cheese and biscuits, thank you.

Marlene: Yes, Griselda's life is like a fairy story, except it starts with marrying the prince.

Griselda: He's only a marquis, Marlene.

Marlene: Well, everyone for miles around is his liege and he's absolute lord of life and death and you were the poor but beautiful peasant girl and he whisked you off. / Near enough a prince.

Nijo: How old were you?

Griselda: Fifteen.

Nijo: I was brought up in court circles and it was still a shock. Had you ever seen him before?

Griselda: I'd seen him riding by, we all had. And he'd seen me in the fields with the sheep.*

Isabella: I would have been well suited to minding sheep.

Nijo: And Mr Nugent riding by.

Isabella: Of course not, Nijo, I mean a healthy life in the open air.

Joan:	*He just rode up while you were minding the sheep and asked you to marry him?
Griselda:	No, no, it was on the wedding day. I was waiting outside the door to see the procession. Everyone wanted him to get married so there'd be an heir to look after us when he died, / and at last he announced a day for the wedding but
Marlene:	I don't think Walter wanted to get married. It is Walter? Yes.
Griselda:	nobody knew who the bride was, we thought it must be a foreign princess, we were longing to see her. Then the carriage stopped outside our cottage and we couldn't see the bride anywhere. And he came and spoke to my father.
Nijo:	And your father told you to serve the Prince.
Griselda:	My father could hardly speak. The Marquis said it wasn't an order, I could say no, but if I said yes I must always obey him in everything.
Marlene:	That's when you should have suspected.
Griselda:	But of course a wife must obey her husband. / And of course I must obey the Marquis.*
Isabella:	I swore to obey dear John, of course, but it didn't seem to arise. Naturally I wouldn't have wanted to go abroad while I was married.
Marlene:	*Then why bother to mention it at all? He'd got a thing about it, that's why.
Griselda:	I'd rather obey the Marquis than a boy from the village.
Marlene:	Yes, that's a point.
Joan:	I never obeyed anyone. They all obeyed me.
Nijo:	And what did you wear? He didn't make you get married in your own clothes? That would be perverse.*
Marlene:	Oh, you wait.
Griselda:	*He had ladies with him who undressed me and they had a white silk dress and jewels for my hair.
Marlene:	And at first he seemed perfectly normal?

Griselda: Marlene, you're always so critical of him. / Of course he was normal, he was very kind.

Marlene: But Griselda, come on, he took your baby.

Griselda: Walter found it hard to believe I loved him. He couldn't believe I would always obey him. He had to prove it.

Marlene: I don't think Walter likes women.

Griselda: I'm sure he loved me, Marlene, all the time.

Marlene: He just had a funny way / of showing it.

Griselda: It was hard for him too.

Joan: How do you mean he took away your baby?

Nijo: Was it a boy?

Griselda: No, the first one was a girl.

Nijo: Even so it's hard when they take it away. Did you see it at all?

Griselda: Oh yes, she was six weeks old.

Nijo: Much better to do it straight away.

Isabella: But why did your husband take the child?

Griselda: He said all the people hated me because I was just one of them. And now I had a child they were restless. So he had to get rid of the child to keep them quiet. But he said he wouldn't snatch her, I had to agree and obey and give her up. So when I was feeding her a man came in and took her away. I thought he was going to kill her even before he was out of the room.

Marlene: But you let him take her? You didn't struggle?

Griselda: I asked him to give her back so I could kiss her. And I asked him to bury her where no animals could dig her up. / It

Isabella: Oh my dear.

Griselda: was Walter's child to do what he liked with.*

Marlene: Walter was bonkers.

Gret: Bastard.

Isabella: *But surely, murder.

Griselda: I had promised.

Marlene: I can't stand this. I'm going for a pee.

MARLENE goes out.

The WAITRESS brings dessert.

Nijo: No, I understand. Of course you had to, he was your life. And were you in favour after that?

Griselda: Oh yes, we were very happy together. We never spoke about what had happened.

Isabella: I can see you were doing what you thought was your duty. But didn't it make you ill?

Griselda: No, I was very well, thank you.

Nijo: And you had another child?

Griselda: Not for four years, but then I did, yes, a boy.

Nijo: Ah a boy. / So it all ended happily.

Griselda: Yes he was pleased. I kept my son till he was two years old. A peasant's grandson. It made the people angry. Walter explained.

Isabella: But surely he wouldn't kill his children / just because –

Griselda: Oh it wasn't true. Walter would never give in to the people. He wanted to see if I loved him enough.

Joan: He killed his children / to see if you loved him enough?

Nijo: Was it easier the second time or harder?

Griselda: It was always easy because I always knew I would do what he said.

Pause. They start to eat.

Isabella: I hope you didn't have any more children.

Griselda: Oh no, no more. It was twelve years till he tested me again.

Isabella: So whatever did he do this time? / My poor John, I never loved him enough, and he would never have dreamt ...

Griselda: He sent me away. He said the people wanted him to marry someone else who'd give him an heir and he'd got special permission from the Pope. So I said I'd go home to my father. I came with nothing / so I went with nothing. I

Nijo: Better to leave if your master doesn't want you.

Griselda: took off my clothes. He let me keep a slip so he wouldn't be shamed. And I walked home barefoot. My father came out in tears. Everyone was crying except me.

Nijo: At least your father wasn't dead. / I had nobody.

Isabella: Well it can be a relief to come home. I loved to see Hennie's sweet face again.

Griselda: Oh yes, I was perfectly content. And quite soon he sent for me again.

Joan: I don't think I would have gone.

Griselda: But he told me to come. I had to obey him. He wanted me to help prepare his wedding. He was getting married to a young girl from France / and nobody except me knew how to arrange things the way he liked them.

Nijo: It's always hard taking him another woman.

MARLENE comes back.

Joan: I didn't live a woman's life. I don't understand it.

Griselda: The girl was sixteen and far more beautiful than me. I could see why he loved her. / She had her younger brother with her as a page.

The WAITRESS enters.

Marlene: Oh God, I can't bear it. I want some coffee. Six coffees. Six brandies. / Double brandies. Straightaway.

Griselda: They all went in to the feast I'd prepared. And he stayed behind and put his arms around me and kissed me. / I felt half asleep with the shock.

Nijo: Oh, like a dream.

Marlene: And he said, 'This is your daughter and your son.'

Griselda:	Yes.
Joan:	What?
Nijo:	Oh. Oh I see. You got them back.
Isabella:	I did think it was remarkably barbaric to kill them but you learn not to say anything. / So he had them brought up secretly I suppose.
Marlene:	Walter's a monster. Weren't you angry? What did you do?
Griselda:	Well I fainted. Then I cried and kissed the children. / Everyone was making a fuss of me.
Nijo:	But did you feel anything for them?
Griselda:	What?
Nijo:	Did you feel anything for the children?
Griselda:	Of course, I loved them.
Joan:	So you forgave him and lived with him?
Griselda:	He suffered so much all those years.
Isabella:	Hennie had the same sweet nature.
Nijo:	So they dressed you again?
Griselda:	Cloth of gold.
Joan:	I can't forgive anything.
Marlene:	You really are exceptional, Griselda.
Nijo:	Nobody gave me back my children.

NIJO cries. The WAITRESS brings brandies.

Source: Caryl Churchill (1993 [1982]) *Top Girls*, London: Methuen, pp.19–25.

14   from *The Homecoming*

Harold Pinter

Act 1

LIGHTS UP.

Night.

TEDDY and RUTH stand at the threshold of the room. They are both well dressed in light summer suits and light raincoats.

Two suitcases are by their side.

They look at the room. TEDDY tosses the key in his hand, smiles.

Teddy: Well, the key worked.

    Pause.

    They haven't changed the lock.

    Pause.

Ruth: No one's here.

Teddy: (*looking up*) They're asleep.

    Pause.

Ruth: Can I sit down?

Teddy: Of course.

Ruth: I'm tired.

    Pause.

Teddy: Then sit down.

She does not move.

    That's my father's chair.

Ruth: That one?

Teddy: (*smiling*) Yes, that's it. Shall I go up and see if my room's still there?

Ruth: It can't have moved.

Teddy: No, I mean if my bed's still there.

Ruth: Someone might be in it.

Teddy: No. They've got their own beds.

    Pause.

Ruth: Shouldn't you wake someone up? Tell them you're here?

Teddy: Not at this time of night. It's too late.

    Pause.

    Shall I go up?

He goes into the hall, looks up the stairs, comes back.

    Why don't you sit down?

    Pause.

    I'll just go up ... have a look.

He goes up the stairs, stealthily.

RUTH stands, then slowly walks across the room.

TEDDY returns.

    It's still there. My room. Empty. The bed's there. What are you doing?

She looks at him.

    Blankets, no sheets. I'll find some sheets. I could hear snores. Really. They're all still here, I think. They're all snoring up there. Are you cold?

Ruth: No.

Teddy: I'll make something to drink, if you like. Something hot.

Ruth: No, I don't want anything.

TEDDY walks about.

Teddy: What do you think of the room? Big, isn't it? It's a big house. I mean, it's a fine room, don't you think? Actually there was a wall, across there ... with a door. We knocked it down ... years ago ... to make an open living area. The structure wasn't affected, you see. My mother was dead.

RUTH sits.

    Tired?

Ruth: Just a little.

Teddy: We can go to bed if you like. No point in waking anyone
          up now. Just go to bed. See them all in the morning ... see
          my father in the morning ...

          Pause.

Ruth: Do you want to stay?

Teddy: Stay?

          Pause.

          We've come to stay. We're bound to stay ... for a few
          days.

Ruth: I think ... the children ... might be missing us.

Teddy: Don't be silly.

Ruth: They might.

Teddy: Look, we'll be back in a few days, won't we?

He walks about the room.

          Nothing's changed. Still the same.

          Pause.

          Still, he'll get a surprise in the morning, won't he? The
          old man. I think you'll like him very much. Honestly.
          He's a ... well, he's old, of course. Getting on.

          Pause.

          I was born here, do you realize that?

Ruth: I know.

          Pause.

Teddy: Why don't you go to bed? I'll find some sheets. I feel ...
          wide awake, isn't it odd? I think I'll stay up for a bit. Are
          you tired?

Ruth: No.

Teddy: Go to bed. I'll show you the room.

Ruth: No, I don't want to.

Teddy: You'll be perfectly all right up there without me. Really you will. I mean, I won't be long. Look, it's just up there. It's the first door on the landing. The bathroom's right next door. You ... need some rest, you know.

Pause.

I just want to ... walk about for a few minutes. Do you mind?

Ruth: Of course I don't.

Teddy: Well ... Shall I show you the room?

Ruth: No, I'm happy at the moment.

Teddy: You don't have to go to bed. I'm not saying you have to. I mean, you can stay up with me. Perhaps I'll make a cup of tea or something. The only thing is we don't want to make too much noise, we don't want to wake anyone up.

Ruth: I'm not making any noise.

Teddy: I know you're not.

He goes to her.

(*Gently*) Look, it's all right, really. I'm here. I mean ... I'm with you. There's no need to be nervous. Are you nervous?

Ruth: No.

Teddy: There's no need to be.

Pause.

They're very warm people, really. Very warm. They're my family. They're not ogres.

Pause.

Well, perhaps we should go to bed. After all, we have to be up early, see Dad. Wouldn't be quite right if he found us in bed, I think. (*He chuckles.*) Have to be up before six, come down, say hullo.

Pause.

Ruth: I think I'll have a breath of air.

Teddy: Air?

Pause.

What do you mean?

Ruth: (*standing*) Just a stroll.

Teddy: At this time of night? But we've ... only just got here. We've got to go to bed.

Ruth: I just feel like some air.

Teddy: But I'm going to bed.

Ruth: That's all right.

Teddy: But what am I going to do?

Pause.

The last thing I want is a breath of air. Why do you want a breath of air?

Ruth: I just do.

Teddy: But it's late.

Ruth: I won't go far. I'll come back.

Pause.

Teddy: I'll wait up for you.

Ruth: Why?

Teddy: I'm not going to bed without you.

Ruth: Can I have the key?

He gives it to her.

Why don't you go to bed?

He puts his arms on her shoulders and kisses her. They look at each other, briefly. She smiles.

I won't be long.

She goes out of the front door.

TEDDY goes to the window, peers out after her, half turns from the window, stands, suddenly chews his knuckles.

LENNY walks into the room from UL. He stands. He wears pyjamas and dressing-gown. He watches TEDDY. TEDDY turns and sees him.

Silence.

Source: Harold Pinter (1991 [1965]) *The Homecoming*, London: Faber and Faber, pp.19–24.

15   from 'Status'

Keith Johnstone

When I began teaching at the Royal Court Theatre Studio (1963), I noticed that the actors couldn't reproduce 'ordinary' conversation. They said 'Talky scenes are dull', but the conversations they acted out were nothing like those I overheard in life. For some weeks I experimented with scenes in which two 'strangers' met and interacted, and I tried saying 'No jokes', and 'Don't try to be clever', but the work remained unconvincing ...

I asked myself for the first time what were the *weakest* possible motives, the motives that the characters I was watching might really have had. When I returned to the studio I set the first of my status exercises.

'Try to get your status just a little above or below your partner's,' I said, and I insisted that the gap should be minimal. The actors seemed to know exactly what I meant and the work was transformed. The scenes became 'authentic', and actors seemed marvellously observant. Suddenly we understood that every inflection and movement implies a status, and that no action is due to chance, or really 'motiveless'. It was hysterically funny, but at the same time very alarming. All our secret manoeuvrings were exposed. If someone asked a question we didn't bother to answer it, we concentrated on why it had been asked. No one could make an 'innocuous' remark without everyone instantly grasping what lay behind it. Normally we are 'forbidden' to see status transactions except when there's a conflict. In reality status transactions continue all the time. In the park we'll notice the ducks squabbling, but not how carefully they keep their distances when they are not.

Here's a conversation quoted by W. R. Bion (*Experience in Groups*, Tavistock Publications, 1968) which he gives as an example of a group not getting anywhere while apparently being friendly. The remarks on the status interactions are mine.

Mrs X: I had a nasty turn last week. I was standing in a queue waiting for my turn to go into the cinema when I felt ever so queer. Really, I thought I should faint or something.

[Mrs X is attempting to raise her status by having an interesting medical problem. Mrs Y immediately outdoes her.]

Mrs Y: You're lucky to have been going to a cinema. If I thought I could go to a cinema I should think I had nothing to complain of at all.

[Mrs Z now blocks Mrs Y.]

Mrs Z: I know what Mrs X means. I feel just like that myself, only I should have had to leave the queue.

[Mrs Z is very talented in that she supports Mrs X against Mrs Y while at the same time claiming to be more worthy of interest, her condition more severe. Mr A now intervenes to lower them all by making their condition seem very ordinary.]

Mr A: Have you tried stooping down? That makes the blood come back to your head. I expect you were feeling faint.

[Mrs X defends herself.]

Mrs X: It's not really faint.

Mrs Y: I always find it does a lot of good to try exercises. I don't know if that's what Mr A means.

[She seems to be joining forces with Mr A, but implies that he was unable to say what he meant. She doesn't say 'Is that what you mean?' but protects herself by her typically high-status circumlocution. Mrs Z now lowers everybody, and immediately lowers herself to avoid counterattack.]

Mrs Z: I think you have to use your will-power. That's what worries me – I haven't got any.

[Mr B then intervenes, I suspect in a low-status way, or rather trying to be high-status but failing. It's impossible to be sure from just the words.]

Mr B: I had something similar happen to me last week, only I wasn't standing in a queue. I was just sitting at home quietly when ...

[Mr C demolishes him.]

Mr C: You were lucky to be sitting at home quietly. If I was able to do that I shouldn't think I had anything to grumble about. If you can't sit at home why don't you go to the cinema or something?...

We've all observed different kinds of teachers, so if I describe three types of status players commonly found in the teaching profession you may find that you already know exactly what I mean. I remember one teacher, whom we liked but who couldn't keep discipline. The Headmaster made it obvious that he wanted to fire him, and we decided we'd better behave. Next lesson we sat in a spooky silence for about five minutes, and then one by one we began to fool about – boys jumping from table to table, acetylene-gas exploding in the sink, and so on. Finally, our teacher was given an excellent reference just to get rid of him, and he landed a headmastership at the other end of the county. We were left with the paradox that our behaviour had nothing to do with our conscious intention.

Another teacher, who was generally disliked, never punished and yet exerted a ruthless discipline. In the street he walked with fixity of purpose, striding along and stabbing people with his eyes. Without punishing, or making threats, he filled us with terror. We discussed with awe how terrible life must be for his own children.

A third teacher, who was much loved, never punished but kept excellent discipline, while remaining very human. He would joke with us, and then impose a mysterious stillness. In the street he looked upright, but relaxed, and he smiled easily.

I thought about these teachers a lot, but I couldn't understand the forces operating on us. I would now say that the incompetent teacher was a low-status player: he twitched, he made many unnecessary movements, he went red at the slightest annoyance, and he always seemed like an intruder in the classroom. The one who filled us with terror was a compulsive high-status player. The third was a status expert, raising and lowering his status with great skill. The pleasure attached to misbehaving comes partly from the status changes you make in your teacher. All those jokes on teacher are to make him drop in status. The third teacher could cope easily with any situation by changing his status first.

Status is a confusing term unless it's understood as something one *does*. You may be low in social status, but play high, and vice versa. For example:

Tramp: 'Ere! Where are you going?

Duchess: I'm sorry, I didn't quite catch ...

Tramp: Are you deaf as well as blind?

Audiences enjoy a contrast between the status played and the social status. We always like it when a tramp is mistaken for the boss, or the boss for a tramp. Hence plays like the *The Inspector General*. Chaplin liked to play the person at the bottom of the hierarchy and then lower everyone...

I ask a student to lower his status during a scene, and he enters and says:

> A: What are you reading?
>
> B: *War and Peace.*
>
> A: Ah! That's my favourite book!

The class laugh and A stops in amazement. I had told him to lower his status during the scene, and he doesn't see what's gone wrong.

I ask him to try it again and suggest a different line of dialogue.

> A: What are you reading?
>
> B: *War and Peace.*
>
> A: I've always wanted to read that.

A now experiences the difference, and realises that he was originally claiming 'cultural superiority' by implying that he had read this immense work many times. If he'd understood this he could have corrected the error.

> A: Ah! That's my favourite book.
>
> B: Really?
>
> A: Oh yes. Of course I only look at the pictures ...

A further early discovery was that there was no way to be neutral. The 'Good morning' that might be experienced as lowering by the Manager, might be experienced as raising by the bank clerk. The messages are modified by the receivers...

Many people will maintain that we don't play status transactions with our friends, and yet every movement, every inflection of the voice implies a status. My answer is that acquaintances become friends when they *agree* to play status games together. If I take an acquaintance an early morning cup of tea I might say 'Did you have a good night?' or something equally 'neutral', the status being established by voice and posture and eye contact and so on. If I take a cup of tea to a friend then I may say 'Get up, you old cow', or 'Your Highness's tea', pretending to raise or lower status. Once students understand that they already play status games with their friends, then they realise that they already know most of the status games I'm trying to teach them.

We soon discovered the 'see-saw' principle: 'I go up and you go down'. Walk into a dressing-room and say 'I got the part' and everyone will congratulate you, but will feel lowered. Say 'They said I was too old' and people commiserate, but cheer up perceptibly...

If I'm trying to lower my end of the see-saw, and my mind blocks, I can always switch to raising the other end. That is, I can achieve a similar effect by saying 'I smell beautiful' as 'You stink'. I therefore teach actors to switch between raising themselves and lowering their partners in alternate sentences; and vice versa. Good playwrights also add variety in this way.

Source: Keith Johnstone (1979) 'Status' in *Impro: Improvisation and the theatre*, London: Faber and Faber, pp.33–8.

16   from *Our Country's Good*

Timberlake Wertenbaker

Scene 2   A lone aboriginal Australian describes the arrival of the first convict fleet in Botany Bay on January 20, 1788

The Aborigine: A giant canoe drifts on to the sea, clouds billowing from upright oars. This is a dream which has lost its way. Best to leave it alone.

Scene 3   Punishment

Sydney Cove. GOVERNOR CAPTAIN ARTHUR PHILLIP, JUDGE CAPTAIN DAVID COLLINS, CAPTAIN WATKIN TENCH, MIDSHIPMAN HARRY BREWER. The men are shooting birds.

Phillip: Was it necessary to cross fifteen thousand miles of ocean to erect another Tyburn?

Tench: I should think it would make the convicts feel at home.

Collins: This land is under English law. The court found them guilty and sentenced them accordingly. There: a bald-eyed corella.

Phillip: But hanging?

Collins: Only the three who were found guilty of stealing from the colony's stores. And that, over there on the Eucalyptus, is a flock of *Cacatua galerita* – the sulphur-crested cockatoo. You have been made Governor-in-Chief of a paradise of birds, Arthur.

Phillip: And I hope not a human hell, Davey. Don't shoot yet, Watkin, let's observe them. Could we not be more humane?

Tench: Justice and humaneness have never gone hand in hand. The law is not a sentimental comedy.

Phillip: I am not suggesting they go without punishment. It is the spectacle of hanging I object to. The convicts will feel nothing has changed and will go back to their ways.

Tench: The convicts never left their old ways, Governor, nor do they intend to.

Phillip: Three months is not long enough to decide that. You're speaking too loud, Watkin.

Collins: I commend your endeavour to oppose the baneful influence of vice with the harmonising acts of civilisation, Governor, but I suspect your edifice will collapse without the mortar of fear.

Phillip: Have these men lost all fear of being flogged?

Collins: John Arscott has already been sentenced to 150 lashes for assault.

Tench: The shoulder-blades are exposed at about 100 lashes and I would say that somewhere between 250 and 500 lashes you are probably condemning a man to death anyway.

Collins: With the disadvantage that the death is slow, unobserved and cannot serve as a sharp example.

Phillip: Harry?

Harry: The convicts laugh at hangings, Sir. They watch them all the time.

Tench: It's their favourite form of entertainment, I should say.

Phillip: Perhaps because they've never been offered anything else.

Tench: Perhaps we should build an opera house for the convicts.

Phillip: We learned to love such things because they were offered to us when we were children or young men.

Surely no one is born naturally cultured? I'll have the gun now.

Collins: We don't even have any books here, apart from the odd play and a few Bibles. And most of the convicts can't read, so let us return to the matter in hand, which is the punishment of the convicts, not their education.

Phillip: Who are the condemned men, Harry?

Harry: Thomas Barrett, aged seventeen. Transported seven years for stealing one ewe sheep.

Phillip: Seventeen!

Tench: It does seem to prove that the criminal tendency is innate.

Phillip: It proves nothing.

Harry: James Freeman, age twenty-five, Irish, transported fourteen years for assault on a sailor at Shadwell Dock.

Collins: I'm surprised he wasn't hanged in England.

Harry: Handy Baker, marine and the thieves' ringleader.

Collins: He pleaded that it was wrong to put the convicts and the marines on the same rations and that he could not work on so little food. He almost swayed us.

Tench: I do think that was an unfortunate decision. My men are in a ferment of discontent.

Collins: Our Governor-in-Chief would say it is justice, Tench, and so it is. It is also justice to hang these men.

Tench: The sooner the better, I believe. There is much excitement in the colony about the hangings. It's their theatre, Governor, you cannot change that.

Phillip: I would prefer them to see real plays: fine language, sentiment.

Tench: No doubt Garrick would relish the prospect of eight months at sea for the pleasure of entertaining a group of criminals and the odd savage.

Phillip: I never liked Garrick, I always preferred Macklin.

Collins: I'm a Kemble man myself. We will need a hangman.

Phillip: Harry, you will have to organise the hanging and
             eventually find someone who agrees to fill that hideous
             office.

Phillip shoots.

Collins: Shot.

Tench: Shot.

Harry: Shot, Sir.

Collins: It is my belief the hangings should take place tomorrow.
             The quick execution of justice for the good of the
             colony, Governor.

Phillip: The good of the colony? Oh, look! We've frightened a
             kankaroo.

They look.

All: Ah!

Harry: There is also Dorothy Handland, eighty-two, who stole a
             biscuit from Robert Sideway.

Phillip: Surely we don't have to hang an eighty-two-year-old
             woman?

Collins: That will be unnecessary. She hanged herself this
             morning.

Source: Timberlake Wertenbaker (1996 [1988]) *Our Country's Good* in *Plays One*,
London: Faber and Faber, pp.186–90.

17   from *Temporary Shelter*

Rose Tremain

Fade up TRIST.

Trist: If you asked me to sum up, I would say that Larry and I
           were both travellers.

           Pause.

           We travelled from – and towards – different places and
           different understandings. We are very different men, and
           though we tried, I don't believe we ever really liked each

other or ever could. But I'll never forget Larry, and though he may want to forget me, I don't think he ever will. Because we met at a point of change; a moment of self-revelation, you might almost say.

Pause.

We met in France, one June, on a municipal campsite to the west of Avignon. I arrived first and then I left again to wander about Provence on my own, going mainly from medieval church to medieval church, looking for 'direction' in alabaster Marys, ebony Christs. During that time, I spoke to no-one except shop assistants or café attendants. I was testing myself, to see if I could keep my own company and not die of tedium or heartbreak.

Pause.

Larry and Marje arrived while I was gone.

Pause. The sounds of early morning on the campsite are heard: dogs barking, cicadas beginning to buzz, movement and an occasional laugh or shout of the campers going to the wash houses, unzipping tents, making breakfast etc.

Marje told me that this was their first holiday for seven years. Larry kept up a lament for the ritzy hotels he couldn't afford. He didn't understand how best to live in a tent.

Hold campsite noises, dipped slightly.

Marje: Aren't you going for your shower, Larry?

Larry: (*seeming not to concentrate*) What, Marje?

Marje: I thought you were off for your shower.

Larry: Yes, I am.

Marje: The toilet paper's in the third from left blue wall pocket.

Larry: Yes. Got it, Marje.

          Pause.

Marje: Off you go then, dear.

Larry: Not the right moment, Marje.

Marje: What?

Larry: No hurry really, is there? It's not a very convenient moment.

Marje: What d'you mean, it's not a 'convenient moment'?

Larry: Nothing, dear. But I'll just hang on a jiffy.

Marje: You know what you said yesterday: better to get to the showers before eight-thirty, otherwise you may have to queue.

Larry: (*in a tight whisper*) Look, Marje, I can't go past Jean-Louis' tent while he and Annette are so obviously ... you know ...

Marje: Oh, good heavens, Larry! They're not going to *see* you. Now please hurry up, dear, and then I can start getting breakfast. And if you could call in at the shop on your way back and get a baguette.

Larry: (*still uneasy*) A what?

Marje: (*patient*) A baguette. That's what it's called, the loaf we like.

Larry: (*with disbelief*) A baguette?

Marje: Yes. Now do go, Larry.

Larry: Okay, Marje, okay. A bag-what?

Marje: A baguette.

Larry: I can't ask for that, Marje.

Marje: Of course you can: 'une baguette, s'il vous plait'.

Larry: How d'you know its 'une' and not 'un'?

Marje: I don't, dear. But I'm sure Madam Bidermann will understand. Larry, I'm trying to get up and you're in the way.

Larry: Okay, Marje. I'm off. Here goes ...

Marje: It's not a high dive contest!

The campsite noises fade.

Trist: It was of course typical – characteristic, you might say – of Larry to be embarrassed by the sexuality of his neighbours. He was the kind of man who has never been, nor wanted to be young.

Pause.

But they interested him, Jean-Louis and Annette. First of all, they were French, and Larry had never met any French people before except one, the proprietor of a restaurant in Bressingham St Mary, Norfolk. And secondly, Jean-Louis was a poet.

Pause.

Larry had never, never met a poet! And never may again. Amateur verse makers, yes, perhaps, but not poets. He told me that he had forgotten, until he ran into Jean-Louis, that poets existed.

Fade up the campsite noises. Dogs barking are now very noticeable.

Marje: (*sighs*) Oh dear, we did come for peace, Jean-Louis, didn't you?

Jean-Louis: (*light*) Oh yes.

Marje: And we didn't expect dogs. I never gave them a thought. Not dogs.

Jean-Louis: I don't think I really hear them.

Marje: Well, I'm surprised. Perhaps it's to do with age. Bark, bark, bark! And I did want a bit of peace, for Larry's sake. He works so hard when we're in England.

Jean-Louis: Does he?

Marje: He works terribly hard. (*Pause. In a confidential whisper*) And I know I can say this to you, Jean-Louise: I've been worried about him. He hasn't been himself at all, not just lately. He's started having these nightmares ...

Jean-Louis: The sunshine will help him, Marje.

Marje: I hope it will. Do you think it will?

Jean-Louis: Yes.

Marje: Dreadful nightmares, he says.

Jean-Louis: About what?

Marje:	Well, that's it, you see. He won't say what they're about. He bottles them up. And I often say, you might feel better if you talked about them, Larry. They might go away.
Jean-Louis:	Perhaps he would tell me, Marje?
Marje:	Oh no! He wouldn't. Larry hardly ever tells people things. I mean, he wouldn't like me talking to you about this. (*Catching sight of LARRY returning*) So don't say a word, will you?
Larry:	(*calls, triumphant*) Got the baguette, Marje!
Marje:	Oh, well done, dear. Coffee's on. It was 'une', wasn't it?
Larry:	Wouldn't know. Said 'une', anyway. Bonjour, Jean-Louis. Had a good night, did you?
Jean-Louis:	Bonjour, Larry.
Larry:	Wouldn't go to the showers yet if I was you. Dreadful queues ...
Marje:	You should have gone before eight-thirty, dear.
Larry:	(*ignoring this*) Get the chairs, shall I, Marje?
Marje:	Yes please, dear. And bring the Nescafé, will you?

Source: Rose Tremain (1985 [1984]) *Temporary Shelter* in *Best Radio Plays of 1984*, London: Methuen/BBC, pp.177–80.

18   from *Cigarettes and Chocolate*

Anthony Minghella

Rob:	Rob. Two-thirty. I'm at work. Call me.
	Tone.
Gail:	(*torrential*) Gemma, it's Gail, I hoped you'd be in because I wanted you to come and look at a flat with me. I'll read you the details, I can never remember whether your machine cuts you off after thirty seconds, I hope not because that drives me crazy, anyway, listen it's in, well the postcode is N19 but it's really Highgate Borders, I

mean the Agents say Highgate which it isn't, but it's not inconvenient and anyway Highgate's ridiculous, as bad as you, it's impossible and this place has got a garden, it says pretty west-facing garden, although it doesn't say a length which is a bad sign, yesterday I saw a place in Camden with a Nice Town Garden, this is true, the details said Nice Town Garden and there was nothing, there wasn't one. There was a back yard where this guy had his bicycle and even that wouldn't stand straight, it was sort of bent up to squeeze it in.

Cut off tone.

Me again. I hate it when that happens. It makes you feel terrible, terribly rejecting, where was I? It's in Hornsey, did I say that, but I measured in the A-Z and it's really no further than, it's not as far north as Muswell Hill, say ... it's about two inches above the Post Office Tower. I can't stand Muswell Hill. I hate the architecture as much as anything else: all those porches and it's smug, it's got smug porches. Will you come and look at this place with me? Two bedrooms, plus a bedroom/study so there's room for the baby, there'll be room for the baby, plus the garden as I said ... reception: fireplace, cornices, 16' x 11' which is okay, and dado rails, dado rails (*Pronounces the 'A' differently, first as in baby then as in far, then sing-song to the tune of 'Let's Call the Whole Thing Off'*). You say Dado and I say Dado, whichever it is, who cares, so, I must hurry before I get cut off ... I've got a scan at three tomorrow and I could go straight from that, so will you phone and let me know yes or no so I can make the appointment? It's much easier when you've got someone with, and Sample has a horror ... actually if I could choose you'd come with me for the scan as well, would you hate

Cut off tone.

Lorna: It's Lorna, Gem, where are you? I'm in a callbox opposite the cinema. Are you on your way? Well, I'm assuming you're on your way. If for any reason you haven't left, I'll leave your ticket at the Box Office, or should I wait? There's a queue, Gem, and it's starting, what do I do? Just hurry up, will you!

Tone.

Rob: It's Rob.

> *Tone.*

ROB sighs, puts the phone down.

> *Tone.*

Source: Anthony Minghella (1997 [1989]) *Cigarettes and Chocolate* in *Plays: 2*, London: Methuen, pp.6–7.

19   from *An Angel at My Table*

Laura Jones

> *The screen is filled with an intensely blue sky; clouds cross the blue. The shape of a person stands dark against the sky. We are looking up, up, from an unseen baby's point of view. There is silence.*

BLACK SCREEN, briefly

> *We see blades and stems of grass and weeds. A baby's tiny hands crawl through grass. The shadow of the crawling baby goes ahead on the grass, as we travel forward with the baby's hands. We hear the sound of the baby's breathing, and movement through the grass.*

BLACK SCREEN, briefly

> *Old, soft cotton, printed with a floral pattern, fills the screen. It is worn by Mum, who holds baby Janet. But we see only the cloth, from Janet's point of view: a floral landscape, with soft light and shade made by Mum's body under the cloth. The flowers are imperceptibly moving with Mum's breathing. There is silence.*

BLACK SCREEN, slightly longer

> *A hand reaches down to sand, and picks up a smooth grey stone. It is Mum's hand. She holds the stone out, turning it.*

Mum: Look, kiddies, a stone.

> *Bruddie and Myrtle stand close to Mum, looking up at the stone in her hand. Janet, held on Mum's hip, looks at the stone at eye-level: a small, mysterious planet; treasure. Janet looks from the stone to Bruddie and Myrtle, mouthing the word soundlessly: STONE. The sound of the ocean.*

BLACK SCREEN

Janet stands in the middle of a long, white, dusty road. She wears a golden velvet dress: her beastie dress. She looks down the road. The gate of her house is on one side of her; the dark, forbidden swamp is on the other side. She looks above her at the telegraph wires. They travel down the road to vanishing point. The sound of the wind in the wires is accentuated, keening, unrelieved. Janet, small and alone, feels the outside world's sadness.

BLACK SCREEN

Janet's hand slides into Dad's best trousers hanging on a hook behind the bedroom door. There is the chink of coins.

Janet stands at the door of the Infants room. She hands each child who comes in a pillow of chewing-gum, naming them: Marjorie, Joy, Billy, and so on.

The children sit at desks in rows, all chewing gum. Two monitors walk up and down the aisles giving out green-covered copy books.

Miss Botting turns from the board where she has lettered the day and date. Not all the children stop chewing as she turns.

Miss Botting:	Billy Delaware. What are you eating?
Billy:	Chewing-gum, Miss Botting.
Miss Botting:	Where did you get it?
Billy:	From Jean Frame, Miss Botting.
Miss Botting:	Dids McIvor, where did you get your chewing-gum?

All the chewing has now stopped, everyone transfixed by the scent of trouble.

Dids:	From Jean Frame, Miss.
Miss Botting:	Jean Frame, where did you get the chewing-gum?
Janet:	From Heath's, Miss Botting.
Miss Botting:	Where did you get the money?
Janet:	My father gave it to me.
Miss Botting:	Where did you get the money? I want the truth.

Janet: Dad gave it to me.

Miss Botting: Come out here.

Janet gets up from her desk and goes to the front of the class.

Miss Botting: Come up here.

Janet climbs up on to the raised platform, where Miss Botting's desk and chair stand, in front of the blackboard.

Miss Botting: Now tell me where you got the money.

Janet: My father gave me the money.

Miss Botting: I want the truth.

Janet: Dad gave it to me.

Miss Botting: Face the blackboard.

Janet turns and faces the blackboard. Miss Botting puts her hand on Janet's back and moves her closer to the board, so she is only a few inches away from the cloudy green board.

Miss Botting: Now you'll stay there until you tell me the truth.

Later, Janet is now alone in the classroom. She is still in the same position, on the platform, in front of the blackboard. The board is now covered in words and simple Infants sentences, in Miss Botting's perfect ball-and-stick lettering.

The high sound of the school at lunch in the playground can be heard.

Janet's eyes roam across the pattern of words and numbers on the board.

Miss Botting, the class seated behind her, stands in front of the platform. Late afternoon sun lights the columns of dust and chalk floating in the air.

Miss Botting: Turn around, Jean Frame.

Janet turns around.

Miss Botting: Are you ready to tell me the truth?

Janet pauses; then finds herself saying, in a small voice.

Janet: I took the money out of my father's pocket.

Miss Botting is pleased; the class gasps.

The next day, Janet walks through the school playground: all the games of hopscotch, jacks, ball, and chasings are going on around her.

We hear a chorus, like cicadas, saying THIEF THIEF THIEF THIEF THIEF. They are not children's voices, but Janet's imagination telling her what everyone must be saying and thinking.

BLACK SCREEN.

Source: Laura Jones (1990) *An Angel at My Table* (TV screenplay based on Janet Frame's autobiography), London: Pandora, pp.1–6.

20   from *The Hours*

David Hare

7. CREDITS. EXT/INT. THE BROWNS' HOUSE. LOS ANGELES. DAWN.

Now a delivery truck moves down a suburban street. A card reads LOS ANGELES. 1951. The credits begin. It is only just past dawn as the truck passes a car coming from the opposite direction. The car approaches a one-level, small detached house, which sits, secure, confident, a familiar image of post-war America. The car draws up in the drive, and from it gets out DAN BROWN, a sturdy, handsome American, just turning 30. He wears suit trousers and a white open-neck shirt, and he is carrying a bunch of white roses. He lets himself in through the front door, and moves, roses in hand, along past the sitting room with its pastel shades and low, sparse furniture into the kitchen. As he reaches for a vase, he looks towards the door of a nearly darkened bedroom which is open at the back of the house. A few rays of light from the window help to pick out shapes. In the bedroom LAURA BROWN, a few years older than DAN, is lying asleep in the bed. She is small, angular and fragile. She turns a moment in her sleep.

8. CREDITS. EXT. HOGARTH HOUSE. RICHMOND. DAWN.

A card reads RICHMOND, ENGLAND 1923. A younger LEONARD WOOLF, only 43, is walking past the church, carrying a newspaper and a pile of envelopes and packages he has collected. This suburban quarter, half an hour away from London, is rich with flowers, lawns, trees. In the other direction come the morning COMMUTERS, dark-coated men, on their way to the station to work. Beside the church is a big gray-stone house, its great face unmoving in the dawn.

9. CREDITS. INT. HOGARTH HOUSE. HALL & GALLERY. DAWN.

LEONARD WOOLF opens the door of the house and goes into the hall, which is lined with paintings. He puts down the packages and paper and looks up in time to see a man in his 60s, obviously a DOCTOR – he carries a doctor's bag and is in a dark coat – coming down the stairs, heading to have a word with him.

Leonard: Ah, Doctor. Good morning.

Doctor: Mr. Woolf. No worse, I think. The main thing is to keep her where she is, keep her calm.

Leonard: Mmm. Friday then?

Doctor: Friday.

Their conversation is left behind. Upstairs, on the first floor, beyond the banisters of an open gallery, is the room the DOCTOR has come out of. Inside the bedroom, a woman is alone. She is lying chastely, blinds down at the windows. She is the younger VIRGINIA WOOLF, now only 41. She is staring up at the ceiling

10. CREDIT. EXT/INT. CLARISSA'S APARTMENT. NEW YORK. DAWN.

A card reads NEW YORK CITY, 2001. A subway train rattles violently past, and a lone WOMAN is left standing on the platform. At street level, the sun is just about to rise down West 10th, one of the leafiest and most pleasant streets in the Village. The woman, SALLY LESTER, is walking quickly down the dawn street, returning home. She is tall, dark, dynamic, in her late 30s, wearing a leather jacket and jeans. She approaches a high red-brick terraced house, goes up the steps and lets herself in through its white-painted front door. SALLY goes up to the first-floor apartment, which she also unlocks. SALLY walks straight through the living room of quiet, Bloomsbury-bourgeois homeliness – terracotta and pine, clay pots, ceramics, plants and massive numbers of books. She goes down a corridor and into a warm-colored bedroom, light beginning to beat now against large blinds. SALLY sheds clothes as she goes, taking off her leather jacket and jeans, stripping down to a T-shirt and knickers. She gets into the bed, doing nothing to wake the apparently sleeping figure beside her. CLARISSA VAUGHAN is short of 50, tall, splendid beside the smaller SALLY. CLARISSA does not react visibly, but a moment after SALLY closes her eyes, CLARISSA opens hers.

11. CREDITS. MONTAGE. ALL OF THE ABOVE. ALL DAWN.

2001, 1951 & 1923. In montage, DAN BROWN stands in the bathroom in front of the mirror, tying his tie. CLARISSA throws back the sheet from the bed and gets up. She comes into the small bathroom in her white night gown, ties her hair back behind her head. LAURA, awake now, reaches for a book which is lying at the side of her bed. As her hand reaches for it, the title is clearly seen: Mrs. Dalloway. VIRGINIA sits alone in her bedroom in her dressing-gown, looking at herself in the mirror, then lifts her fingers to adjust her hair. Water pours onto CLARISSA'S face in the shower as she reaches her naked arm out in front of her to grope for the tap, invisible in steam. DAN sets out the breakfast things at the kitchen table for three people, then goes and spoons Nescafé for himself into a mug. He pours on hot water. CLARISSA, in a robe, goes to fill her percolator from a kitchen sink which is full of live crabs, in water. VIRGINIA completes dressing, checks herself neatly in the mirror, walks down the corridor and stands for a moment at the top of the stairs, readying herself. CLARISSA comes into her living room, stands in the middle with her remote control and adjusts the lighting, then turns on a classical radio station. LAURA arranges the pillows to enjoy a luxurious few moments of reading. She turns to listen for the sound of her husband in the kitchen.

In succession, the three women, suspended: VIRGINIA pausing, CLARISSA looking around satisfied with the environment she has created, LAURA listening. Then one thing disturbs CLARISSA: a bunch of sorry-looking dead flowers in the corner of the room. She shakes her head in irritation. DAN brings his roses from the sink and puts the vase on the kitchen table. As he does so, another vase is put down by a MAID'S hands, this time with a bunch of blue cornflowers. As it goes down, echoing the identical motion from 28 years later, the credits end.

12. INT. HOGARTH HOUSE. HALL & GALLERY. DAY.

1923. The vase of cornflowers is seen to be on a table in the open hall of Hogarth House. LEONARD WOOLF is sitting eating toast, drinking coffee, and already proof-reading a manuscript. He looks up at the sound of VIRGINIA appearing from upstairs.

Virginia: Good morning, Leonard.

Leonard: Good morning, Virginia. How was your sleep?

Virginia: Uneventful.

Leonard: The headaches?

Virginia: No. No headaches.

Leonard: The doctor seemed pleased.

VIRGINIA helps herself to tea from the table and nods at the mail.

Virginia: That's all from this morning?

Leonard: Yes. This young man has submitted his manuscript. I've found three errors of fact and two spelling mistakes and I'm not yet on page four.

LEONARD is watching her all the time and sees that she is not planning to sit down.

Leonard: Have you had breakfast?

Virginia: Yes

Leonard: Liar

LEONARD'S tone is casual. He has the quiet, tactful manner of a good nurse.

Leonard: Virginia, it is not at my insistence. It's the wish of your doctors.

VIRGINIA just looks at him, not answering.

Leonard: I'm going to send Nelly up with a bun and some fruit.

Again, VIRGINIA looks at LEONARD, disobediently.

Leonard: Very well, then. Lunch. A proper lunch. Husband and wife sitting down to soup, pudding and all. By force, if necessary.

Virginia: Leonard, I believe I may have a first sentence.

LEONARD looks her in the eye, knowing how stubborn she is.

Leonard: Work, then. But then you must eat.

13. INT. HOGARTH HOUSE. STUDY. DAY.

VIRGINIA goes into her plain, serene study and sits down, picking up a board on which she writes. There is an inkwell, a fountain pen. She lights a cigarette. Then, charged with quiet excitement, she opens a clean notebook. The blank page. Then a feeling of pleasure appears on her face in the hushed room. Before writing she tries her sentence out loud.

Virginia: Mrs. Dalloway said she would buy the flowers herself.

14. INT. BROWNS' HOUSE. LOS ANGELES. DAY.

1951. LAURA is lying in the bed, luxuriating in a moment of being alone. She reaches for the copy of Mrs. Dalloway beside her bed and she opens it. She smiles in anticipated pleasure. She speaks out loud.

Laura: 'Mrs. Dalloway said she would buy the flowers herself.'

15. INT. CLARISSA'S APARTMENT. NEW YORK. DAY.

2001. CLARISSA is standing in the middle of the living room, frowning, as if wondering what she should do. Then she calls out to SALLY, unseen in the other room.

Clarissa: Sally! I think I'll buy the flowers myself.

Source: David Hare (2002) *The Hours* (screenplay based on the novel by Michael Cunningham), New York: Miramax, pp.3–9.

21   from *The Singing Detective*

Dennis Potter

Marlow lies on his hospital bed, not quite able to stifle a cry of pain. He starts remembering.

In the Forest, the small boy is climbing the special tree, his face contorting with effort, concentration, and perhaps a little fear as hand over hand, grappling, branch upon branch, he ascends higher and higher into the magnificent old oak.

... Birdsong takes over, liquid, slightly amplified. And the soft, sea-like Hush-u-shush-hh of a breeze stirring through the myriads of summer leaves. Philip, the boy, has reached his treetop perch, and is able to look out and around at the forest spreading in every direction. There seem to be no other sights but the undulating treetops, no other sounds but the trilling birds and the wind in the branches. Philip's face is troubled. It is streaked with recent tears.

Philip: (*Strong accent*) Our Father which art in Heaven Hallowed be thy name Thy kingdom come Thy will be done ...

Music, quickly swelling, drowns his frightened, intense voice: it is from a wireless set.

In a small room in a cottage in the village, there is one tiny sash window, in the sill of which sits an accumulator-charged wireless, loudly playing 'Don't Fence Me In'. Listening, and too crowded, are Grancher, hunched in a sagging chair by the coal grate; Gran, pinafore-ed; Mr Marlow, and Mrs Marlow, an attractive young (30-ish) woman. All except Grancher are at the table, eating bread and jam.

Gran: (*Forcefully*) Putt thik racket, off, ut?

Grancher: Oy. Tis, yunnit? Get on thee wick.

Mr Marlow gets up and switches the wireless off. But he looks at his wife, slightly timidly, as he comes back the two paces to the table.

Mrs Marlow: I like the Andrews Sisters. I like Bing Crosby.

Unlike the others, she has a London accent.

Mr Marlow: (*Nervously*) Oh ay. Well. And I do.

End of conversation. Black looks around the table. Grancher has a tin-tack rattle in his chest caused by silicosis. He suddenly gasps and wheezes into a truly awful hawking cough from somewhere deep in his diseased lungs and – phlop! – a nasty gobbet of phlegm lands on the bars of the grate, where it sizzles, oozes, and elongates. An entirely matter-of-fact expectoration. Mrs Marlow has just taken a mouthful of bread and jam. She stops chewing. Distress, distaste, on her face, she looks sidelong at her husband, who, although painfully aware of her feelings, affects not to notice.

Gran: Lovely bit o' plum, yunnit? Thou costn't byut [*beat*] plum, not for jam. I don't care what nobody d'say …

Once again, the tin-tack chest rattle, the preliminary to another foul performance. But Grancher momentarily holds it back.

Grancher: (*Gasp*) Cosn't cook a plum. A plum don't like cooking. Him a' got too much skin. Give I stro'bry jam any day of the wik – I'd rather have me a –

But his observations have to remain unfinished. The rattle gets too much for him. The hawking cough starts all over again, and concludes with an equally emphatic spit into the grate. Crash! Mrs Marlow, flushed, throws her knife down on to her plate, with an exaggerated clatter, and pushes back her chair with a loud scrape.

Mrs Marlow: God Almighty.

Mr Marlow: What – ? What's the matter?

Mrs Marlow: What's the matter – What's matter – ! How can anybody eat with that going on?

Gran: (*To Mr Marlow*) What's up wi' her now?

Mr Marlow: (*Mildly, to Mrs Marlow*) Him cont help it, now can 'a? It chunt no joke, mind. That coal dust in the lungs. What's our Dad supposed to do – ?

Grancher: (*Offended*) Eh? What? What's that?

Mrs Marlow: He can go outside! When we're eating –

Gran: Oh, aye. Whose house is it? Tell me that! Have him got to go outside for a bit of a cough in his own whum!

There is an obvious tension and dislike between the two women.

Mrs Marlow: A bit of a cough. You call that a bit of a cough! More like a bleed'n avalanche!

Gran: Langwidge.

Grancher: (*Plaintive*) You try it o'butty. Thou try a chest like mine!

Mr Marlow: (*Unhappily*) It's all right, Dad –

Mrs Marlow: It's not all right!

Mr Marlow:	All right. All right.
Mrs Marlow:	It turns me right off, and you know it does! I'd just put some food into my mouth. It was as much as I could do to get it down.
Gran:	Fuss! Fuss!

The door opens and the boy Philip stands looking at them, pale, withdrawn, anxious. And not coming any further into the room. His father, Mr Marlow, notices him with relief, hoping for some sort of distraction to halt the brewing row.

Mr Marlow:	Where's thou been, our Philip? Tea's bin ready half-hour agoo.
Mrs Marlow:	It's not fuss, not at all. It turns me up.
Gran:	(*Nastily*) Then thee's know what thous can do doosn't!
Mr Marlow:	(*Unhappily*) Now, our Mam.
Mrs Marlow:	(*Jeer*) 'Now our Mam.' 'Ooh, our Mam.' Why don't you stick up for me for a change! Christ Almighty.
Gran:	Langwidge!

The boy is watching, wide-eyed, his back against the latched door.

Grancher:	Let's have no an-i-mos-ity. Not in my house. I don't want it.
Gran:	Whosc housc is it – that's all I'da want to know? Whose feow sticks of furniture – ? Have Dad and me got to be told what to do at our time of life in our own place – Whose house! Tell me that!
Mrs Marlow:	Is that all you can say? Do you ever say anything else? Can't you change the bloody tune sometimes?

Grancher half rises from his sagging fireside chair, greatly offended.

Grancher:	No cussing! No cussing here! If you please!
Gran:	I won't have you talking to me like that, my girl – Not in my own –

Mr Marlow:	(*Sharper*) Mam!
Gran:	We never wanted this. Never wanted to end up like this!
Mr Marlow:	Oh, let's have our bit tea. For goodness' sake, don't let's have all this squabbling! I be sick at heart with it all.

A small, hostile pause – and, almost simultaneously, they all seem to turn their eyes to Philip.

Mrs Marlow:	(*Sharply*) Where have you been? Why are you always late for tea?
Mr Marlow:	You heard your mother. Where've you bin?
Mrs Marlow:	I've been calling all over for you. Didn't you hear me?
Philip:	(*Barely audible*) No-o.
Mr Marlow:	You bin mooching about in them woods agyun – on thee own? Is that it? Stuck up top of a tree.
Gran:	Chunt natural.
Mrs Marlow:	I never know where you are. Wanted you to go to the shop. Calling, calling! I'd a good mind you wouldn't get any tea at all, if you can't come in on time –
Gran:	Oh, him a got to have his little bit of tay –
Grancher:	'Course him have, a growing lad like Philip – (*To the silent boy*) Got to put some gristle in them arms, antcha o'butty?
Gran:	Come th'on. Sit up at table. There's a good boy. Make a soldier of tha, eh?

Mrs Marlow, made edgy, and already very unhappy with her situation in this tiny squabbling-box of a house, all but yells out –

Mrs Marlow:	I'll decide that! That's for me to say! He's my son! Philip! No tea for you!
Mr Marlow:	Oh now Betty – doosn't say –
Mrs Marlow:	(*Yell*) You gutless bugger!

Gran:	I've never heard the like! Not in all my born days! Ted – bist thou going to put up with that or – I'd smack her one, that I'ood!
Mrs Marlow:	(*To GRAN*) Shut up! Keep your nose out of it. You interfering old cow!

Gran rises from the table, utterly shocked.

Gran:	What? What did you? Get out! Get theeself out! Get out of this house – !
Mr Marlow:	(*Desperate*) Don't, our Mam – don't – holt on!
Mrs Marlow:	(*Shrill*) I would! I would! If your son was any sort of man –
Mr Marlow:	Betty.
Mrs Marlow:	– It's his job to find us a place, his wife and his son – Instead of being squashed up in this poky hole –
Gran:	Hole!
Grancher:	Poky! You calling it poky!
Mr Marlow:	Her don't mean it –
Mrs Marlow:	Yes, I do!

Philip stays with his back flat against the latched door, his eyes wide in his pale, freckled face, the angry adult words sinking under his unhappy thoughts.

Philip:	(*Thinks*) My fault. Me. It's me. Me. It's all my doing. Me. It's me. My fault. Mine. Our Father which art in heaven Hallow'd be Thy name ...

The boy's gabbled voice is quickly fading over the face of the distressed man he is to become, in the hospital ward.

Source: Dennis Potter (1986) *The Singing Detective*, London: Faber and Faber, pp.64–70.

22   from *The Hours*

Michael Cunningham

Mrs. Dalloway said she would buy the flowers herself.

For Lucy had her work cut out for her. The doors would have to be taken off their hinges; Rumpelmayer's men were coming. And then, thought Clarissa Dalloway, what a morning – fresh as if issued to children on a beach.

It is Los Angeles. It is 1949.

Laura Brown is trying to lose herself. No, that's not it exactly – she is trying to keep herself by gaining entry into a parallel world. She lays the book face down on her chest. Already her bedroom (no, their bedroom) feels more densely inhabited, more actual, because a character named Mrs. Dalloway is on her way to buy flowers. Laura glances at the clock on the nightstand. It's well past seven. Why did she buy this clock, this hideous thing, with its square green face in a rectangular black Bakelite sarcophagus – how could she ever have thought it was smart? She should not be permitting herself to read, not this morning of all mornings; not on Dan's birthday. She should be out of bed, showered and dressed, fixing breakfast for Dan and Richie. She can hear them downstairs, her husband making his own breakfast, ministering to Richie. She should be there, shouldn't she? She should be standing before the stove in her new robe, full of simple, encouraging talk. Still, when she opened her eyes a few minutes ago (after seven already!) – when she still half inhabited her dream, some sort of pulsating machinery in the remote distance, a steady pounding like a gigantic mechanical heart, which seemed to be drawing nearer – she felt the dank sensation around her, the nowhere feeling, and knew it was going to be a difficult day. She knew she was going to have trouble believing in herself, in the rooms of her house, and when she glanced over at this new book on her nightstand, stacked atop the one she finished last night, she reached for it automatically, as if reading were the singular and obvious first task of the day, the only viable way to negotiate the transit from sleep to obligation. Because she is pregnant, she is allowed these lapses. She is allowed, for now, to read unreasonably, to linger in bed, to cry or grow furious over nothing.

She will make up for breakfast by baking Dan a perfect birthday cake; by ironing the good cloth; by setting a big bouquet of flowers (roses?) in the middle of the table, and surrounding it with gifts. That should compensate, shouldn't it?

She will read more pages. One more page, to calm and locate herself, then she'll get out of bed.

What a lark! What a plunge! For so it had always seemed to her, when, with a little squeak of the hinges, which she could hear now she had burst open the French windows and plunged at Bourton into the open air. How fresh, how calm, stiller than this of course, the air was in the early morning; like the flap of a wave; the kiss of a wave; chill and sharp and yet (for a girl of eighteen as she then was) solemn, feeling as she did, standing there at the open window, that something awful was about to happen; looking at the flowers, at the trees with the smoke winding off them and the rooks rising, falling; standing and looking until Peter Walsh said, 'Musing among the vegetables?' – was that it? – 'I prefer men to cauliflowers' – was that it? He must have said it at breakfast one morning when she had gone out on to the terrace – Peter Walsh. He would be back from India one of these days, June or July, she forgot which, for his letters were awfully dull; it was his sayings one remembered; his eyes, his pocket-knife, his smile, his grumpiness and, when millions of things had utterly vanished – how strange it was! – a few sayings like this about cabbages.

She inhales deeply. It is so beautiful; it is so much more than ...well, than almost anything, really. In another world, she might have spent her whole life reading. But this is the new world, the rescued world – there's not much room for idleness. So much has been risked and lost; so many have died. Less than five years ago Dan himself was believed to have died, at Anzio, and when he was revealed two days later to be alive after all (he and some poor boy from Arcadia had had the same name), it seemed he had been resurrected. He seemed to have returned, still sweet-tempered, still smelling like himself, from the realm of the dead (the stories you heard then about Italy, about Saipan and Okinawa, about Japanese mothers who killed their children and themselves rather than be taken prisoner), and when he came back to California he was received as something more than an ordinary hero. He could (in the words of his own alarmed mother) have had anyone, any pageant winner, any vivacious and compliant girl, but through some obscure and possibly perverse genius had kissed, courted, and proposed to his best friend's older sister, the bookworm, the foreign-looking one with the dark, close-set eyes and the Roman nose, who had never been sought after or cherished; who had always been left alone, to read. What could she say but yes? How could she deny a handsome, good-hearted boy, practically a member of the family, who had come back from the dead?

So now she is Laura Brown. Laura Zielski, the solitary girl, the incessant reader, is gone, and here in her place is Laura Brown.

One more page, she decides; just one more. She isn't ready yet; the tasks that lie ahead (putting on her robe, brushing her hair, going down to the kitchen) are still too thin, too elusive. She will permit herself another minute here, in bed, before entering the day. She will allow herself just a little more time. She is taken by a wave of feeling, a sea-swell, that rises from under her breast and buoys her, floats her gently, as if she were a sea creature thrown back from the sand where it had beached itself – as if she had returned from a realm of crushing gravity to her true medium, the suck and swell of saltwater, that weightless brilliance.

She stiffened a little on the kerb, waiting for Durtnall's van to pass. A charming woman, Scrope Purvis thought her (knowing her as one does know people who live next door to one in Westminster); a touch of the bird about her, of the jay, blue-green, light, vivacious, though she was over fifty, and grown very white since her illness. There she perched, never seeing him, waiting to cross, very upright.

For having lived in Westminster – how many years now? over twenty, – one feels even in the midst of the traffic, or waking at night, Clarissa was positive, a particular hush, or solemnity; an indescribable pause; a suspense (but that might be her heart, affected, they said, by influenza) before Big Ben strikes. There! Out it boomed. First a warning, musical; then the hour, irrevocable. The leaden circles dissolved in the air. Such fools we are, she thought, crossing Victoria Street. For Heaven only knows why one loves it so, how one sees it so, making it up, building it round one, tumbling it, creating it every moment afresh; but the veriest frumps, the most dejected of miseries sitting on doorsteps (drink their downfall) do the same; can't be dealt with, she felt positive, by Acts of Parliament for that very reason: they love life. In people's eyes, in the swing, tramp, and trudge; in the bellow and the uproar, the carriages, motor cars, omnibuses, vans, sandwich men shuffling and swinging; brass bands; barrel organs; in the triumph and the jingle and the strange high singing of some aeroplane overhead was what she loved; life; London; this moment of June.

How, Laura wonders, could someone who was able to write a sentence like that – who was able to feel everything contained in a sentence like that – come to kill herself? What in the world is wrong with people? Summoning resolve, as if she were about to dive into cold water, Laura closes the book and lays it on the nightstand. She does not dislike her child, does not dislike her husband. She will rise and be cheerful.

At least, she thinks, she does not read mysteries or romances. At least she continues to improve her mind. Right now she is reading Virginia Woolf, all of Virginia Woolf, book by book – she is fascinated by the idea of a woman like that, a woman of such brilliance, such strangeness, such immeasurable sorrow; a woman who had genius but still filled her pocket with a stone and waded out into a river. She, Laura, likes to imagine (it's one of her most closely held secrets) that she had a touch of brilliance herself, just a hint of it, though she knows most people probably walk around with similar hopeful suspicions curled up like tiny fists inside them, never divulged. She wonders, while she pushes a cart through the supermarket or has her hair done, if the other women aren't all thinking, to some degree or other, the same thing: Here is the brilliant spirit, the woman of sorrows, the woman of transcendent joys, who would rather be elsewhere, who has consented to perform simple and essentially foolish tasks, to examine tomatoes, to sit under a hair dryer, because it is her art and her duty. Because the war is over, the world has survived, and we are here, all of us, making homes, having and raising children, creating not just books or paintings but a whole world – a world of order and harmony where children are safe (if not happy), where men who have seen horrors beyond imagining, who have acted bravely and well, come home to lighted windows, to perfume, to plates and napkins.

What a lark! What a plunge!

Laura gets out of bed. It is a hot, white morning in June. She can hear her husband moving around downstairs. A metal lid kisses the rim of its pan. She takes her robe, pale aqua chenille, from the newly reupholstered chair and the chair appears, squat and fat, skirted, its nubbly salmon-colored fabric held down by cord and salmon-colored buttons in a diamond pattern. In the morning heat of June, with the robe whisked away, the chair in its bold new fabric seems surprised to find itself a chair at all.

She brushes her teeth, brushes her hair, and starts downstairs. She pauses several treads from the bottom, listening, waiting; she is again possessed (it seems to be getting worse) by a dreamlike feeling, as if she is standing in the wings, about to go onstage and perform in a play for which she is not appropriately dressed, and for which she had not adequately rehearsed. What, she wonders, is wrong with her. This is her husband in the kitchen; this is her little boy. All the man and boy require of her is her presence and, of course, her love. She conquers the desire to go quietly back upstairs, to her bed and book. She conquers her irritation at the sound of her husband's voice, saying something to Richie about napkins (why does his voice remind her sometimes of a potato being grated?). She descends the last three stairs, crosses the narrow foyer, enters the kitchen.

She thinks of the cakes she will bake, the flowers she'll buy. She thinks of roses surrounded by gifts.

Her husband has made the coffee, poured cereal for himself and their son. On the tabletop, a dozen white roses offer their complex, slightly sinister beauty. Through the clear glass vase Laura can see the bubbles, fine as grains of sand, clinging to their stems. Beside the roses stand cereal box and milk carton, with their words and pictures.

'Good morning,' her husband says, raising his eyebrows as if he is surprised but delighted to see her.

'Happy birthday,' she says.

Source: Michael Cunningham (1999) *The Hours*, London: Fourth Estate, pp.37–43.

23   from *Her Big Chance*

Alan Bennett

Lesley is in her early thirties. She is in her flat. Morning.

I shot a man last week. In the back. I miss it now, it was really interesting. Still, I'm not going to get depressed about it. You have to look at the future. To have something like that under your belt can be quite useful, you never know when you might be called on to repeat the experience.

It wasn't in the line of duty. I wasn't a policewoman or someone who takes violence in their stride. It was with a harpoon gun actually, but it definitely wasn't an accident. My decision to kill was arrived at only after a visible tussle with my conscience. I had to make it plain that once I'd pulled the trigger things were never going to be the same again: this was a woman at the crossroads.

It wasn't Crossroads, of course. They don't shoot people in Crossroads, at any rate not with harpoon guns. If anybody did get shot it would be with a weapon more suited to the motel ambience. I have been in Crossroads though, actually. I was in an episode involving a fork lunch. At least I was told it was a fork lunch, the script said it was a finger buffet. I said to the floor manager, I said, 'Rex. Are you on cans because I'd like some direction on this point. Are we toying or are we tucking in?' He said, 'Forget it. We're losing the food anyway.' I was playing Woman in a Musquash Coat, a guest at a wedding reception, and I was scheduled just to be in that one episode. However in my performance I tried to suggest I'd taken a fancy to the hotel in the hope I might catch the director's eye and he'd have me stay on after the fork lunch for the following episode which involved a full-blown weekend. So I acted an interest in the soft furnishings, running my fingers over the formica and admiring the carpet on the walls. Only Rex came over to say that they'd put me in a musquash coat to suggest I was a sophisticated woman, could I try and look as if I was more at home in a three star motel. I wasn't at home in that sort of motel I can tell you. I said to the man I'd been put next to, who I took to be my husband, I said, 'Curtains in orange nylon and no place mats, there's not even the veneer of civilisation.' He said, 'Don't talk to me about orange nylon. I was on a jury once that sentenced Richard Attenborough to death.' We'd been told to indulge in simulated cocktail chit-chat so we weren't being unprofessional, talking. That is something I pride myself on, actually: I am professional to my fingertips.

Whatever it is I'm doing, even if it's just a walk-on, I must must must get involved, right up to the hilt. I can't help it. People who know me tell me I'm a very serious person, only its funny, I never get to do serious parts.

The parts I get offered tend to be fun-loving girls who take life as it comes and aren't afraid of a good time should the opportunity arise-type-thing. I'd call them vivacious if that didn't carry overtones of the outdoor life. In a nutshell I play the kind of girl who's very much at home on a bar stool and who seldom has to light her own cigarette. That couldn't be more different from me because for a start I'm not a smoker. I mean, I can smoke if a part requires it. I'm a professional and you need as many strings to your bow as you can in this game. But, having said that, I'm not a natural smoker and what's more I surprise my friends by not being much of a party-goer either. (Rather curl up with a book quite frankly.) However, this particular party I'd made an exception. Thing was I'd met this ex-graphic designer who was quitting the rat race and going off to Zimbabwe and he was having a little farewell do in the flat of an air hostess friend of his in Mitcham, would I go? I thought, well it's not every day you get somebody going off to Zimbabwe, so I said 'Yes' and I'm glad I did because that's how I got the audition.

Now my hobby is people. I collect people. So when I saw this interesting-looking man in the corner, next thing is I find myself talking to him. I said, 'You look an interesting person. I'm interested in interesting people. Hello.' He said, 'Hello.' I said, 'What do you do?' He said, 'I'm in films.' I said, 'Oh, that's interesting, anything in the pipeline?' He said, 'As a matter of fact, yes,' and starts telling me about this project he's involved in making videos for the overseas market, targeted chiefly on West Germany. I said, 'Are you the producer?' He said, 'No, but I'm on the production side, the name's Spud.' I said, 'Spud! That's an interesting name, mine's Lesley.' He said, 'As it happens, Lesley, we've got a problem at the moment. Our main girl has had to drop out because her back's packed in. Are you an actress?' I said, 'Well, Spud, interesting that you should ask because as a matter of fact I am.' He said, 'Will you excuse me one moment, Lesley?' I said, 'Why, Spud, where are you going?' He said, 'I'm going to go away, Lesley, and make one phone call.'

It transpires the director is seeing possible replacements the very next day, at an address in West London. Spud said, 'It's interesting because I'm based in Ealing.' I said, 'Isn't that West London?' He said, 'It is. Where's your stamping ground?' I said, 'Bromley, for my sins.' He said, 'That's a far-ish cry. Why not bed down at my place?' I said, 'Thank you, kind sir, but I didn't fall off the Christmas tree yesterday.' He said, 'Lesley, I have a son studying hotel management and a daughter with one kidney. Besides, I've got my sister-in-law staying. She's come up for the Ideal Home Exhibition.'

The penny began to drop when I saw the tattoo. My experience of tattoos is that they're generally confined to the lower echelons, and when

I saw his vest it had electrician written all over it. I never even saw the sister-in-law. Still traipsing round Olympia probably.

Go to black.

Source: Alan Bennett (1993 [1988]) *Talking Heads*, London: BBC Books, pp.56–8.

24   from *Last Orders*

Graham Swift

Vic takes the jar and starts to ease it back in the box but it's a tricky business and the box slides from his lap on to the floor, so he puts the jar on the bar.

It's about the same size as a pint glass.

He says, 'Bern!'

Bernie's at the other end of the bar, usual drying-up towel over his shoulder. He turns and comes towards us. He's about to say something to Vic, then he sees the jar, by Lenny's pint. He checks himself and he says, 'What's that?' But as if he's already worked out the answer.

'It's Jack,' Vic says. 'It's Jack's ashes.'

Bernie looks at the jar, then he looks at Vic, then he gives a quick look round the whole of the bar. He looks like he looks when he's making up his mind to eject an unwanted customer, which he's good at. Like he's building up steam. Then his face goes quiet, it goes almost shy.

'That's Jack?' he says, leaning closer, as if the jar might answer back, it might say, 'Hello Bernie.'

'Jesus God,' Bernie says, 'what's he doing here?'

So Vic explains. It's best that Vic explains, being the professional. Coming from Lenny or me, it might sound like a load of hooey.

Then I say, 'So we thought he should have his last look-in at the Coach.'

'I see,' Bernie says, like he don't see.

'It's a turn-up,' Lenny says.

Vic says, 'Get me a large scotch, Bernie. Have one yourself.'

'I will, thank you, I will, Vic,' Bernie says, all considered and respectful, like a scotch is appropriate and it don't do to refuse a drink from an undertaker.

He takes two glasses from the rack and squeezes one up against the scotch bottle, two shots, then he takes just a single for himself. He turns and slides the double across to Vic. Vic pushes over a fiver, but Bernie holds up a hand. 'On the house, Vic, on the house,' he says. 'Aint every day, is it?' Then he raises his glass, eyes on the jar, as if he's going to say something speechy and grand but he says, 'Jesus God, he was only sitting there six weeks ago.'

We all look into our drinks.

Vic says, 'Well here's to him.'

We lift our glasses, mumbling. JackJackJack.

'And here's to you, Vic,' I say. 'You did a good job Thursday.'

'Went a treat,' Lenny says.

'Don't mention it,' Vic says. 'How's Amy?'

'Managing,' I say.

'She hasn't changed her mind about coming then?'

'No, she'll be seeing June, as per usual.'

Everyone's silent.

Vic says, 'Her decision isn't it?'

Lenny sticks his nose in his glass like he's not going to say anything.

Bernie's looking at the jar and looking anxiously round the bar. He looks at Vic like he don't want to make a fuss but.

Vic says, 'Point taken, Bernie,' and takes the jar from where it's sitting. He reaches down for the fallen box. 'Not much good for business, is it?'

'Aint helping yours much either, Vic,' Lenny says.

Vic slides the jar carefully back into the box. It's eleven twenty by Slattery's clock and it feels less churchy. There's more punters coming in. Someone's put on the music machine. *Going back some day, come what may, to Blue Bayou* ...That's better, that's better.

First wet rings on the mahogany, first drifts of blue smoke.

Vic says, 'Well all we need now is our chauffeur.'

Lenny says, 'They're playing his tune. Wonder what he'll bring. Drives something different every week, these days, far as I can see.'

Bernie says, 'Same again all round?'

As he speaks there's a hooting and tooting outside in the street. A pause, then another burst.

Lenny says, 'Sounds like him now. Sounds like Vincey.'

There's a fresh round of hooting.

Vic says, 'Isn't he coming in?'

Lenny says, 'I reckon he wants us out there.'

We don't go out but we get up and go over to the window. Vic keeps hold of the box, like someone might pinch it. We raise ourselves up on our toes, heads close together, so we can see above the frosted half of the window. I can't quite, but I don't say.

'Jesus Christ,' Lenny says.

'It's a Merc,' Vic says.

'Trust Big Boy,' Lenny says.

I push down on the sill to give myself a second's extra lift. It's a royal blue Merc, cream seats, gleaming in the April sunshine.

'Jesus,' I say. 'A Merc.'

Lenny says, it's like a joke he's been saving up for fifty years, 'Rommel *would* be pleased.'

Source: Graham Swift (1996) *Last Orders*, London: Picador, pp.10–12.

25 from *Be Near Me*

Andrew O'Hagan

Before we'd started the soup, the postman came to the door and hammered on it with his usual disregard. 'Nothing gets your attention like a knock at the door,' said Mrs Poole, and she went out. I spent a moment playing a phrase on the piano, placing my foot on a dull brass pedal. Then I stopped and cocked an ear before putting Chopin into the CD player; I could hear very clearly what the postman was saying to Mrs Poole.

'How's yer English priest getting on then?'

'He's not English,' she said. 'He was born in Edinburgh.'

'Don't kid yerself,' said the postman. 'Yer man's as English as two weeks in Essex. Get a load ae that rug lying there!'

'What are you talking about?'

'That thing under yer feet,' he said. 'They didnae have that in Father McGee's day. That's a pure English rug, that.'

'Just go about your business and stop coming round here talking nonsense,' said Mrs Poole. 'This is a Persian rug.'

'That's Iran or Iraq,' he said. 'You want to get rid ae that.'

As he laughed he sent a menacing splutter into the hall. 'There's blood in they carpets. Our troops are over in that place and they're not buildin' sandcastles. There's young men dying out there. You have to watch out for the Iraqis.'

I'm sure there's an essay in which Liszt writes of Chopin's apartment on the chaussée d'Antin, the room with a portrait of Chopin above the piano, and the belief of the younger musician that the painting must have been a constant auditor of the sound that once flamed and lived in that room, bright and brief as a candle.

'The postman?' I said.

Mrs Poole put a letter into its envelope and folded the whole thing in three. She creased it as people do who never file their letters, holding the stiff paper in her hand like a small baton. 'Aye,' she said. 'Just another of yer local idiots.'

'Isn't Good Friday a bank holiday? Don't they get the day off?'

'Not in Scotland,' she said. 'That's an English thing.'

She seemed more than slightly annoyed with the postman, as if his careless and brash way of talking had added some terrible degree of insult to the letter he had given her, the letter she now stuffed into the front pocket of her apron.

'Are you all right?'

She smoothed one lip against the other. 'In this country,' she said, 'they prefer to have an extra holiday on the second of January. They ignore Good Friday but they don't ignore the second of January.'

'Really?'

'Of course,' she said. 'The second is the day after New Year's Day, and they'd much sooner have an extra day with alcohol than an extra day with God.'

'You're very severe, Mrs Poole.'

'No wonder,' she said. 'The idea of a person like that being responsible for bringing the post.'

Source: Andrew O'Hagan (2006) *Be Near Me*, London: Faber and Faber, pp.12–13.

26   On the genesis of *Be Near Me*

Andrew O'Hagan

I was alone in a cafe near the Rue Balzac when the first seeds of *Be Near Me* were planted. I hardly ever go to Paris, but it was one of those blue nights that make you think you ought to go to Paris more often, and the room was bustling and crowded in the way of those famous paintings. I remember noticing a grey-haired priest who was sitting alone at a table beneath the window. He stared at his hands and after a while he stirred his coffee and a tear rolled down his cheek.

Back home, I began to hear the voice of Father David at the shaving mirror. There was something lovely but annoying in his voice – something both wise and deluded at the same time. I could hear he liked wine and poetry, cared for gardening and music, and quickly I decided he went to school at Ampleforth and came from a long line of recusants. After some months, I resolved that he went to Balliol College, Oxford, and the English College in Rome. None of these things had happened to me personally, so I went in search of the facts and the dates and the flavours. I walked through the parks in Rome where he would have walked and I took notes at the bases of statues and dreamed of his boyhood hours on the Lancashire coast.

In Scotland, I took a boat to Ailsa Craig and was forced back by the weather.

Writing a novel is an act of self-annihilation as much as self-discovery. You can kill whole appetites and flood whole depths while plumbing them, but if you are serious about it you also get to put something into the world that wasn't quite there before. I've been asked which of the other arts novel-writing is most like, and I have come to believe it is acting. Of course, in terms of pattern it can be like music, in terms of structure it can be like painting, but the job to me is most like acting. You give life to these characters and you inhabit them at some cost to yourself, while also realising yourself in the process.

Be Near Me really came alive when I went to the scene of a mob demonstration in the north of England. There were people outside a priest's house – placards, cameras, ice-creams – and looking up at one of the bedrooms I saw the net curtain twitch. There is a human being up there, I thought. And suddenly I knew this story was about a very human struggle – a struggle of individuals and communities in various guises – and I knew, too, that the book was asking for everything I had. After some weeks, I could see each of my characters in their exact colours: some knew how to live naturally and practically, while others lived opportunistically; some had faith and a care for the beauty of life, while others simply hid in tradition or eloquence, or existed defensively or in company with ugliness. I worked with each character in relation to the others, and I began to feel the novel was my own. I knew Mark and Lisa; I knew Mrs Poole. And my greatest job was to help readers to know my narrator, Father David, better than he knows himself.

There's a horrible fallacy that exists in the popular discussion of fiction these days: the idea that a successful central character need be "likeable" or "sympathetic". It is surely more important that they be human, no? More crucial that they breathe? The idea that people in novels should be more sympathetic than people in life simply baffles me. The characters I have loved most in Dickens, in Evelyn Waugh, or F Scott Fitzgerald have been, at best, morally ambiguous, and that state of being can only add to the joy of the book for me. Father David, as I say, had something not quite right about him from the beginning: he could be lovable and terrible, an enabler and a snob, a poet and a holy fool, and that made him just the perfect person to narrate this particular story.

A novel is a machine made up of pure essentials, where every part is crucial to the overall effect. My narrator surprised me at first, but then possessed me. I worked hard to protect his narration from my own arguments: the sentences I gave him don't express an editorial or form a manifesto (only fools think novels do that), but they may animate a true moral drama in the mind of a sensitive reader. I say true, and I mean that. A novel that is any good will know how to be true to itself if nothing else.

Source: Andrew O'Hagan (2007) 'Andrew O'Hagan on the genesis of *Be Near Me*', *Guardian*, 14 July.

27 from *Tragedy at Bethnal Green*

L.R. Dunne

On the night of the 3rd March the alert sounded at 8.17 p.m. precisely. By this time it was estimated that about 500–600 people were already in the shelter. The gates had all been opened some time prior to the alert. The chances of a raid were freely discussed but the people were perfectly orderly and normal in the manner of their entry up to the time of the sounding of the alert. Immediately the alert was sounded a large number of people left their homes in the utmost haste for the shelter. A great many were running. Two cinemas at least in the near vicinity disgorged a large number of people and at least 3 omnibuses set down their passengers outside the shelter. From 8.17 and for the next 10 minutes there was a hurried convergence of hundreds of people towards, and at, the gates of the shelter. The people were nervous and anxious to get under cover. The entrance of the shelter was densely packed though there was no actual disorder, and the people were able to enter the shelter in a hurried but orderly stream. As fast as they passed down the stairs, numbers were converging at the entrance behind them. In the 10 minutes succeeding the alert it is estimated that some 1,500 people entered the shelter. A number of these had had advance warning before the actual alert from the fact that their relay wireless had gone off. This, apparently, is a nearly certain sign that an alert will follow. The proportion of women and children was large. At this time there was gunfire, but it was distant and, according to numerous witnesses, not very alarming. No bombs or other missiles had fallen within a radius of some miles of the shelter.

At precisely 8.27 p.m. a salvo of rockets was discharged from a battery some third of a mile away. This caused a great deal of alarm. Some people on their way to the shelter lay down in the road and then ran on. There were some cries reported that 'they were starting dropping them': that it was a land mine; and other alarming observations. The crowd surged forward towards the entrance carrying in front of it those who were entering the shelter, and placing a severe and sudden pressure upon the backs of those already descending the nearly dark stairway.

Either as a result of this sudden pressure from behind, or, by an unlucky coincidence simultaneously with the pressure reaching the people immediately behind her, a woman, said to have been holding or leading a child, fell on the third step from the bottom. This was observed both by a witness on the landing below and by at least 2 people in the crowd on the stairs behind her. As a result or, again, simultaneously, a man fell on her left. This occurred in the right half of the stairway. So great was the pressure from behind that those impeded by the bodies were forced down on top of them with their heads outwards and towards the landing. In a matter of seconds there was built an immovable and interlaced mass of bodies 5 or 6 or more deep against which the people above and on the stairs continued to be forced by the pressure from behind.

Source: L.R. Dunne (1999 [1945]) *Tragedy at Bethnal Green: Report on an inquiry into the accident at Bethnal Green tube station shelter*, London: The Stationery Office, pp.8–10.

28   from *Half of a Yellow Sun*

Chimamanda Ngozi Adichie

Master was a little crazy; he had spent too many years reading books overseas, talked to himself in his office, did not always return greetings, and had too much hair. Ugwu's aunty said this in a low voice as they walked on the path. 'But he is a good man,' she added. 'And as long as you work well, you will eat well. You will even eat meat every day.' She stopped to spit; the saliva left her mouth with a sucking sound and landed on the grass.

Ugwu did not believe that anybody, not even this master he was going to live with, ate meat *every day*. He did not disagree with his aunty, though, because he was too choked with expectation, too busy imagining his new life away from the village. They had been walking for a while now, since they got off the lorry at the motor park, and the afternoon sun burned the back of his neck. But he did not mind. He was prepared to walk hours more in even hotter sun. He had never seen anything like the streets that appeared after they went past the university gates, streets so smooth and tarred that he itched to lay his cheek down on them. He would never be able to describe to his sister Anulika how the bungalows here were painted the colour of the sky and sat side by side like polite, well-dressed men, how the hedges separating them were trimmed so flat on top that they looked like tables wrapped with leaves.

...

Master grunted in response, watching Ugwu and his aunty with a faintly distracted expression, as if their presence made it difficult for him to remember something important. Ugwu's aunty patted Ugwu's shoulder, whispered that he should do well, and turned to the door. After she left, Master put his glasses back on and faced his book, relaxing further into a slanting position, legs stretched out. Even when he turned the pages he did so with his eyes on the book.

Ugwu stood by the door, waiting. Sunlight streamed in through the windows, and from time to time, a gentle breeze lifted the curtains. The room was silent except for the rustle of Master's page turning. Ugwu stood for a while before he began to edge closer and closer to the bookshelf, as though to hide in it, and then, after a while, he sank down to the floor, cradling his raffia bag between his knees. He looked up at the ceiling, so high up, so piercingly white. He closed his eyes and tried to reimagine this spacious room with the alien furniture, but he couldn't. He opened his eyes, overcome by a new wonder, and looked around to make sure it was all real. To think that he would sit on these sofas, polish this slippery-smooth floor, wash these gauzy curtains.

...

After Ugwu watched Master drive out of the compound, he went and stood beside the radiogram and looked at it carefully, without touching it. Then he walked around the house, up and down, touching books and curtains and furniture and plates, and when it got dark, he turned the light on and marvelled at how bright the bulb that dangled from the ceiling was, how it did not cast long shadows on the wall like the palm oil lamps back home. His mother would be preparing the evening meal now, *akpu* in the mortar, the pestle grasped tightly with both hands. Chioke, the junior wife, would be tending the pot of watery soup balanced on three stones over the fire. The children would have come back from the stream and would be taunting and chasing one another under the breadfruit tree. Perhaps Anulika would be watching them. She was the oldest child in the household now, and as they all sat around the fire to eat, she would break up the fights when the younger ones struggled over the strips of dried fish in the soup. She would wait until all the *akpu* was eaten and then divide the fish so that each child had a piece, and she would keep the biggest for herself, as he had always done.

Ugwu opened the fridge and ate some more bread and chicken, quickly stuffing the food in his mouth while his heart beat as if he were running; then he dug out extra chunks of meat and pulled out the wings. He slipped the pieces into his shorts' pockets before going to the bedroom. He would keep them until his aunty visited and he would ask her to give them to Anulika. Perhaps he could ask her to give some to Nnesinachi too. That might make Nnesinachi finally notice him. He had never been sure exactly how he and Nnesinachi were related, but he knew they were from the same *umunna* and therefore could never marry. Yet he wished that his mother would not keep referring to Nnesinachi as his sister, saying things like, 'Please take this palm oil down to Mama Nnesinachi, and if she is not in, leave it with your sister.'

Nnesinachi always spoke to him in a vague voice, her eyes unfocused, as if his presence made no difference to her either way. Sometimes she called him Chiejina, the name of his cousin who looked nothing at all like him, and when he said, 'It's me,' she would say, 'Forgive me, Ugwu my brother,' with a distant formality that meant she had no wish to make further conversation. But he liked going on errands to her house. They were opportunities to find her bent over, fanning the firewood or chopping *ugu* leaves for her mother's soup pot, or just sitting outside looking after her younger siblings, her wrapper hanging low enough for him to see the tops of her breasts. Ever since they started to push out, those pointy breasts, he had wondered if they would feel mushy-soft or hard like the unripe fruit from the *ube* tree. He often wished that Anulika wasn't so flat-chested – he wondered what was taking her so long anyway, since she and Nnesinachi were about the same age – so that he could feel her breasts. Anulika would slap his hand away, of course, and perhaps even slap his face as well, but he would do it quickly – squeeze and run – and that way he would at least have an idea and know what to expect when he finally touched Nnesinachi's.

...

In the following weeks, the weeks when he examined every corner of the bungalow, when he discovered that a beehive was lodged in the cashew tree and that the butterflies converged in the front yard when the sun was brightest, he was just as careful in learning the rhythms of Master's life. Every morning, he picked up the *Daily Times* and *Renaissance* that the vendor dropped off at the door and folded them on the table next to Master's tea and bread. He had the Opel washed before Master finished breakfast, and when Master came back from work and was taking a siesta, he dusted the car over again, before Master left for the tennis courts. He moved around silently on the days that Master retired to the study for hours. When Master paced the corridor talking in a loud voice, he made sure that there was hot water ready for tea. He scrubbed the floors daily. He wiped the louvres until they sparkled in the afternoon sunlight, paid attention to the tiny cracks in the bathtub, polished the saucers that he used to serve kola nut to Master's friends. There were at least two visitors in the living room each day, the radiogram turned on low to strange flutelike music, low enough for the talking and laughing and glass clinking to come clearly to Ugwu in the kitchen or in the corridor as he ironed Master's clothes.

He wanted to do more, wanted to give Master every reason to keep him, and so one morning, he ironed Master's socks. They didn't look rumpled, the black ribbed socks, but he thought they would look even better straightened. The hot iron hissed and when he raised it, he saw that half of the sock was glued to it. He froze. Master was at the dining table, finishing up breakfast, and would come in any minute now to pull on his socks and shoes and take the files on the shelf and leave for work. Ugwu wanted to hide the sock under the chair and dash to the drawer for a new pair but his legs would not move. He stood there with the burnt sock, knowing Master would find him that way.

'You've ironed my socks, haven't you?' Master asked. 'You stupid ignoramus.' *Stupid ignoramus* slid out of his mouth like music.

'Sorry, sah! Sorry, sah!'

'I told you not to call me sir.' Master picked up a file from the shelf. 'I'm late.'

'Sah? Should I bring you another pair?' Ugwu asked. But Master had already slipped on his shoes, without socks, and hurried out. Ugwu heard him bang the car door and drive away. His chest felt weighty; he did not know why he had ironed the socks, why he had not simply done the safari suit. Evil spirits, that was it. The evil spirits had made him do it. They lurked everywhere, after all. Whenever he was ill with the fever, or once when he fell from a tree, his mother would rub his body with *okwuma*, all the while muttering, 'We shall defeat them, they will not win.'

He went out to the front yard, past stones placed side by side around the manicured lawn. The evil spirits would not win. He would not let them defeat him. There was a round, grassless patch in the middle of the lawn, like an island in a green sea, where a thin palm tree stood. Ugwu had never seen any palm tree that short, or one with leaves that flared out so perfectly. It did not look strong enough to bear fruit, did not look useful at all, like most of the plants here. He picked up a stone and threw it into the distance. So much wasted space. In his village, people farmed the tiniest plots outside their homes and planted useful vegetables and herbs. His grandmother had not needed to grow her favourite herb, *arigbe*, because it grew wild everywhere. She used to say that *arigbe* softened a man's heart. She was the second of three wives and did not have the special position that came with being the first or the last, so before she asked her husband for anything, she told Ugwu, she cooked him spicy yam porridge with *arigbe*. It had worked, always. Perhaps it would work with Master.

Ugwu walked around in search of *arigbe*. He looked among the pink flowers, under the cashew tree with the spongy beehive lodged on a branch, the lemon tree that had black soldier ants crawling up and down the trunk, and the pawpaw trees whose ripening fruits were dotted with fat, bird-burrowed holes. But the ground was clean, no herbs; Jomo's weeding was thorough and careful, and nothing that was not wanted was allowed to be.

The first time they met, Ugwu had greeted Jomo and Jomo nodded and continued to work, saying nothing. He was a small man with a tough, shrivelled body that Ugwu felt needed a watering more than the plants that he treated with his metal can. Finally, Jomo looked up at Ugwu. '*Afa m bu Jomo*,' he announced, as if Ugwu did not know his name. 'Some people call me Kenyatta, after the great man in Kenya. I am a hunter.'

Ugwu did not know what to say in return because Jomo was staring right into his eyes, as though expecting to hear something remarkable that Ugwu did.

'What kind of animals do you kill?' Ugwu asked. Jomo beamed, as if this was exactly the question he had wanted, and began to talk about his hunting. Ugwu sat on the steps that led to the backyard and listened. From the first day, he did not believe Jomo's stories – of fighting off a leopard barehanded, of killing two baboons with a single shot – but he liked listening to them and he put off washing Master's clothes to the days Jomo came so he could sit outside while Jomo worked. Jomo moved with a slow deliberateness.

...

He had been with Master for four months when Master told him, 'A special woman is coming for the weekend. Very special. You make sure the house is clean. I'll order the food from the staff club.'

'But, sah, I can cook,' Ugwu said, with a sad premonition.

'She's just come back from London, my good man, and she likes her rice a certain way. Fried rice, I think. I'm not sure you could make something suitable.' Master turned to walk away.

'I can make that, sah,' Ugwu said quickly, although he had no idea what fried rice was. 'Let me make the rice, and you get the chicken from the staff club.'

'Artful negotiation,' Master said in English. 'All right, then. You make the rice.'

'Yes, sah,' Ugwu said. Later, he cleaned the rooms and scrubbed the toilet carefully, as he always did, but Master looked at them and said they were not clean enough and went out and bought another jar of Vim powder and asked, sharply, why Ugwu didn't clean the spaces between the tiles. Ugwu cleaned them again. He scrubbed until sweat crawled down the sides of his face, until his arm ached. And on Saturday, he bristled as he cooked. Master had never complained about his work before. It was this woman's fault, this woman that Master considered too special even for him to cook for. Just come back from London, indeed.

When the doorbell rang, he muttered a curse under his breath about her stomach swelling from eating faeces. He heard Master's raised voice, excited and childlike, followed by a long silence and he imagined their hug, and her ugly body pressed to Master's. Then he heard her voice. He stood still.

Source: Chimamanda Ngozi Adichie (2007 [2006]) *Half of a Yellow Sun*, London: Harper Perennial, pp.3–22.

29   from 'In the Pit'

Annie Proulx

'Blue,' said his mother, looking like Charles Laughton in a flowered wrapper, 'won't you do this one little thing for me?' She tapped her cigarette ash into a ceramic sombrero on the dinette table. Papers, magazines, letters, bills, offers to develop her film in twenty-four hours or insure her credit cards against loss, fliers and folders spilled around her. Her white hair was rumpled like a cloud torn by wind, her eyes the common pastel of greeting-card rabbits. Blue looked away from the heavy sleeves of flesh that hung from her upper arms, from the smoke curling out of her nose.

'Now. It's in here somewhere, and full of spelling mistakes.' She shuffled a deck of envelopes. 'Here, sheriff writes blah, blah, vandals broke in. Threw chairs and furniture over the ledge, smashed dishes, broke windows, and they don't know who did it.' The letter grated across spilled sugar as she slid it under her coffee cup.

'You could drive up in a couple of hours, Blue, see how bad it is, put on a lock or whatever. Revisit the scenes of your childhood,' she said, puffing her mocking voice out with the smoke, 'those happy hours you spent in the loft while your father and I shouted at each other.'

He remembered the neatness of the camp, the moon-blonde kitchen with its silvery pots and pans on hooks, the blue shutters, the narrow clenched spirals of the braided rug, so different from this apartment where his mother's carnival-tent clothes hung on the chairs and shoes sprawled like dead fish. She saw his look. 'I don't know how I did it in those days, keeping everything cleansy-weansy, always bent over that damn little sink the size of a sardine tin. Honey, I don't know how I did it.' She threw a few envelopes into the air and let them fall in disorder.

'You're a wild woman, mother,' he said.

Blue was visiting to show photographs of his wife Grace and their adopted daughter, Bonnie. The pool, little Bonnie and her pony, even Grace's richly colored hair and nails demonstrated his success after years of failed starts at one thing and another. Blue had made his life over, had repaired himself through a class in Assertiveness Training, had learned how to look into others' eyes, to clasp their hands firmly, to bend them to his will. He had dieted eighteen pounds away through willpower and dressed his new shape with style. A dark, wavy hairpiece gave his fleshy face with its long sheep's mouth a kind of springing vigor.

He had two weeks for everything, the travel, the photographs, the overhaul of memories. This was the first time he had seen his mother since the funeral in Las Cruces seven years earlier. She had arrived late from the airport in a mocha-colored limousine, accompanied by an unknown man wearing saddle oxfords.

...

On the main highway the resentful landscape showed itself to him, a stiff, hard country with rigid trees, frost-shattered masses of rock and shadowy gorges. The road to the shopping mall in Canker looped and doubled like intestine, ran between a stream and the leaning cliffs. Ravens flew up from crushed mats of fur and gristle at the rushing approach of his car, and dropped again before he was out of sight. The sky was filled with raw, bunched clouds. He crossed a bridge where a bicycle leaned against the guardrail like a tired animal.

Mr. Fitzroy, wearing old-fashioned overalls with wide, simple legs, was a mile farther on, his hand uplifted at the sound of Blue's car. Blue stopped and opened the door.

'Hello, Mr. Fitzroy. What's wrong with your bicycle?'

...

'What do you get for water rights?' asked Blue.

'Water rights! Just drill a deep well if you got to, or find a fresh spring. Track them wild horses, see where they drink, and that's your water.'

'Um,' said Blue, thinking of the parched, pale land and the tufts of bunchgrass spaced far apart like the repeated pattern on wallpaper, the place where land without water was worthless, and there was a lot of worthless land.

Light was shining out of the milkroom window, and Mr. Fitzroy went in, leaving the door open, while Blue pulled the bicycle free.

'Come in and say howdy to my partner,' shouted the old man.

The big stainless steel tank was gone, replaced by odd pieces of furniture, a frowsty bed, a table with bulbous legs. On the table in a welter of newspapers, beer cans and dirty plates was a gleaming toaster with a fleur-de-lis design on its side, and he knew it immediately. It was their old toaster from the camp.

Once he had tried to grill a cheese sandwich in that toaster and the bread caught fire, black smoke as though from burning tires billowed out of the chrome. His parents shouted. His mother flapped the air with a towel and screamed, 'You damn little fool to try to make a sandwich in a toaster!' and his father hurled words like clods of dirt. 'What do you expect, the kid has never seen any kind of food fixed except cornflakes and canned soup.' She threw the toaster as hard as she could, and his father caught it, hot and smoking, strings of cheese looping across the floor. Blue ran up to the loft where he cried for the cheese sandwich as though it were the last one in the world, and the shouting below went on and on, and then the brown sofa creaked as though they were tearing it apart. The next day his father's hands were bandaged, but the toaster still worked and they had kept on using it.

'Meet Gilbert,' said Mr. Fitzroy. The lamp was behind the seated figure and he seemed, for a minute, to be edged in a rim of fire, with round eyeglasses glinting like circles of steel. Then Gilbert teetered on his chair legs and looked to the side. His crimpy, tan hair was arranged in three large standing waves across the top of his head. His face was the color of a cracker, as stiff as if it had been baked, his eyes like a hen's, yellow and ignorant.

...

He knocked on the milk room door and waited a long time before Mr. Fitzroy opened it. The old man's eyes were as red as a St. Bernard's, his mouth slack. He was wearing a long green flannel nightgown.

'I want the toaster,' said Blue. His voice was firm, but not hard, full of the quiet strength learned in the Strength Through Will seminars. He tried to look in Mr. Fitzroy's eyes, but they stared away at some ghostly thing in the trees.

'I'm not going to say anything to the sheriff about how Gilbert messed up our camp unless I have to, but I want that toaster,' said Blue. He tried to step into the milk room, but Mr. Fitzroy set his hands on each side of the doorframe and blocked him, still staring out and away as if directions for what to do next were printed in the sky. Blue pulled at the old man's arms. They were as corded and hard as alder branches. He heaved and twisted, first at one arm, then the other, until he pried Mr. Fitzroy loose.

'Gilbert,' called the old man in the mangled voice of someone having a nightmare. But Gilbert slept like a dead hog under the covers of the bed he and Mr. Fitzroy shared, nor did he move when Blue seized the toaster and carried it to his car. Light glinted on the old man's wet lip.

Source: Annie Proulx (1995) *Heart Songs*, London: Fourth Estate, pp.103–14.

30   'That First Time'

Christopher Coake

Bob Kline was sitting at his computer, reading and then deleting a number of old letters from his soon-to-be ex-wife Yvonne, when he received an email from a sender he didn't know. Its subject line contained a name – Annabeth Cole – he didn't recognise either. The email read:

> Is this the Bobby Kline who went to Westover High in 1988? If so, I'm sorry to tell you that Annabeth Cole died several months ago. She wanted you to know. If you have any questions, call me. Sorry to bring bad news.

At the bottom of the message was a number and a name: Vicky Jeffords.

Bob stared at the email for a long time, not understanding it at all, eyes still damp and blurred from the hour he'd spent reading Yvonne's old love letters. In the early days of their marriage her job had kept her travelling, and she'd sent him dozens of them, each one impossibly sweet. *I'm just looking out over the ocean and missing you.* He tried now to pull his thoughts together.

Annabeth Cole? He was the Bob Kline this Vicky wanted, but as far as he could remember, he'd never gone to school with an Annabeth. He dug for a while in his closet, pulled out his yearbook. He didn't see an Annabeth – or a Vicky, for that matter.

He went to the kitchen of his apartment and opened a can of beer. Then he punched the number from the email into his cell phone. A woman answered after two rings.

This is Bob Kline, he said. You emailed me – ?

Bobby! she said. This is Vicky. Thanks for calling.

Her voice was completely unfamiliar.

Sure, he said. Listen – I'm the guy you want, but I have to say I'm a little confused. I don't remember going to school with an Annabeth.

Annabeth *Cole*, Vicky said.

Help me out. How did I know her? Did I know *you*?

After a few seconds of silence, she said, Not as well as you knew Annabeth. You slept with her once. If that narrows it down any.

I did?

She and I went to East Oaks. She met you at a –

And then Bob knew. *Annie*? he said. Holy shit.

He sat down hard on the couch and put a hand over his eyes. Annie. It had been what – eighteen years? He'd forgotten her last name. And if she'd ever told him her full name was Annabeth, he'd forgotten that too. A picture of her came into his mind: a small, slender girl, long sandy-coloured hair, glasses. He'd only known her a week, if that. They *had* slept together, just once, when he was seventeen.

She's dead? he asked. How?

Cancer. Non-Hodgkin's lymphoma.

Vicky told him the story while he stared at the beer can on his knee. She had been Annabeth's – Annie's – best friend since grade school. And Bobby had met Vicky soon after he met Annabeth – did he remember? At the pizza place? He told her he did, but this was mostly a lie. He remembered a girl, sitting across the booth, while he flirted with Annie. A place-holder shape in his memory. Was she tall? Maybe blonde?

Vicky told him she went to stay with Annabeth in Chicago for the month before she'd died. Towards the very end they talked a lot about the old days, and about what to do when Annabeth was gone, and Annabeth had written Bob's name on a list of people who might want to hear the news. Then Vicky tracked him down on the web.

There are a lot of Bob Klines, she said. You're a hard man to find ...

Vicky then told him about the service, three months past, but he didn't listen. When she was quiet again he said, Look, I guess I don't remember Annie and I ... ending up on the best of terms. Back then.

I don't either, Vicky said.

Was she – was she still angry with me?

It was a stupid question, and he knew it the moment the words were in the air.

Vicky said, Well, you were her first time.

Yeah, he said, rubbing a knot at the base of his skull.

And it was kind of intense. I mean the whole thing. She was pretty messed up, after you dumped her.

Yeah, he said again.

Vicky said, Well. She thought you might remember her. And that you'd want to know.

I do, he said. Thank you. Listen, Vicky –

He could barely believe he was saying this.

I'm not like I was then. I mean, I was seventeen. She was such a sweet girl. If I could do it over –

Hey, Vicky said, we were kids.

He couldn't even picture the outlines of the girl Vicky had been, but he could see her now, on the other end of the phone: a woman with her head in her hand, tired and sad. He wanted to say something else to her, to console her. But while he was thinking of what that might be, she said, I should go. I'm sorry, Bobby.

When she'd hung up Bob went to the patio doors and opened the blinds. He lived in an apartment overlooking downtown Indianapolis, fifteen floors up. The sun was setting, and the city lights were coming on, which was more or less the best thing that happened to him any more. He'd been separated from Yvonne for six months, and hadn't been doing much since but working and then coming home to sit out on the balcony at night, drinking and watching the lights, telling himself he'd done the right thing.

His head was pounding now. He decided the circumstances called for a switch from beer to bourbon. For a little impromptu wake.

Bob picked up a bottle and glass from the kitchen, and took them both outside on to the balcony. A helicopter darted overhead. Next door he could hear a lot of people talking, the sound of music playing – jazz. He had classy neighbours on that side.

He finished the bourbon in his glass and tried to find grief for poor Annie in his swimming head. He couldn't. It was somewhere outside of him, but faint, like the music he could just hear through the walls from next door.

Annie Cole. He'd broken her heart. Not on purpose, but all the same he had. He meant what he'd said to Vicky – she had been a sweet girl, and he'd been stupidly cruel. When he'd thought of her these past eighteen years, it was to wish her a happy life, a good husband, a big yard with kids and dogs. Had she told him she wanted those things? Or had he simply given them to her, in his mind? He couldn't remember.

He lifted his glass, first to the party next door, then to the big glittery mirror-windowed office building across the street, where a few sad souls still worked; in this light he could just see them, ghostlike, through the reflective glass. To Annie, he thought. He wasn't a religious man, but for her sake he hoped there was a heaven, someplace far away from sickness, from people like him.

A week went by. Bob's settlement hearing with Yvonne was coming up in another two. As the day pulled closer he grew more and more impatient, more restless.

He ran his own business, a house-painting company. As he worked that week, balanced carefully on his ladder, he found himself thinking more and more about Annie Cole. He'd been so shocked to hear the news that he'd asked Vicky almost nothing about her. In his head she was still the tiny slip of a girl he'd known for a week in high school; he couldn't picture her as a grown woman, let alone someone pale, bald, suffering. Dying, and then dead.

Then, Bob remembered: he might still have a picture of Annie, packed away in storage. She'd sent one to him, after, and he didn't think he'd ever had the heart to throw it out. When he came home from work that night he unlocked his basement storage cage and dug out the box labelled HIGH SCHOOL. He lugged it upstairs and emptied it on the living-room floor.

He set aside his diploma, and a bunch of old report cards, all relentlessly unexceptional. For the first time in years he looked at his senior prom picture, with Yvonne. In her gown she looked fabulous, proud; he looked confused, maybe even a little scared. But then he'd been stoned that night.

Scattered on the bottom of the box were several loose photos. Sure enough Annie's was one of them: a wallet-sized picture, well tattered. In it she leaned against a tree, wearing a baby-blue sweater and a tan skirt. She was smiling shyly, and wasn't wearing her glasses. Her hair fell thick and glossy over her shoulder. On the back of the photo was a girl's handwriting: *To Bobby. I'll never forget. Love, Annie.*

By the time Annie sent him this picture he'd known he'd never speak to her again. He set it down on the carpet, right next to the prom photo. And there they were: the triangle Yvonne had never known about.

Bob had already been in love with Yvonne the summer he and Annie met. That was the whole problem. Yvonne, his first girlfriend, the first person *he'd* slept with. That summer – 1988 – they'd briefly broken up, while she prepared to leave Indiana for college in Maryland. Bob's folks had just split, and for complicated reasons he had to spend the summer in his father's house in little East Oak, fifty miles from Westover. There Bob had a jumbled basement room with its own bathroom and exterior door. His father was away a lot on business, and Bob was in a town he didn't know well, and in which he wouldn't stay past summer's end. Everything, even the ground under his feet, felt impermanent.

He worked part-time in a restaurant, and met a lot of East Oak kids there. He was a decent-looking guy, and thanks to friends back in Westover he always had pot, so he found himself, that summer, strangely popular. He took advantage. In the month after Yvonne broke things off, he brought three different girls back to his basement room. Why not? He didn't know then whether what he felt was freedom or despair. When he was in his room, smoking a joint, or stripping off the panties of a girl he'd just met, he was able to believe it was freedom.

He'd met Annie at the East Oak park, while he was waiting with his friend Lew for their turn at a game of pickup hoops. Annie sat in the grass next to them with a friend – it must have been Vicky – watching boys she knew on the other team. Who had talked first? Bob couldn't remember. But they'd introduced each other, chatted, joked.

He looked down at the picture in his hands. He would have noticed Annie's hair first. And then – her voice. He remembered it. Deep, a little husky – like she smoked, even though she didn't, usually. He remembered her long thin legs, her white tennis shoes. He and Lew got up to play their game, and when he came back twenty minutes later Annie had left. But she'd written her number on a slip of paper and tucked it beneath his keys.

Bob called her that afternoon and a couple of nights later they met up at the Pizza King downtown. Annie brought Vicky and he brought Lew. Bob sat next to Annie in the booth. She was wearing a short skirt, and was laughing and wild and flirty, turning in the seat to face him and, once, putting her hand on his knee.

Later that night, down in his basement room, he was shocked when Annie told him it was her first time. Why me? he asked her. You barely know me.

Annie, curled up beside him on the bed, laughed and blushed and said, I feel like I do. Like you're right for me.

Bob put down the photo. Against whatever judgement he had left, he called Yvonne. She didn't answer. He left her a message: A friend of mine from high school died. It's thrown me for a loop. I'd really like to see you before next week –

He realized what he was saying and quickly hung up. Then, without setting down the phone, he dialled Vicky's number.

While her phone rang he stood out on the balcony, 150 feet above the city streets. Off to the east a thunderhead had massed; lightning flickered down over the suburbs. If it rained tomorrow there'd be no painting; he'd have nothing at all to do. The thought filled him with panic.

Vicky, he said when she answered. It's Bob Kline.

Oh! I thought the number looked familiar.

Is it a bad time? I can let you go.

No. I'm fine, really. How are you?

I don't know, he said. Leaves blew on to his balcony, from some place in the city that had trees. I guess I'm a little curious, he said.

He listened to the long silence.

Is it alright if I ask about her? he said. I don't want to put you in a bad spot –

No! Ask. Please.

Her voice was strange. Was she crying? He couldn't tell.

He said, I forgot to ask whether she was happy. I want to know if she – if she was in a good place.

Yes, Vicky said. Until she got sick, she was very happy.

Was she married?

Yes.

Nice guy?

Yeah. They were good for each other.

Kids?

No. She wanted them. But no.

Bob stood and leaned against the rough concrete wall of the building. Rain was starting to fall through the glow of the patio light, the drops appearing frozen for an eye-blink.

What did she do? he asked.

She was a lawyer.

He laughed.

Is that funny?

I'm in the middle of a divorce, he said. Or at the end, I guess I mean. I make a lot of lawyer jokes.

She was a prosecutor.

Well, I've steered clear of those, he said, taking a sip of his drink. I guess that's all right.

She was quiet on the other end. He said, Hey, I can let you go. I'm just shooting the shit now.

It's all right, Vicky said. I'm – I get a little defensive about her.

Can I ask another question? Do you mind?

Sure.

Was it – He ran a hand through his hair. Did she suffer? Was it bad?

Another long quiet. It was cancer, Vicky said.

You were with her.

Yes. Me and Rick and her folks.

That must have been –

It was hard.

He said the next part quickly, meaning every word of it: I don't know you, or even her, really. But it sounds to me like she was real lucky in her friends.

The line was so empty that he had to check the screen on his phone to make sure he hadn't lost the call.

Thanks, Vicky said. A little burble of sound in the machine next to his ear. It's – it's been rough. I miss her.

Bob wanted to say, I do too – but that would be stupid. Up until a week ago he hadn't missed her at all. But he did, now that he thought about her. He missed the girl touching his knee at the Pizza King. That feeling of invitation.

Listen, he said. You said you live in Indy?

Yeah.

You want a drink? I'm just sitting around here thinking about this. If it'll help – I mean if you want to – I'm glad to meet you someplace.

He hadn't planned on saying that, but once he had, he hoped dearly Vicky would say yes. But why would she? She didn't know a thing about him except that he'd screwed over her friend in the eleventh grade. He paced back and forth and wondered at his own stupidity.

But then Vicky said, Sure. Okay.

It turned out she lived not very far from him, out in the neighbourhoods to the east, right underneath the lightning and the smudge of rain. She gave him the name of a bar halfway between them.

Bob spent a few minutes in the bathroom, taking a quick shower, shaving off two days' worth of stubble, looking with dismay at his jowls, rubbing some gel in his hair. He was thirty-five, but he looked older. He had some grey at his temples. Years working in the sun had done a number on his skin. He was tanned, at least, didn't look unhealthy. Vicky would be remembering the seventeen-year-old he'd been: long, greasy hair, bloodshot eyes, a wispy goatee. Whatever he was now would have to be an improvement. He put on a nice polo shirt and clean blue jeans and black shoes.

Bob squared himself up in the mirror. After the attention, he still looked just like he felt: lonely, a little drunk, probably on his way to making a mistake.

Just before Bob walked into the bar, he realized he'd forgotten to ask what Vicky looked like. She hadn't asked him either.

But it was a Tuesday night and the bar wasn't busy. After his eyes adjusted to the light he spotted Vicky right away, sitting at a small table against the outer wall. She was the only woman in the place who looked as though someone close to her had just died, her face a white, sad oval in the low, warm light. Whatever he looked like, she spotted him too; she stood the moment he met her eyes, offering a half-wave.

He'd been trying to remember a blonde, but Vicky was a redhead, her hair in a pixie cut, though her face was a little too round for that to work. She'd dressed in a light-green blouse and black slacks. Work clothes, he thought. On the whole she looked nice, but not done up.

Bobby, she said.

Vicky.

Then she smiled at him, crookedly, maybe happy or sad or both at once – and right there, he remembered her, sitting across the table from him at the Pizza King. The smile was the key. While Annie flirted with him, Vicky's smile had gone more and more lopsided, tipping through sadness and into panic; her laughter had gotten louder and louder. The best friend getting left behind.

He held out a hand to her, but Vicky shrugged and gave him an embrace instead, quick and clumsy. When they pulled apart she said, You haven't changed a bit.

I remembered you, he said, but I wasn't sure I'd recognize you.

Vicky laughed a little. Her cheeks were dotted with freckles, and the low neckline of her blouse showed him more. He didn't remember those, but he liked them.

So, you want a drink? she said. First round's on me.

Thanks, he said. Bourbon?

Vicky walked over to the bar and Bob sat at her table. An empty margarita glass stood next to her car keys. Beside her keychain was a small photo album, closed with a clasp. She'd brought pictures of Annie along. Bob wished he had the bourbon in him already.

Vicky came back with their drinks. She sat and sighed, and said, Bobby Kline.

You know, he said, I go by Bob these days.

Oh, right. I don't know if I can do that. You've been Bobby for eighteen years.

Fair enough. You mind if I keep calling Annabeth Annie?

Her eyes flickered up. I guess not.

And you're Vicky.

And Vicky I shall remain.

He liked her. Had he expected not to? He lifted his glass, and she followed suit; they clinked rims. Thanks for this, he said.

Well, you're buying the next one.

I will. But I mean meeting me.

She shrugged, smiled her half smile. I've been spending a lot of time in my head, you know? It's good to be out.

This your bar?

One of them.

It's nice.

She nodded and took a sip of her drink. Oh, Bobby, she said. I don't know if I can do small talk.

She levelled her eyes at him, which were very green.

He said, I guess now that I've got you here, I don't know what to ask.

Vicky said, You can't figure out why she wanted me to call you.

He laughed, surprised – that was it all right. Yeah, he said.

You weren't the only person I called. The only ex boyfriend.

I'd be real sorry if I was.

Vicky kept her eyes on him. She was very good at that.

He said, I guess for my sake I was kind of hoping I wasn't ... still important.

Vicky said, You were the first guy she ever slept with. You never forget your first, right?

Bob remembered Yvonne, in the back seat of his old Impala, grinning, unbuttoning his jeans, guiding his hand underneath her skirt. You better be sure, she'd told him. This is the big time.

He'd felt the warm inside of her thigh with wonder and said, I am absolutely, positively sure.

Yeah, he told Vicky. You never do.

Annabeth was obsessed with you, Vicky said. Right from the start, when she talked to you in the park. She was crushed for months, after you dumped her.

It hurt him to hear, but he had no place to hide from it.

I was an asshole, he said. I admit it.

You were a total fucking prick, is what you were.

He kept his eyes on his drink.

I'm sorry, Vicky. I wish I could have apologized to her.

So why didn't you?

I don't know. I always thought about looking her up, but at a certain point I figured the past is the past, you know?

He was lying. It had never occurred to him to call Annie, or any of the other women he'd slept with that summer, before Yvonne showed up at his doorstep and said she wanted him back. Sure, he'd treated Annie badly, but Yvonne had come back for him, and once that happened, he couldn't turn around and stare for even a second at where he'd been. Or what he'd done.

A furrow was deepening between Vicky's eyebrows.

He said, I don't want to excuse myself, okay? I feel like shit. It's why I called you. I can't stop thinking about how terrible it is that this happened.

You can't, huh.

Do you need to tell me off? he asked. Would that make it better?

No, Vicky said. Her face was clouding. It wouldn't.

Bob wished he hadn't called her, that he hadn't come. He took another drink and turned to look over his shoulder. It had gotten dark, and the rain was coming down hard.

He asked, Did she hate me?

Vicky might have been gearing up for it for a while, but after that question, out of nowhere, she dropped her head and began to cry.

Not noisily; she ducked her head and tears rolled out of her eyes, and she fumbled for a napkin.

After a while she shook her head and said, She wasn't like that.

She had to. At least a little.

Vicky jerked her head up. She wanted you to remember! Is that so fucking hard to figure out? She was dying! She shared something really special with you. Maybe she thought you might still have a heart in there, huh?

Over Vicky's shoulder the bartender was giving them both the eye. Other people were looking, too.

Vicky's voice quavered. She was the one who told *me* not to hate you –

Bob stood up. Vicky had started to sound too much like Yvonne, like every phone call he'd taken from her late at night, when she'd had to accuse him of anything and everything, and he had to agree.

Look, he said. I'm sorry. I didn't mean to upset you. I'll go.

Vicky buried her face in her hands. You don't have to go, she said. I'm sorry.

Annie was a good girl. Better than me. I'll always remember her. Okay?

Vicky didn't say anything, or lift her eyes from behind her fingers. Her shoulders shook. Bob stood at her side for a few seconds, unsure whether to say anything more, or squeeze her shoulder, or what. She still didn't move. Finally he figured he'd done enough damage and he walked out of the front door. The heavy rain gave him an excuse to jog the half block to his car, to pile in and drive away as fast as he could.

Inside his parking garage he didn't get out of the car. He couldn't bring himself to go home yet. What had Vicky said? She'd been in her head too much. That was about right – so had he. If he went inside he'd call Yvonne, he knew it. Better to keep both of his hands on the wheel and manoeuvre the downtown streets. He had a little too much drink in him, so he stopped at a drive-though for a black coffee and sipped it carefully while he drove.

He'd lied to Vicky. He'd said he'd always remember Annie. But he couldn't remember everything that happened, at least not in the way Annie had always believed. He remembered meeting her, remembered flirting with her. Remembered taking her to his room.

But the sex, the actual first time Annie had chosen him for – he couldn't remember any of it.

He remembered pulling a handful of beers for the two of them out of his father's refrigerator. He remembered Annie asking him if he had any pot – she said she'd heard that if you got high before you did it, it wouldn't hurt as much. He told her he did have pot, but that it might hurt anyway. Its okay, she said. I'm ready.

He remembered her body; she undressed in front of him, blushing, smiling through the thick curtain of her hair. Without her clothes she seemed even smaller, her arms and legs too thin, her chest barely bigger than a boy's. He undressed for her, feeling strangely shy.

When he took off his underwear she reached over and curled her hands around his penis, then withdrew her fingers, as though she'd done something she shouldn't have. Even then that just about broke his heart.

They hadn't rushed. But why? He'd been plenty excited. For a long time they sat side by side, naked hips touching. He put on music and they talked and shared a joint and drank the beer. Relaxing. It was hot, even after the sun went down, and they opened a window to let in a breeze.

But all the beer and the pot did its work; he remembered the two of them listening to Pink Floyd for a while, and after that the night went blank.

Then it was morning. He woke with Annie's head tucked against his shoulder, one of her legs flung across him. He nudged her awake. They were both hungover, and he took her to a diner on the interstate for coffee, which he found she'd never tried before. She made a face and joked about how sex was easier, the first time. They both joked about how much trouble she'd be in, for staying out all night without permission. It was worth it, she said. You sure? he asked. I'm sure. He dropped her off down the block from her house. When he got back home he saw the blood on his sheets, and that was really the last thing he remembered: sitting hungover out behind the house, wadding up his sheets into a five-gallon bucket full of bleach and stirring them around with a stick.

Annie called him that night, in tears, to tell him she was grounded for two weeks. She told him she missed him. He told her he missed her too. He was sure he meant it.

And then a week later Yvonne called him, for the first time in a month. He remembered that call with great clarity; he'd been hoping for it all summer, jumping to his feet whenever the phone rang. I can't do this, she told him, crying, while he listened in disbelief. She said, I can't live without you. He told her to come over, and she did. They lay together on his clean sheets, and she said, Bobby, make love to me, and if he thought about Annie Cole, or any of the other girls, it was only to hope he hadn't missed cleaning any trace of them out of the room. Yvonne took off his clothes and he took off hers and they cried together, and made love, and in the early morning he said, I think we ought to get married, as soon as we can. And she said, Of course we should. We're meant for each other. He remembered, and would always remember, kissing her then, his hands cupping her cheeks, while she pressed her entire length against him; afterward she stared into him with her big unblinking eyes.

Annie called again two days later, and that was when he'd begun to hurt her. She'd left a message on the machine: how she wanted to see him, how she was thinking about him all the time, how she was worried because he hadn't called. Yvonne was in the shower when he listened, and he was afraid she'd hear too. He hit the Erase button before the message was over.

Annie left two more messages, her voice growing sadder and sadder. The last time she cried. I can't understand this, she said, over and over. He erased it. He came home two days later and found a letter taped to his door.

No getting around it. He'd been a kid, sure, but an asshole was an asshole. He tore up the letter without opening it. After that he never heard from her again. And if he felt bad, there was Yvonne, talking about their wedding, the kids they'd have, the names they'd give them.

Yvonne used to like to say to him, I feel safe with you.

As Bob drove through the city, he imagined what it would have been like, if he'd chosen differently. If whatever had happened with Annie had made him love her, instead of Yvonne. Annie with her tiny body and her gravelly laugh. Her long silky hair. He imagined the two of them going off to school together. Marrying their sophomore year. Maybe they would have been able to have kids. Maybe they would have had something to talk about, these last five years.

But whatever they would have been, Annie would still have gotten sick and died, and he would have had to watch.

Maybe, he thought, it would be better that way – maybe it was better to love someone who died than it was to fall out of love with someone living.

Here was a first time for Vicky, one he'd never forget: the first time he cheated on Yvonne. This was three years ago. Yvonne was out of town, at her sister's. He'd started a fight just before she got on the plane, and she'd left tight-lipped, furious. He sat at home thinking about what she was saying to her sister until he couldn't stand it any more. He walked to a bar downtown and traded drinks with a woman ten years younger than him, who was only weeks away from going off to grad school. At the end of the night they shared a taxi home. While they were parked at the kerb she said, Why don't you come in? He gave her a look, and she gave it back. She said, It's what you think.

I'm married, he said.

She was twenty-two, blonde, impossible. One of the straps of her dress had fallen off her shoulder. I won't tell, she said. Come on in.

He had. And he remembered damn near everything.

Bob tried and tried to avoid it, but after an hour of driving aimlessly he found himself in Yvonne's neighbourhood, up in Carmel. She lived in a nice apartment complex, behind a gate, and at eight o'clock, after circling her block five times, he gave up and turned the wheel into the entrance. He hadn't seen her in two months. He punched her number into the security box. She answered straight away.

It's me, he said.

What do you want?

To talk to you.

I don't think so. Are you drunk?

No, he said. Five minutes, that's all.

Bob –

Five minutes, he said. I don't even have to come in. We can even do it like this, if you want.

She didn't say anything. But after several seconds the gate buzzed open, and he drove slowly through. He parked in one of the Visitor slots, which, for a moment, made him want to cry.

Yvonne answered the door in a little black dress and heels. Immediately he smelled her perfume; it made him want to reach for her. She'd dyed her hair a dark maroon; the last time he saw her it was long, but she'd had it cut short. It showed off her neck. He thought she might have lost a little weight, too. Her mouth was pursed, and she didn't look at him, beyond an initial once-over.

You *are* drunk, she said. You shouldn't be driving.

I'm all right, he said. You look great, by the way.

I'm about to go out.

A guy?

She laughed and crossed her arms. Like I'd tell you?

He figured that meant no; these days she would tell him.

So what do you want? she asked. Four minutes, and I've got to go.

Bob peered at her again, trying to see the girl she'd been, the one he'd taken to prom. He could feel her anger swelling while he did.

I've just been thinking about us, he said. Trying to make sense out of it.

She laughed, without any humour. Join the club.

He said, How did this happen?

You told me you didn't love me any more, is what happened.

He ran a hand through his hair. What if it wasn't true? What if I got it wrong?

Well, it's too late for that now, she said, and glanced theatrically at her watch. That was a favourite line of hers, right up there with *Maybe you should have thought of that before you fucked all those girls.*

I did love you, he said. I know that, and you do too.

And you felt the need to drive over here and tell me?

Can I ask you something?

Two minutes.

Would you have done things differently? If you'd known?

What – if I knew we'd end up like this?

Yes.

She laughed again. Of course I would have, she said. I married you; I didn't think I was taking out a fucking lease. Seriously, Bob. Would *you* have?

I don't know if I could have stopped myself, he said. That's how in love I was.

I'm leaving, she said. Right after you.

Yvonne grabbed her purse off the kitchen table and gestured towards the door. She was still beautiful, still smarter and better than him. And Bob was everything she said he was, believed him to be. It was better for them to be apart. Better for her. He knew that.

But Yvonne was so beautiful – spectacular, really, in her dress and good shoes, smelling of flowers, her new hair shimmering around her neck. He couldn't help it.

Von, are you really going to hate me the rest of my life?

She stared at him.

He said, If I died tomorrow, would you still hate me?

Yvonne pressed her lips together and pointed at the door.

Come on, he said. Next week it's permanent. Answer me.

For a second he saw something else in her eyes, a moment of – of what? Sadness? Remorse? She still didn't answer him.

His next words surprised him. Let me kiss you again, he said. Once more, while I'm still your husband.

Uh-uh. Absolutely not.

I don't remember the last time we kissed, he said.

This was true; it had been bothering him. The last one had probably been nothing but a meaningless kiss goodbye, some morning as they left for work. His closed lips against her turning cheek.

She opened the door for him. Her voice still shaking, she said, Well I do.

Bob drove home quickly, with only one stop, at the liquor store for a bottle of Maker's Mark. There was nothing more to do tonight but get blind drunk, and if that was the case he might as well go down in style.

Inside his apartment he sat on the couch with a drink in one hand and the old pictures – Annie, he and Yvonne at prom – in the other. Both women looking up at the camera, happy, expectant. And him looking dull, stoned. Maybe a little scared. How had that skinny kid in the tux managed to cause so much pain? He looked at Yvonne, eighteen, thrilled to be alive holding his hands. He turned over Annie's picture and read the inscription again. Why had they trusted him with anything?

His phone buzzed then against his hip; he dug it out. Yvonne, he thought. She'd probably thought up some good lines, or was going to give him the AA speech again.

But instead he saw Vicky's number on the screen. He told himself, Don't answer. Do her a favour and never speak to her again.

But he couldn't help it.

Bobby, she said. Thanks for picking up.

Did you think I wouldn't?

She sighed. I wouldn't blame you. Listen. I'm sorry. I went off on you and I shouldn't have.

Vicky, he said, touched. Come on. It was my fault, too.

This is really hard on me, she said. But I wouldn't want someone calling me on shit I did when I was seventeen, either.

Its okay, he said. My wife does all the time.

He thought he heard her lighting a cigarette. She said, It's just that I feel like I have to honour her, you know? But I'm too unstable to do it right. She wouldn't have wanted me to yell at you.

He swirled the bourbon in his glass and looked at the pictures in front of him. He said, Tell me something I don't know about her. What would she have wanted me to know?

Vicky was quiet for a while. Then she said, She would have wanted you to know she was strong.

She seemed plenty strong to me. Sure of herself.

Yeah, but as an adult. A woman. She'd want you to know she was *tough*. She grew up and put bad guys in jail. She was proud of that.

Another silence, and he knew they were coming to the end of things.

After they hung up there'd be no reason for either of them to call again. But he didn't want to hang up. Vicky might be crazy, but he liked her voice on the other end of the phone. He thought again of the freckles on her chest, and wondered what kind of man that made him.

She surprised him. Hey, Bobby, she said, do you still get high?

What?

That was your rep, she said. You were the Westover guy with the good pot. Annie was all nuts about you, and the first thing I said was, The pot guy?

Jesus, he said, leaning his head back on the couch. Yeah, he said, Sure I do. But I don't exactly have the supply I used to.

Listen, she said. I've got some. You want to come by? If we're going to talk about Annie – let's talk about Annie.

He sat up and looked at the clock. Was she really inviting him over?

Vicky, it's almost midnight.

I know. I don't sleep much. Not these days.

Half an hour later, showered, in a change of clothes and wearing aftershave, Bob knocked at Vicky's door. She lived in a nice new brownstone town house, not two miles from his apartment building. While he waited for her to open the door, he saw a tiger-striped cat watching him from the windowsill, its tail lashing. He tapped a finger against the glass; it fled instantly.

Vicky answered the door. Her eyes were red, a little glassy; she might not have waited for him to light up. Bobby, she said, with her crooked smile. Come on in.

She was dressed in a pyjama top and cut-off shorts, and was barefoot. One of her ankles was ringed with some kind of tribal tattoo. Her thighs were freckled too.

He followed her into the town house. Nice place, he said, even though it was a mess. Her living room was full of books, and every surface was dusty. Through an arched doorway he could see a kitchen counter piled with dishes. The air smelled like incense and weed and maybe some kind of Mediterranean food.

Thanks for calling, he said, trying for some kind of charm.

Thanks for coming, she said. Then she stopped and leaned forward and hugged him, as awkwardly as she had at the bar. She sniffled in his ear. She might be high, but she was still sad, too.

You want a drink? she asked. I've only got wine. Red.

I'll take some, sure.

Wine and bourbon. He might not survive the morning. From the couch, he heard the kitchen faucet come on, water splashing. Music was playing softly from speakers he couldn't see – a woman and an acoustic guitar; he couldn't make out the words. He looked over the walls. Even the spaces that weren't covered by bookshelves had books stacked against them, as high as his chest.

On the end table, next to his elbow, was a photograph in a wooden frame. He turned it to get a better look. It showed Vicky – in college, he guessed – and another woman, standing together in bikinis, on a dock someplace blue and tropical.

He'd stared a few seconds before he recognized the other woman as Annie.

He picked up the photo and peered closely. Annie hadn't remained a skinny little girl. She'd grown up and out – she'd become a knockout, in fact, tanned and curvy. The Vicky next to her   tall, angular, sunburnt across her forehead – seemed to know it, too; she was shrinking into herself, her smile as uncertain as it had been back in East Oak. She knew she was completely outmatched.

This was the picture Vicky kept out for herself to see.

She came back from the kitchen and handed him a generous glassful of wine. That's my favourite picture of her, she said.

She's beautiful.

Yeah. She always was. Vicky took the photo from him and held it against her chest. You want to see more pictures?

Did he? Vicky wanted him to, at least, and he didn't want to disappoint her. Sure, he said.

Vicky disappeared for a few seconds, then returned with the little photo album he'd seen earlier that evening, on the table at the bar.

She sat next to him on the couch and put the album between them, balanced on her knees. He resisted the impulse to put his arm around her shoulders. He hadn't picked up anything from her, that way, since arriving, and he felt a little sheepish. He wished he hadn't put on aftershave, but if she noticed it, she gave no sign.

She opened the album. That's us in elementary school, she said.

Looking at the pictures was the strangest thing he'd done in a long time. He turned the pages and watched Annie slowly age, from a little kid with braces into a tomboy, and from there into the skinny long-haired girl he remembered.

In college Annie suddenly blossomed, and not just her body; there was something in her face that hadn't been there, before. She and Vicky toasted the camera with martini glasses. Was it that she seemed calmer? A sudden intuition told him: there was someone on the other side of the camera she liked.

Then on to adulthood. Annie and Vicky sitting at a New Year's party, wearing hats. A man sat next to Annie, smiling at the camera, his hand over hers. An average-looking guy, thin, with a full beard.

Rick? he said.

That's him.

Only two pictures in the album didn't have Vicky in them. The first was a wedding picture, in black and white: Annie in her gown, caught in a swirl of activity, at the reception probably – she looked to be on a dance floor, surrounded by blurred bodies. Annie was grinning, eyes and teeth shining, her face turning back to look at the camera over he shoulder. Bob thought of the pictures he had of Yvonne, looking like that, and had to pinch the bridge of his nose.

The second picture – the last one – showed Annie sick. She was sitting on a deep couch, looking up at the camera, a blanket on her lap and a mug in her hands. She was wearing a bulky sweatshirt, but her face and her wrists were shockingly thin, and he was sure the hair on her head was a wig. Her skin was as white as paper.

Vicky said, I thought she'd be mad at me taking that one. I don't even know why I keep it in here.

He didn't know either. He wished, looking at it, that he'd seen only the pictures of Annie happy.

Vicky said, I still think she's beautiful. Even then.

She put a hand over her mouth and began to shiver, staring down at the picture.

Bob closed the album.

Its okay, she said. You can keep looking. But tears were rolling down her cheeks.

He put his arm around her shoulders, and she collapsed – he could feel her tumbling into herself, inside, even as she leaned into him.

Its okay, he said. It's all right.

No, it's not.

You did what you could, he said, hoping it was what she needed.

I didn't.

She groaned, and then said, I loved her, Bobby. I loved her for years, and I never told her. I never told anybody.

She was your best friend, he said. She knew you loved her –

Vicky lifted her head and fixed her wet eyes on him.

That's not what I mean.

He had to turn the words over for a few seconds before he understood.

Oh, he said.

Vicky sat up and reached for a tissue from the end table, her lips trembling. Yeah.

Did she know? I mean, that you were –

That I'm what? A lesbian?

He was the stupidest man on earth. Yeah, he said.

Vicky shook her head. Annabeth knew, but I didn't – I didn't bring it up much.

Bob thought of the wedding picture: Annie twirling, with no groom in sight.

How long did you know? he asked. About Annie.

Vicky shook her head. For ever. When I got jealous of her boyfriends in high school, I figured it was just because she was more popular than me. For sure in college. After I came out.

Vicky sniffled and kneaded the pillow.

That was right when Annabeth met Rick, and after she told me she was in love with him I went to my room and threw up and was in this panic –

She looked off to the side, like she was seeing Annie, there in the corner of the room.

And then she got married, and she was happy, so I tried to keep my distance, and had my own things going on, but then when she got sick, she called me and said Rick needed help –

And you went.

Yeah.

He tried to imagine what she must have gone through. What it would have been like to be close to Yvonne all those years – loving her, but never having it returned, never being able even to say it. Look at tonight. Even now that things were over, he'd been unable to keep his mouth shut when it counted. Vicky had been quiet for twenty years.

Vicky whispered then, I'm jealous of you.

Bob's stomach sank. Don't be, he said. There's nothing to be jealous of.

She was staring at him. Sure there is, she said.

We were kids, he said. We were stoned and drunk. We didn't take home any medals, okay?

Vicky took a breath and held it. He braced himself for her anger.

But she said, Tell me about her.

You know her so much better –

Vicky's cheeks were scarlet.

No, she said. I mean – I mean *during*. When you were ... together.

I can't, he said, his mouth dry.

It's the only way I'll ever know, she said. Who else could I ask? Rick?

He thought of Vicky, across the table at the Pizza King, her face just a blur in the background, while Annie touched his knee. He thought of erasing Annie's message, her voice cutting off mid-word.

Please, Vicky said.

So he took a deep breath and told her what he could. Vicky leaned closer. He told her all the details he could remember: Annie touching his knee. Twining her fingers in his as he drove to his apartment. Murmuring while he kissed her. Taking off her clothes.

Was she beautiful? Vicky asked. Like that?

He told her about the way Annie's hair looked, falling across her shoulders. The shape of her body. How, when Annie was naked, she'd asked, Is this all right? The two of them lying back against a pile of pillows, smoking a joint, Annie warm and smiling against his chest.

Vicky took a drink, her fingers white around her glass. She whispered the next question: Tell me what it was like.

Bob wanted to tell her, but he'd reached the limit of his memories.

It was great, he said.

How?

Vicky had closed her eyes, was waiting.

He couldn't remember. He really couldn't. But Vicky needed more.

Then the solution came to him.

Carefully, without using her name, he told Vicky instead about Yvonne – about that first time, right after Yvonne came back to him. He told Vicky about a beautiful girl naked beneath the blankets, laughing; about the silky feel of her body; about how she never stopped moving against him, almost like water. About the surprising strength of her kisses. He told her about the sweet taste of her skin and lips. How, when they were done, she took his hand and kissed his palm, right in the centre. How she said, This is special.

Vicky's eyes were still closed. She spoke so softly he could barely hear the words: She really tasted sweet?

He thought of Yvonne's clean wet hair, smelling of apples; of the vanilla gloss she used to put on her lips.

Yeah, he said. She really did.

I knew it, Vicky said, and smiled. I just knew it.

Source: Christopher Coake (2007) 'That First Time' in Ian Jack (ed.), *Granta*, 97, Spring 2007, pp.49–70.

31   from *A History of the World in 10½ Chapters*

Julian Barnes

I taught for a term at a crammer half a mile from my home ...

It was the grandfather who had founded the school, and he still lived on the premises. Although in his mid-eighties, he had only recently been written out of the curriculum by some crafty predecessor of mine. He was occasionally to be seen wandering through the house in his cream linen jacket, college tie – Gonville and Caius, you were meant to know – and flat cap (in our house a flat cap would have been common; here it was posh and probably indicated that you used to go beagling). He was searching for 'his class', which he never found, and talked about 'the laboratory', which was no more that a back kitchen with a bunsen burner and running water. On warm afternoons he would sit outside the front door with a Roberts portable radio (the all-wood construction, I learned, gave better sound quality than the plastic or metal bodies of the transistors I admired), listening to the cricket commentary. His name was Lawrence Beesley.

...

Fifty-two years before I met him, Lawrence Beesley had been a second-class passenger on the maiden voyage of the *Titanic*. He was thirty-five, had recently given up his job as science master at Dulwich College, and was crossing the Atlantic – according to subsequent family legend, at least – in half-hearted pursuit of an American heiress. When the *Titanic* struck its iceberg, Beesley escaped in the underpopulated Lifeboat 13, and was picked up by the *Carpathia*. Among the souvenirs this octogenarian survivor kept in his room was a blanket embroidered with the name of the rescuing ship. The more sceptical members of his family maintained that the blanket had acquired its lettering at a date considerably later than 1912. They also amused themselves with the speculation that their ancestor had escaped from the *Titanic* in women's clothing.

...

Lawrence Beesley made no mention of female dress in his book *The Loss of the Titanic*. Installed at a Boston residential club by the American publishers Houghton Mifflin, he wrote the account in six weeks; it came out less than three months after the sinking it describes, and has been reprinted at intervals ever since. It made Beesley one of the best-known survivors of the disaster, and for fifty years – right up to the time I met him – he was regularly consulted by maritime historians, film researchers, journalists, souvenir hunters, bores, conspiracy theorists and vexatious litigants. When other ships were sunk by icebergs he would be telephoned by newsmen eager for him to imagine the fate of the victims.

Forty or so years after his escape he was engaged as a consultant on the film *A Night to Remember*, made at Pinewood. Much of the movie was shot after dark, with a half-size replica of the vessel poised to sink into a sea of ruckled black velvet. Beesley watched the action with his daughter on several successive evenings, and what follows is based upon the account she gave to me. Beesley was – not surprisingly – intrigued by the reborn and once-again-teetering *Titanic*. In particular, he was keen to be among the extras who despairingly crowded the rail as the ship went down – keen, you could say, to undergo in fiction an alternative version of history. The film's director was equally determined that this consultant who lacked the necessary card from the actor's union should not appear on celluloid. Beesley, adept in any emergency, counterfeited the pass required to let him board the facsimile *Titanic*, dressed himself in period costume (can echoes prove the truth of the thing being echoed?) and installed himself among the extras. The film lights were turned on and the crowd briefed about their imminent deaths in the ruckled black velvet. Right at the last minute, as the camera were due to roll, the director spotted that Beesley had managed to insinuate himself to the ship's rail; picking up his megaphone, he instructed the amateur imposter kindly to disembark. And so, for the second time in his life, Lawrence Beesley found himself leaving the *Titanic* just before it was due to go down.

...

On 25th August 1891, James Bartley, a thirty-five-year-old sailor on the *Star of the East*, was swallowed by a sperm whale off the Falkland Islands:

> I remember very well from the moment that I fell from the boat
> and felt my feet strike some soft substance. I looked up and saw a
> big-ribbed canopy of light pink and white descending over me, and
> the next moment I felt myself drawn downward, feet first, and I
> realised that I was being swallowed by a whale. I was drawn lower
> and lower; a wall of flesh surrounded me and hemmed me in on

every side, yet the pressure was not painful and the flesh easily gave way like soft india-rubber before my slightest movement.

Suddenly I found myself in a sack much larger than my body, but completely dark. I felt about me; and my hands came in contact with several fishes, some of which seemed to be still alive, for they squirmed in my fingers, and slipped back to my feet. Soon I felt a great pain in my head and my breathing became more and more difficult. At the same time I felt a terrible heat; it seemed to consume me, growing hotter and hotter. My eyes became coals of fire in my head, and I believed every moment that I was condemned to perish in the belly of a whale. It tormented me beyond all endurance, while at the same time the awful silence of the terrible prison weighed me down. I tried to rise, to move my arms and legs, to cry out. All action was now impossible, but my brain seemed abnormally clear; and with a full comprehension of my awful fate, I finally lost all consciousness.

The whale was later killed and taken alongside the *Star of the East*, whose crewmen, unaware of the proximity of their lost comrade, spent the rest of the day and part of the night flensing their capture. The next morning they attached lifting tackle to the stomach and hauled it on deck. There seemed to be a light, spasmodic movement from within. The sailors, expecting a large fish or perhaps a shark, slit open the paunch and discovered James Bartley: unconscious, his face, neck and hands bleached white by the gastric fluids, but still alive. For two weeks he was in a delirious condition, then began to recover. In due course he was returned to normal health, except that the acids had removed all the pigmentation from his exposed skin. He remained an albino until the day he died.

Source: Julian Barnes (1990 [1989]) *A History of the World in 10½ Chapters*, London: Picador, pp.171–80.

Acknowledgements

Grateful acknowledgement is made to the following sources for permission to reproduce material in this book.

Parts 1–3

Page 17: 'We Remember Your Childhood Well' is taken from *The Other Country* by Carol Ann Duffy published by Anvil Press Poetry in 1990;

Pages 114–16: Screenplay by Hart, J. (1992) *Bram Stoker's Dracula* © 1992 Columbia Pictures Industries, Inc. All rights reserved. Courtesy of Columbia Pictures;

Pages 188–9: Chaudhuri, A. (2002) 'Prelude to an Autobiography: A fragment', *Real Time*, Pan Macmillan Ltd. Copyright © Amit Chaudhuri, 2002;

Page 212: Plath, S. (1965) 'You're', *Ariel*, Faber and Faber Ltd. Reprinted by permission of HarperCollins Publishers. Copyright © 1965 by Ted Hughes;

Page 221: McMillan, I. 'Branwell Brontë is Reincarnated as a Vest', *Perfect Catch*, Carcanet Press Limited. Copyright © Ian McMillan 2000;

Pages 222–3: France, L. (1994) 'Little Dogs Laugh', *The Gentleness of the Very Tall*, Bloodaxe Books Ltd. Copyright © Linda France 1994;

Pages 232 and 237–8: Bishop, E. 'One Art' and 'A Miracle for Breakfast', *The Complete Poems 1927–1979*, The Hogarth Press. Farrar, Straus & Giroux, LLC;

Page 242: Graves, R. (1996) 'With Her Lips Only', *Robert Graves: Poems Selected by Himself* (1996), Penguin Books Ltd, By permission of A.P. Watt Ltd on behalf of The Trustees of the Robert Graves Copyright Trust;

Page 242: Fennelly, B.A. (1998) 'Poem Not to be Read at Your Wedding', *A Different Kind of Hunger*, Texas Review Press;

Pages 243–4: Reid, C. (1998) 'Fly', *Expanded Universes*, Faber and Faber Ltd;

Page 244: Douglas, K. 'Landscape with Figures 2' in Graham, D. (ed.) (1990) *Keith Douglas: Complete Poems*. By permission of Oxford University Press;

Page 245: Muldoon, P. (2006) 'The Old Country', *Horse Latitudes*, Faber and Faber Ltd/Farrar, Straus & Giroux, LLC;

Part 4

Reading 13: Churchill, C. (1993) *Top Girls*, Methuen Drama, an imprint of A & C Black Publishers;

Reading 14: Pinter, H. (1991) *The Homecoming*, Faber and Faber Ltd;

Reading 15: Johnstone, K. (1981) 'Status', *Impro: Improvisation and the theatre*. Methuen Drama, an imprint of A & C Black Publishers 1992. Faber and Faber Ltd;

Reading 16: Wertenbaker, T. (1996) *Our Country's Good*, in *Plays One*, Faber and Faber Ltd;

Reading 17: *Temporary Shelter* © by Rose Tremain, 1984 is reproduced by permission of Sheil Land Associates;

Reading 18: Minghella, A. (1997) *Cigarettes and Chocolate, Minghella: Plays 2*, Methuen Drama, an imprint of A & C Black Publishers;

Reading 19: Jones, L. (1990) *An Angel at My Table: the screenplay*, Pandora Press, an imprint of Unwin Hyman Ltd. (from the autobiography of Janet Frame). Copyright © Laura Jones and Janet Frame. The Wylie Agency (UK) Ltd. And Hisbiscus Film;

Reading 20: Hare, D. (2000) *The Hours: a screenplay*, based on the novel by Michael Cunningham, Miramax Books. Copyright © 2002 Paramount Pictures Corporation. Courtesy of Miramax Film Corp;

Reading 21: Potter, D. (1986) *The Singing Dectective*, Faber and Faber Ltd

Reading 22: Cunningham, M. (1999) *The Hours*, Fourth Estate. Reprinted by permission of HarperCollins Publishers Ltd. © Michael Cunningham;

Reading 23: Extract from *Her Big Chance* by Alan Bennett from *Talking Heads: Volume 1* (© Forelake Ltd. 1988) is reproduced by permission of PFD (www.pfd.co.uk) on behalf of Forelake Ltd.

Reading 24: Excerpted from *Last Orders* by Graham Swift. Copyright © 1996 Graham Swift. Reprinted by permission of Pan Macmillan, London, A P Watt Ltd and Random House Canada;

Reading 25: O'Hagan, A. (2006) *Be Near Me*, Faber and Faber Ltd, McClelland & Stewart, AP Watt Ltd and Houghton Mifflin Harcourt Publishing Company. Copyright © 2006 Andrew O'Hagan;

Reading 26: O'Hagan, A. 'Andrew O'Hagan on the genesis of *Be Near Me*', *The Guardian*, 14 July 2007. Copyright © Guardian Newspapers Limited 2007;

Reading 27: Dunne, L.R. (1999) *Tragedy at Bethnal Green: Report on an inquiry into the accident at Bethnal Green tube station shelter*. Crown

Index